GLOBAL EQUITY MARKETS: TECHNOLOGICAL, COMPETITIVE, AND REGULATORY CHALLENGES

GLOBAL EQUITY MARKETS: TECHNOLOGICAL, COMPETITIVE, AND REGULATORY CHALLENGES

Edited by

Robert A. Schwartz

NEW YORK UNIVERSITY SALOMON CENTER
Leonard N. Stern School of Business

IRWIN
Professional Publishing

Chicago • Bogotá • Boston • Buenos Aires • Caracas
London • Madrid • Mexico City • Sydney • Toronto

This publication is designed to provide accurate and
authoritative information in regard to the subject matter
covered. It is sold with the understanding that neither the
author or the publisher is engaged in redering legal, accounting,
or other professional service. If legal advice or other expert
assistance is required, the services of a competent professional
person should be sought.

*From a Declaration of Principles jointly adopted by a Committee
of the American Bar Association and a Committee of Publishers.*

Executive editor: Ralph Rieves
Project editor: Denise Santor-Mitzit
Production supervisor: Ann Cassady
Designer: Larry J. Cope
Compositor: J. Cozby
Printer: Buxton-Skinner

Library of Congress Cataloging-in-Publication Data

Global equity markets : technological, competitive, and regulatory
   challenges / edited by Robert A. Schwartz.
      p.   cm.
   ISBN 1-55623-844-4
   1. Stock exchanges.   2. Program trading (Securities)
   I. Schwartz, Robert A. (Robert Alan)
   HG4551.G633   1995
   332.64' 2—dc20   94–24024

Printed in the United States of America

1 2 3 4 5 6 7 8 9 0   Bux   0 9 8 7 6 5 4

FOREWORD

Development of efficient domestic capital markets, especially for equities, carries with it significant potential benefits in terms of both the quantitative and qualitative dimensions of economic growth. These are achieved through improved static and dynamic properties of the domestic financial market, better liquidity, lower transactions costs, enhanced linkage to international sources of portfolio investment, and overall improvements in the process of domestic and cross-border capital allocation.

A prerequisite for achieving many of these gains is an efficient basic domestic financial market "infrastructure" that helps to link securities intermediaries and the ultimate buyer with the ultimate seller of equities, in both primary and secondary market transactions. It comprises a "value-chain" of services, optimally supplied to market participants on the basis of quality and price (value-added) by competing private-sector vendors of information services, analytical services, trading services and information processing, credit services, enhanced custody and safekeeping, and analytical services.

The higher the information costs, transactions costs, and risks associated with the basic domestic securities infrastructure are, the more retarded will be the development of the national financial market and its ability to link effectively into the international capital flows. By building an infrastructure that delivers liquidity, transparency, reliability, and hence low transactions and information costs, the interests of both active securities traders and buy-and-hold investors—as well as issuers—are served and, in turn, assure a more efficient allocation of capital.

This volume examines a major part of the financial market infrastructure, specifically market mechanisms associated with transactions in equity securities. It is an issue that remains full of controversy, both in terms of the comparative static and dynamic efficiency properties of competing approaches and in terms of enormous vested interests—public and private—in existing and proposed systems. By addressing in turn the technological and competitive challenges, as well as the various critical regulatory issues in both a U.S. and global context, the volume is unique in the scope and the quality of its coverage.

The professional standing of the authors and discussants, as well as the effort that went into their contributions, made this conference an outstanding success. The care that went into editing this volume makes this book no less of a success. The editors and the authors are to be congratulated in producing a definitive work—one that is fully in the tradition of projects conducted under the auspices of the New York University Salomon Center.

Ingo Walter
Director
New York University
Salomon Center

CONTENTS

CONTRIBUTORS

Yakov Amihud   Professor of Finance and Yamaichi Faculty Fellow, Salomon Center for Research in Securities Markets, Stern School of Business, New York University

Janet Angstadt   Associate, Schiff Hardin & Waite, and formerly Senior Counsel, Division of Market Regulation, Office of Automation and International Markets, U.S. Securities and Exchange Commission

Brandon Becker   Director, Division of Market Regulation, U.S. Securities and Exchange Commission

Harold S. Bradley   Vice President and Director, Equity Trading, Investors Research Corporation

Rolf-E. Breuer   Member of the Board of Managing Directors, Deutsche Bank AG

Corinne Bronfman   Assistant Professor of Finance, University of Arizona

David C. Cushing   Director of Research, ITG, Inc.

Ian Domowitz   Professor of Economics, Northwestern University

William H. Donaldson   Chairman and CEO, New York Stock Exchange

Nicholas Economides   Associate Professor of Economics, Stern School of Business, New York University

Gene Finn   Vice President and Chief Economist, NASD/The NASDAQ Stock Market

Eric Fisher   Vice President, TIAA-CREF

Edward Fleischman   Partner, Rosenman & Colin

Reto Francioni   Member of the Executive Board, Deutsche Börse AG

William C. Freund   Professor of Economics and Director of the Center for the Study of Equity Markets, Lubin School of Business, Pace University

Bernardo González-Aréchiga   Executive Vice President, Planning Division, Bolsa Mexicana de Valores

Jacques Hamon   Professor of Finance, CEREG, Université Paris Dauphine

Puneet Handa   Associate Professor of Finance, College of Business Administration, University of Iowa

Oliver Hansch   Ph.D. Candidate, Institute of Finance and Accounting, London Business School

Lawrence Harris   Professor of Finance and Business Economics, School of Business Administration, University of Southern California

Joel Hasbrouck   Associate Professor of Finance, Stern School of Business, New York University

Roger D. Hendrick   Vice President, Corporate Marketing, Chicago Stock Exchange

Chris Hynes   Senior Vice President, State Street Global Advisors

Bertrand Jacquillat   University Professor, Université Paris Dauphine and Associés en Finance

Raymond L. Killian   President and CEO, ITG, Inc.

Andrew Large   Chairman, Securities and Investments Board

Kenneth Lehn   Professor of Business Administration and Director of the Center for Research & Contracts & the Structure of Enterprise, Joseph M. Katz Graduate School of Business, University of Pittsburgh

Kevin McCabe   Associate Professor of Accounting, University of Minnesota

Jianping Mei   Associate Professor of Finance, Stern School of Business, New York University

Haim Mendelson   James Irwin Miller Professor of Business Administration, Graduate School of Business, Stanford University

Anthony Neuberger   S. G. Warburg Research Fellow, Institute of
     Finance and Accounting, London Business School

Kazuhisa Okamoto   Managing Director and CEO Japan/Asia Group,
     Wells Fargo Nikko Investment Advisors Japan Limited

Junius W. Peake   Monfort Professor of Finance, University of
     Northern Colorado

Stephen Rassenti   Assistant Director, Economic Science Laboratory,
     University of Arizona

Robert A. Schwartz   Professor of Finance and Economics and
     Yamaichi Faculty Fellow, Stern School of Business, New York
     University

James E. Shapiro   Managing Director, Research and Planning, New
     York Stock Exchange, Inc.

Vernon Smith   Regents' Professor of Economics and Director of
     Research and Education, Economic Science Laboratory,
     University of Arizona

Chester Spatt   Professor of Finance, Graduate School of Industrial
     Administration, Carnegie Mellon University

Sanjay Srivastava   Professor of Finance, Graduate School of Industrial
     Administration, Carnegie Mellon University

Hans R. Stoll   Anne Marie & Thomas B. Walker Professor of Finance
     and Director of the Financial Markets Research Center, Owen
     Graduate School of Management, Venderbilt University

Ingo Walter   Professor of Finance and Director, Salomon Center for
     Research in Securities Markets, Stern School of Business, New
     York University

Bruce W. Weber   Assistant Professor of Information Systems, Stern
     School of Business, New York University

Stephen Wells   Chief Economist, London Stock Exchange

Yimin Zhou   Graduate Student, College of Insurance

INTRODUCTION

ADDRESSING THE NEEDS OF BUY-SIDE TRADERS

Robert A. Schwartz

Remarkable change, brought about by technology, deregulation, and the introduction of new financial instruments, has characterized the securities industry since the early 1970s. Three powerful forces are now accelerating the rate of change. First, trading and markets are rapidly becoming more global. Second, buy-side participants, primarily the mutual and pension funds, are becoming far more aware of the extent to which trading costs impair portfolio performance and are increasingly demanding better market performance. Third, new trading systems are attracting the attention of an appreciable number of buy-side participants; and, increasingly, these systems are exerting competitive pressure on traditional sell-side broker/dealer firms and market centers.

A two-day conference was held in October 1993 at New York University's Leonard N. Stern School of Business and sponsored by the Salomon Center to assess these developments in the securities markets. Both buy-side participants (investors—both retail and institutional—who buy marketability services) and sell-side participants (broker/dealer intermediaries who sell marketability services) were present, as were government regulators, academicians, and other students of the market. Organizations from three different parts of the industry sponsored the conference: the New York Stock Exchange (a traditional market center), the Investment Technology Group (a proprietary trading system and brokerage firm), and the Investors Research Corporation, manager of the

1

Twentieth Century Mutual Funds (a buy-side participant). This book contains the papers presented at that conference. Together, they address the technological, competitive, and regulatory challenges facing the industry as it heads toward the year 2000 in an increasingly global environment.

TECHNOLOGY AND COMPETITION

Information technology is the single most important driving force behind the current developments in securities markets. The computer, of course, has long since found its way onto trading floors and trading desks, and the pros and cons of electronic trading have been debated for a good 20 years (see, for example, Peake, Mendelson, and Williams, 1976).[1] For the most part, however, the computer has been used for order routing and information dissemination, not trade execution. Clearly, a large-scale integration of computerized trading into an agency/auction market, such as the New York Stock Exchange (NYSE), or a competitive dealer market, such as NASDAQ, would have a profound effect on these market centers. It would also have major implications for the profitability of the brokerage houses and dealer firms that are their members.

Technological inertia, the vested interests of sell-side participants, and the very complexity of trading itself account for the slow pace of the computer's adoption. But the impediments are starting to be overcome. Electronic information systems enable quantitative investment/trading programs to be run profitably if—and only if—transaction costs are kept low.[2] The computer has allowed trade data to be captured and analyzed, and the analysis has revealed the cost of trading, not just to the quantitative managers, but to buy-side participants in general. And, the reality is sinking in that, with computer technology, natural buyers and natural sellers can find and trade with each other without the intervention of intermediaries.

With electronic speed, orders are now routed to foreign markets, for both foreign and domestic issues. That is, a U.S. fund manager will buy U.S. as well as British shares in London if doing so lowers trading costs. Similarly, a German or Swiss fund may trade its domestic securities in London. In good part due to this competitive pressure, plans are in process in Germany and Switzerland to introduce new, state-of-the-art electronic markets. Fundamental change is also being considered in England, France, and elsewhere on the continent. In general, from China to

Mexico, new markets are emerging around the globe, and as they do, cross-border competition is intensifying.

Within the United States, proprietary trading systems (PTS), though still small, are beginning to exert substantial pressure on the traditional market centers. These systems include Instinet's electronic continuous market and crossing network, the Investment Technology Group's (ITG) Posit (an electronic crossing network), and the Arizona Stock Exchange's (AZX) electronic call market.

The proprietary trading systems are owned by equity shareholders. As such, they are not membership associations, as is the New York Stock Exchange, where members own seats. The profit incentive of their owners provides an incentive for the proprietary trading systems to listen to the needs of their customers, the buy-side participants, with a different receptivity than do the seat holders of the major market centers. In contrast, traditional membership organizations view their members as their customers, and that which is best for the member-customers is that which maximizes the price of a seat on the exchange. Indeed, the price of a seat reflects the value of access privileges given to members. Herein lies a conflict: an innovation that might decrease the cost of trading shares (and in so doing raise share prices) for the membership organization (for instance, a more efficient order handling procedure) might not also raise but, in fact, could lower the value of a seat (if that system also reduces the need to use broker/dealer intermediaries).[3] Consequently, membership organizations cannot be relied upon to undertake all the innovations that would be efficient from the point of view of the ultimate investors.

The ultimate investors, of course, are the public traders. Currently, 75 to 80 percent of NYSE average daily volume is estimated to be institutional trading.[4] Can institutions trade in a liquid, transparent environment without destabilizing the markets, with immediacy, at low cost? They cannot. To address their needs, market structure issues must be assessed from their viewpoint.

MARKET STRUCTURE ISSUES

The issues concerning market structure include transparency, liquidity, consolidation of the order flow, accurate price discovery, reasonable price stability, fairness, regulatory simplicity, and low transaction costs.

In addition, it is widely believed that buy-side participants demand immediacy. Let us consider these issues.

Transparency Transparency is typically taken to mean that quote (pretrade) and last sale (post-trade) information is widely available on a real time basis.[5] The quality of pretrade information is impaired when market makers widen their quotes, understate the number of shares they would be willing to trade at the quotes, and then give within the spread transactions of larger size. The quality of post-trade information is impaired when trades are not reported quickly (or at all) to the market, as is the case for large orders in London's SEAQ market, U.S. trades that are made in after-hours proprietary systems such as Instinet's crossing network and the Arizona Stock Exchange, and U.S. trades made abroad (largely in London).

Although not widely discussed, transparency also involves participants' disclosing their orders. Unfortunately, revealing information concerning a willingness to trade can be detrimental to a trader—it may result in the loss of anonymity, costly information signaling, and having one's orders front-run. Data collected by the Plexus Group indicate that 40 percent of the orders given to buy-side trading desks (including the smaller investment managers) are greater than a stock's average daily trading volume.[6] Orders of this size cannot be disclosed immediately to the market. What is the total size of orders that are not revealed because their rapid injection into the market would trigger excessive, adverse price moves? How much would trading volume increase if participants did reveal their orders more fully? Can trading be structured so that institutions will not under-reveal their orders to the system?

Liquidity Institutional order flow is characteristically lumpy and may be one-sided (buyers only or sellers only). Can the market makers cope? Will they provide sufficient liquidity? Can institutions provide liquidity to themselves? Are other innovations in market structure needed?[7]

Consolidation of the Order Flow Consolidating orders makes it easier for counterparties to a trade to find each other and to transact at reasonable prices with minimal sell-side intervention. Orders can be consolidated in two ways: spatially (geographically) and temporally (over time). To date, attention has focused almost exclusively on spatial consolidation. Would temporal consolidation facilitate order handling for the institutions? Would it enable a better integration of institutional and retail order flow?

Price Discovery Price discovery is the process by which a market attempts to find transaction prices that are in reasonable alignment with theoretically desirable equilibrium values that are themselves rapidly changing. Equilibrium prices are rarely attained in the securities markets, largely because buy-side participants commonly do not reveal their full demand to the market.[8] Although it is now recognized to be a complex, imperfect process, price discovery has been given insufficient attention in the debates about market structure. Why? Are the deviations of transaction prices from equilibrium values a significant trading cost for the institutions? Might this cost be controlled by a trading system's design?

Price Stability It is widely believed that intraday price movements are excessively volatile.[9] This may largely be attributable to insufficient liquidity and to inaccuracies in price discovery. Can the sell-side, by itself, provide sufficient stability to the market?

Fairness Fairness means that all participants in the marketplace operate under similar conditions and that some do not have persistent advantages over others in terms of either position or the receipt of information (both fundamental and market information). Are the institutions unfairly disadvantaged by sell-side participants in our current markets? Are the retail customers? How is fairness affected by a trading system's design?

Regulatory Simplicity The continuous market is an inherently complex environment to operate in and to regulate.[10] Symptomatic of the difficulty, exchange specialists commonly stop orders and do not display all limit orders to the market. Knotty regulatory issues range from front running to payment for order flow. Would the temporal consolidation of orders simplify the resolution of some of these issues?

Transaction Costs The complexity of operating within a continuous market is also reflected in trading costs. Bid-ask spreads exist, market impact is accentuated, and orders are more easily front-run. The bid-ask spread is eliminated in call market trading. How much would market impact costs be reduced if buy-side traders had the alternative of directing their orders to a call market several times a day? How much might trading costs be lowered by introducing decimal pricing, thereby reducing the minimum tick size of $\frac{1}{8}$ of a point?[11]

Immediacy Most equity markets have continuous trading because buy-side participants are assumed to demand immediacy (that is, wish to be able to transact whenever they choose during a trading day). Do the funds really have a fundamental need for immediacy? To what extent is the demand for immediacy a product of a continuous trading environment? If the sale of immediacy were unbundled from the act of trading by offering both call and continuous systems, how much immediacy would be demanded by the institutions?[12]

One more question must be addressed: are the nine items set forth above mutually attainable? Eight of them might be. As noted, reasonable price stability requires accurate price discovery, and accurate price discovery requires transparency, liquidity, and sufficient order flow consolidation. If transparency is attained and order flow consolidated, then fairness is enhanced, the regulatory environment may be simplified, and transaction costs may be kept low. However, it might not be possible to achieve transparency, liquidity, and immediacy at the same time.[13] Contrasting London's SEAQ and Paris's CAC, which are both continuous systems, illustrates the problem. London market makers provide liquidity, but SEAQ is not transparent because of the expressed needs of the market makers for opacity.[14] CAC, on the other hand, provides more transparency but attracts less liquidity from broker/dealer firms. The Securities and Exchange Commission's (SEC) Division of Market Regulation argues in its Market 2000 Report, however, that "because transparency increases the integrity of the securities markets and fosters investor confidence in those markets, it encourages greater participation by investors. Such participation, in turn, increases market liquidity." (p. IV-3).

But transparency and liquidity do not appear to be fully consistent attributes in a continuous market. One might expect that their mutual attainment would be facilitated by unbundling the act of "trading" from the sale of "immediacy." However, while transparency and liquidity have been widely discussed, it has generally been assumed without question that participants demand immediacy and are willing to pay its price. Certainly, some investors choose not to pay the price. The list includes limit order traders, passive investors, and others who desire lower trading costs.[15] Moreover, the demand for immediacy may in part be endogenous to the continuous market, as participants attempt to trade quickly so as to preserve anonymity and to avoid front-running. Perhaps if it were realized that, given its price, immediacy may not be so important to many traders, market structure and regulation problems that have remained unsettled after two decades of public debate could be resolved more easily.

REGULATION OF THE MARKETS

Largely in response to global pressures, the emergence of the PTSs, and continued concerns about market fragmentation, the U.S. Securities and Exchange Commission launched its "U.S. Equity Market Structure Study" (widely referred to as the Market 2000 study) in July 1992 and released its final report in February 1994. The study is the first major reassessment of regulatory issues since the Securities Acts Amendments of 1975.[16]

The Securities Acts Amendments of 1975 mandated the development of a National Market System (MNS) and effectively thrust the SEC into the business of directly managing market design. In the nearly two decades that have followed, the SEC has played an active role in the development of the Intermarket Trading System (ITS),[17] the Consolidated Tape Association (CTA), and the Consolidated Quotations System (CQS); in enforcing the partial removal of the NYSE's order consolidation Rule 390[18]; and in allowing a carefully controlled emergence of the proprietary trading systems. Now, the SEC and others have questioned the desirability of the agency's activist role.[19] In its July 1992 request for public comment, the SEC's Division of Market Regulations itself stated,

> The Division is not trying to dictate what the structure of the equity markets should be in the year 2000. That determination should be made by the markets and their participants as a result of competition. However, that competition should not be skewed by inequitable regulation or allocation of self-regulatory costs, beyond that which is necessary for the protection of investors (Release No. 34-30920, p. 14).

The Market 2000 Report itself contains proposals concerning transparency (the display of customer orders should be improved and the minimum allowable price change for shares reduced from an eighth of a point to a penny), the fair treatment of investors (payments for order flow should be disclosed and soft dollar practices improved), fair market competition (third market surveillance and order handling should be strengthened and the Commission's review process for market center system changes expedited), and open market access (the restrictions on off-board trading of listed stocks by member firms should be relaxed for after-hours trading and delisting made easier for NYSE-listed firms). No clear regulatory constraint on the PTSs has been proposed. However, the report also reaffirms the SEC's commitment to the National Market System mandate of the 1975 Securities Acts Amendments, which suggests that the Commission's involvement with market issues will continue.

Keeping the hands of a regulator out of market structure issues and letting competition be the engine for change is not easy. First, a regulator might point out that competition has been blocked in a number of ways. Indeed, it has been seriously stymied by institutional rigidities, soft-dollar arrangements, the vested interests of various sell-side participants, and the inordinate difficulty a new market has "priming the pump" by attracting order flow when it does not have order flow to begin with. Nevertheless, the inexorable pressure of competition should not be underestimated. Increasingly, institutional investors are demanding anonymity and direct access to markets, and big traders are willing to sacrifice transactional immediacy to lower their trading costs. A market that caters to this reordering of priorities will gain order flow.

Second, another reason for regulatory intervention in market structure issues is to ensure that markets are fair and orderly for a broad spectrum of participants. When questions of fairness and market quality arise, disadvantaged parties naturally look to Washington for solutions. The regulators are apt to respond because fairness is, of course, desirable. But care must be taken not to stifle effective competition in the name of fairness. Competition is never entirely fair, and fairness can always be used as an excuse to regulate.

Third, a regulator might argue, and correctly so, that consolidation of the order flow is desirable, all else equal, and that order flow might, with undesirable consequences, fragment as satellite markets free-ride on the price discovery and other services provided by a major market center.[20] But all else is not equal. Forced consolidation of the order flow prevents competition between market centers that offer different trading technologies. Consequently, fragmentation of the order flow between technologically different markets must be allowed if the impediments to change presented by technological inertia and vested interests are to be overcome. Let us consider this more closely.

FRAGMENTATION: FRACTURED ORDER FLOW OR HEALTHY COMPETITION?

Some dealer houses, using automation to achieve fast execution, are now paying roughly a penny a share for the orders of retail brokerage firms, and satellite markets more generally (including regional exchanges) are posting computer determined quotes that are based on values established on a primary market.[21] The concern is that these practices, known as "payment for order flow" and "auto-quoting" (or "quote matching") impair liquidity and the accuracy of price discovery.[22]

Remarkably, controversy over fragmentation of the order flow has not been resolved after roughly 20 years of analysis and debate. However, a critical difference now exists: the complexity of competition in the securities markets is better recognized today. In the 1970s, it was thought that interdealer competition needed strengthening and that the desired product of competition would be tighter bid-ask spreads. Now there is a growing sense that interdealer competition does not necessarily result in tighter posted spreads, as noted by Joel Hasbrouck in chapter 12 in this book. In both the United States and Britain, dealers commonly post wider spreads and then give executions within the quotes, especially when others free-ride on their prices. The practice might be a good competitive response; but for the aggregate market, it impairs transparency.

In the 1990s, competition is increasingly seen as occurring between markets that offer different trading technologies. The desired product of competition is now recognized to include both lower execution costs (including bid-ask spreads and market impact) and sharpened price discovery.[23] Without question, the efficiency of the U.S. markets has benefited from the traditional battle for listings between the agency/auction exchanges (NYSE, the American Stock Exchange, and so forth) and NASDAQ. Now, intermarket competition is being further strengthened by the arrival of the proprietary trading systems. The enriched set of alternatives enables buy-side customers to "vote" by directing their order flow to those market centers that give them the best results.

But it is one thing to argue for competition in the abstract and another to adhere to a truly competitive stance in relation to specific issues. For instance, consider the challenges involved when a satellite market attracts order flow away from a major market center such as the NYSE. The exchange has certain options; it could make adjustments in its trading system, or it could seek regulatory support in requiring order flow consolidation.[24] Assume the NYSE seeks regulatory support—that is, pressures the SEC to keep Rule 390, to disallow payment for order flow, and to constrain the development of the satellite market—and does not innovate with regard to its own trading system. How should the SEC respond?

A standard regulatory approach would be to consider the arguments concerning each issue and to decide the preferred market structure "by committee." Alternatively, the agency could let the market decide. This would mean (1) allow Rule 390 to stand because the NYSE, as a competitive player in the market, believes it to be in its best self-interest to impose an order focusing rule on its members, (2) allow payment for order flow, and (3) allow the satellite market to operate without undue regulatory restriction because alternative trading technologies put competitive pressure on a major market center to innovate.

The second alternative may be difficult to select, especially because externality arguments concerning payment for order flow are valid. However, regulation itself can have complex, unintended effects, as noted by Corinne Bronfman in Chapter 13 in this book. With the intricacies of both competition and regulation more fully perceived, the opinion has been broadly voiced that the regulators should rein in their desire to control market structure.[25] Given the competition that now exists and the advances in market structure that sophisticated technology will no doubt enable in the future, designing market structure by the regulatory process is more apt to impair the efficiency of competition, than it is to bring us trading systems that will better service the needs of buy-side participants.

OVERVIEW OF THE BOOK

The book is divided into three sections. The first deals with technological and competitive challenges, the second with regulatory challenges, and the third with global challenges.

Technological and Competitive Challenges

The first four chapters in this section present a broad overview of the competitive environment. James Shapiro focuses on the forces generating new competition and on how they will drive the evolution of U.S. securities trading as manifested at the NYSE. Roger Hendrick surveys developments over the past 15 years in the U.S. equity markets, highlighting ways in which the market has fragmented. He emphasizes that the exchanges need to reintegrate pieces of the markets to maximize liquidity while providing a fair playing field. Gene Finn discusses key microstructure differences between dealer and agency processes and presents recent evidence of the costs to institutions of trading in the NASDAQ market. Raymond Killian and David Cushing consider the development of proprietary trading systems, noting that PTS alternatives to the central market fill a niche that the central market does not itself fill at the current time. They predict that the electronic layer now provided by the PTSs will become the marketplace of the future, instead of just a gateway, as it is today.

The next three chapters in this section deal with specific issues concerning the provision of liquidity and the magnitude of transaction costs. Jacques Hamon, Puneet Handa, Bertrand Jacquillat, and Robert Schwartz, noting that buy-side market participants can be classified as either liquidity suppliers or liquidity demanders, examine the profitability of limit order trading on the NYSE and Paris Bourse. Their findings suggest that, despite structural differences, both of these markets compensate public limit order traders for supplying liquidity to the market. Focusing on the temporal consolidation of orders, Nicholas Economidies shows how the provision of liquidity is enhanced by call market trading. He proposes that transaction fees in call market trading be time differentiated so as to encourage early order placement, thereby enhancing the transparency and liquidity of the market. Hans Stoll estimates the magnitude of equity trading costs (both commissions and market impact) from the aggregate revenue of securities firms in the years 1980–1992. He presents estimates of public trading costs, as a proportion of portfolio value, and of securities firms revenues, relative to their trading volume.

The last two chapters of the section discuss two new approaches for analyzing the effect of market structure on performance. Kevin McCabe, Stephen Rassenti, and Vernon Smith focus on the use of experimental economics to design electronic auctions and to assess the quality of market performance. Bruce Weber shows how a simulated environment, where a live player enters orders into a computer-simulated market, can be used to compare alternative market designs and to measure the player's performance.

Regulatory Challenges

The first seven chapters in this section deal with issues relating to the SEC's Market 2000 study. Brandon Becker presents the considerations of a regulator, based on his experience as director of the SEC's Division of Market Regulation, which had responsibility for producing the report. His chapter, coauthored with Janet Angstadt, is titled "Market 2000: A Work in Progress." It captures the reality that work on the complex issues involved is never totally complete. The next three chapters consider issues relating to the report, such as transparency, fragmentation, and the role of regulators in the design of market architecture. Kenneth Lehn discusses the main issues of the Market 2000 study. He recommends that the SEC not lay down a regulatory blueprint, as this would impede innovation, given the substantial technological changes that will no doubt occur in the near future. In focusing on transparency issues, Joel Hasbrouck considers how disclosure requirements impose private costs on the parties who produce information and stresses that fragmentation does impose a cost on an exchange such as the NYSE. Corinne Bronfman comments on the changing regulatory role in the United States, paying particular attention to the futures markets. She addresses the issue of whether the goals of protecting investors and facilitating competition are consistent.

The next three chapters in this section deal with market structure issues from the users' point of view. Harold Bradley urges the SEC to affirm the proprietary trading systems because they provide low cost, instant access to a transparent marketplace as well as other benefits. He further states that the NYSE should supplement traditional continuous markets with a call market structure at the open and the close, and he predicts that strategic alliances will be formed in the future as the distinction between money management firms and broker/dealer firms blurs. Eric Fisher, in dealing with the fragmentation issue, stresses that the proprietary trading systems offer much lower commissions and market impact costs, which increases liquidity. Chris Hynes, while considering the issues of segmentation, payment for order flow, and soft-dollar arrangements, urges the SEC to let the markets develop flexibility so as to best meet the needs of different types of investors.

The next two chapters consider fundamental issues concerning the organization of a securities market. Chester Spatt and Sanjay Srivastava look at the rules underlying the design of the NYSE's agency/auction market and consider their implications for the market's dynamics. Lawrence Harris analyzes the economic forces that cause markets to consolidate, fragment, and coalesce into a unified complex of diverse segments. He explains that different traders, solving different problems, prefer different market mechanisms, and that trader-coordinated price formation across various market structures is possible.

The last three chapters in the section present specific regulatory proposals. Junius Peake proposes that the current minimum price variation of ⅛ of a point be eliminated in favor of decimal pricing (a major recommendation in the Market 2000 report). He suggests that the change would save investors more than a billion dollars annually, while making the markets more efficient and less volatile. Yakov Amihud and Haim Mendelson discuss the effects of liquidity on asset prices in multimarket trading and propose that a company have the legal right to determine the specific global markets in which its stock can be traded (which is in harmony with the recommendation in the Market 2000 report that delisting requirements be eased for NYSE-listed companies). Edward Fleischman describes the major features of the model for federal regulatory reform proposed by the Chicago Mercantile Exchange and explains the reasons for and likely impact of the consolidation of all financial agencies into a single cabinet-level department, organized along functional lines, and structured to encourage innovation and adaptation in international markets.

Global Challenges

The first five chapters of this section deal with fundamental issues concerning the globalization of trading. William Donaldson addresses the issue of how to keep national securities regulation in harmony with a global marketplace. In so doing, he notes that the NYSE is working on technological innovations that will make 24-hour trading, and trading in multiple currencies, a reality on the NYSE in the not-too-distant future. William Freund discusses two implications of international equity trading: (1) cross-country listings of equities must bend to the information disclosure standards of major global markets, rather than to the preference of domestic regulators, and (2) trade reporting must recognize the realities of global institutional trading and its effect on transnational liquidity. Rolf-E. Breuer provides an overview of global developments in the equity markets, including the growth of institutional investors and the advent of electronic trading. He discusses the concept of a single European Stock Exchange in the year 2000 and considers its consequences for market participants. Ian Domowitz looks at issues of market transparency and fragmentation, while considering the European community's Investment Services Directive (ISD) as a basis for regulating markets in locations such as London and Paris. In so doing, he shows how automation has changed both dealer and auction market structures and has thus far encouraged fragmentation. Andrew Large makes a strong point that regulators must take a fresh look at problems and not just keep doing things the way they have always been done. Specifically, he states that mechanisms are needed to bring harmonization to global markets, but with as little regulation as possible.

The next seven chapters deal with developments in various international market centers. Stephen Wells describes the London equities market, an institutional electronic market that has become decentralized. He addresses regulatory challenges brought on by the ISD and diverging user needs with respect to regulation and trading costs. Anthony Neuberger examines the cost of doing large vs. small trades on the London Stock Exchange. He looks at the overall profitability of order matching and position taking and finds that order matching is the only way to make profits consistently. Turning to the French market, Bertrand Jacquillat, Robert Schwartz, and Jacques Hamon describe the introduction of a facility, PIBAL, that would enable companies to be the source of additional liquidity for their own shares and, in so doing, bring additional liquidity to the Paris Bourse. Reto Francioni explains the new German Exchange Organization founded in 1993 and the structure of its cash and derivatives market. In so doing, he discusses the future potential of the German financial markets, the growing role of electronic trading in the cash market, and offers insights into how these developments will further be effected by the ISD. Bernardo González-Arichéga describes the Bolsa Mexicana, including its second-tier market introduced in 1993, which is organized as an electronic call market. Jianping Mei discusses the growth of the Shanghai equities market. He considers both primary and secondary operations, including the problems and opportunities the Chinese market faces in the near future. Kazuhisa Okamoto reviews the past and present condition of Japanese pension fund management and analyzes the current situation. He points out that pension fund returns are currently deteriorating and that investment advisory companies are beginning to take a more active role in the management of these funds.

Acknowledgements

Through the various stages of this project, from the organization of the conference to the publication of this volume, a number of people have been helpful. In particular, I wish to express my thanks to Ingo

Walter, Roy Smith, Mary Jaffier, Karen Golis, and Jim Cozby. The project could not have been undertaken without them.

NOTES

1. Junius Peake, Morris Mendelson, and R. T. Williams, Jr., "The National Book System: An Electronically Assisted Auction Market," Proceedings of the National Market Advisory Board of the Securities and Exchange Commission, April 30, 1976.
2. See Eric Fisher, "Comments on Market Fragmentation: The User's Perspective," chapter 15 of this book.
3. See Dale Oesterle, Donald Winslow, and Seth Anderson, "The New York Stock Exchange and Its Out Moded Specialist System: Can the Exchange Innovate to Survive?" *The Journal of Corporation Law,* Winter 1992.
4. See Brandon Becker and Janet Angstadt, "Market 2000: A Work in Progress," chapter 10 of this book.
5. See Harold Bradley, "Market 2000: The User's Perspective"; Ian Domowitz, "Financial Market Automation and the Investment Services Directive"; and Joel Hasbrouck, "Trade and Quote Transparency: Principles and Prospects for the Year 2000," chapters 14, 25, and 12, respectively, of this book.
6. Mark Edwards and Wayne Wagner, "Best Execution," *Financial Analysts Journal,* January/February 1993.
7. See Bertrand Jacquillat, Robert Schwartz, and Jacques Hamon, "A Program to Increase the Liquidity of Shares in the French Equity Market," chapter 29 of this book.
8. See Thomas Ho, Robert Schwartz, and David Whitcomb, "The Trading Decision and Market Clearing under Transaction Price Uncertainty," *Journal of Finance*, March 1985; Corinne Bronfman and Robert Schwartz, "Price Discovery Noise," New York University working paper, 1993; and Puneet Handa and Robert Schwartz, "Dynamic Price Discovery," New York University working paper, 1993.
9. See, for instance, Joel Hasbrouck and Robert Schwartz, "Liquidity and Execution Costs in Equity Markets," *Journal of Portfolio Management,* Spring 1988.
10. See Lawrence Harris, "Consolidation, Fragmentation, Segmentation, and Regulation," chapter 18 of this book.
11. See Junius Peake, "Brother, Can You Spare a Dime? Let's Decimalize the U.S. Equity Markets!" chapter 19 of this book.
12. I have, with reference to an agency/auction market such as the NYSE or a dealer market such as NASDAQ, elsewhere proposed that the electronic call be used to open a continuous market at twelve noon and once again to close the market. See Kalman Cohen and Robert Schwartz, "An Electronic Call Market: Its Design and Desirability," in Henry Lucas and Robert Schwartz (eds.), *The Challenge of Information Technology for the Securities Markets: Liquidity, Volatility, and Global Trading,* Dow Jones–Irwin, 1989; and Nicholas Economidies and Robert Schwartz, "Electronic Call Market Trading," *Journal of Portfolio Management*, winter 1995.
13. See William Freund, "Two SEC Rules in an Era of Transnational Equities Trading," and Ian Domowitz, "Financial Market Automation and the Investment Services

Directive," chapters 23 and 25, respectively, of this volume.

14. Large trades are not reported for 90 minutes in the SEAQ market, and very large trades are not reported for five days. Moreover, the London market makers commonly post relatively wide bid-ask spreads and then give executions within the touch (the market bid-ask spread).

15. See Nicholas Economidies and Robert Schwartz, "Electronic Call Market Trading," New York University working paper, 1994; and Nicholas Economidies, "How to Enhance Market Liquidity," chapter 6 of this book.

16. See Brandon Becker and Janet Angstadt, "Market 2000: A Work in Progress"; Corinne Bronfman, "In the Public Interest? Reassessing the Regulatory Role in the Financial Markets"; Joel Hasbrouck, "Trade and Quote Transparency: Principles and Prospects for the Year 2000"; and Kenneth Lehn, "The Market for Marketplaces: Reflections on the SEC's Market 2000 Report," chapters 10, 13, 12, and 11, respectively, of this book.

17. The Intermarket Trading System is an electronic execution and linkage system that displays quotes for exchange-listed securities to market makers on national and regional exchanges and in the over-the-counter (OTC) market.

18. NYSE Rule 390 prohibits NYSE member firms from entering into principal executions in exchange-listed securities away from an exchange floor. The scope of the rule was narrowed in July 1980, when the SEC instituted Rule 19c.3, which allows exchange members to make off-board markets for issues listed after April 26, 1979.

19. Many of the comment letters submitted in response to the release have urged that competition, not legislative interference, be relied on to drive markets toward greater efficiency.

20. For an early presentation of this argument, see Ernest Bloch and Robert Schwartz, "The Great Debate over NYSE Rule 390," *Journal of Portfolio Management,* Fall 1978.

21. See James Shapiro, "U.S. Equity Markets: Recent Competitive Developments," chapter 1 of this book.

22. A fundamental economic question relates to these practices. Who should have the property rights to the prices that are established in a market: the market center itself, the traders whose (limit) orders have established the prices at which others might trade, and/or the brokerage houses that provide the information and other services that bring the customers to the market? The answer might well be all three.

23. In the standard microeconomic paradigm, competition is typically in terms of price. However, in a dynamic, technologically sophisticated environment, competition can also be in terms of technology itself.

24. For instance, appreciable order flow could be recaptured by the exchange in the absence of an order focusing rule if it were to introduce an electronic call market into its system. I have argued elsewhere (Schwartz, "Competition and Efficiency," in Kenneth Lehn and Robert Kamphuis (eds.), *Modernizing U.S. Securities Regulation: Economic and Legal Perspectives,* Business One Irwin, 1993, and Schwartz and Economidies, "Electronic Call Market Trading," op. cit.) that free riding on price discovery is more difficult in a call market than in a continuous market environment.

25. See Kenneth Lehn, "The Market for Marketplaces: Reflections on the SEC's Market 2000 Report," chapter 11 of this book.

PART ONE

TECHNOLOGICAL AND COMPETITIVE CHALLENGES

CHAPTER 1

U.S. EQUITY MARKETS: RECENT COMPETITIVE DEVELOPMENTS

James E. Shapiro

INTRODUCTION

Since 1987 there has been an apparent quickening of the pace of competition in the trading of equities in the United States. Without a doubt, the New York Stock Exchange (NYSE)—the dominant central market—faces new and potent competitive challenges. In this chapter I will briefly outline some of the forces generating new competition and comment on how these competitive forces are likely to drive the evolution of U.S. securities trading.

The broad contours of the competitive environment in the United States can be discerned from Figure 1–1. While the NYSE clearly dominates trading, as measured by dollar volume, NASDAQ, a screen-based quotation system that facilitates over-the-counter trading in both over-the-counter and exchange-listed securities, has grown significantly in recent years. Volume data from dealer markets (such as NASDAQ) and from auction markets (such as the NYSE) are not strictly comparable because of the different market structures and different proportions of

The opinions expressed in this chapter are those of the author and do not necessarily represent those of the NYSE, its Board of Directors, or its officers.

FIGURE 1–1
Distribution of Trade[a] in U.S. Equities

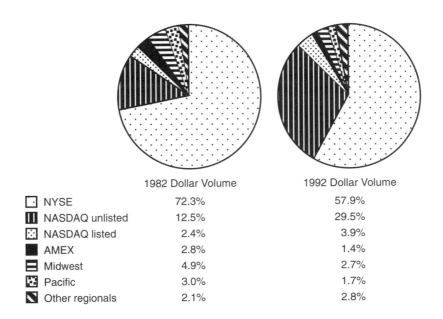

	1982 Dollar Volume	1992 Dollar Volume
NYSE	72.3%	57.9%
NASDAQ unlisted	12.5%	29.5%
NASDAQ listed	2.4%	3.9%
AMEX	2.8%	1.4%
Midwest	4.9%	2.7%
Pacific	3.0%	1.7%
Other regionals	2.1%	2.8%

[a] Includes foreign stocks traded in the United States but does not include off-shore trading, pink sheets, or Fourth Market trading (Instinet, POSIT, etc.)

customer/dealer trading. Nevertheless, the trend in recent years is clear: trading effected through dealers in the over-the-counter (OTC) market has grown as a share of total reported trading.

Traditionally, the role of the OTC market was limited to those equities considered too small or closely held to support auction market trading and which, therefore, required dealer support to maintain liquidity. Today, OTC trading has grown to become significant, even in stocks liquid enough to support auction market trading.

In the market for NYSE-listed stocks, the NYSE still retains over 80 percent of the volume. But the NYSE's share has declined appreciably since 1987, and nearly all of that decline can be attributed to increased competition from dealers—either NYSE member firms who "internalize" customer orders to trade against them as principal rather than send them to the NYSE's auction market or to third market firms who make over-the-counter markets in NYSE-listed stocks.[1]

DIVERSION OF SMALL ORDERS IN NYSE-LISTED STOCKS

While the NYSE still clearly dominates the overall market for NYSE-listed stocks, its position is substantially eroded if certain segments are examined separately. In trades of 100 to 2,099 shares, for example, the NYSE currently accounts for around 65 percent of the share volume. In part because the competition is fiercest for these small, typically retail orders, this sector raises several interesting issues and deserves closer scrutiny.

Following the Securities Acts Amendments of 1975, the SEC tried to promote the development of a National Market System (MNS) based on the notion that market centers would compete for order flow by disseminating superior quotations and that brokers would route orders to the market with the best quotation.[2]

Despite the Commission's quotation-based model of an NMS, the competition that has actually materialized in the listed equity market has little to do with quotations. While some markets occasionally disseminate quotations superior to the NYSE (the "primary" market), the competition that has developed involves nonprimary markets pricing transactions derivately off the best advertised bid or offer, which is usually in the primary market. For the month of September 1993, for example, there were 3,447,735 trades in the 2,278 NYSE common stocks across all market centers, including the National Association of Securities Dealers (NASD). Among them, 3,168,917 (92 percent) trades occurred when the NYSE had the best consolidated bid, and 91 percent (3,137,575) of the trades occurred when the NYSE had the best consolidated offer.[3]

Many factors affect the decisions by broker/dealers to route customer orders to one execution facility rather than another—only rarely is best quote one of them. Because the nonprimary markets are required to disseminate quotations, there is a proliferation of meaningless "auto-quotes"—computer-generated quotes at the same price or an eighth outside the primary market quote. These auto-quotes, which are typically for the minimum 100-share round lot, have little effect on the information content of the quotes and have little to do with broker decisions about where to route an order. Despite the fact that the NYSE quote is the best consolidated bid or offer more than 90 percent of the time, far fewer than 90 percent of the *orders* to trade NYSE-listed stocks are routed to the NYSE.

The lack of quote-based or explicit price competition among markets and dealers is particularly interesting, given the way that the theoretical finance literature has almost completely ignored the phenomenon. While there are many models of nonprice competition in the industrial organization literature, models of financial markets have nearly always assumed that price competition is at least one of the primary determinants of the bid-ask spread. To some degree, this gap may be related to the fact that the primary concern of financial models has always been the pricing of assets, rather than the pricing of the services relating to the trading of those assets. As the competition for these "exchange" services heats up and gets more interesting, the theoretical literature will likely explore these issues as it has in other nonfinancial markets.

Of course, the fact that there is nonprice competition does not mean that there *is not* price competition. Markets and dealers cannot ignore the best prevailing price. In most cases they must match it, either by advertising a quote as good as the best bid or offer or by guaranteeing a price "as good as anyone else's advertised price."

Nonprice competition in U.S. equity markets appears closely related to intraquote trading. On the NYSE, for example, in September 1993, 28 percent of *all* trades in NYSE common stocks occurred between the NYSE bid and offer. When the spread is greater and $^1/_8$ of a dollar, the majority of trades (66 percent) occurred between the NYSE quote.

Why has competition failed to produce even narrower spreads? It may be that effective spreads rather than quoted spreads are the proper metric and that effective spreads are "appropriately" narrow, despite wider quoted spreads. This is an empirical issue which will not be sorted out easily. But, leaving aside the issue of whether advertised spreads are too narrow or too wide, my reading of the available evidence is that these spreads do not appear to shrink in the face of competition, at least as much as we might expect them to. Table 1–1 illustrates a related fact. Examining data from September 1993, it is clear how little the NYSE's competition attempts to rely on better quotes to attract business. It is also clear how muchwider advertised spreads are on these alternative markets.

TABLE 1–1
Trading in NYSE Common Stocks (September 1993)

Exchange[a]	Trades	Volume	Trade-weighted Spread[b] (cents)
Boston	115,543	71,353,600	43.3
Cincinnati	143,145	87,122,400	32.0
Chicago	286,392	285,579,700	40.0
NYSE	2,148,008	5,417,248,858	20.0
Pacific	255,611	139,383,000	35.7
NASDAQ	370,187	296,990,300	28.5
Philadelphia	128,849	84,905,500	49.7
Total	3,447,735	6,382,582,358	26.1

[a] The American Stock Exchange is not shown here because it does not trade any NYSE-listed common stocks.
[b] The trade-weighted spread is defined as

$$\frac{\sum_{i=1}^{n}(\text{offer}_i - \text{bid}_i)}{n}$$

where i indexes the bids and offers in effect on each market at the time each of the n trades occur.

It has been suggested that relaxing the minimum tick would cause advertised spreads to narrow—and presumably this logic is behind a recent SEC proposal to move to decimal pricing.[4] But it is by no means clear—at least to me—whether relaxing the minimum tick size on the NYSE would result in narrower spreads, given the current state of quote-based competition.[5]

A second hypothesis is that intermarket competition among decentralized (and imperfectly linked) markets or dealers is less effective at reducing spreads than intramarket competition among limit orders.[6] There arc two reasons why this may be the case. First, if time priority and other secondary priority rules are not enforced across dealers or markets, then limit orders will have less incentive to reveal themselves to the market. The role such limit orders plays in narrowing the spread on the NYSE is substantial. Second, if order exposure rules are not enforced across markets, intermarket competition through quote matching may lead to less willingness to reveal limit orders to narrow the advertised quote, because revealing a limit order allows others simply to trade elsewhere *at* your quote but not *with* you.

A final hypothesis is that increasing competition among dealers (as opposed to competition among customer limit orders) does not necessarily lead to narrower spreads because dealers have strong incentives to maintain wide spreads. For example, despite the fact that in the highest capitalization NASDAQ stocks—household names like Apple, Microsoft, etc.—there are 30 or more competing dealers, spreads remain surprisingly wide.[7] Competition between these dealers does not reduce the advertised spread as effectively as one might imagine. In fact, the average spread is approximately twice as large as the spread for similarly active and large stocks traded on the NYSE. One explanation of this phnomenon is that dealers may find it desirable *not* to compete by narrowing the spread, because a relatively large spread (greater than the minimum tick size) facilitates interdealer transactions within the spread. This wider spread, in turn, may make it easier (through interdealer trades) for one dealer with a customer's buy order to share the quoted spread with another dealer with a customer's sell order. Until we know more about the volume of interdealer trading on NASDAQ, it will be difficult to evaluate this—and other—hypotheses of why spreads remain so wide on that market.

Agency Problems

For smaller orders under 1,000 shares, the most important reason for the fact that trades are increasingly diverted away from the NYSE is that dealer markets provide profitable opportunities for dealers to trade for their own account. Own-account trading has become increasingly important as competition has sharply reduced commission income—to around 15 percent of gross income for NYSE member firms[8] (See Figure 1–2). For dealers, a small retail order offers the best risk/reward ratio because it is very unlikely to move the price of a security.

When brokers buy or sell stock on a customer's behalf, they act as agents. When the interests of an agent are different from those of the agent's customer, we have what is commonly referred to as an "agency problem." The fact that dealer trading of small orders is so lucrative poses a potentially serious agency problem. Most investors do not choose the market in which they trade—their brokers do. When retail investors give their orders to their brokers, they rarely specify where the

FIGURE 1–2
**Securities Commissions, Trading and Investment Revenues of
NYSE Member Firms**

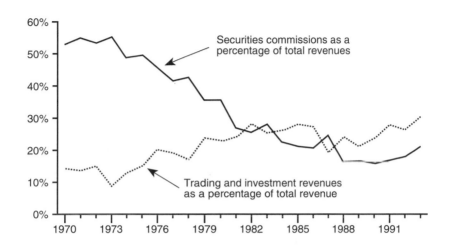

order should be executed. Retail customers typically either assume that NYSE-listed stocks are always traded on the NYSE, or they do not care because they assume that as long as they get the best quoted bid or offer they are receiving the best possible execution.

Unfortunately, the assumption that where a small order executes does not affect the quality of execution appears to be mistaken. Several empirical studies using trade-by-trade transaction data have found that small orders sent to the NYSE receive, on average, better executions than those sent elsewhere.[9]

This is particularly disturbing because much of the small investor order flow is being "sold" by retail brokerage firms to automated dealer systems which offer quick execution at the best bid or offer. Small investors in particular—even if provided with specific disclosure of payments as the SEC is proposing—are the least able to effectively monitor the quality of their trading through agents. As additional empirical evidence accumulates, policy makers will be more able to judge the degree to which retail investors are disadvantaged by the sale of their orders to dealer execution systems. Unfortunately, even if small retail investors are disadvantaged by this practice, the economic incentive for broker/ dealers to trade against their retail order flow is so powerful that there is little likelihood of this practice abating without at least some regulatory intervention.

For the NYSE, competition from dealers for small retail trades presents difficult choices. Would it be wise to adopt the practices of our competitors, executing small orders at the bid and offer and paying for order flow? Because this would be difficult to accomplish without "dealerizing" our own small trades, it poses obvious philosophical problems. If we cannot or are unwilling to dealerize small trades ourselves, the key issue becomes *what can the NYSE do to narrow the spreads in those stocks where dealer competition is greatest?* One obvious suggestion is to reduce the minimum tick size. But, as noted above, it is not at all clear that this will be effective in narrowing spreads. Clearly, the more we know about market structure—the influence of tick size, priority rules, limit order submission, and so forth—the better we will be able to find an answer.

Under current conditions, it is hard to see how an auction market like the NYSE can compete effectively by paying for order flow, for the simple reason that neither the exchange nor the specialists on the floor earn the entire spread, as off-exchange dealers do. The spread on the floor is dissipated among customers. Every time two customer orders meet, one of them saves—or both of them share—the spread. Because 82 percent of NYSE volume is transacted without NYSE specialists taking the other side, it would be impossible for NYSE specialists to pay as much for order flow as "pure" dealers do.

Competition is fierce in the U.S. equity markets, in part because of deliberate and effective regulations to encourage it. As U.S. equity markets evolve, however, care is needed to ensure that public policies which are intended to benefit investors by encouraging competition (through, of course, quote competition) do not merely enrich intermediaries (by, for example, increasing the percentage of trading done through dealers).

FOREIGN TRADING OF NYSE-LISTED STOCKS

The threat to the NYSE that organized exchanges overseas will take away trading in NYSE-listed stocks is more potential than real at the present time. Blue chip U.S. companies are currently listed on major exchanges around the world and have been for some time. But, except for London, trading on these exchanges is relatively modest.

Currently, reported trading in NYSE-listed stocks is about 4.5 million shares a day in London and about 300,000 to 400,000 shares in each of the other major markets, Tokyo, Paris, and Frankfurt. Trading of U.S. stocks in other non-U.S. markets is negligible.

In addition to *reported* trading of NYSE stocks overseas, however, there is a substantial amount done in a variety of ways off exchange and "sort of" off exchange (see Figure 1–3). To give an example, a foreign subsidiary of a U.S. broker/dealer may be active in London without becoming a member of the London Stock Exchange. Such a firm's over-the-counter trades in NYSE stocks would not be *publicly* reported, although they would be reported to the British self-regulatory organization, the Securities and Futures Authority. (Estimates of this activity are included in "other foreign trading" in Figure 1–3.)

A large portion of non-U.S. activity in NYSE-listed stocks consists of off-hours program trading, largely done by NYSE member firms sending a fax to a foreign branch. The NYSE's Crossing Session II, introduced June 13, 1991, was an attempt to repatriate this type of activity by allowing firms to "fax" these trades to the NYSE where they can be reported. To date, Crossing Section II has repatriated over half this activity. Neither we nor the organized exchanges in the countries where the faxes are sent are likely to find a way to structure this business to make it a significant revenue generator. But the NYSE (and presumably the SEC) believes it is useful to have it occur in the United States for regulatory purposes.

In addition, there is an unknown (and, to some extent, unknowable) amount of offshore trading in NYSE-listed stocks which is done by non-NYSE member firms. The number used in Figure 1–3 for "other foreign trading" includes a rough estimate of this activity, based on anecdotal sources.

The NYSE still dominates international trading in NYSE issues. This home market domination is the rule not only in the United States but also throughout the world. However, the increasing number of exceptions to this rule indicate that it would be foolish to plan on its continuing forever. Foreign trading now accounts for over 7 percent of NYSE volume, and in absolute terms it has been rising rapidly in 1993 as U.S. investor interest and the number of foreign-listed companies have grown (see Figure 1–4). U.S. investors make up the largest and

FIGURE 1–3
Off-Hours and Foreign Trading in NYSE-Listed Issues (first half of 1993)

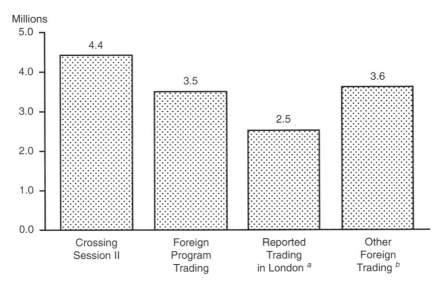

Millions

a Reported trading by London Stock Exchange member firms.
b Estimated.

richest investor base in the world. This concentration of investors, as well as the lack of competing major foreign markets in overlapping time zones, will tend to work in favor of the NYSE and other U.S. financial markets as international competition for transnational trading heats up.

ALTERNATIVE TRADING MECHANISMS WITH DIRECT INSTITUTIONAL ACCESS

Institutional trading is of increasing importance to the NYSE. While the percentage of NYSE trading initiated by institutions has varied over time, it appears to be growing as more and more marketable assets come under the control of U.S. institutions.

These institutions appear to be increasingly attracted to crossing networks and other nontraditional trading mechanisms, because they

FIGURE 1–4
NYSE Average Daily Volume in Foreign Stocks

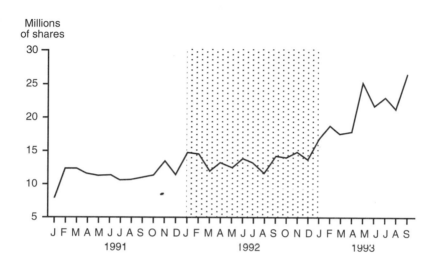

want to interact with each other and cut out the middlemen. Nontraditional trading mechanisms typically bypass both the organized exchanges and the exchange's members.

This is a significant challenge to all organized exchanges and their member firms. Alternatives to exchange-based trading are growing, and the virtues of this direct institution-to-institutuion approach—often referred to as the "fourth market"—are being touted by users with missionary zeal. It is in the users' interest to induce more participants into these systems to increase liquidity. Also, the users are generally young and find these new trading systems in harmony with their attraction to technology.

Right now, the most frequently used mechanisms are POSIT (run by ITG), the Crossing Network, Instinet (both owned by Reuters), and the Arizona Stock Exchange (operated by AZX Inc.). (See Figure 1–5.)

POSIT, which stands for Portfolio System for Institutional Trading, began operating in October 1987. Its hours of operation are 7 a.m. to 7 p.m. on days when primary markets are open. There are many pricing options, but the most commonly used appears to be the midpoint of the bid and ask, during preset windows. Users have a variety of options

FIGURE 1–5
Estimated 1993 Average Daily Volume (NYSE issues only) [a]

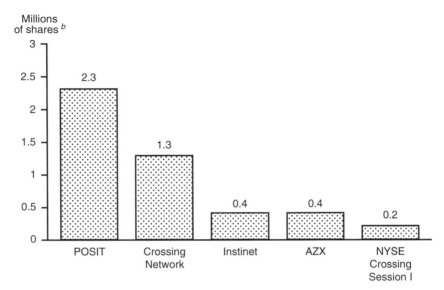

Millions of shares [b]

POSIT: 2.3
Crossing Network: 1.3
Instinet: 0.4
AZX: 0.4
NYSE Crossing Session I: 0.2

[a] Excludes AMEX, OTC, and London issues.
[b] Counting only one side of each trade.

about disclosing their identity. Most transactions are done during regular NYSE hours (9:30 a.m. to 4 p.m.). Since ITG is a member of the NASD, these trades are reported to the consolidated tape as NASD-sold sales. Trading outside regular hours is reported to the NASD and, therefore, to the SEC on Form T, which is not publicly available. According to industry reports, this later activity averages about 600,000 shares per day.

Instinet is Reuters's system operating during regular trading hours. Its success in NYSE issues has been modest compared with its success in OTC issues where they claim to execute 15 percent of NASDAQ volume. Reuters's after-hours system, the Crossing Network, which began operations in October 1986, has been more successful in NYSE issues. The Crossing Network accepts orders during the day and attempts computerized matches between 6 p.m. and 7 p.m. Both POSIT and the Crossing Network staffs have the right to solicit counterparties for orders, but they claim they do not. Pricing options include the primary market close for listed stocks, the mean of the closing bid and ask for over-the-counter stocks and a weighted average price for the day.

All of the Crossing Network's activity is after consolidated tape hours (9:30 a.m. to 5:15 p.m.). Consequently, these trades are also reported to the NASD on Form T and not made public. The estimate of two million shares a day is only an informed guess, based on anecdotal evidence.

What is the appeal of these nontraditional trading systems? Users point to the following characteristics:

- The explicit costs (commissions and fees) are low.
- The users are often institutional invetors who believe that intermediaries are unnecessary to them.
- Some of these users distrust the broker/dealer community. These systems permit the institution to initiate a trade without revealing their intentions to a broker/dealer.
- The systems permit institutions to control how much information is revealed to their fellow institutional investors.
- Many of these users are among the growing number of patient investors who do not demand the immediate liquidity of a continuous NYSE-style market.

Despite the growth of institutional trading and the proliferation of alternative trading mechanisms for institutional investors, the portion of large trades (in NYSE-listed stocks) executed on the NYSE has actually increased slightly in the last few years, hovering around 90 percent (see Figure 1–6). Why is this? Technology experts have been predicting the end of hte NYSE for decades—presumably because institutions would prefer to trade large trades among themselves. But the difficulties of designing a direct institution-to-institution trading system that provides greater liquidity than the NYSE floor trading system have been nontrivial. Despite the desire of many institutional investors to use alternative trading mechanisms as much as possible, they still find themselves coming to the floor for liquidity and for the flexibility that floor brokers can offer in terms of timing and order exposure.

Block Trading

About half of the NYSE's trading volume is "block" volume—that is, trades of 10,000 shares or more. Many people believe that all block trades are facilitated by "upstairs" desks and then brought to the floor to be printed. This misconception is the result of not differentiating be-

FIGURE 1–6
NYSE Market Share of Trades Greater Than 10,000 Shares [a]

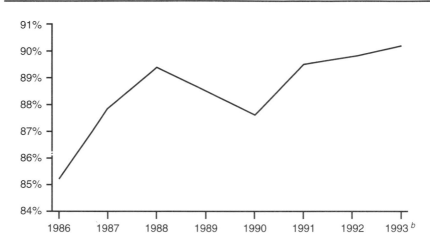

[a] NYSE-listed common and warrants only.
[b] Through September 30.

tween *upstairs-facilitated* and *block* trades. Only about one quarter of block volume is facilitated by upstairs trading desks of NYSE member firms. In other words, about 12.5 percent—or one eighth—of NYSE volume is facilitated by upstairs trading desks.

The NYSE requires a precise definition of block trading for proper enforcement of certain rules, and any trade which satisfies the definition's size requirements qualifies as a block trade, even if there are multiple buyers or sellers on one or both sides of the trade. The definition of a block trade does not require *any* upstairs participation. For the purposes of reporting "block volume," which is published in major newspapers and other media outlets each day, a block is simply a trade of 10,000 shares or more.

An upstairs-facilitated trade refers to a trade, or a portion of a trade, in which both the buyer and the seller are represented by the same member firm. Because member firms do not lable trades as "upstairs," we can only estimate upstairs-facilitated trading. NYSE Research and Planning has done some preliminary work along these lines, based on NYSE audit information.

As we would expect, upstairs trading is more common when the liquidity on the floor is not sufficient to fill an order without disrupting the price or restricting the speed of execution. For very large trades (100,000 plus shares) in the "least active stocks," upstairs trading is particularly important. However, trades of more than 10,000 shares are frequently executed without any upstairs participation. Even 100,000 shares trades, worth approximately $3 million, often rely solely on the floor for liquidity.

Will the NYSE continue to dominate the market for large trades? Perhaps. At the moment, the floor of the NYSE appears to work better than any alternatives for the execution of reasonably large trades. But it is by no means perfect, and there is no doubt that in the future it will evolve in ways that serve the needs and desires of institutional customers—including the ones who appear to have strong preferences for off-floor or non-intermediated systems. Ironically, as the number of trading systems proliferates, they may be making liquidity harder, rather than easier, to locate away from the NYSE. But alternative trading mechanisms are working every day to increase their attractiveness and liquidity. Fortunately, so is the New York Stock Exchange.

NOTES

1. NYSE Rule 390 is often misunderstood as a ban on off-exchange trading by NYSE member firms. In fact, Rule 390 only restricts NYSE member firms from trading certain NYSE-listed stocks as dealers or "crossing" two customer orders, away from an organized exchange. It is a rule designed to ensure that member firms expose their customers' order to all other orders in the market. Rule 390 in no way constrains NYSE members in trading single-sided customer orders as agent. Also, the rule only applies to NYSE-listed stocks which were listed before April 26, 1979. In all other "19c.3" issues—which now account for more than half of all NYSE-listed stocks and about half of all volume—Rule 390 does not restrict member trading.
2. For further discussion of the National Market System in this context, see the NYSE's comment letter on the SEC Division of Market Regulation's release announcing its Market 2000 study of the U.S. securities markets.
3. Lee (1992) and Blume and Goldstein (1992) find similar percentages in earlier sample periods. Hasbrouck (1993) also examines the degree to which other markets price transactions off the primary market.
4. See the recent proposed rule on Payment for Order Flow, Security and Exchange Commission, Release No. 34-33026.
5. In addition, there are other reasons why reducing the minimum tick size may—at least in theory—widen rather than narrow the quoted spread. For a discussion of some of these issues, see Lawrence E. Harris (1990).

6. See Lawrence R. Glosten (1993).
7. See "Comparison of Quote Spreads on Actively Traded NYSE and NASDAQ Stocks," NYSE Research & Planning.
8. Despite this fact, principal activity by NYSE member firms on the NYSE is still secondary to the interaction of public orders. In 1992, principal trading (purchases and sales) by specialists was 9.8 percent of total purchases and sales. Principal trading (purchases and sales) by other member firms was 12.8 percent of total purchases and sales. For more detail and historical data, see NYSE Fact Book, 1992 Data.
9. See, for example, Lee (1992), Blume and Goldstein (1992), and Petersen and Fialkowski (1994).

REFERENCES

Blume, Marshall, and Michael Goldstein. (1992). "Displayed and Effective Spreads by Market." Rodney L. White Center for Financial Research working paper no. 27–92.

Glosten, Lawrence. (1993). "Intra- and Inter-Market Competition." Columbia Business School working paper.

Harris, Lawrence. (1990). "Liquidity, Trading Rules, and Electronic Trading Sytems." New York University Salomon Center Monograph Series in Finance and Economics.

Hasbrouck, Joel. (1993). "One Security, Many Markets: Determining the Contributions to Price Discovery." New York University working paper.

Lee, Charles. (1993). "Market Integration and Price Execution for NYSE-listed Securities," *Journal of Finance,* 48: 3, pp. 1009–38.

New York Stock Exchange. (1992a). "Comparison of Quote Spreads on Actively Traded NYSE and NASDAQ Stocks." Research and Planning, New York Stock Exchange, Inc.

New York Stock Exchange. (1992b). "Comment Letter on the Market 2000 Study of the U.S. Securities Markets."

Petersen, M., and D. Fialkowski. (1994). "Posted vs. Effective Spreads: Good Prices or Bad Quotes?" Journal of Financial Economics, 35: 3 (June).

Securities and Exchange Commission. (1993). "Proposed Rule on Payment for Order Flow." Release no. 34-33026.

CHAPTER 2

THE CHANGING ROLE OF EXCHANGES

Roger D. Hendrick

Managing money and trading equities have changed radically during the past 20 years. Stock exchanges and their regulatory structure were designed in response to the needs of investors of the 1920s. Exchanges have tried to preserve their historic roles, while trying to adapt to the demands of 1990s investors. What follows will explore the evolution of the trading process, how these forces of change have challenged the traditional role of the exchanges, and what the appropriate future role for exchanges should be.

EXCHANGE REGULATION

U.S. securities markets have historically had broad participation from individual investors. Since the review of the markets after the 1929 crash, the Securities and Exchange Commission (SEC) and the exchanges have had the primary role of protecting the individual investor. The SEC and the exchanges are bound by the Securities Act of 1934 to consider the implications of any rule changes on the customer. Some of these rules include financial disclosure and reporting by corporations, prohibitions on insider trading, and limitations of selling short. In addition, issues like transparency (the ability to see the accurate price), timely reports, market manipulation, and the adequacy of capital requirements are concerns of both the exchanges and the SEC.

A significant departure from the investor protection standard occurred when the SEC approved a process for selling securities to a limited set of qualified investors with lower financial reporting and disclosure requirements. This process operates under a set of guidelines called Rule 144a, under which issues are allowed to meet a lower standard of disclosure if they sell to a set of institutions able to "fend for themselves." The 144a provisions are generally used by foreign issuers attempting to tap the resources of the U.S. capital market. The provisions have also been used by U.S. issuers as an alternative to issuing securities in the Euromarket.

The review process by the SEC requires the evaluation of the adherence of rule changes like these to the Securities Acts of 1933 and 1934 with regard to protecting individual investors. One of the central arguments of the exchanges in their letters of response to the SEC's study of the markets (called Market 2000) was that nonexchange markets are not held to the same standards of regulatory oversight. These nonexchange markets are systems generally owned and operated by broker/dealers. These systems are able to modify procedures and rules without approval by the SEC. Exchanges are burdened by the regulatory process in their ability to adapt to market demands and compete with proprietary systems on an equitable basis.

EXCHANGE VS. DEALER MARKETS

Exchange markets are bound by the standard that customer orders always have priority over dealer orders. In comparison, in dealer markets like NASDAQ, customer orders have no standing and are not represented in quotes. Opening trades in exchange issues all receive the same opening price. On NASDAQ, buy orders pay the offer, sell order receive the bid. The intervention of a dealer on each trade prevents buyer and seller from meeting and reaching an improved execution. This is illustrated in Figure 2–1, which shows the impact of spreads when stocks move from NASDAQ to the NYSE or AMEX. Recently, exchanges have begun trading selected NASDAQ issues in an effort to bring the investor the same standard of protection as in listed issues.

As noted in the August 16, 1993, *Forbes* article, "Fun and Games

FIGURE 2–1
"When Fat Spreads Thin Out"—Example of Change in Impact of Spreads When a Stock Moves from NASDAQ to the NYSE or AMEX

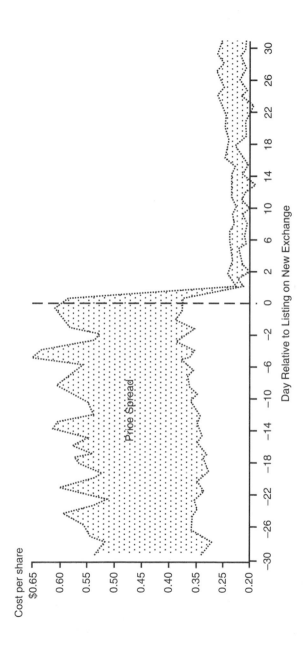

on NASDAQ," the economics of trading are more favorable for dealers in dealer markets than in exchange trading. Under the existing regulatory environment, dealer trading can exist in the same issues as exchange trading. Combined with the low level of influence that individual traders have in directing their order, dealers have purchased and traded against orders from other brokers. This has resulted in the growth of the NASD market share of trades in listed issues from 2 percent in 1985 to almost 11 percent in 1992.

TRADING

The relative percentage ownership of securities by individuals has gradually declined in importance. Individuals are often beneficial owners through their participation in company-sponsored retirement plans or by investment in mutual funds. In 1993 there were more mutual funds in existence than stocks listed on the NYSE.

During the past 30 years more and more money has become controlled by pension plans and their investment managers. The total equity holdings of pension plans and plan sponsors increased from almost $9 billion in 1950 to over $2 trillion in 1992 (see Figure 2–2). The equity holdings represented a larger commitment of the funds' portfolios, from 10 percent in 1950 to 30 percent in 1989.[1] The concentration of the holdings are reflected in the ownership of all equities by institutions, increasing from 6 percent in 1950 to over 43 percent in 1992.[2]

The ability to manage money invested in equities was enhanced by four converging developments. There were (1) the reduction of trading costs, (2) the introduction of index futures trading in February 1982, (3) the development of computerized technology, and (4) the growing interest in performance monitoring by plan sponsors.

Reduction of Trading Costs

The experience of exchanges worldwide has been that the reduction of trading costs increases volume. This can be expressed in terms of the size of the quote or the commission cost. Lower costs make a broader variety of trading strategies worthwhile. In Far East exchanges, such as Bangkok or Hong Kong, spreads are equivalent to two or three cents. This compares to 2.5 to 25 cents in the U.S. markets. The cost of trading

FIGURE 2–2
Holdings of Corporate Equities in the United States (end of period)

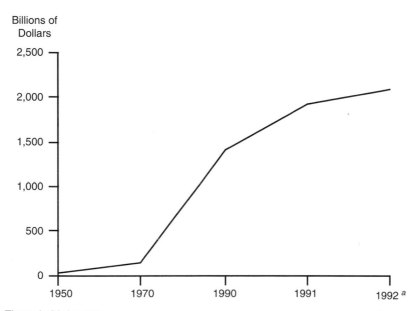

Billions of
Dollars

a Through third quarter.

Source: NYSE 1992 Fact Book

in and out is so low in these markets that it encourages speculation and liquidity.

In the United States, the drop in fixed commissions of 15 to 20 cents per share down to 4 to 6 cents has had a similar impact. This drop makes more active trading strategies viable, as shown by an increase in share turnover. This is reflected in daily share volume of NYSE-listed issues, which has gone from 19 million in 1975 to 245 million in 1992. However, the drop in commission rates also caused brokerage firms to examine their trading styles.

After the brokers experienced heavy losses during the 1987 crash, many concluded that they were not adequately compensated for trading as principal. Most reduced their capital commitments to institutions. The rationale was that if the commissions do not cover mistakes, then the broker will only trade when he is right. This magnified the adversarial relationship between institutions and brokers when brokers traded as principal and, in turn, has damaged the level of trust between them.

Index Futures Trading

Index futures impacted trading by dramatically lowering the cost of managing a portfolio. The S&P 500 Index became the measurement standard for performance on money managers. This led to index trading or commoditization of stocks, where individual stocks were traded based on their contribution to the index, rather than their own merits. According to Wayne Wagner of Plexus, "one of the results of the futures trading was the resounding acceptance of low-cost passive management." One third of all equity money under management was managed by index fund managers in 1992, according to *Pension and Investment* (January 1993).

The focus of trading for indexers became the elimination of unplanned tracking error and reduction of transaction costs. The S&P 500 future became an extremely inexpensive way to quickly shift exposure in equities. In addition, this product allowed traders to execute an exposure shift in a single trade and not be bound by short-selling restrictions in individual issues. When the NYSE introduced a product to trade all 500 issues in the S&P Index, a user had to pay $420 in exchange fees and clearing charges on individual issues to trade. A similar trade in the futures contract cost only 70 cents. While the NYSE portfolio product did receive regulatory relief for short sales, it was clear from the start that the NYSE service was doomed from cost disadvantages.

Technology

Technology has facilitated innovation and trading efficiencies in the securities industry. In many ways, technology was initially used to integrate the markets. The InterMarket Trading System (ITS) is an example of how technology was used to link the markets to ensure the maximum available liquidity for orders. This system connects each of the national exchanges and provides incentives and protection for displayed orders in the system. ITS eliminated the strategy of arbitrage between exchanges. As Figure 2–3 shows, ITS activity has grown steadily since its introduction in 1982.

The lower cost of computers allowed money managers to analyze trading opportunities and act while the profit was available. Computer

FIGURE 2–3
Average Daily Trades on the InterMarket Trading System (ITS)

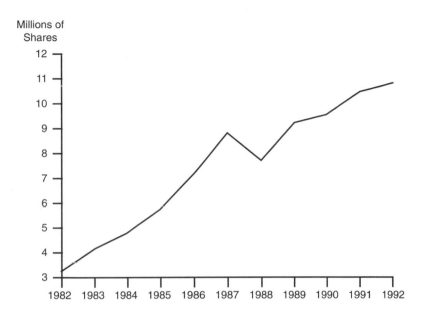

trading facilitated arbitrage between the S&P futures and the underlying equities and execution of large numbers of orders to rebalance portfolios. The advent of the NYSE Designated Order Turnaround system (DOT) and other exchange systems for electronic delivery made the process much more efficient than earlier manual processes.

Further evolution and competition between systems has led to automated execution of orders without the intervention of either broker or specialist. This resulted in extremely efficient order processing and execution for the broker community. Technology is a necessary element to handle the high volume activity that occurs routinely in the 1990s.

As technology has become more sophisticated, it has led to the development of systems which fragment the markets. As brokers have looked for more efficient ways to trade and the costs of computing have come down, private exchanges have been developed. These private exchanges have prospered in the semiregulated environment of proprietary systems. Similar pressures by money managers have led to the development of a number of alternative execution locations.

The proprietary systems fall into three categories. The first category includes the various periodic crossing systems. Examples include POSIT, Instinet's Crossing Network, and the Arizona Stock Exchange (AZX). The second category includes the trade management systems like Fidelity's ILN or First Boston's Lattice system. The third category is the group of in-house trading systems which either deliver the order to an exchange or execute against the broker's principal trading account.

Reuters's Instinet has developed a very successful network for trading primarily NASD issues. This system provides direct access by institutions and the ability to display orders at better than the NASD quote. Instinet gave institutions a significant advantage over giving orders to a broker where the order was not displayed. Instinet technology, however, was not a critical element to its success. Instinet's success can be attributed to better service to the customer and more flexible rules than the NASD market makers.

While these systems have developed as sources of liquidity, they require users to have multiple terminals to access. this has created the demand for a service that can integrate the systems through a single network. There are firms, such as Merrin or Thomson Financial, who are developing systems for this application. However, users are apprehensive about the potential for misuse of the control of order routing by these independent firms. These systems should be an industry-owned utility that has no potential conflicts on directing or capturing the order traffic.

Performance Measurement

Technology has not only brought about efficiency but also the ability to capture trade information from the point of investment decision to execution. This gives the plan sponsor the ability to monitor many facets of performance.

The monitoring of a trader's performance by money managers is being refined as sophistication and experience grows. There is wide acceptance of the need to measure performance. However, the standard for measuring execution costs ranges from "gut feeling" to a sophisticated analysis of the cost of *not trading*. While there is little standardization in the process, most managers measure total commissions paid and the market impact of individual trades. The plan sponsors are the force behind performance measurement. The sponsors are motivated by a combination of ERISA requirements and their own accountability to their plan participants.

Performance measures have found that the market impact of a trade is far more significant than the commissions paid to the broker. Studies on performance have found that the market impact of a trade varies with the relative liquidity in an issue, compared to the size of the order. One study showed that the spread in NYSE issues ranged from 0.76 percent in the top decile stock to 5.49 percent in the tenth decile.[3] These spreads are quite a bit larger than commissions, which are about 0.15 percent. This causes money managers to ask how they can reduce market impact. Many have concluded that the less liquid the stock, the more important it becomes to use passive trading strategies.

In addition to execution costs, firms are trying to measure the risk reward performance of their portfolios. The objective is to identify both tracking risk and performance risk. As Figure 2–4 shows, a key element in evaluating exposure is to identify overweighting or underweighting of elements in a "perfect" portfolio. For example, portfolios that are managed by multiple managers need to be compared to each other and the overall target of the portfolio manager. Filling holes or eliminating overlaps is a necessary step to eliminate tracking errors and reducing uncompensated risk.

FIGURE 2–4
"When the Sponsor Can't Sleep"—Serious Misfit Risk

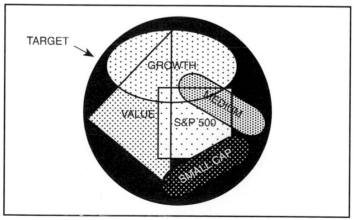

Source: Virginia Retirement System

Exchanges need to be cognizant of this as a trend so that they can develop systems for brokers to improve their own execution performance. For example, the Chicago Stock Exchange's entry into over-the-counter (OTC) trading has allowed institutions to trade inside the NASDAQ market, thus improving their overall performance and execution costs in trading OTC issues.

MARKET INNOVATION

Because of studies on performance, institutions examined their trading strategies and the technological resources to implement these strategies. Institutions that tracked their performance to an index viewed the ideal system as one in which the commission cost was low, there was little or no market impact, and the liquidity was high enough to execute a large portion of their order over some extended but acceptable period of time.

Institutions that were information-driven looked at an ideal system as one that had enough liquidity to execute their order immediately with the smallest market impact possible. Institutions also began to look to ways to execute all orders with one trade, to minimize operational expenses and costs of implementing trading strategies. Two of these strategies are the development of crossing systems and package trading.

Crossing Systems

Initial systems were developed specifically in response to the institutional requirements of no market impact and low cost. Instinet's Crossing Network was one of the first examples of such a system. The crossing systems like Instinet, Jefferie's POSIT, and AZX are unique in comparison to the national exchanges in that they allow direct access by institutions. Such direct access to exchanges has been prohibited by Congress in the Securities Acts Amendments of 1975. The NYSE after-hours trading session also matches orders, although only brokers have access. These systems price from a neutral source, such as the NYSE closing price for the consolidated quote.

There is very little order disclosure or price discovery in the systems, although the AZX system has a facility for disclosure. Orders are entered in a system and matched at the neutral price. These systems satisfy the requirements of low commission costs and low market impact, but fall short on liquidity. Even though there are millions of shares entered on these systems, generally only a very small portion of the shares match.

The Chicago Stock Exchange (CHX) is introducing a system to bring together features of the exchange market with features of the crossing systems. This institutional trading system, called Match Market Exchange (MMX), allows for the direct participation of both institutions and brokers, incorporate the features of nondisclosure for those wishing low market impact, disclosure for users interested in price discovery, and the use of premiums and discounts to improve the likelihood of matching. In addition, the system will be able to deliver unmatched orders to brokers for negotiation. MMX also integrates floor orders into the system providing them with the highest priority and order protection.

Package Trading

Another application of technology to trading has been the execution of packages of trades. The electronic execution of large numbers of orders was originally done through existing services, like the Chicago Stock Exchange's automated execution system, MAX, or the New York Stock Exchange's DOT. Most of the recent development has now been done by brokers. These systems have allowed institutions to trade packages of stocks without disclosing individual orders.

The trading of packages of stocks has been accomplished by using exchange systems or upstairs dealer bids. When exchange systems are used, individual orders are delivered to the floor for execution and re-porting. When dealer bids are used, the trade is effected relative to some basis, like the prior night's close, and is reported to the dealer's office in London or Tokyo after NYSE trading hours. This volume is not publicly reported, although brokers do file a report with the NASD on their activity. By executing trades through brokers and reporting overseas, custom-ers avoid disclosing their trading activity and any SEC fees normally associated with trades in the United States.

The systems for package trading have the advantage of liquidity and controlled market impact but suffer from high costs. Generally, dealers that bid on packages of stocks are exposed to "ignorance risk." That is, because they do not know the particular issues and sizes of orders, they must build in higher commissions in their bid to compensate for their risk. Many traders have found the implicit costs of package trading to be three to four cents per share. The other disadvantage of this approach to trading is that it places a burden on the institutional trader to categorize his portfolio by nature of the issue, liquidity demands of his portfolio, and tracking accuracy to some index. Institutions need a certain level of sophistication to use this approach.

Exchanges are burdened by requirements to trade each stock individually. It would be difficult to conform to the SEC requirements of transparency and to protect individual orders if package trading were to occur on exchanges.

CONCLUSION

The securities industry is in a period of great change. Many different elements of the industry are experimenting and developing new systems to satisfy particular trading needs. With that experimentation, fragmentation has developed. This fragmentation creates operational issues as well as investor protection issues. How can a trader be sure he has received the best execution for an order without testing every source of liquidity? How are orders in one system protected against trades in another system? Exchanges represent the best institution to accommodate the technological needs of investors while protecting the rights of individual orders.

The exchange's best role is to reintegrate the pieces of the securities markets to maximize liquidity while providing a fair and neutral playing field for all participants. By understanding the demands of the new trading styles of institutional participants, exchanges will be able to adapt current rules to include, rather than exclude, these orders in the markets. This is a role that cannot be filled by a proprietary trading system. In the interest of public policy, it is a role that should be encouraged by regulators and investors alike.

NOTES

1. Robert A. Schwartz, *Reshaping the Equity Markets: A Guide for the 1990s,* New York: Harper Business (1991), p. 197.
2. From Federal Reserve, *Flow of Funds* (1993).
3. Wayne Wagner (ed.), *The Complete Guide to Securities Transactions,* New York: John Wiley & Sons (1989), p. 211.

CHAPTER 3

INSTITUTIONS IN NASDAQ'S COMPETING DEALER MARKETS

Gene Finn

INTRODUCTION

It is ironic that the conventional wisdom continues to reflect a perception that competing dealer markets are less efficient than agency markets while economic forces continue to operate in ways that result in dealer market dominance of securities market trading. There are several misconceptions respecting the operation of agency and dealer markets that are held by researchers, investors, and even professional brokers and dealers.

Institutional experience in the NASDAQ market is the context that I have chosen to review some of these misperceptions. Institutional transactions data files are increasingly available, eliminating the need for much of the guesswork respecting microstructure differences that affect trading data. This chapter reviews some key microstructure differences and some recent evidence respecting the immediacy and liquidity services received and the apparent costs paid by institutions in the NASDAQ competing dealer process as compared to transactions in the market for exchange-listed stocks, with its greater mix of agency transactions.

INSTITUTIONALIZATION OF THE NASDAQ
STOCK LIST

The movement of institutions into NASDAQ over the past 13 years has been phenomenal (see Figure 3–1). Institutional holdings, approximated 15 percent of market value in 1979 the first year of such tabulations. They accounted for over 46 percent of market value in 1992. The average number of institutional positions per NASDAQ stock has been rising as a rate approximating 2 per year with, on average, 29 positions per company in March 1993. How much volume is accounted for by institutions is anyone's guess. Clearly, 60 to 70 percent of public average daily volume would not be an unreasonable assumption.

The institutionalization of NASDAQ actually is greater in degree than the institutionalization of the NYSE. It is apparent from Figure 3–2 that the percentage of market value held by institutions is greater for NASDAQ National Market stocks than for NYSE stocks in every market value category except the very smallest.

This makes economic sense. The potential value added by pooling

FIGURE 3–1
NASDAQ Market Value Held by Institutions

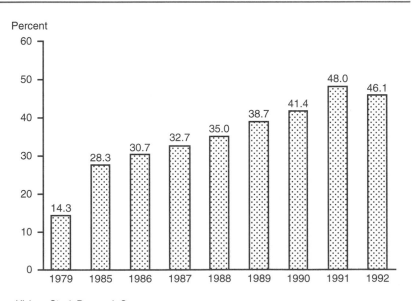

Source: Vickers Stock Research Corp.

FIGURE 3–2
Distribution of Institutional Holdings by Market and
Market Value

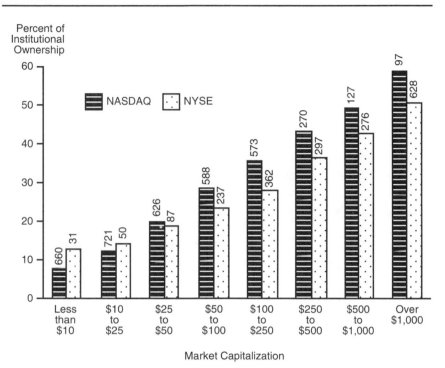

Source: Vickers Stock Research Corp.

and by money management to investment in small- and mid-cap stocks that are individually less diversified is greater than is the case for multibillion dollar firms. There ought to be a greater proportionate flow of funds through pooled investments in small- and mid-cap companies than in the billion dollar and up category corporations that already incorporate a substantial degree of diversification.

However, many still assume that more institutions will hold a stock after listing on an exchange than held it before listing. The fact is that the growth in institutional positions in NASDAQ stocks has been so rapid that the growth must be controlled for even over the four- to six-month time gaps in before-and-after listing comparisons.

DOMINANCE OF COMPETING DEALER MARKETS

The breast-beating over the prospect of dealerization of equity markets contrasts with the fact that the preponderance of securities market activity in the United States already is accomplished through competitive dealer processes. Indeed markets generally held up as the most efficient markets in the world are dealer markets. The U.S. government securities market is the most obvious example. If agency processes are naturally more efficient, why is that market not an agency market? The same question could be asked of currency markets, the municipal securities market, the corporate bond market, and the markets for government guaranteed debt securities.

Moreover, the leading U.S. agency market in equities, the NYSE, has a member participation rate equivalent to 45 percent of volume occurring on the floor, not to mention the 20 percent of volume in NYSE-listed securities that occurs in the third market and on regional exchanges. Most offboard volume is at-risk principal in character. It is probable that less than 40 percent of the volume in NYSE-listed stocks is accounted for by broker-to-broker trades (that is, agency transactions that do not involve the participation of an intermediary as principal on one side or the other). The current high level of intermediation in exchange market trading is not just true of recent periods. A high level of intermediation has been present historically on the New York Stock Exchange (see Table 3–1). The participation rate of exchange members acting as principal in transactions on the floor of the NYSE has fluctuated over the past four decades between 45 and 59 percent.

It is important to note that changes in the NYSE member participation rate are not attributable to the elimination of NYSE Rule 394 on agency trades in 1975 or to the adoption of SEC Rule 19c.3 in the early 1980s. Rule 394, the predecessor to Rule 390, required all agency and principal trades of NYSE members to be executed on an exchange. It was eliminated with respect to noncross agency trades in December 1975. Following the elimination of Rule 394 on agency trades and adoption of SEC Rule 19c.3, third-market competition became intensely competitive for retail order flow in NYSE stocks. However, this shift of retail volume apparently has not significantly affected the member participation rate. This suggests that much of that order flow was executed against members' accounts, even when it was accomplished on the exchange floor.

TABLE 3-1
New York Stock Exchange Member Participation Rate

Year	Total Member Purchases & Sales, as a Percentage of		Year	Total Member Purchases & Sales, as a Percentage of	
	NYSE-Reported Sales	NYSE-Reported Sales & Purchases		NYSE-Reported Sales	NYSE-Reported Sales & Purchases
1955	48.1%	24.1%	1974	48.4%	24.2%
1956	51.2	25.6	1975	46.8	23.4
1957	50.7	25.4	1976	46.2	23.1
1958	49.9	25.0	1977	47.2	23.6
1959	53.7	26.9	1978	48.8	24.4
1960	53.0	26.5	1979	50.0	25.0
1961	51.4	25.7	1980	53.0	26.5
1962	50.3	25.2	1981	53.2	26.6
1963	47.1	23.6	1982	55.4	27.7
1964	47.3	23.6	1983	57.1	28.5
1965	48.5	24.3	1984	55.7	27.9
1966	53.3	26.6	1985	52.6	26.3
1967	52.2	26.1	1986	55.9	27.9
1968	51.8	25.9	1987	53.2	26.6
1969	50.4	25.2	1988	45.7	22.9
1970	48.4	24.2	1989	47.5	23.7
1971	49.4	24.7	1990	46.0	23.0
1972	50.2	25.1	1991	46.4	23.2
1973	49.4	24.7	1992	45.3	22.7

If dealer intermediation has been the dominant force in markets, why then do we continued to find a preoccupation with the protection of or encouragement of agency processes? Why is so much effort focused on protecting or expanding that portion of trading activity that economic forces, in spite of regulatory protection, have relegated to a relatively small share of trading markets? While it is true that facilities have not encouraged agency processes in the competing dealer markets, I submit that there is an inadequate appreciation of the efficiency and competitiveness of dealer processes and an exaggeration of the true benefit/cost ratio of the agency process. Investors and their brokers appear to be responding to quality of service and net trade proceeds incentives in choosing markets, while much of the research and policy debate focuses on gross trade prices and ignores important service quality factors—a situation that favors agency processes in the debate, but dealer processes in the execution.

MICROSTRUCTURE DIFFERENCES BETWEEN DEALER AND AGENCY PROCESSES

Much microstructure research assumes away or ignores key differences in dealer and agency processes that, if properly quantified, would dramatically alter findings respecting the relative performance of dealer and agency markets. What are some of these assumptions?

- *That gross price trade reports and net price trade reports are equivalent and investor costs can be inferred without adjustment.* In dealer markets, institutions and possibly some other large traders do not pay commissions. They deal net. The prices quoted and reported are the net prices received or paid by the customer without further deduction of a commission. In such markets, the bid and offer quotation spreads and last-sale price differences incorporate a larger percentage of the total transaction costs of investors than do the quotation spreads and last-sale price divergences in an agency market. In agency trades, commissions are yet to be deducted from the transaction price to arrive at the investor's net price. Thus, average spreads and price differences will tend to be wider in net markets than in agency (commission) markets, even though the net proceeds to investors is the same. This is an important factor because institutions account for more than one half of trading in both exchange-listed and NASDAQ stocks.

- *Services received by investors and time lapses are assumed equivalent in every respect from the entry of the order by the investor to the trade report time stamp.* Evaluations of comparative transaction costs in agency and dealer markets frequently use trade report data which are available; and they ignore differences in commissions and in the immediacy, depth, and liquidity provided to the broker and his investor clients for which data are generally not as available. An immediate execution of the whole order at the bid/ask while on the first telephone call saves time of both investor and broker. Also differences exist in the time lapses between entry of the order, execution, and recordation of the trade report in the file ultimately used in analyses. Automated executions result in real-time trade reports. Nonautomated trade reports can take up to 90 seconds longer.

- *It is often assumed that both sides in an agency transaction benefit when intermediation by broker/dealer principals is avoided.* Limit order option costs, working order waiting costs, and the opportunity costs of missed executions often are ignored. Also not considered is the option value to unexposed bids and offers of market order exposure from the chance to improve on the quoted price if they choose. The fact that these costs are borne by public investors and are not transparent or quantified does not validate their omission in interpretations of comparative analyses of the dealer/agency processes. Moreover, the time-value costs incurred by brokers and customers in terms of their own time used to communicate and monitor pending orders and to activate reinvestment decisions for sales proceeds are not considered.

  In contrast, there is no waiting on either public side of the market when principal intermediation occurs. Both sides receive immediate executions, generally while on the telephone. The service value of participant time saved is incalculable.

- *Dealer inventory driven quotations are assumed equivalent to agency market order driven quotations even though there are important critical differences.* Dealer market size quotations are minimums rather than fixed quantities. Currently, because of the Small Order Execution System (SOES) parameter and exposure limit requirements, the minimum at-risk dealer exposure in many NASDAQ National Market stocks is 5,000 shares. In contrast, agency market size quotations reflect orders or batches of orders; and quotation prices and sizes change much more in response to trades, as the orders that form the basis of the quotation are executed.

  Also, the splitting of orders is not a problem in intermediated markets. Order sizes need not match for orders to be executed at a single price. Separate execution of odd lots does not occur.

- *An assumption if frequently made that reported share volume overstates "true" volume and that volume should be reduced to reflect only the public sides of trades.* Ignored is the fact that the immediacy being received by investors in intermediated processes is usually double the immediacy received in pure agency processes. For example, when one customer buys from a dealer and ten minutes later another customer sells to a dealer, both customers receive immediacy. Conversely, when one customer's order reposes or waits in the market for another customer's order to match, only one of the two public sides receives immediacy.

- *Finally, it is sometimes assumed, again incorrectly, that dealers virtually always buy below and sell above the midpoint of the bid/ask spread.* NASD research staff tested this assumption against NASD market surveillance and audit trail data and found it to be incorrect by a substantial margin.

One or more of the above microstructure assumptions or misconceptions is commonly present in analyses of the relative merits of competing dealer and agency processes. Moreover, their effects are often exacerbated by an overriding problem: differences in company characteristics that are reflected in market measures, such as bid/ask spreads. Many of the above assumptions and misconceptions are avoided if markets are analyzed from the investor side and on a net basis. In other words, after allowance for service quality, commissions, and trading costs, is the investor better off, worse off, or optimized in the choice of processes that is being made?

INSTITUTIONAL EXPERIENCE IN NASDAQ's COMPETING DEALER MARKET

When studies focus on total transactions costs and from the investor side, we find that institutions are finding liquidity and immediacy at competitive transaction costs in the competing dealer market. Two recent studies using institutional transactions data provide an investor-side basis for comparing NASDAQ and exchange-listed markets.

NASD sponsored a study of institutional transactions costs by Josef Lakonishok and Louis Chan at the University of Illinois utilizing data of SEI Corporation. SEI provided a client database covering 33 large money-management firms. The data file contains information respecting the details of transactions by institutions in NASDAQ- and exchange-listed stocks, including the prices at which transactions were executed and the commissions paid on exchange-listed stocks. The database used by Lakonishok and Chan included over 1.7 million trades during the period from January 1, 1989, through December 31, 1991.

They developed comparative total transaction cost statistics for

NASDAQ- and exchange-listed stocks following procedures that they had followed in prior studies. They focus on position changes called "trade packages." A package is defined as a buy or sell series of trades in a stock from the first day it was traded until a break of more than five consecutive days without a trade. Packages are categorized on the basis of company market capitalization and complexity of the trade package (that is, shares traded as a percentage of outstanding shares).

Trading costs are calculated from pre-execution and postexecution benchmarks including the opening price on the day of the first trade and the closing price five days after the last trade in the package. The upper limit of the five company-size groups are $180 million, $480 million, $1.2 billion, $4.5 billion, open-end. The five complexity classes are: bottom 50 percent, 50–75 percent, 75–90 percent, and 95 and over. The SEI data reveal the following respecting the experience of institutions in NASDAQ stocks:

Liquidity   The average size of trade purchase package in four out of five company market value size categories is found to be larger for NASDAQ National Market stocks than for exchange-listed stocks (Figure 3–3). With respect to sale packages larger average-size trade packages were reported for NASDAQ National Market stocks in each market value size category (Figure 3–4).

Likewise, when the size of trade packages were calculated as a percentage of outstanding equity, the relative size of trade packages executed by institutional managers was found to be larger for NASDAQ National Market stocks in every market value category. This was true for both buy and sell packages (Figures 3–5 and 3–6).

Immediacy   Lakonishok and Chan also provide data with respect to the duration of time required to execute the trade packages. Sale packages in every market value category were sold in a shorter time period for NASDAQ National Market stocks than was true for exchange-listed stocks (Figure 3–7). For purchase packages, the NASDAQ National Market stocks were executed in a shorter time duration in the three smallest market value ranges but took slightly longer than the NYSE stocks in the two larger market value ranges (Figure 3–7).

It is clear from these data that institutional investors have executed in at least as large a size and with at least as great immediacy in the competing dealer market process as they appear to have executed in the exchange agency process. The differences clearly favor the competing dealer process.

FIGURE 3–3
Average Size of Trade Packages by Institutional Money Managers for Buys,[a] 1989–1991

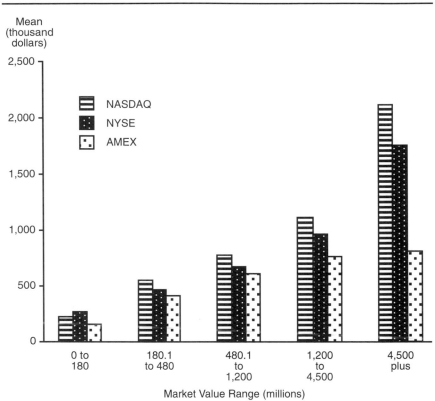

[a] A buy package is defined as the same money manager executing successive purchases of the same stock with a break of less than five days between successive trades.

Source: "A Cross-Exchange Comparison of Institutional Trading Costs" by L. Chan and J. Lakonishok, University of Illinois at Urbana-Champaign.

Transaction Costs   As noted above, institutions deal net in the competing dealer market with net prices reported. They deal with commissions included and gross prices reported in exchange-listed stocks. A net price is a price that reflects the per-share value actually received by the institution or transactor. A gross price is a price that still must be reduced or increased by commissions or retail markup charges to arrive at the net per share value received or paid by the customer. Trade report prices mix gross and net trades, and bid/ask prices tend to reflect all

FIGURE 3–4
Average Size of Trade Packages by Institutional Money
Managers for Sells,[a] 1989–1991

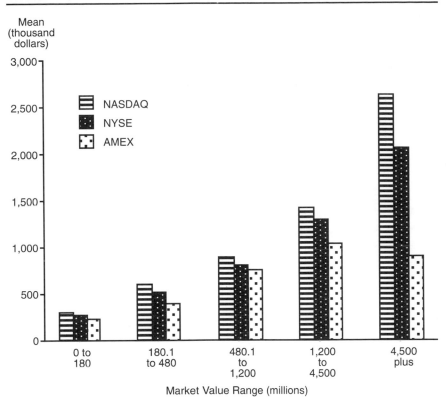

Mean
(thousand
dollars)

Market Value Range (millions)

[a] A sell package is defined as the same money manager executing successive purchases of
the same stock with a break of less than five days between successive trades.

Source: "A Cross-Exchange Comparison of Institutional Trading Costs" by L. Chan and J. Lakonishok,
University of Illinois at Urbana-Champaign.

transactions costs in net markets. The objective of the Lakonishok and
Chan study was to generate comparative data respecting the total transaction costs experienced by institutions.

Three variations of measured cost are used: principal-weighted cost,
equal-weighted cost, and money-manager cost. Principal-weighted cost
weights each trade cost, using relative trade principal values. Equal-
weighted treats each package cost as equivalent, regardless of size, and
money-manager cost is the median or typical money manager cost for

FIGURE 3–5
Average Size of Packages Relative to Outstanding Equity by Institutional Money Managers for Buys,[a] 1989–1991

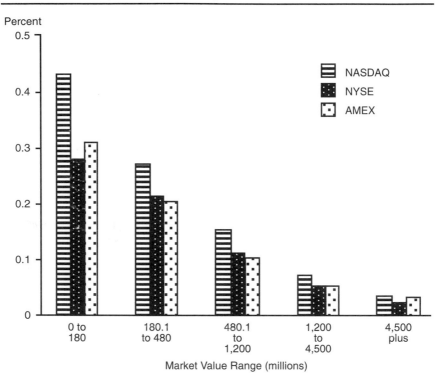

Market Value Range (millions)

[a] A buy package is defined as the same money manager executing successive purchases of the same stock with a break of less than five days between successive trades.

Source: "A Cross-Exchange Comparison of Institutional Trading Costs" by L. Chan and J. Lakonishok, University of Illinois at Urbana-Champaign.

packages of each size and complexity.

The median is chosen for purposes of comparisons of round-trip cost, because the within-group variances are large, the arithmetic mean statistics are affected by skewed distributions within groups, and the number of trade packages varies across cells. The median, of course, is the typical package, with one half costing more and one half costing less. The median return from buy packages and the median of the sell packages is summed in each complexity and market value cell to generate round-trip costs. The values in Tables 3–2 through 3–4 are stated in terms of basis points.

FIGURE 3–6
Average Size of Packages Relative to Outstanding Equity by Institutional Money Managers for Sells,[a] 1989–1991

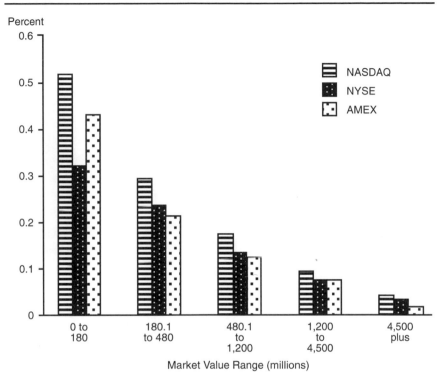

[a] A sell package is defined as the same money manager executing successive purchases of the same stock with a break of less than five days between successive trades.

Source: "A Cross-Exchange Comparison of Institutional Trading Costs" by L. Chan and J. Lakonishok, University of Illinois at Urbana-Champaign.

We find the NASDAQ (competing dealer) medians equivalent to or with some advantage over the NYSE (exchange agency) medians in most comparisons. This is true for each of the various measures of round-trip costs. When principal-weighted cost is used, the NASDAQ median looks better in 15 to 17 of the 25 cells on both a pre-execution and postexecution basis (Table 3–2). The results are roughly equivalent when equal-weighted cost or the median (money-manager) measures are used (Tables 3–3 and 3–4); but in the case of each of the three measures, the competing dealer process comes out equivalent or slightly better. Across cells, there is a pattern of NASDAQ advantage in the

FIGURE 3–7
Package Duration by Institutional Money Managers for Buys,[a]
1989–1991

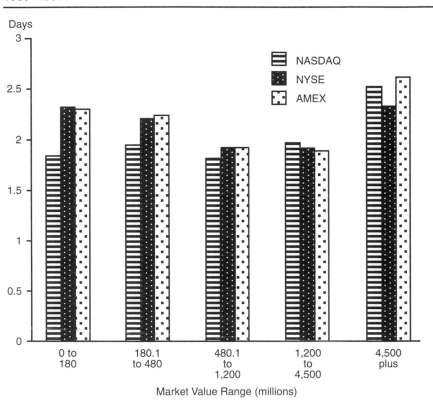

a A buy package is defined as the same money manager executing successive purchases of the same stock with a break of less than five days between successive trades.

Source: "A Cross-Exchange Comparison of Institutional Trading Costs" by L. Chan and J. Lakonishok, University of Illinois at Urbana-Champaign.

small- and mid-cap stocks and some NYSE advantage in the large (over $4.5 billion) stock group, where there were only five NASDAQ companies (three computer and two telecommunications).

Overall, when the typical (median) intermarket differences of the managers is combined for the three different measures, two benchmarks, five complexity, and five company size groups (150 cells), managers cost data reveal that NASDAQ costs were lower in 88 cells, and higher in 62 cells. These data and findings, while suggestive, are not statisti-

FIGURE 3–8
Package Duration by Institutional Money Managers for Sells,[a]
1989–1991

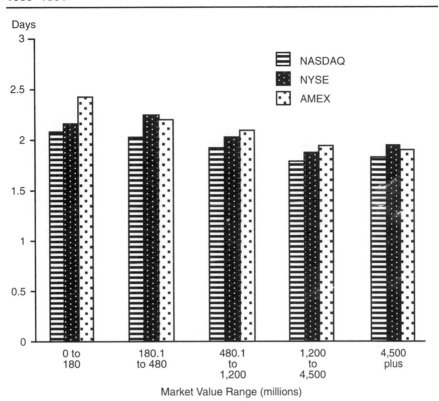

Market Value Range (millions)

[a] A sell package is defined as the same money manager executing successive purchases of the same stock with a break of less than five days between successive trades.

Source: "A Cross-Exchange Comparison of Institutional Trading Costs" by L. Chan and J. Lakonishok, University of Illinois at Urbana-Champaign.

cally significant.

The key fact is that, if one utilizes total transactions costs instead of just trading costs, competing dealer markets are at least as cost-efficient as are agency processes and, indeed, may have an edge.

Wayne Wagner and Mark Edwards[1] have reported similar results using a different institutional data set. They analyzed 64,000 orders of institutions for the second quarter of 1992. They broke transactions costs into four components: (1) commission, (2) price impact (difference be-

TABLE 3–2
Median Round-Trip Return from Packages—Principal-Weighted Cost

Panel A: Postexecution Benchmark (+ benefit, – cost)
Cell Advantage (postexecution): NASDAQ – 17; NYSE – 8

		Market Value Range				
		(Small)				(Large)
Complexity		1	2	3	4	5
(Easy) 1	NASDAQ	0.17625	0.14770	0.02021	−0.75225	−0.34736
	NYSE	−0.87505	−0.29532	−0.45630	−0.29409	−0.51382
2	NASDAQ	−0.11348	0.65705	0.45598	0.40679	−0.95856
	NYSE	−1.27560	−0.66372	0.13090	−0.43505	−0.16702
3	NASDAQ	−0.34171	0.74022	0.24011	0.21412	−0.61912
	NYSE	−1.00468	−0.79471	−0.68111	0.02585	−0.25946
4	NASDAQ	−1.52300	0.36220	−0.10034	−0.88027	−0.48587
	NYSE	−1.71988	−0.17005	0.50459	0.25301	0.09308
(Hard) 5	NASDAQ	−1.80864	−0.40149	−1.85515	−0.25240	−1.72516
	NYSE	−2.27068	−1.12252	−0.86617	−1.02123	−0.01082

Panel B: Pre–execution Benchmark (– benefit, + cost)
Cell Advantage (pre-execution): NASDAQ – 15; NYSE – 10

		Market Value Range				
		(Small)				(Large)
Complexity		1	2	3	4	5
(Easy) 1	NASDAQ	1.44987	0.81557	0.94385	0.68825	0.58256
	NYSE	2.26667	1.13355	0.94553	0.67680	0.35188
2	NASDAQ	2.45421	0.99491	0.87740	0.58787	0.14763
	NYSE	2.69542	1.21718	0.89678	0.84080	0.37505
3	NASDAQ	1.81142	1.49492	0.26785	0.86501	1.26724
	NYSE	2.86570	1.58651	0.99851	0.65495	0.77503
4	NASDAQ	2.36303	1.82839	1.93106	1.95464	1.98214
	NYSE	3.19947	1.81209	1.96584	1.20454	1.56486
(Hard) 5	NASDAQ	3.00583	2.03200	1.46979	2.45849	2.60576
	NYSE	4.61790	2.87081	1.46247	1.49461	1.20138

TABLE 3–3
Median Round-Trip Return from Packages—Equal-Weighted Cost

Panel A: Postexecution Benchmark (+ benefit, – cost)
         Cell Advantage (postexecution): NASDAQ – 14; NYSE – 11

				Market Value Range		
		(Small)				*(Large)*
Complexity		1	2	3	4	5
(Easy) 1	NASDAQ	–.014508	–0.10722	–0.03188	–0.79947	–1.15760
	NYSE	–0.88198	–0.56032	–0.56291	–0.18607	–0.39504
2	NASDAQ	–0.28196	0.19315	0.45682	–0.16314	–0.55629
	NYSE	–1.15028	–0.70492	–0.04748	–0.24547	–0.26813
3	NASDAQ	–0.57485	0.85284	0.27150	0.41408	0.05387
	NYSE	–0.44312	–0.54120	–0.53256	0.05887	–0.24901
4	NASDAQ	–1.68696	0.69268	–0.27000	–0.31843	–0.23180
	NYSE	–1.55256	–0.53360	0.62964	0.58506	0.01198
(Hard) 5	NASDAQ	–0.93533	–0.65664	–1.94350	–1.31538	–0.98990
	NYSE	–2.96766	–1.18789	–0.16578	–0.63493	0.04759

Panel B: Pre-execution Benchmark (– benefit, + cost)
         Cell Advantage (pre-execution): NASDAQ – 12; NYSE – 13

				Market Value Range		
		(Small)				*(Large)*
Complexity		1	2	3	4	5
(Easy) 1	NASDAQ	1.68135	1.01750	1.02903	0.72240	0.76187
	NYSE	2.22883	1.41241	0.85779	0.63622	0.45611
2	NASDAQ	2.64546	0.69339	0.82150	0.79786	0.37795
	NYSE	2.83581	1.36928	0.90751	0.75878	0.55642
3	NASDAQ	2.37574	1.56346	0.30048	0.87814	1.05556
	NYSE	3.10301	1.36147	1.06878	0.77820	0.86128
4	NASDAQ	1.55178	1.95783	0.38684	2.29250	2.14105
	NYSE	3.24173	2.06462	1.98466	1.14059	1.45652
(Hard) 5	NASDAQ	4.09482	2.49879	1.43462	1.78857	2.30040
	NYSE	4.78454	1.99930	1.11475	1.29195	1.40217

TABLE 3–4
Median Round-Trip Return from Packages—Median Cost

Panel A: Postexecution Benchmark (+ benefit, – cost)
Cell Advantage (postexecution): NASDAQ – 15; NYSE – 10

		Market Value Range			
		(Small)				*(Large)*
Complexity		1	2	3	4	5
(Easy) 1	NASDAQ	−0.08000	0.04000	0.23300	−0.58700	−1.67920
	NYSE	−1.14000	−0.39000	−0.51000	−0.27000	−0.41900
2	NASDAQ	−0.47860	0.47750	0.22000	0.70500	−0.55500
	NYSE	−0.81110	−0.54000	0.06000	−0.35350	−0.37450
3	NASDAQ	0.25050	1.12900	−0.15000	1.04500	0.14000
	NYSE	−0.34500	−0.16600	−0.13300	−0.04000	−0.06000
4	NASDAQ	−1.29000	1.43418	−0.60629	−0.15654	−0.23180
	NYSE	−1.23169	0.10900	−0.31610	0.13000	−0.16800
(Hard) 5	NASDAQ	−0.89000	−0.17000	−1.08000	−0.24717	−0.35046
	NYSE	−2.95072	−0.60000	0.73000	−0.68000	0.04300

Panel B: Pre-execution Benchmark (– benefit, + cost)
Cell Advantage (pre–execution): NASDAQ – 13; NYSE – 12

		Market Value Range			
		(Small)				*(Large)*
Complexity		1	2	3	4	5
(Easy) 1	NASDAQ	0.85000	0.83000	0.82000	0.55520	0.77000
	NYSE	2.10000	1.24000	0.78000	0.52000	0.40000
2	NASDAQ	2.45473	1.45250	0.95000	0.65000	0.46546
	NYSE	2.862220	1.08500	1.04000	0.77000	0.60000
3	NASDAQ	1.97470	1.52000	0.92920	1.20000	1.09000
	NYSE	3.19000	1.92000	1.06000	0.88500	0.71000
4	NASDAQ	2.05227	1.82502	0.86000	1.97372	1.86420
	NYSE	3.56910	1.63358	1.64000	1.03000	1.28000
(Hard) 5	NASDAQ	3.78000	2.88000	1.89000	1.75050	1.93884
	NYSE	4.84853	1.99930	2.40740	1.07000	1.63000

tween the price at which a trade was revealed to a broker and the execution price), (3) timing cost (the price move prior to being able to trade), and (4) opportunity cost (the cost of failing to find the liquidity to complete the trade).

Wagner and Edwards data show that:

- Exchange-listed commissions averaged 5.6 cents per share;
- Impact and spread costs are lower in NASDAQ stocks for liquidity-demanding orders, higher for neutral orders, and the same as in exchange-listed stocks for liquidity-supplying orders;
- Timing costs are higher for NASDAQ stocks for liquidity-demanding orders but lower for neutral and for liquidity-supplying orders;
- Opportunity costs (portions of orders not executed) are not broken down between exchange-listed and NASDAQ.

Numerous analyses, focused on displayed spreads and trade price differentials, have inferred, suggested, or concluded that transaction costs are larger in the competing dealer processes. Studies using investor-side data and focused on total transactions costs, including commissions, clearly are contradicting such conclusions, at least for institutions.

The findings of these investor-side cost studies are particularly significant, because they are also not adequately controlling for company-specific differences. Differences in key company characteristics, such as stock price, size, industry product mix, expected growth rates, average daily volume, and leverage, which affect the market spread and trading impact costs of stocks, can be expected to affect intermarket transaction cost comparisons as well. McInish and Wood, utilizing a linear programming technique to create equivalent portfolios, may have solved this problem.[2]

The purpose here is not to suggest that only investor-side studies of transaction costs should be pursued, but to point out the importance of the microstructure and company equivalence assumptions that are often implicitly being made when markets are being compared.

Also, this is not meant to suggest that agency processes and order-driven systems are not important. Indeed, NASDAQ established a limit order file in SOES in 1989 and the order-driven Selectnet system in late 1990. In addition, the NASD Board took an important action at its September 1993 meeting to raise the quality of service provided limit orders in the NASDAQ Stock Market. These actions recognize that the markets that investors and brokers desire will not be all dealer but rather some optimum mix of agency and dealer services that competitive forces are yet to determine.

A reasonable question to ask is, "What about individual investors?" The answer is that trading data from the market side are too incomplete to answer that question also. Investor-side order, cost, and value of service information is needed. A commonly held assumption that small investors do better in an agency process is probably also erroneous.

NOTES

1. Wayne H. Wagner and Mark Edwards, "Best Execution," *Financial Analysts Journal*, January-February 1993.
2. Thomas H. McInish and Robert A. Wood, "Volatility of NASDAQ/NMS and Listed Stocks," in *The Competition for Order Flow and Market Efficiency,* Memphis State University, November 1992.

CHAPTER 4

THE EFFECT OF LIQUIDITY ON ELECTRONIC ORDER ROUTING

Raymond L. Killian
David C. Cushing

INTRODUCTION

The debate about where the U.S. equity market should be headed in terms of regulation and structure has become increasingly heated over the last few years. The Market 2000 study sponsored by the Securities and Exchange Commission (SEC) has fanned the flames of this debate, and at least some changes seem sure to come from it.

One of the unspoken and seldom-challenged tenets underlying the great market debate is "the evolution and application of new technology is affecting market liquidity." The most frequently heard rejoinder along these lines is that proprietary electronic trading systems are fragmenting or "Balkanizing" liquidity.

This logic puts the cart before the horse. The truth of the matter is that liquidity and the quest for liquidity are really the driving forces and that trends and developments in electronic order routing are really just consequences of institutional demands for liquidity. If the current market structure truly satisfied institutions' needs, the thrust of technology development would be directed toward improving that structure—making it faster, easier to use, and more efficient. Since many institutions' needs are not being met by the current market structure, a significant proportion of technology resources have gone into the development of proprietary trading systems and routing vehicles to help reach those systems.

We will attempt to identify and interpret some of the trends we are seeing today in trading technology and how those trends are being shaped by the liquidity needs of institutional investors.

THE EQUITY MARKET TODAY

While markets are always changing, the pace of change in the U.S. equity market only seems to accelerate. Liquidity sources are growing at a rate that boggles the imagination. A partial listing of current liquidity sources is shown in Table 4–1. Viewed schematically, the lay of the land today looks something like Figure 4–1.

Each of these alternative to the New York Stock Exchange (NYSE) arose and thrives due to a special need or niche. For example,

- The regional stock exchanges (for example, Boston, Philadelphia, and Pacific) paid attention to local stocks—they promoted them, liquidity grew, and institutions sought to trade there.

- NASDAQ made listing easier for small stocks and provided a competing market maker system. Volume and liquidity exploded.

- The "upstairs" market made available a significant amount of capital to service the emerging block trading market, a need which undercapitalized specialists were unable to provide.

- The third market provided "anytime, anywhere" trading and generally lower commissions.

- Crossing systems satisfied list traders' need for confidentiality, while eliminating the spread and charging low commissions.

- Off-Board market makers, such as Madoff, D. E. Shaw & Co., and Tri-Mark Securities exploited two main inefficiencies of the specialist system: fixed minimum spreads, and the specialists' inability to diversify his or her portfolio. This enabled them to offer a competitive level of price improvement, eliminate floor brokerage charges, and *pay* clients a small inducement for using their services.

TABLE 4–1
A Partial List of Sources of Liquidity

Source	Description/Comments
Exchanges [a]	
New York Stock Exchange (NYSE)	Primary listed stock trading location.
American Stock Exchange (AMEX)	Alternative listed stock trading location, specializing in smaller stocks, listed derivatives, and other unusual equity securities.
NASDAQ	Primary over-the-counter stock trading location.
Upstairs Market	Manual block trade crossing and capital commitment, primarily by NYSE member firms.
Third Market	Manual block trade crossing and capital commitment, primarily by nonmember firms.
Off-Board Electronic Market Makers	Electronic execution systems operated on a proprietary basis. Compete with the NYSE for DOT order flow. Guarantee best bid/offer. Users paid for order flow.
Electronic Crossing Systems	
POSIT	Dominant intraday call market. Operated by ITG Inc.
Instinet	Dominant continuous proprietary electronic trading system. Bulk of trading occurs in over-the-counter issues.
The Crossing Network	After-hours, closing price call market. Operated by Instinet.
SelectNet	Continuous electronic trading of over-the-counter stocks. Operated by NASDAQ. Available only to NASDAQ market makers.
Arizona Stock Exchange (AZX)	After-hours single price auction.
ILN, Match Plus, Lattice	Continuous intraday crossing systems operated on a proprietary basis by various broker/dealers.

[a] Defined as a "location" (electronic or physical) where there are indications to buy to sell stocks.

FIGURE 4–1
Markets Today—A Crowded Field

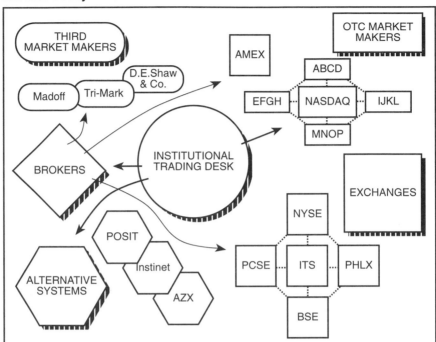

OTHER TRENDS

In addition to the proliferation of liquidity sources, several other trends are worth mentioning since they relate to our analysis of institutions' responses.

- Trading is now viewed as a source of added value in the total portfolio management process. It is no longer viewed as a "service bureau" type of operation. Many manager searches today hinge on innovations in managers' approach to implementation.

- Portfolio managers are including ever greater numbers of issues in their portfolios. This trend sharply compounds the liquidity access complexity problem.

- Money management strategies are becoming increasingly complex and short-term.

- Information is available more cheaply and quickly and can be filtered more efficiently. Computers continue to offer improving price/performance.

INSTITUTIONAL RESPONSE

The proliferation of liquidity sources, in combination with the other trends noted above, have given investors an unprecedented level of flexibility and choice in tailoring their overall investment process of maximize returns. However, along with flexibility usually comes complexity, and this situation is no exception. Managing that complexity has given rise to a daunting new set of requirements. Brokers and other vendors in the 1990s face a major challenge in trying to serve these new needs for their clients. Some of the new tools and capabilities that institutions need to handle their increasingly complex business include the following:

Electronic Order Management

- *Position Keeping*   Institutions must know the status of their portfolios in real time.

- *Trade Analysis*   Traders are demanding increasingly sophisticated analysis of their trade lists—before, during, and after the trade.

- *Efficient Clearing and Settlement*   Trades must be processed quickly, cheaply, and accurately.

Electronic Order Routing

- *Seamless, Easy-to-Use Electronic Access to Multiple Liquidity Sources*   Traders need the ability to route their orders quickly and easily to many different locations. For situations where electronic access is not available, traders need an efficient manual interface to feed executions back into the system.

- *Ability to Process Large Trade Volumes Paperlessly*   Implicit in this discussion is the need to weed out as much paper as possible. If even 10 percent of the process involves paper, any electronic system will be greatly underutilized. Also implied is the requirement for any system to handle *volume*. People laughed when the

NYSE planned for 600 million share days after the 1987 crash. They're not laughing anymore.

- *Intelligent Order Setting and Routing*   When should I trade? How much should I trade? At what price? Should I use limit or market orders? By virtue of the sheer volumes they will be handling, traders will continue to rely increasingly on electronic support to answer these questions.

A LOOK TOWARD THE FUTURE

The investment community is at a crossroads today, with a tremendous appetite for fast, powerful, easy-to-use, integrated portfolio management and trading tools.

As noted above, there are many liquidity sources available today and each source has different characteristics. Even though all sources might be important to a given investor, there are time and opportunity costs associated with moving around from place to place. The aggressive use of technology can break down the barriers between sources and dramatically lower the cost of moving around—effectively allowing you to have your cake and eat it, too.

Fortunately, the price/performance of computer technology today makes satisfying these needs more attainable than ever. Unfortunately, as an industry, we are still a long way from providing a meaningful answer to these needs.

If the past is any guide, the changes required to meet the needs of investors will occur by evolution, not revolution. The first noticeable change (which is already happening) is that participants will be able to move from one liquidity source to another with increasing ease and speed.

However, an even more interesting change will also begin unfolding: *The electronic layer that is used to access all of the various liquidity sources will gradually become the marketplace, instead of just a gateway to the various marketplaces and liquidity sources.*

Figure 4–2 represents how the market will start to look. Represented schematically in Figure 4–2 are the various market participants interacting directly and electronically via a market network, which is effectively a "trading superhighway." Shown as nodes on the diagram are the four fundamental participant types: fiduciaries, principals, bro-

FIGURE 4–2
The Market of the Future?

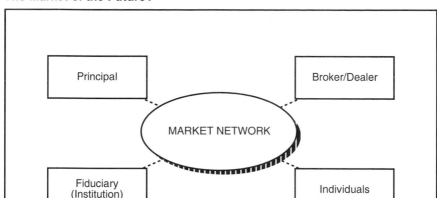

kers, and individuals. In this scheme, the fiduciary box covers invest-ment managers, plan sponsors, and others who invest assets in a fidu-ciary capacity. A principal is defined here as a hedge fund, market maker, or other entity who invests risk capital in a nonfiduciary capacity. The broker will continue to function as a provider of advice, recommen-dations, and execution services. The individual is shown interacting di-rectly with the market network in this scheme, but many will probably continue to seek the services of a broker.

Following are some of the direct implications of how this shift will affect the future of investing:

- Institutions will have more and more opportunities to interact directly with each other.

- As described above, participants will come to be classified more along functional lines. An investment manager or pension sponsor will be known more for its role of "fiduciary" than "client," as opportunities to interact directly expand and as the traditional client/broker framework breaks down.

- Fiduciaries will begin earmarking capital for market making. This will be viewed as part of an evolutionary change as this group pursues shorter and shorter term strategies.

- As the "brokerage" part of the broker/dealer function declines in significance, more attention will be directed to market making and proprietary trading strategies. Sales of research, investment advice, and execution/clearing services for commissions will continue, albeit in a reduced form.

- At the same time, brokers have traditionally done a better job than the exchanges of understanding client needs for execution services. As such, brokers can be expected to take a leading role in building and providing technology-based execution systems.

- Partnerships between institutional brokers and technology vendors will form as part of an effort to deliver these execution systems.

- Niche liquidity sources will become more important as they are more tightly integrated into the electronic layer.

- Technology will drive down costs as monopoly and special interests decline in value to the investor.

HOW DO WE GET THERE?

We are perhaps well on our way to arriving at the vision of the future described above. It is certainly within technological reach as computers get cheaper and faster, while the much-vaunted "information superhighway" continues to extend its reach. The main barriers to the evolution of the market of the future are political ones; and for good reason: there are literally billions of dollars of monopoly profits at stake.

"Following the money" raises another important question: who would "own" this new market? Initially, the vendors of electronic routing and order management systems would, and they would (and do) charge either fees or commissions or both for shares traded through their systems. As the distinctions among systems gradually blur and electronic routing becomes a commodity, these fees would gradually decline, causing a consolidation of competing systems. The resulting oligopoly or monopoly could then be subject to regulation or outright nationalization by the government (although they wouldn't call it that!).

But we are still a long way from that day. Indeed, the demise of the NYSE and other membership-based trading cartels has been predicted almost since the time of their founding, yet volume (though not market share) continues to grow on all exchanges. Nevertheless, the future, and the battlefield for control of the future, is beginning to take shape through the technology offerings of firms like ITG, Instinet, Bloomberg, AZX, and the Crossing Bridge, to name a few. Strategic links and alliances are being formed, and truly meaningful electronic access to multiple liquidity sources has become reality.

CONCLUSIONS

What conclusions can be drawn from this look at the interaction of electronic order routing and liquidity? Some final thoughts and observations follow:

- Specialized investors' needs have been served historically by creative liquidity niches, and this trend will continue.

- Sophisticated order routing layers are evolving to minimize the cost of properly using these niches. Technology will continue to drop in price, further reducing the cost of accessing routing layers. Software and systems that capitalize on this improved price/performance will continue to evolve.

- A multiplicity of competing systems will initially compete to provide investors' order management and routing needs. Ultimately, the field will consolidate, leaving only the stronger systems. At the same time, the electronic layer or trade routing highway will gradually evolve to become "the" marketplace, as multiple liquidity sources become connected electronically and investors get more and more opportunities to interact without intermediaries.

- Interestingly, the resulting network will start to look and feel like the National Market System mandated by Congress in 1975. Best of all, market forces, not the burden of regulation, will have driven the change.

- Most importantly, *all* investors benefit from these trends as technology reduces many of the costs of trading.

CHAPTER 5

MARKET STRUCTURE AND THE SUPPLY OF LIQUIDITY

Jacques Hamon
Puneet Handa
Bertrand Jacquillat
Robert A. Schwartz

INTRODUCTION

For a securities market to function, some traders must supply liquidity and other who demand it must pay an appropriate price for the service. In the New York Stock Exchange (NYSE), there are two categories of liquidity suppliers: (1) the specialist assigned to a specific stock and (2) limit order traders who trade either for proprietary reasons (such as portfolio rebalancing) or to make the markets. The Paris Bourse (CAC), on the other hand, is a fully automated order-driven exchange where liquidity is supplied solely by the market participants and not by any assigned individual. Hence, a market participant faces a choice and needs to make a decision whether to trade by market order, thereby demanding liquidity, or to trade by limit order, thereby supplying liquidity.

Two recent paper examine the supply of liquidity at the New York Stock Exchange (Handa and Schwartz, 1993) and the Paris Bourse (Hamon, Handa, Jacquillat, and Schwartz, 1993). In specific, they examine the profitability of limit order trading relative to trading by market order at the two exchanges. Here we examine the implications of market structure on the supply of liquidity at the New York Stock Exchange and at the Paris Bourse.

Recently, there has been a great deal of interest in trading via limit orders. In particular, the debate has centered around the put option nature of limit order trading. Consider an investor who arrives at the marketplace to sell stock. The investor can sell shares to the market at the best bid or place a limit order to sell near the ask price. Depending on the liquidity in the market and on the asking price of the investor, the limit order may or may not execute, and the further the asking price is from the best ask in the market, the longer it would take for the order to execute. If price follows a random walk, however, any time the price crosses the asking price of the investor, he or she would be *bagged* in the send that the price would be higher than the price obtained by the investor. On the other hand, if price never rose to the asking price of the investor, he or she would fail to sell at the asking price, resulting in a *nonexecution cost.*

The issue then is, if placing a limit order is equivalent to writing a free put option, then why do investors even choose to trade by limit orders? Handa and Schwartz (1993) provide a detailed examination of the issue. The argument is that, if prices follow a random walk, it is suboptimal for any trader to trade by limit order. This, in turn, means that in order-driven markets, such as the Paris Bourse and the NYSE, trading will come to a halt if no participant chooses to trade via limit order and thereby to supply the market with liquidity.

Also, if prices follow a mean reverting process, an order-driven market is viable: relatively patient participants submit limit orders, and relatively eager participants submit market orders. Moreover, Handa and Schwartz (1993) show that a viable order-driven market requires that prices follow a mean reverting process. Mean reversion in prices implies a tendency of prices to rebound and to have additional volatility over short horizons, over and above their long-run volatility. For the market ecology to be in balance, the mean reversion must be just sufficient to compensate the marginal limit order traders adequately. Hence, in equilibrium, an optimal level of mean reversion in prices will coexist with an optimal proportion of limit orders to market orders.

If the Handa-Schwartz conjecture is to hold, trading via limit order must be profitable in any order-driven market, irrespective of its design. The Handa-Schwartz results on the NYSE and the Hamon-Handa-Jacquillat-Schwartz results on the Paris Bourse allow us to compare and contrast the profitability of limit order trading at these two exchanges and thereby draw inferences on the implications of market structure on the supply of liquidity. The sample of stocks in Handa-Schwartz consists of the 30 Dow Jones Industrial stocks at the New York Stock Exchange. As opposed to this, the Hamon-Handa-Jacquillat-Schwartz sample consists of all stocks traded on the Paris Bourse cash and futures markets. Further, there is diversity across the time periods over which these two exchanges are examined. These factors allows us to examine the robustness of the Handa-Schwartz conjecture. Overall, there is broad-based support for the conjecture that limit order traders profit from mean reversion in securities prices.

MARKET STRUCTURE OF THE NEW YORK STOCK EXCHANGE

At the NYSE, liquidity is supplied by (1) the specialist assigned to a stock and (2) limit order traders. The exchange opens at 9:30 a.m. and trading starts in most Dow Jones Industrial stocks soon thereafter with an opening call. Prior to the call, the specialist gives some indication of interest on both sides of the market, but the order is not displayed. The exchange functions as a continuous agency-auction market after the opening call until the close at 4 p.m.

Specialist participation in the trades that take place in their stocks is a function of trading volume. For example, in 1990 the largest 100 stocks at the New York Stock Exchange, which accounted for 45 percent of trading volume, had a specialist participation rate of 15 percent *of trading volume*. The smallest 700 stocks had a specialist participation rate ranging from 30 to 40 percent *of trading volume*. The average specialist participation rate was 18 percent *of trading volume*. Hence, at the NYSE, specialist participation in trades is somewhat limited. The bulk of the trading takes place between market participants, and the liquidity in these instances is supplied by limit order traders.

In spite of the low participation rate, the specialist is a key player in the trading process. Most trading activity takes place through or close to the specialist in the so-called downstairs market. There is a small percentage of large-volume trades that are negotiated in the upstairs market. These trades, although arranged upstairs, must be reported downstairs to the specialist. All individuals who want to supply liquidity to the downstairs market must do so through the specialist. Hence, all individuals who wish to trade via limit orders must place these orders on the limit order book with the specialist.

The specialist is the sole repository of information in the limit order book, and one might conjecture that this provides the market maker with a limited amount of monopoly power.[1] Based on all information available, including that in the limit order book, the specialist posts a quote. A quote may represent the specialist's own trading interest, trading interest in the crowd, or the limit orders in the limit order book. A quote consists of a bid price and a bid depth (sometimes called bidsize), and an ask price and an ask depth (sometimes called asksize). The bid price is the price at which the specialist, acting on his own account or on behalf of the other liquidity suppliers, commits to buy a maximum number of round lots given by the bid depth. Similarly, the ask price is the price at which the specialist commits to sell a maximum number of round lots given by the ask depth.

The specialist's quotes represent his commitment to buy or sell. Hence, it is the specialist's responsibility to ensure that trades take place at prices no worse than disseminated quotes. It is possible for trades to take place at prices better than the quoted price or for larger trades (than the posted depth) at worse prices. However, the specialist may not display the entire depth or interest near the quote and may be in a position to allow larger trades to take place at the quoted price. Typically, if a trader wants to sell more round lots than the posted bidsize (or to buy more round lots than the posted asksize), the specialist reserves the right to change the bid price (or the ask price). Alternatively, it is often possible to trade within the spread, either with the specialist, with another trader on the floor, or even against the book. Price improving orders should be displayed, especially if the trader so requests, but this does not always occur in practice.[2] Blume and Goldstein (1992) refer to the phenomenon of trading at prices better than the quote as *price improvement.* They document that a high percentage of trades at the New York Stock Exchange are at improved prices.

Since the specialist is the largest supplier of liquidity on the floor and the sole repository of the information in the limit order book, it is not unreasonable to view the specialist as a strategic participant. In addition, there is no reason to believe that the other suppliers of liquidity would choose to deviate from a strategy adopted by the specialist.[3] In this sense, the actual trading practice at the New York and American

Stock Exchanges may not be very different from the framework assumed in information models, such as Admati and Pfleiderer (1989). Of course, whether perfect competition prevails or the specialist can, in fact, act strategically as predicted by Admati and Pfleiderer (1989), is an empirical issue.

MARKET STRUCTURE OF THE PARIS BOURSE

The Paris Bourse is an electronic, automated and transparent exchange with no market makers or specialists. Liquidity is provided solely by the limit order traders. Hence, an investor who wishes to trade must decide either to place a limit order and thereby supply liquidity or to place a market order and thereby demand liquidity. In this sense the Paris Bourse represents an ideal order-driven market to test the Handa-Schwartz conjecture on limit order trading.

Trading starts at the Paris Bourse at 10 a.m. and continues until 5 p.m. In the hour preceding the opening, buy and sell orders are accepted by the system but remain unexecuted until the opening. In this period, the entire limit order book is shown on the screens within the brokerage houses (*sociétés de bourses*), but only the five best limits are shown on the screens of individual investors. A theoretical transaction price is constantly computed and displayed during the period. At the open, an attempt is made to come up with the first transaction price using all limit orders available in the limit book up to that point. Failing this, market orders are used to come up with the first price.

As an example of the opening procedure, consider Rhône Poulenc Certificates (CIP) on July 31, 1992, from 9:01 a.m. to 9:59 a.m. During this period, 64 orders were entered in the limit order book: 31 buy orders with price limits between 185 and 578 francs and 33 sell orders up to 680 francs. The cumulative buy quantity was 4,400 shares, and the cumulative sell quantity was 8,975 shares. The modal order quantity was 25 shares, both on the buy and sell sides, the median being 50 shares. There were two orders of 1,000 shares or more on the buy side and three such orders on the sell side. At 10 a.m., the five best limits on the order book are shown in Figure 5–1.

The details of the 18 orders representing the five best price limits at the opening of the trading session on July 31 for Rhône Poulenc appear in Table 5–1. At 10 a.m., the system computed the first transaction price following a two-stage procedure. First, all limit orders were examined and indicated that the highest price that the less demanding buyer accepted to pay (FF 578) was less than the lowest price that the less demanding seller accepted to receive (FF 582). Thus, no trade was possible with limit orders only. In the second stage, market orders were executed. In this example, a sell order of 50 shares was executed against the best limit order in the book (i.e., at FF 578). This procedure resulted in the first transaction price of 578 FF. Moreover, the limit order continued to stay in the book for 50 shares. The absolute spread after the first price was FF 582, less FF 578 (i.e., FF 4), and the relative spread was 0.69 percent.

Starting at 10 a.m., all new orders that enter the system can generate a trade and, thus, a new transaction price. If the order cannot be executed immediately, it is put in the limit order book, and the first-in, first-out priority rule applies. The limit orders on the book are displayed throughout the day during continuous trading.

In the French market, the CAC, stocks are traded in the forward market (*règlement mensuel* or RM) or in the cash market (which includes the "official market" and also a "Second Marché"). This distinction is primarily based on the characteristics of the companies trading on the CAC system, which are quite heterogeneous. Shares traded on the RM market normally have a higher transactions frequency and a smaller relative spread.

The Hamon-Handa-Jacquillat-Schwartz study is over the period from March 1990 to April 1991, during which a fee was charged by the central market on executed orders only; but placing an order in the order book was free of charge (the billing of orders, whether or not they are executed, started in July 1991, and the trading of stocks listed in the third group by a fixing twice a day started in December 1991). The reservation procedure is an old tradition at the Paris Bourse.

During the sample period, and for the stocks traded on the RM market, a price change of 10 percent relative to the closing price of the previous trading session triggered a trading halt of 30 minutes. Trading resumed at a new price 5 percent below the last market price before the halt. The procedure could be repeated once with a new price 5 percent below the previous one. The theoretical price variation during a trading session was thus 20 percent on the RM. On the cash market, the filters were, respectively, 3 percent at the opening and an additional one percent after 1 p.m. This practice, which limited the potential zone of price

FIGURE 5–1
Limit Order Book for Rhône Poulenc CIP on July 31, 1992, at 10 a.m.

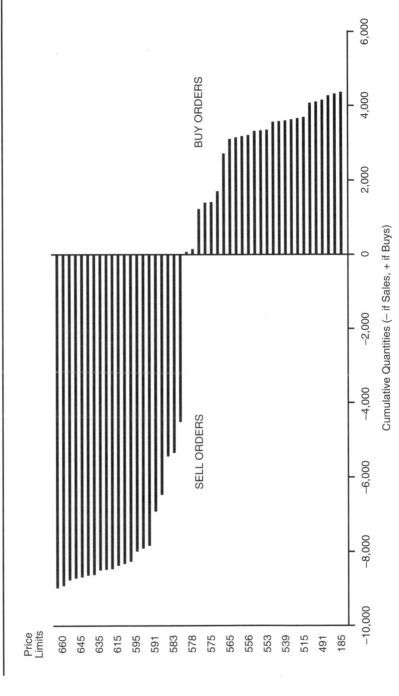

TABLE 5–1
The Five Best Limits on Rhône Poulenc on July 31, 1992, at
10 a.m. at the Paris Bourse

Time	Price (FF)	Sell		Buy	
		Quantity	Cumulative	Quantity	Cumulative
9:37:45	591	500	6,925		
9:50:52	590	1,000	6,425		
9:19:18	590	25	5,425		
9:28:03	585	25	5,400		
9:01:21	585	25	5,375		
9:52:42	583	750	5,350		
9:44:10	583	100	4,600		
9:58:36	582	4,000	4,500		
9:55:30	582	500	500		
9:59:48	578			100	100
9:59:47	578			75	175
9:48:59	577			1,000	1,175
9:30:30	577			175	1,350
9:30:30	577			100	1,450
9:01:04	575			25	1,475
9:58:48	568			300	1,775
9:49:18	566			1,000	2,775
	Market	(50)			

variation tended to reduce the size of the price reversals and may reduce the profitability of a limit order strategy.

COMPARATIVE RESULTS AND IMPLICATIONS

Handa and Schwartz (1993) examine the profitability of limit order trading at the NYSE. Their sample consists of the 30 Dow Jones Industrial firms for the year 1988. The Paris Bourse is examined in Hamon, Handa, Jacquillat, and Schwartz (1993) who monitor 909 CAC stocks over the period from March 1990 to April 1991. A common limit order strategy is tested by both papers in two distinctly different environments.

The trading strategy requires the specification of the following parameters: the length of the trading window, the length of the investment window, and the difference (expressed as a percentage) between the current price and the limit order price. For simplicity, one parameter, x, is used to reflect all three variables. For example, let $x = 2$ specify a two-day trading window, a two-day investment window, and a buy limit order that is $(1 - 0.02)$ percent of the opening price in the trading window.

Proper specification of x is critical. The trading window must be large enough to allow a liquidity event to occur, and the investment window must be large enough to allow the order imbalance to be corrected and price to mean revert. Because the investment window begins on the day immediately following the initial purchase, we need not be concerned, however, about the trading window being too long. Neither need we worry about the investment window being too long, although the power of our tests is greater if the investment window does not exceed the period over which prices might mean revert. In this chapter, we present graphical summaries for only three strategies (corresponding to $x = 1$, 2, and 3 days) from both exchanges and draw implications from their results.

A market buy order at a current price is compared with a limit buy order place x percent below the current price. The limit order is followed until it executes or until the last price in the trading window is reached. The purchase price of the limit order is its limit price if the stock trades below the limit price during the x-day trading window. If the limit order does not execute during the trading window, it is purchased at the opening price on the day following the trading window. For each trading window, all prices are standardized by setting the current price equal to 100.

Results on the overall profitability of limit orders, as measured by the unconditional purchase price, appear in Figure 5–2. For all categories of limit orders, the French Bourse cash and forward markets show a lower unconditional purchase price than market orders. On the NYSE, however, limit order trading performs marginally worse than market order trading for the 1 and 2 percent categories, but significantly worse for the 3 percent category. Overall, for the three markets, for the 2 percent and 2 percent categories, limit order trading does not perform significantly worse than market order trading. A limit order trader, not facing stiff competition from a specialist, performs better at the Paris Bourse.

In case a limit order fails to execute and the limit order trader is forced to buy by market, the purchase price should average higher than the market order price at the start of the trading strategy. This is indeed

FIGURE 5–2
Unconditional Purchase Price of Limit Orders at the NYSE, the
Paris Bourse Cash Market, and the Paris Bourse Forward Market
(Market Order Purchase Price = 100)

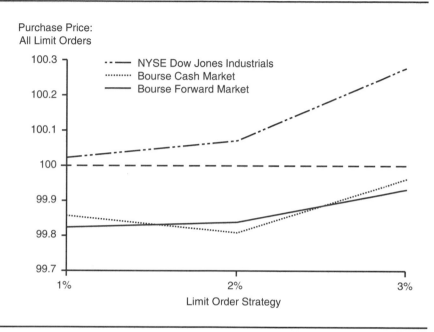

the case, as Figure 5–3 indicates. The purchase price paid at the three exchanges deteriorates as the *x* parameter increases from 1 to 3. All three exchanges show positive nonexecution costs, as Handa and Schwartz conjecture. The French forward exchange has the highest nonexecution costs, followed by the NYSE and the French cash market. This is likely to discourage investors who gain some consumer surplus from trading via limit orders at the forward market.

Execution rates are shown in Figure 5–4. Notice that the ordering of exchanges is again similar to the nonexecution cost graph (Figure 5–3). Execution rates are best at the forward market, followed by the NYSE and the cash market. Handa and Schwartz (1993) claim that high nonexecution costs may be balanced by high execution rates in equilibrium. This is clearly evident in the French Bourse forward market. Similarly, the lower nonexecution costs in the cash market are counterbalanced by lower execution rates.

FIGURE 5–3
Purchase Price of Unexecuted Limit Orders at the NYSE, the
Paris Bourse Cash Market, and the Paris Bourse Forward Market
(Market Order Purchase Price = 100)

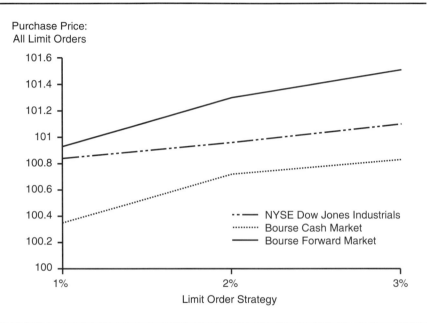

Rates of return for the 2 percent limit order strategy appear in Table 5–2. Examination of the table reveals that, in terms of rates of return, limit order trading outperforms trading via market order on all exchanges. Further, trading via limit orders is profitable when the order executes, implying negative bagging costs as predicted by Handa-Schwartz. Limit order trading is marginally worse than trading via market order when the limit order fails to execute at the French cash market.

The results from the 1 percent and 3 percent limit order strategies, available in the two relevant papers, are similar. The limit order trading strategy continues to dominate trading via market order. There are negative bagging costs as the limit order strategy, upon execution, outperforms trading via market order. Finally, nonexecution costs are positive and the limit order strategy, conditional upon nonexecution, is marginally worse than trading via market order.

Overall, our results present strong support for the Handa-Schwartz conjecture. Limit order trading is a profitable way of trading for all

FIGURE 5–4
Percentage of Limit Orders that Executed Naturally at the NYSE,
the Paris Bourse Cash Market, and the Paris Bourse Forward
Market

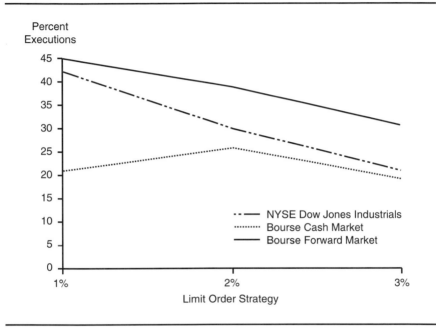

TABLE 5–2
Summary of Market Order and Limit Order Returns for the Two
Percent Strategy at the NYSE and at the Paris Bourse Cash and
Forward Markets

	Market Order Return	Overall Limit Order Return	Return to Naturally Executed Limit Order	Return to Forced Executed Limit Order
NYSE Dow Jones Industrials	0.056	0.100	0.237	0.042
Paris Bourse Cash	0.020	0.230	0.850	0.000
Paris Bourse Forward	–0.060	0.130	0.290	0.020

traders and particularly for traders who do not bear nonexecution costs at both the NYSE and at the Paris Bourse. A natural balance of execution rate and nonexecution costs appears to exist in a securities exchange that promotes trading via limit order and makes a securities market viable.

We can conclude that market structure can only lead to second order effects on the basic compensation that traders require to supply liquidity to a securities market. In equilibrium, patient traders (that is, traders who may choose not to trade at all if the price changes unfavorably) will tend to supply liquidity and gain as suppliers of liquidity. On the other hand, eager traders (traders who gain high consumer surplus from trade) will tend to demand liquidity and pay a price as demanders of liquidity. In an exchange such as the Paris Bourse, the lack of a designated supplier of liquidity does not deter the supply of liquidity: market participants, acting rationally, choose to supply liquidity whenever the marginal gains from supplying liquidity exceed the cost.

NOTES

1. The specialist's monopoly position may hold even when the markets are thick, primarily because the limit order traders face an even worse adverse selection problem than the specialist: they are not only writers of a free put option but also subject to gaming by the specialist (Rock, 1990).
2. See McInish and Wood (1992).
3. Information models such as Admati and Pfleiderer (1988, 1989) consider multiple market makers, and quote determination involves the selection of the best bid and the best ask quote each period. A unified *strategic* response is possible if the first participant chooses an action, and if deviation by a subsequent participant results in both participants being worse off.

REFERENCES

Admati, Anat R., and Paul Pfleiderer. (1988). "A Theory of Intraday Patterns: Volume and Price Variability," *The Review of Financial Studies,* 1: 1, pp. 3–40.

Admati, Anat R., and Paul Pfleiderer. (1989). "Divide and Conquer: A Theory of Intraday and Day-of-the-Week Mean Effects," *The Review of Financial Studies,* 2: 2, pp. 189–223.

Blume, Marshall, and Michael Goldstein. (1992). "Differences in Execution Prices among the NYSE, the Regionals, and the NASD." The Wharton School, University of Pennsylvania working paper.

Hamon, Jacques, Puneet Handa, Bertrand Jacquillat, and Robert A. Schwartz. (1993). "The Profitability of Limit Order Trading on the Paris Stock Exchange." New York University working paper.

Handa, Puneet, and Robert A. Schwartz. (1993). "Limit Order Trading." New York University working paper.

McInish, Thomas H., and Robert A. Wood. (1992). "Hidden Limit Orders on the NYSE." Memphis State University working paper.

Rock, Kevin. (1990). "The Specialist's Order Book and Price Anomalies." Harvard Business School working paper.

CHAPTER 6

HOW TO ENHANCE MARKET LIQUIDITY

Nicholas Economides

Exchanges in financial markets may be diversified in a variety of dimensions. They may differ in the attributes of the traded assets, in the location of the exchanges, in the time of the transaction, and in the manner that the transaction takes place. Further, markets differ in the degree of participation of intermediaries and in the role they play in the market.

Certain aspects of diversification are inherently desirable to market participants. Some types of financial exchange diversification are necessary for the particular way that the market works, including the way in which price is discovered in the market. Still other types of diversification arise naturally out of competition among exchanges. The variety of possible organizations of financial markets allows for comparisons among them. First, we need to define the criteria of evaluation.[1]

A financial exchange should be structured so as to maximize the satisfaction of participants and potential participants. This is accomplished by minimizing transaction costs, establishing market prices that accurately reflect the underlying equilibrium prices, and by reducing the uncertainty that traders face in market interactions. In a related paper, Economides and Schwartz (1993) discuss in detail how the introduction of electronic calls in the presence of a continuous market may have very

The author thanks Kalman Cohen, Bob Wood, Bob Schwartz, and the participants of the Global Equity Markets conference for their comments and suggestions.

significant benefits. They discuss the benefits of the call in enhancing liquidity, order handling, information revelation, market transparency, market anonymity, and avoidance of free-riding. The aspect on which we focus in this chapter if liquidity. We will argue that call markets provide coordination of trades in the time dimension and, thus, increase expected profits for traders. We further discuss how to best coordinate traders in their order placement in a call market, so as to achieve the highest possible marketwide profits.[2]

Liquidity plays a crucial role in financial exchange markets. Without the availability of counteroffers, markets cease to exist, and they are replaced by individualized bilateral contracts. Thus, some liquidity is necessary even for the *existence* of a financial exchange market. Further, high liquidity expands the set of potential counteroffers and enhances the probability of a favorable match. Thus, higher liquidity increases the expected level of satisfaction (utility) of market participants.[3] This is true irrespective of the particulars of the organization of the market. However, the realization of the enhancing role of market liquidity has very important implications on the relative benefits and drawbacks of different market organizations. Clearly, *spatial consolidation* of markets tends to increase liquidity. To increase liquidity further, we consider next the effects of *time consolidation* of markets in the form of an electronic call market.

Continuous markets tend to exhibit little *inherent* liquidity. In these markets, liquidity is provided to a large extent by special intermediaries, market makers, and specialists. However, the artificial creation of liquidity increases transaction costs in such markets. In contrast, electronic call markets inherently exhibit high liquidity because they implement the bunching of orders over time and their simultaneous execution. Thus, potentially call markets can offer lower transaction costs than continuous markets.

An electronic call market may be organized as a price scan double-sided auction.[4] The call, or market clearing, happens at a prespecified time T. Market participants are connected to the auctioneer at the exchange through a network of electronic terminals. Orders are taken by the exchange from time $t_0 < T$ up to time T. Orders without contingencies (or with contingencies that have been met) are displayed in aggregate form to all market participants.[5] Thus, in the time interval $[t_0, T]$ preceding the call, every trader is able to see the evolving aggregate demand and supply in the upcoming call market.

We model call markets in the presence of a continuous market that is functioning in parallel during the period in which orders are submitted to the call market. In deciding to participate in the electronic call, many traders accept to delay their market participation. That is, many traders have decided well before the call to trade but wait for the call, instead of sending their orders to the continuous market that is still in operation in the interval $[t_0, T]$. In marking such a choice, a trader evaluates the lower transaction fees and reduced market uncertainty in the call market in comparison to the risk of price changes during the waiting period between the decision to trade and the call. Economides and Heisler (1994b) discuss the choices of traders under these circumstances.

It is generally assumed that market participants demand immediacy, that is, immediate execution of their transactions. This is disputed by Economides and Schwartz (1993), who see the present demand for immediacy less as an inherent demand but rather as an effect of the present market organization. Economides and Schwartz (1994) developed a questionnaire (distributed through Trader Forum of the *Institutional Investor*, winter 1994, that attempts to evaluate the demand for immediacy by assessing how much delay traders are willing to accept in return for a reduction in transaction fees.

The extent of liquidity at the call is crucial. The more liquid the call, the more attractive it is to traders. This mechanism is self-reinforcing: the more traders participate, the more liquid the call becomes. The self-reinforcing mechanism could exist in expectations of trader participation that get realized (fulfilled) at the time of the call. That is, a large number of traders anticipate (expect) that a large number of other traders will participate in the call; therefore, they themselves participate in the call, and the expectation of large participation is fulfilled. This is certainly an equilibrium, but it is hardly the only one. In fact, it is not difficult to show that *any size of participation is an equilibrium, including zero participation*. If everyone expected no one else to participate in the call, he would not participate himself, and the market would not exist. Given the wide multiplicity of expectations equilibria, it is clear that *there is a need to create a specific mechanism that can support a single equilibrium of large participation.*[6]

The mechanism we propose utilizes two elements: (1) *commitments to trade* and (2) *discounts in fees and/or commissions*. Large participation can be supported as an equilibrium if it is the result of a series of sequential commitments by traders over time (in the interval $[t_0, T]$).

Each commitment to participate induces further commitments by others. The level of participation at the call (and other features of the outcome) is an easy projection of the accumulated committed orders in the final moments before the call. Thus, given the sequence of commitments, the role of expectations in determining the equilibrium outcome is significantly diminished.[7]

What form does the commitment of the traders take? In placing an order at time t, a trader commits not to withdraw the order until the call. If he withdraws the order, he is charged a fee equal to the fee that he would have been charged if his order had stayed in and had been executed at the call.[8] Therefore, everything else being equal, a trader may want to delay his commitment until the last second before the call. Such behavior would completely defeat the mechanism. To avoid such behavior, *the exchange induces traders to commit early by rewarding early commitment.* Thus, the exchange offers lower fees to traders who commit at an earlier time to participate in the upcoming call.[9] Traders self-select the time at which they enter their order. Less risk-averse, more patient traders with low demand for immediacy will commit earliest. More risk-averse traders will commit later.[10] The profit maximizing fee structure of a monopolist-auctioneer of a call market is established in Economides and Heisler (1994a).[11] The same paper establishes social welfare maximizing fee structure.

The lower fee for early entrants rewards the extra liquidity that an early entrant brings to the call in inducing others to participate in the market in the remaining time up to the call. These early entrants allow the call to be a focal point in the competition with a continuous market.

The fee structure that gives the highest benefit to the call market auctioneer makes the last participant of the call (who signs up just before time T) indifferent between participating at the call and participating at the continuous market. All participants who committed earlier pay strictly lower fees and are strictly better off by participating in the call market, rather than at a continuous market. Some very early traders may even be subsidized (that is, charged a fee below cost) to be compensated for the very large positive externality that they create in the market. Economides and Heisler (1994a) also show that, once entry has started, there are no gaps in trader arrival. That is, if the first trader enters at t_1, $t_0 < t_1 < T$, there is always some trader who enters at every instant between t_1 and T.

The profit-maximizing call market auctioneer internalizes some of the externality of liquidity provision by early entrants, but he does not fully internalize the externality. Maximization of the total benefit to society from the call market requires even lower fees to be charged to early participants. A perfectly price discriminating monopolist call market auctioneer can decentralize the total social benefit maximizing solution. However, the auctioneer in a typical call market is unable to implement price discrimination, and therefore he cannot achieve social benefit maximization.

The self-reinforcing nature of liquidity, as of any other network externality, creates the possibility that often small-size financial exchange networks will not be observed. That is, there exists some positive size of a network, named *critical mass*, n^{CM}, below which no network is observed. Thus, either no market of this type is observed, or a market of at least size n^{CM} is observed. It follows that one should not be surprised by very sudden growth of certain financial networks, including call markets, as conditions change that make a market of critical mass just sustainable.

We have shown earlier that the self-reinforcing nature of liquidity and the dependence on beliefs and expectations of the size of the market (in the absence of the explicit mechanism we propose) leads to a multiplicity of equilibria. Therefore, *history matters*. That is, historical events may define which of the equilibrium outcomes is realized and, in particular, which markets exist and which do not. In that respect, it is important to note that there may be crucial time inconsistencies. The technological conditions of yesterday may lead to the selection of environment X, but the conditions of today may make system Y the inevitable choice if we had not selected anything before. But it is possible that, if we had selected X yesterday, today we may still want to continue with X. That is, it may take a very drastic improvement in certain dimensions to make Y the best choice, given the earlier selection of X. This process is further complicated by the fact that the profits accruing to different parties will be different in different environments and systems, and therefore the incentives for change will not in general be coordinated.

Continuous markets are praised for their production of up-to-the-minute market-relevant information, most notably market clearing bid and ask prices. This creates a potentially significant criticism of traditional nonelectronic call markets, which were essentially infrequent exchanges of particular stocks. However, in an electronic market structured in the way described in this chapter, every participant can calculate the market clearing price during the period $[t_0, T]$. Thus, although there are no transactions until time T, at any time t in $[t_0, T]$ there is an easy-to-calculate price that reflects the equilibrium price if a clearing would have happened at that point in time. Further, this price is validated by the cumulative orders on both sides of the market up to that point t. Thus, even though this "would-be" clearing price at time t is not announced, it is validated by a larger volume of orders than any particular clearing price at any point in time in a continuous market.[12] Therefore, *the electronic call market produces timely information of superior quality and cannot be criticized on informational grounds.* The volume-validated "would-be" clearing price may serve as a better base for derivative instruments calculations rather than the price in the continuous market.

Price piracy is easy and common in financial markets. For example, prices established at the NYSE are used on regional exchanges and proprietary systems in place of price discovery. This free-riding on information weakens the exchanges where price is discovered as well as the validity of the market price. The existence of piracy has created incentives for the exchanges not to reveal the equilibrium price with accuracy. Thus, *piracy can hurt transparency in financial markets.* Price piracy can similarly affect call markets by creating fragmentation, reducing liquidity, and diminishing the validity of the discovered price. It is hard to eliminate the incentive for price piracy without administrative measures.

In summary, this short chapter focused on liquidity considerations in financial markets. We demonstrated the liquidity advantages of call markets over continuous markets. Further, we analyzed a structure of time-differentiated fees in a call market that guarantees high liquidity. We also discuss the importance of critical mass and the creation and acquisition of price information on market equilibrium and, ultimately, on the market structure of financial exchanges.

NOTES

1. See Economides (1993a) for a discussion of a financial market as a *network*.
2. For many noneconomists, coordination to an equilibrium that is better for all traders seems utopian, if not quite impossible. However, it is truly possible to create trading environments and mechanisms that do better than other environments for all traders,

i.e., are *Pareto superior* to other environments. Disbelief of this fact is similar to the widespread disbelief among noneconomists of the fact that bilateral trade can be beneficial to all parties involved.

3. See Economides and Siow (1985, 1988), and Economides (1992).

4. For a description of the specifics of the market clearing mechanism, see Economides (1993b).

5. The call market can accommodate *stock-specific* contingencies and *marketwide* contingencies. For example, a *stock-specific* contingency may require that the orders of an individual trader do not exceed a certain percentage of the orders on the other side of the market. A *marketwide* contingency may require that the after-the-call exposure of a trader in the whole market (or for a specific collection of stocks) is limited to a certain value.

6. In this analysis, we knowledge on *network externalities* developed in the New Theory of Industrial Organization. A *network externality* is a production or consumption positive-size externality. In a typical network, the addition of a new customer (or network node) increases the willingness to pay for network services by all participants. In a financial exchange network, high liquidity in a particular market is a network externality, since it increases the willingness of all traders to participate in that market, and traders receive this effect for free.

7. Thus, the proposed mechanism transforms orders into durable goods of varying durations. Since orders are durable, they can be counted cumulatively, and the level of participation at time T follows easily. See Economides and Himmelberg (1993) for a study of networks of durable and nondurable goods.

8. Of course, no fees will be paid for an order that does not execute in the call because no suitable match was found.

9. In practice, the electronic market of the Arizona Exchange (AZX) utilizes differential fees to induce early commitments to trade in the call.

10. Also, traders with large orders may be at greater risk of moving the market price in small liquidity markets and, therefore, may prefer the call more than the continuous market.

11. This mechanism is reminiscent of pricing by a price discriminating monopolist in Mussa and Rosen (1978). The good "participating in the call market" is differentiated in quality (vertically differentiated) so that all traders would prefer to enter later, everything else being equal. The auctioneer of the call market sells the higher quality goods (entry near T) at a higher price. However, he cannot fully implement an optimal price discrimination scheme that would require selling at different prices (fees) to different traders who arrive at the same time, as well as prohibiting arbitrage among entry times.

12. Of course, the volume of accumulated orders increases as time approaches T.

REFERENCES

Economides, Nicholas. (1992). "Liquidity and Markets," in *The New Palgrave Dictionary of Finance.*

Economides, Nicholas. (1993a). "Network Economics with Application to Finance," *Financial Markets, Institutions, and Instruments.* 2: 5, pp. 89–97.

Economides, Nicholas. (1993b). *Proposal to the Bank of Greece on the Organization of Primary and Secondary Markets in Greek State Bills, Notes, and Bonds.*

Economides, Nicholas, and Jeff Heisler. (1994a). "Fee Structure in Electronic Call Markets," New York University, Stern School of Business discussion paper EC-94-15.

Economides, Nicholas, and Jeff Heisler. (1994b). "Co-existence of Call and Continuous Markets," mimeograph.

Economides, Nicholas, and Charles Himmelberg. (1993). "Critical Mass and Network Size," mimeograph.

Economides, Nicholas, and Robert A. Schwartz. (1993). "Electronic Call Market Trading." New York University, Stern School of Business discussion paper EC-93–19, and forthcoming in *Journal of Portfolio Management* (winter 1995).

Economides, Nicholas, and Robert A. Schwartz. (1994). *Making the Trade: Equity Trading Practices and Market Structure.*

Economides, Nicholas, and Aloysius Siow. (1985). "Liquidity and the Success of Futures Markets." Columbia Business School, Center for the Study of Futures Markets, working paper no. CSFM-118.

Economides, Nicholas, and Aloysius Siow. (1988). "The Division of Markets Is Limited by the Extent of Liquidity," *American Economic Review,* 78: 1, pp. 108–21.

Mussa, Michael, and Sherwin Rosen. (1978). "Monopoly and Product Quality," *Journal of Economic Theory,* 18: pp. 16–37.

Rohlfs, Jeffrey. (1974). "A Theory of Interdependent Demand for a Communications Service," *Bell Journal of Economics,* 5: pp. 16–37.

Schwartz, Robert A. (1988). "A Proposal to Stabilize Stock Prices," *The Journal of Portfolio Management,* 15: 1, pp. 4–11.

Schwartz, Robert A. (1991). *Reshaping the Equity Markets: A Guide for the 1990s.* New York: Harper Business.

Schwartz, Robert A. (1993). "Competition and Efficiency," in Kenneth Lehn and Robert Kamphuis (eds.), *Modernizing U.S. Securities Regulation: Economic and Legal Perspectives.* Burr Ridge, IL: Irwin Professional Publishing.

CHAPTER 7

THE IMPORTANCE OF EQUITY TRADING COSTS: EVIDENCE FROM SECURITIES FIRMS' REVENUES

Hans R. Stoll

Investors pay trading costs in the form of commissions and market impact. Commissions are easily measured by investors since they are clearly reported on the trade confirmation. The market impact cost arises because investors sell at bid prices and buy at ask prices and because prices may move against investors. Measuring the extent to which prices move against investors is difficult, and this problem has spawned studies by Arnott and Wagner (1990); Beebower, Kamath, and Kurtz (1985); Berkowitz, Logue, and Noser (1988); Bodurtha and Quinn (1990); Perold (1988); Chan and Lakonishok (1991); and Keim and Madhavan (1991), who examine samples of institutional trades. Schwartz and Whitcomb (1988) provide a comprehensive overview and analysis of institutional investor trading costs and trading practices. Wagner and Edwards (1993) provide a framework for analyzing market impact costs.

This chapter is based in part on an earlier paper, Stoll (1993b), "Equity Trading Costs in-the-Large." The project was supported by a grant from the Institute of Chartered Financial Analysts and by the Financial Markets Research Center at Vanderbilt University. Helpful comments from Gilbert Beebower, Bill Christie, Gene Finn, Roger Huang, Philip Steele, and Ted Sternberg are gratefully acknowledged.

A variety of academic papers also focus on market impact costs as reflected in market transactions data (rather than the data of particular institutional investors). Studies in this vein include Hasbrouck (1990), Roll (1984), and Stoll (1989). These studies provide estimates of the market impact of trades from observable transaction prices, without knowing the identity of traders.

Instead of relying on transactions data to measure impact costs, this study measures trading costs on the basis of aggregate revenues of securities firms. Revenues of securities firms are trading costs to investors. This procedure cannot provide detailed information on the costs incurred by particular investors or with respect to particular types of stocks, but it can provide a baseline against which other estimates of costs can be evaluated.

In the first section I provide a brief overview of the alternative measures of market impact cost based on trading data. The data on securities industry revenues are next described. Estimates of the public's trading costs as a proportion of portfolio value are presented first. Next, the public's trading costs, based on securities firms' revenues, are stated in cents per share traded by the public and as a percent of trade value traded by the public. I also compute securities firms' revenues relative to securities firms' volume. Per share trading costs to the public are not necessarily the same as per share revenues to the securities industry, since securities firms do not participate in every trade. The chapter ends with a summary.

MEASUREMENT OF MARKET IMPACT COST
FROM TRADING DATA

The market impact cost associated with the placement of a market order covers three major costs—order processing, risk bearing, and adverse information. A market order demands immediacy—a dealer, for example—must be compensated for the costs of processing an order, such as telephone, computer, clearing fees, wages, and other costs. Second, the supplier of immediacy bears inventory risk for which compensation is demanded. Third, the supplier of immediacy faces the danger that incoming orders posses special information, and therefore the bid-ask spread is wider than it would otherwise be.

Figure 7–1 depicts hypothetical price changes associated with an

FIGURE 7–1
Implementation Short Fall and Price Reversal of a Sale at 30.75

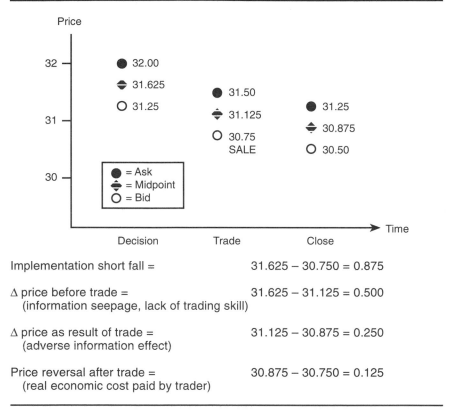

Implementation short fall =	31.625 – 30.750 = 0.875
Δ price before trade = (information seepage, lack of trading skill)	31.625 – 31.125 = 0.500
Δ price as result of trade = (adverse information effect)	31.125 – 30.875 = 0.250
Price reversal after trade = (real economic cost paid by trader)	30.875 – 30.750 = 0.125

investor's sale of stock. The investor makes the decision to sell the stock when the midpoint between the bid and ask is 31.625. By the time the trade takes place, the midpoint has fallen to 31.125, and the stock sells at the bid of 30.75. By the end of the day, the midpoint is at 30.875.

The market impact cost is measured by comparing the trade price to another price which serves as a standard of where the stock could have or should have traded. The broadest measure is Perold's (1988) implementation shortfall in which the trade price is compared to the midpoint at the time of the decision to trade. In Figure 7–1, the implementation shortfall is 31.625 – 30.75 = 0.875. One component of the shortfall is the price change in the midpoints between the time the portfolio manager decides to trade and the time the trader executes the trade, 0.50. In an efficient market, in which portfolio manager cannot pick stocks, one would expect this change to average zero. However, if the portfolio manager has special information or stock selection skill, unskilled trading may reduce or eliminate portfolio management profits. For example, if the trader is slow to act, the portfolio manager's information may become public and cause a stock price decline prior to the time of the trade. However, this price change does not measure the cost to society of providing trading services, since information about the company would eventually cause the price to fall whether a trade takes place or not. It is not appropriate to designate as an economic cost of trading a price change that would take place whether or not a trade takes place. The price change is, however, important to the money manager who is interested in the timing of trades and would rather not hold a stock prior to a price decline.

A second component of the shortfall is the change in the midpoint associated with the sale—$31.125 - 30.875 = 0.25$. The change in the midpoint reflects the expected value of the adverse information contained in the trade. Since sales, on average do convey bad news, this price change is not an economic cost, but only a warranted price change reflecting the information in the trade. The trick is to convince the market that one does not possess adverse information. The change in the midpoint is thus not a gain or loss in economic resources, but only an adjustment to reflect the new equilibrium price.

The final component of the shortfall is an economic cost. It measures the extent to which the stock is sold below its equilibrium value, where the equilibrium value is measured by the midpoint at the end of the day. In Figure 7–1, the reversal is $30.875 - 30.75 = 0.125$. If prices reverse in this manner, suppliers of immediacy make money and demanders of immediacy sell at a cost.[1] Studies of block trading, such as Kraus and Stoll (1972) and Holthausen, Leftwich, and Mayers (1987), indicate that prices reverse after sales but not after purchases, which implies that sales have a market impact cost, but that purchases do not. Chan and Lakonishok (1991) examine packages of institutional trades and reach a similar conclusion. They find that prices after the completion of a package of sales tend to reverse by about 0.10 percent whereas prices tend to continue after a package of purchases. Assuming an average stock price of \$35, a 0.10 percent reversal is 3.5 cents per share. Huang and Stoll (1993) calculate 5 minute and 30 minute reversals after every trade in 343 S&P 500 stocks in the years 1987 to 1991. For trades at or below the bid, they find a reversal of about 3.1 cents, and for trades at or above the ask, they find a reversal of about 2.5 cents.

Although reversals are small and, as Chan and Lakonishok indicate, often difficult to detect, they must exist if suppliers of immediacy are to make trading gains. A dealer that buys at the bid earns revenues only if he sells at a higher price at a later time. Similarly, a dealer that sells at the ask earns revenues only if he buys at a lower price. On the NYSE, immediacy is supplied to market orders not only by the specialist and other professional traders in the crowd but also by limit orders. If limit orders are picked off or are unable for other reasons to earn reversals, the average reversal over all participants can be less than the reversal earned by a dealer.

In this chapter, rather than measuring reversals directly, I infer on the basis of securities firms' revenues the investor trading costs per share paid to the securities industry. Data on securities firms' revenues make it possible to infer both commission costs and market impact costs.

SECURITIES INDUSTRY DATA

All registered securities firms complete the Securities and Exchange Commission's FOCUS report that provides detailed standardized data on revenues, expenses, and balance sheet items. Aggregated results are reported in the SEC's Annual Report, by various self-regulatory bodies, and by the Securities Industry Association publication, *Securities Industry Trends.* Aggregated income and expense data used in this study, "Part II – Financial and Operational Combined Uniform Single Report, Aggregate Data" and "Part IIA – Financial and Operational Combined Uniform Single Report, Aggregate Data," were supplied by the SEC for calendar years 1980 to 1992.[2] Part II firms carry customer accounts or clear trades. In 1992, there were 911 firms fitting this description. Part IIA firms neither carry public account nor clear trades. In 1992, these firms numbered 6,842. Part II firms accounted for 81 percent of industry revenues from commissions and trading gains in 1992.

Two sources of securities firms' revenues were used in estimating trading costs—commissions and trading gains—and results are reported for these categories. Firms acting in an agency capacity earn commissions; firms acting as principals, such as dealers, earn trading gains. Excluded were gains on firms' investment accounts, underwriting revenue, fees for account supervision, and other sources of revenue. The calculations are conservative since some investor trading costs may be reported in these other accounts. Revenues are also categorized by locus of trading—exchange-listed equities or NASDAQ equities. Revenues on debt trading and on options are excluded. Brokerage commissions and clearing fees paid to other brokers are netted out. Details of the calculations are contained in the appendix to this chapter.

The results are sensitive to the interpretation of the FOCUS data and to the accuracy of reporting on the FOCUS reports. This is particularly so when commission revenues and trading gains are allocated to exchanges and NASDAQ. The FOCUS report has no category for commissions earned in NASDAQ trading. Over-the-counter commissions are reported in an "all other" category, of which 85 percent is assumed to be NASDAQ commissions. Trading gains in OTC stocks are reported for Part II firms; but for Part IIA firms, trading gains are detailed for options trading but are not split out for NYSE, NASDAQ, or debt. Trading gains of nonpublic Part IIA firms are assumed to reflect the gains of specialists on exchanges, and the gains of the public Part IIA firms are assumed to be 50 percent from debt trading and 50 percent from NASDAQ trading. It is also not always clear, especially for the NASDAQ market, whether revenue figures correspond to the volume data. For example, the FOCUS report gives commissions and trading gains for all OTC stocks, including those not in NASDAQ, while volume data are for NASDAQ. In spite of these problems, it is interesting to determine if the data conforms to *a priori* expectations and reflect known time trends.

The aggregate data for commissions and trading gains derived from these calculations are presented in Table 7–1. In 1992, for example, commissions on exchange-listed and NASDAQ equities amounted to $11,099 million, and trading gains amounted to $4,753 million. Also listed in Table 7–1 are the market value of equities traded on exchanges and on NASDAQ, the share volume of trading, and the dollar volume of trading.

Until June 5, 1992, volume reporting procedures differ for NASDAQ stocks, according to whether they are National Market System (NMS) or not.[3] For non-NMS stocks, each market maker reports volume at the end of the day as the greater of purchases or sales in each stock in which he makes a market. If a market maker buys 500 shares during the day and sells 400 shares during the day, volume in that stock would be

TABLE 7-1
Aggregate Securities Industry Revenues from Equities, Market Value and Volume of Equities, and Member Firm Participation (all data in millions, except participation)

	1980	1981	1982	1983	1984	1985	1986	1987	1988	1989	1990	1991	1992
Commissions[a]													
Exchanges	4,100	3,830	4,318	5,919	4,970	5,760	7,213	8,709	6,180	7,253	6,146	7,244	7,731
NASDAQ	869	944	999	1,721	1,501	1,855	2,395	2,899	2,291	2,356	2,275	2,857	3,368
Trading gains[a]													
Exchanges	749	747	1,098	1,202	1,571	1,913	2,117	1,854	2,255	2,756	830	1,838	960
NASDAQ	864	750	795	1,741	1,138	1,601	2,260	2,354	1,847	2,004	1,887	3,143	3,793
Market Value													
Exchanges[b]	1,349,200	1,238,200	1,289,700	1,608,800	1,587,300	1,951,800	2,205,300	2,205,100	2,455,100	3,009,000	2,765,900	3,642,100	3,958,128
NASDAQ[c]	122,400	124,800	153,100	229,300	206,954	287,332	340,915	325,544	338,702	386,343	310,848	508,300	615,100
Share volume													
Exchanges[b]	15,584	15,969	22,492	30,316	30,548	37,188	48,581	64,083	52,666	54,417	53,746	58,296	63,202
NASDAQ[c]	6,692	7,823	8,432	15,909	15,159	20,699	28,737	37,890	31,070	33,530	33,380	41,311	48,455
NASDAQ restated[d]	10,038	11,735	12,643	21,182	18,380	23,738	32,320	42,214	34,875	37,254	36,543	44,638	49,808
Dollar volume													
Exchanges[b]	476,501	491,017	603,094	958,304	951,318	1,200,128	1,707,117	2,286,903	1,587,951	1,847,767	1,616,798	1,778,398	2,047,088
NASDAQ[c]	68,669	71,057	84,189	188,285	153,454	233,454	378,216	499,855	347,089	431,381	452,430	693,852	890,785
NASDAQ restated[d]	103,004	106,586	126,229	250,694	186,063	267,729	425,376	556,896	389,598	479,292	495,299	749,727	915,671

Member firm participation as a fraction of volume

Exchanges[e]	0.262	0.263	0.274	0.284	0.277	0.262	0.278	0.265	0.228	0.237	0.230	0.231	0.225
NASDAQ[f]	0.5	0.5	0.5	0.5	0.5	0.5	0.5	0.5	0.5	0.5	0.5	0.5	0.5

[a] Based on FOCUS reports as described in the appendix to this chapter.

[b] Data on market value and volume of stocks listed on the NYSE, AMEX, and regional exchanges is from SEC Annual Report, 1992, except for 1992 which is estimated from NYSE data. Market values are at year-end.

[c] NASDAQ market values and volume are from the NASD Fact Book.

[d] NASDAQ volume data is restated to account for underreporting of non-NMS volume relative to NMS volume. NMS share volume as a proportion of total OTC shares volume is 0.0 before 1982 and 0.001 for 1982, 0.277 for 1983, 0.50 for 1984, 0.637 for 1985, 0.686 for 1986 0.71 for 1987, 0.691 for 1988, 0.717 for 1989, 0.775 for 1990, 0.789 for 1991, and 0.85 for 1992.

[e] Specialists and other member firms' purchases plus sales as a fraction of twice total volume. Data are from the NYSE Fact Book.

[f] Market-maker participation of 0.5 assumes a NASDAQ market-maker participates in each trade on one side or the other.

reported as 500 shares. In this example, the market maker's inventory change is 100 shares. NMS stocks follow last-sale reporting procedures, as is the case on exchanges. Under last-sale reporting, every sale is reported. Under that procedure, volume would be 900 shares, not 500 shares—500 shares sold by the public to the market maker and 400 shares sold by the market maker to the public. The volume reporting procedure for non-NMS NASDAQ stocks thus understates volume substantially, relative to NMS stocks.

To convert aggregate non-NMS share volume to what would be reported under last-sale reporting, the following procedure is followed. Let V_1 be non-NMS volume and let V_2 be the corresponding last-sale volume. Then

$$V_2 = 2(V_1 - \frac{1}{2} \Delta I)$$

where ΔI is the average absolute inventory change of market makers. For 1980, it is assumed that $\Delta I = .5V_1$, so that $V_2 = 1.5V_1$. Non-NMS volume is restated by the factor 1.5 and added to NMS volume to give the resulting restated total NASDAQ volume, which is reported in Table 7–1. In subsequent years, the factor is decreased as active stocks switch to NMS, leaving less active stocks with larger absolute inventory changes in the non-NMS category.[4]

Because a large fraction of reported volume is for the account of securities firms, public volume is substantially less than total volume. The last rows of Table 7–1 contain estimates of the proportion of volume executed for the account of securities firms. The data for exchanges are taken from the NYSE *Fact Book* and represent purchases plus sales of specialists and other member firms as a percent of twice reported volume.[5] There appears to have been a decline in member firm trading to 22.5 percent in 1992 from 26.2 percent in 1980 and a prior high of 27.8 percent in 1986.

For NASDAQ stocks, market-maker participation is calculated in the same way as it is for exchange stocks—purchases plus sales divided by twice volume. In the example used above, this amounts to purchases plus sales of 900, divided by twice-reported volume of 1,800, or 0.50. If a market maker participates on one side of every trade, market-maker participation is 0.50. If there were public-to-public volume, market-maker participation would be less than 0.50; if there were trading between market makers, market-maker participation would be greater than

0.50. I assume market-maker participation of 50 percent of NASDAQ restated volume.

TRADING COSTS AS A PROPORTION OF PORTFOLIO VALUE

The aggregate data in Table 7–1 indicate that, in 1992, net securities commission income on exchanges and on NASDAQ stocks amounted to $7,731 million and $3,368 million, respectively. Trading gains in equity securities amounted to $960 million and $3,793 million, respectively, in the two categories of stocks. Aggregate securities firms' revenues from commissions and trading gains in 1992 thus totaled $15,852 million, an amount that represents direct trading costs to the public. This is up from a total of $6,582 in 1980.

Revenues reported as commissions and trading gains constitute less than half the revenues of securities firms. To the extent that other revenues of securities firms include payment for trading services, the trading cost figures are conservative. For example, the revenues from underwriting new equity issues, which for clearing and carrying firms amounted to $2,305 million in 1992, are not included.[6] Although this chapter focuses on secondary market trading costs, the cost of the initial trade to bring stock public might reasonably be included as a cost of trading that is borne by investors. Also excluded are "fees for account supervision," "other revenue," and "gains from firms' investment accounts," which could include some compensation for trading services. In 1992, clearing and carrying firms received $3,359 million, $22,300 million, and $533 million, respectively, in these three categories. Finally, the trading cost figures do not include costs incurred directly by investors, such as payments for research material and the opportunity cost of their time in managing assets.

On the basis of the data in Table 7–1, Table 7–2 reports trading costs as a proportion of the value of securities outstanding at year-end for the years 1980 to 1992. For example, in 1992, total trading costs of $15,582 million amount to 0.347 percent of the combined market value of stocks on the NYSE, AMEX, and NASDAQ. This percentage is down from a high of 0.625 percent in 1987 and from 0.447 percent in 1980. The trend over time reflects the trend in turnover, which peaked in 1987, and the trend in trading costs per share, which have declined over time. Table 7–2 does show that

TABLE 7-2
Equity Trading Costs as a Percent of Market Value[a]

	1980	1981	1982	1983	1984	1985	1986	1987	1988	1989	1990	1991	1992
Exchanges													
Commissions	0.304	0.309	0.311	0.368	0.313	0.295	0.327	0.395	0.252	0.241	0.222	0.199	0.195
Trading Gains	0.056	0.060	0.079	0.075	0.099	0.098	0.096	0.084	0.092	0.092	0.030	0.055	0.032
Total	0.360	0.369	0.390	0.443	0.412	0.393	0.423	0.479	0.344	0.333	0.252	0.254	0.227
NASDAQ													
Commissions	0.710	0.757	0.653	0.750	0.725	0.645	0.702	0.891	0.677	0.610	0.732	0.562	0.548
Trading gains	0.705	0.601	0.519	0.759	0.550	0.557	0.663	0.723	0.545	0.519	0.607	0.600	0.592
Total	1.415	1.358	1.172	1.509	1.275	1.202	1.365	1.614	1.222	1.129	1.339	1.162	1.140
Total Exchanges and NASDAQ													
Commissions	0.338	0.350	0.345	0.416	0.361	0.340	0.377	0.459	0.303	0.283	0.274	0.243	0.243
Trading gains	0.110	0.110	0.123	0.160	0.151	0.157	0.172	0.166	0.147	0.140	0.088	0.122	0.107
Total	0.448	0.460	0.468	0.576	0.512	0.497	0.549	0.625	0.450	0.423	0.362	0.365	0.350

[a] Calculated from Table 7–1 as trading costs (commissions or trading gains) divided by market value (exchanges or NASDAQ)

trading costs in NASDAQ stocks exceed one percent of the market value of those stocks, substantially more than for NYSE stocks. This reflects the higher turnover of NASDAQ stocks and the greater trading cost per share traded. In 1980, turnover, calculated from the data in Table 7–1 as the ratio of annual dollar trading volume to market value, was 0.35 on exchanges and 0.84 on NASDAQ (using restated volume). In 1987, these figures were 0.77 and 1.25, respectively. Since 1987, turnover has declined more on exchanges (to 0.52 in 1992) than on NASDAQ (to 1.53 in 1992), which has resulted in a smaller decline in trading costs as a fraction of market value on NASDAQ than on exchanges.

Although they have declined over time, trading costs as a percentage of the total value of all stocks are substantial at about 0.40 percent. Portfolios that are actively traded, of course, bear a larger cost, and portfolios that do not trade bear no trading cost. When trading costs are combined with other fees, such as for underwriting and account management, and with investment management fees of money managers, the total costs of trading and managing the nation's equity portfolio very probably exceeds one percent of the market value of all stocks each year, an economically significant cost relative to the average return per year.

TRADING COSTS RELATIVE TO VOLUME

Trading costs are usually measured in cents per share or as a percent of the value of the trade. These data are derived from Table 7–1 by dividing revenues by twice public volume, and the results are reported in Tables 7–3 and 7–4. The figures in Table 7–3 represent the trading costs on one side of the trade in cents per share. For example, the commission of 8.73 cents calculated for exchanges in 1989 represents the commission to the buyer or the seller. Similarly, the trading gain on exchanges of 3.32 cents in 1989 represents one half the market impact cost on a round-trip transaction. The figures in Table 7–4 represent the trading costs on one side of the trade as a percent of trade value.

Clearly evident in Tables 7–3 and 7–4 is the dramatic decline in exchange commissions between 1980 and 1992—in cents per share, from 17.81 cents to 7.89 cents; and in percent, from 0.583 percent to 0.244 percent. The decline in commissions reflects the fact that commission rates declined for almost all investors and the fact that the composition of trading has become more concentrated in institutional investors,

TABLE 7–3
Equity Trading Costs in Center per Share Traded[a]

	1980	1981	1982	1983	1984	1985	1986	1987	1988	1989	1990	1991	1992
Exchanges													
Commissions	17,81	16.26	13.23	13.64	11.25	10.49	10.29	9.25	7.60	8.73	7.42	8.08	7.89
Trading gains	3.25	3.17	3.36	2.77	3.56	3.48	3.02	1.97	2.77	3.32	1.00	2.25	1.28
Total	21.06	19.43	16.59	16.41	14.81	13.97	13.31	11.22	10.37	12.05	8.42	10.33	9.17
NASDAQ													
Commissions	8.66	8.05	7.90	8.12	8.16	7.81	7.41	6.87	6.57	6.32	6.32	6.40	6.76
Trading gains	8.60	6.39	6.29	8.22	6.19	6.74	6.99	5.58	5.30	5.38	5.16	6.84	7.32
Total	17.26	14.44	14.19	16.34	14.35	14.55	14.40	12.45	11.87	11.70	11.39	13.24	14.08
Total Exchanges and NASDAQ													
Commissions	15.03	13.53	11.74	11.83	10.34	9.68	9.38	8.51	7.29	7.98	7.06	7.52	7.51
Trading gains	4.88	4.24	4.18	4.56	4.33	4.47	4.27	3.08	3.53	3.96	2.28	3.78	3.32
Total	19.91	17.77	15.92	16.39	14.67	14.15	13.65	11.59	10.82	11.94	9.34	11.30	10.83

a Calculated from Table 7–1 as dollar trading costs (commissions or trading gains) as a percent of twice public share volume. Public share volume is share volume reported in Table 7–1 less the proportion of volume done by securities firms.

TABLE 7-4
Equity Trading Costs as a Percent of Trade Value [a]

	1980	1981	1982	1983	1984	1985	1986	1987	1988	1989	1990	1991	1992
Exchanges													
Commissions	0.583	0.529	0.493	0.431	0.361	0.325	0.293	0.259	0.252	0.257	0.247	0.265	0.244
Trading gains	0.106	0.103	0.125	0.088	0.114	0.108	0.086	0.055	0.092	0.098	0.033	0.074	0.040
Total	0.689	0.632	0.618	0.519	0.475	0.433	0.379	0.314	0.344	0.355	0.280	0.339	0.284
NASDAQ													
Commissions	0.844	0.886	0.792	0.686	0.806	0.693	0.563	0.521	0.588	0.492	0.459	0.381	0.368
Trading gains	0.838	0.704	0.630	0.694	0.611	0.598	0.531	0.423	0.474	0.418	0.381	0.407	0.398
Total	1.682	1.590	1.422	1.380	1.417	1.291	1.094	0.944	1.062	0.910	0.840	0.788	0.766
Total Exchanges and NASDAQ													
Commissions	0.616	0.575	0.531	0.471	0.414	0.373	0.333	0.296	0.298	0.291	0.282	0.290	0.271
Trading gains	0.200	0.180	0.189	0.181	0.173	0.172	0.151	0.107	0.144	0.091	0.146	0.120	
Total	0.816	0.755	0.720	0.652	0.587	0.545	0.484	0.403	0.442	0.435	0.373	0.436	0.391

[a] Calculated from Table 7–1 as dollar trading costs (commissions or trading gains) as a percent of twice public dollar volume. Public dollar volume is dollar volume reported in Table 7–1 less the proportions of volume done by securities firms.

who pay the lowest commission rates. The decline in commissions is significant in view of the generally accepted fact that soft dollar services have increased during the 1980s. NASDAQ commissions in cents per share are always less than exchange commissions in cents per share, which reflects the fact that a considerable amount of NASDAQ trading is "net." Institutional investors generally do not pay commissions. NASDAQ commissions also fell, from 8.66 cents to 6.76 cents, but not as much as exchange commissions.

On exchanges, the average trading gain per share—the market impact cost of a trade—is always less than half the minimum bid-ask spread of 6.25 cents per share. The largest gain per share of 3.56 cents, 57 percent of the minimum half-spread, occurred in 1984. That the trading gain is less than the half-spread reflects the fact that prices tend to move against a dealer after a trade and the fact that transactions occur inside the spread. Some estimated market impact costs are quite low— one cent per share in 1990 and 1.28 cents per share in 1992. Apparently these were poor years for the securities firms' trading operations, or, alternatively, there may have been some errors in the data. Even if one ignores these two years, the data suggest that exchanges' trading gains per share have declined over time. Trading gains in NASDAQ are higher than on exchanges and reflect the higher spreads of NASDAQ stocks and the fact that trading gains are a more important source of revenue than are commissions. During the 1980s, NASDAQ trading gains fell somewhat, from an average of 7.5 cents in 1980–1981 to an average of 5.27 cents in 1989–1990. Since 1990, trading gains have increased somewhat.

Average trading gains on exchanges are comparable in magnitude to average reversals reported by Chan and Lakonishok (1991) and Huang and Stoll (1993). In these studies, which are based on data from the years 1986 to 1991, reversals are about 2 to 4 cents per share. These reversals are about the same as the average per-share trading gains shown in Table 7–3 that range between 1.97 cents and 3.32 cents in the years 1987 to 1991, excluding 1990.

The market impact costs calculated from securities firms' revenues do not include market impact costs paid by some public investors to other public investors. For example, public market orders may pay a market impact cost to public limit orders. If the per-share market impact costs paid to securities firms are the same as the average reversal over all trades, as the results of Chan and Lakonishok and Huang and Stoll suggest, the implication is that limit orders earn no compensation for providing immediacy. If they did, the average per-share reversal (over all shares traded) paid by market orders should exceed the average per-share trading gain (over all shares traded) paid to securities firms.

In cents per share, NASDAQ total trading costs have ranged between 17.26 cents (1980) and 11.39 cents (1990), and exchanges' trading costs have ranged between 21.07 cents (1980) and 8.43 cents (1990). As a percent of trade value, NASDAQ trading costs are substantially larger than exchanges' costs, ranging from 1.682 percent (in 1980) to 0.766 percent (in 1992), as compared with a range of 0.689 percent (in 1980) to 0.280 percent (in 1990) for exchanges. In part, this reflects the fact that the average share price in the NASDAQ market is much lower than on exchanges. In 1989, the average price of shares traded on NASDAQ was about one third the average share price on exchanges ($12.87 versus $37.03), as it was during all of the 1980s. By 1992 the ratio had fallen to two to one ($18.38 in NASDAQ versus $34.05 in exchanges).

SECURITIES FIRMS' REVENUES RELATIVE TO THEIR VOLUME

Securities firms' trading gains per share or per dollar traded are not necessarily equal to public costs per share or per dollar. If securities firms participate in less than 50 percent of volume, their trading revenues per share or per dollar traded will be greater than public costs per share or per dollar traded. This is because public costs are expressed relative to public volume, whereas securities firms' are expressed relative to firms' volume. In the case of commissions per share or per dollar, the figures are the same for the public and the securities firms under the assumption that a securities firm participates as an agent whenever the public trades. Table 7–5 presents estimates of securities firms' trading revenues in cents per share traded by securities firms and as a percent of the value of shares traded by securities firms. The data simply take securities firms' revenues relative to securities firms' trading volume (rather than public volume).

The data for NASDAQ market makers are the same as public trading costs shown in Tables 7–3 and 7–4 because a market-maker participation rate of 50 percent is assumed. For exchanges, securities firms'

TABLE 7–5
Securities Firms' Trading Gains Relative to Securities Firms' Share and Dollar Volume [a]

	1980	1981	1982	1983	1984	1985	1986	1987	1988	1989	1990	1991	1992
As percent of twice firms' share volume													
NASDAQ	8.602	6.391	6.288	8.217	6.189	6.742	6.993	5.576	5.296	5.379	5.164	6.837	7.316
Exchanges	9.188	8.904	8.894	6.980	9.292	9.833	7.830	5.458	9.400	10.702	3.361	7.503	4.432
As percent of twice firms' dollar volume													
NASDAQ	0.838	0.704	0.630	0.694	0.611	0.598	0.531	0.423	0.474	0.418	0.381	0.407	0.398
Exchanges	0.300	0.290	0.332	0.221	0.298	0.305	0.223	0.153	0.312	0.315	0.112	0.246	0.137

[a] Calculated from Table 7–1 as trading gains taken as a percent of twice securities firms' share or dollar volume

average revenues per share exceed the public's average post per share because securities firms are involved in substantially less than 50 percent of volume. For example, in 1989, the public paid an average market impact cost of 3.32 cents per share (Table 7–3) but securities firms earned average trading gains of 10.7 cents per share (Table 7–5). On NASDAQ, the market impact cost that year is estimated at 5.38 cents per share. In 1992, securities firms earned an average trading gain of 4.43 cents per share from trading on exchanges, but the public paid an average of 1.28 cents per share to securities firms. On NASDAQ, the market impact cost in 1992 paid by investors and received by securities firms is estimated at 7.32 cents per share.

SUMMARY

Estimates of equity trading costs are computed for the years 1980 to 1992 based on revenue data from securities firms. During this period, annual equity trading costs (commissions and market impact costs), stated as a percent of the market value of outstanding equity shares on exchanges and the NASDAQ market, ranged between 0.347 percent (in 1992) and 0.625 percent (in 1987). Over time, trading costs as a percent of market value have declined somewhat despite an increase in turnover.

On exchanges, commissions per share traded by the public declined from 17.81 cents to less than 8 cents; and in NASDAQ, from 8.66 cents to less than 7 cents. On exchanges, the market impact cost of a trade, measured as trading gains of securities firms relative to public volume, declined from about 3.25 cents per share in 1980 to less than 2 cents per share in 1992. In NASDAQ, the estimated market impact cost declined from 8.6 cents per share in 1980 to less than 6 cents per share in the years 1987 to 1990, and have increased recently to 7.32 cents in 1992. As a percent of trade value, trading costs are substantially higher in the NASDAQ market than on exchanges because share prices are lower on NASDAQ.

Trading costs presented in this study provide new evidence that can be used to evaluate and can be evaluated against other studies of trading costs based on data from institutional investors and on markets data. Market impact costs measured from transactions data face a number of difficulties. The trade price must be compared to some standard price that is difficult to choose. The direction of a price impact depends on whether the buyer or seller is the active party, something that is often impossible to determine. Trading costs measured from securities firms' revenues avoid some of these difficulties, but face others. In particular, trading costs based on securities firms' revenues cannot provide much information about differences in trading costs across stocks or across different traders. The accuracy of trading costs measured in this way depends on the accuracy of accounting data provided by securities firms and on certain assumptions about how costs should be allocated. Per-share data depend on the accuracy of volume data. Improvements in the quality of the data, especially in the breakdown of revenues by market and type of security, would increase the reliability and usefulness of in-the-large measures.

Despite these difficulties, trading costs based on securities firms' revenues appear reasonable, particularly for exchanges. Estimated commissions reflect the known decline in commissions per share in the last 13 years. The implied market impact cost of a trade is of the same magnitude as the price reversal measure of market impact calculated from transactions data.

NOTES

1. The price reversal as a measure impact was first used by Scholes (1972). See also Kraus and Stoll (1972).
2. I thank Van Anthony for help with the data.
3. On June 15, 1992, non-NMS NASDAQ securities switched to last-sale reporting. This group of about 1,700 stocks is now called the NASDAQ Small Cap Market.
4. The NMS category was introduced in 1982. The proportions of reported NASDAQ volume which were in NMS stocks are as follows, according to the NASDAQ *Fact Book*:

'82	'83	'84	'85	'86	'87	'88	'89	'90	'91	'92
.001	.277	.500	.637	.686	.710	.691	.717	.755	.789	.850

I assume the daily dealer inventory change of non-NMS stocks increased over time because the less active stocks remained in the non-NMS category. I assume $DI = .5 + .15p$, where p = the proportion of reported share volume in NMS stocks. The effect of this assumption is to decrease the adjustment factor from 1.5 in 1980 to 1.3725 in 1992.

On June 15, 1992, when the remaining non-NMS NASDAQ securities switched to last-sale reporting, reported share volume for the small cap issues increased by 17.5 percent, as compared with 4.2 percent for NMS issues. (I thank Philip Steele of the American Stock Exchange for providing these data). This implies $V_2 = 1.15\ V_1$, a smaller adjustment factor than I used. This factor implies an average dealer inventory change of 85 percent of the greater of his daily purchases or sales, which seems a bit large, even for small inactive stocks.

To reflect the switch to last-sale reporting by non-NMS stocks in the middle of the year, the restated NASDAQ volume reported in Table 7–1 is an average of (1) restated total volume, if no switch to last-sale reporting by non-NMS securities had taken place, and (2) reported total volume.

5. Reported volume is total sales (which equals total purchases). Since specialist and member firms' purchases and sales are aggregated, dividing by twice reported volume (which is aggregate purchases plus sales) is appropriate. See Stoll (1985) for more discussion of specialists' participation.

6. Equity underwriting fees earned by firms that clear or carry were the following for the years 1980 to 1990 (in millions of dollars): 420, 444, 343, 770, 260, 775, 1426, 1278, 1234, 781, 735, 1894, 2305.

REFERENCES

Arnott, Robert D., and Wayne H. Wagner. (1990). "The Measurement and Control of Trading Costs," *Financial Analysts Journal,* November/December, pp. 73–80.

Beebower, Gilbert, Vasant Kamath, and Ronald Surz. (1985). "Commission and Transaction Costs of Stock Market Trading." SEI Corporation working paper (July).

Berkowitz, Stephen, Dennis Logue, and Eugene Noser. (1988). "The Total Cost of Transactions on the NYSE," *Journal of Finance,* 43: March, pp. 97–112.

Bodurtha, Stephen, and Thomas Quinn. (1990). "Does Patient Program Trading Really Pay?" *Financial Analysts Journal,* May/June, pp. 35–42.

Chan, Louis K. C., and Josef Lakonishok. (1991). "Institutional Trades and Intraday Stock Price Behavior." University of Illinois, College of Commerce and Business Administration working paper 91–0167 (October).

Hasbrouck, Joel. (1993). "Assessing the Quality of a Security Market: A New Approach to Transaction-Cost Measurement," *The Review of Financial Studies,* 6: pp. 192–212.

Huang, Roger, and Hans Stoll. (1993). "Anatomy of Trading Costs." Vanderbilt University working paper (October).

Holthausen, Robert, Richard Leftwich, and David Mayers. (1987). "The Effect of Large Block Transactions on Security Prices: A Cross-sectional Analysis," *Journal of Financial Economics,* 19: December, pp. 237–67.

Keim, Donald, and Ananth Madhavan. (1991). "The Upstairs Market for Large-Block Transactions: Analysis and Measurement of Price Effects." The Wharton School, Finance Department working paper (November).

Kraus, Alan, and Hans Stoll. (1972). "Price Impacts of Block Trading on the New York Stock Exchange," *Journal of Finance,* 27: June, pp. 569–88.

Perold, Andre F. (1988). "The Implementation Shortfall: Paper versus Reality," *Journal of Portfolio Management,* Spring, pp. 4–9.

Roll, Richard. (1984). "A Simple Implicit Measure of the Bid-Ask Spread in an Efficient Market," *Journal of Finance,* 39: September, pp. 1127–39.

Scholes, Myron. (1972). "The Market for Securities: Substitution versus Price Pressure and the Effects of Information on Share Price," *Journal of Business,* 45: April, pp. 179–211.

Schwartz, Robert A., and David K. Whitcomb. (1988). "Transaction Costs and Institutional Investor Trading Strategies." New York University, Stern School of Business, Salomon Center for Financial Studies Monograph Series 1988–2/3.

Stoll, Hans. (1989). "Inferring the Components of the Bid-Ask Spread: Theory and Empirical Tests," *Journal of Finance,* 44: March.

Stoll, Hans. (1993a). *Equity Trading Costs.* Charlottesville VA: Institute of Chartered Financial Analysts.

Stoll, Hans. (1993b). "Equity Trading Costs in-the-Large," *Journal of Portfolio Management,* 19: Summer, pp. 41–50.

Wagner, Wayne, and Mark Edwards. (1993). "Best Execution," *Financial Analysts Journal,* January/February, pp. 65–71.

APPENDIX TO CHAPTER 7
Calculation of Trading Costs from FOCUS Data

All registered securities firms are required to submit detailed standardized data on income and expense items as well as balance sheet items. For the years 1980 through 1990, the Securities and Exchange Commission kindly supplied aggregated income and expense data categorized into two sets of firms. Firms carrying customer accounts or clearing trades were aggregated under the heading, "Part II – Financial and Operational Combined Uniform Single Report, Aggregate Data." At year-end 1989, there were 1,094 such firms, all but 45 of which did a public business. Firms that neither carry accounts nor clear trades were aggregated under the heading, "Part IIA—Financial and Operational Combined Uniform Single Report, Aggregate Data." At year-end 1989, there were 7,718 such firms, all but 3,061 of which did a public business. For each category— Part II or Part IIA—the breakdown into firms doing a public business and not doing a public business was available. A sample of the Part II and Part IIA data is in Appendix B of Stoll (1993a) or may be obtained from the author.

The description below gives the line number from the Part II or Part IIA forms that are added or subtracted in the calculation of commissions and trading gains on exchanges and on the over-the-counter market. A verbal description of the data item is also given. For example, the notation "II.1.A." signifies line number 1.A of the report for Part II firms. Sometimes a line number is multiplied by a factor (k, k´, k*, k‡, a, b). these factors are defined after the summation in which they first appear. The resulting aggregate amounts are in the first four rows of Table 7–1.

Commissions on Exchanges

+   [II.1.A. Commissions in listed equity on an exchange by firms carrying public accounts or clearing trades.]
–k [II.16. Floor brokerage paid to certain brokers.]
–k [II.17. Commissions and clearance paid to all other brokers.
+   [IIA.1.A. Commissions in listed equity on an exchange by firms not carrying public accounts and not clearing.]
–k´ [[IIA.12. Commissions paid to other broker dealers.]
     where k = II.1.A/II.1.E, fraction of total commissions of carrying/clearing firms for transactions on an exchange.
     where k´ = IIA.1.A/IIA.1.D, fraction of total commissions of noncarrying/ nonclearing firms for transactions on an exchange.

Commissions in NASDAQ

+a [II.1.D. All other securities commissions by firms carrying public accounts or clearing.]
–k* [II.16. Floor brokerage paid to certain brokers.]
–k* [II.17. Commissions and clearance paid to all other brokers.]
+a [IIA.1.C. All other securities commissions by firms not carrying public accounts or clearing.]
–k‡ [IIA.12. Commissions paid to other broker/dealers.]
     where a = estimated proportion of "All other securities commissions" for NASDAQ equity. Calculations assume a = 0.85. Remaining proportion assumed to be for non-NASDAQ equity commissions (such as Bulletin Board stocks and pink sheet stocks) and for nonequity commissions.
     where k* = a (II.1.D)/(II.1.E), fraction of total commissions of carrying/ clearing firms for NASDAQ equity trading.
     where k‡ = a (IIA.1.C)/(IIA.1.D), fraction of total commissions of noncarrying/nonclearing firms for transactions NASDAQ.
     Note: Commissions for listed equity executed in NASDAQ are not reported because volume and NASDAQ market value do not include listed securities.

Trading Gains on Exchanges

+   [II.2.D. Gains from trading other than options, debt, or OTC equity.]
+   [IIA.2.B, nonpublic only. Part IIA firms reporting exchange trading gains and not doing a public business include exchange specialists (nonpublic option market makers report separately on line 2.A.)]

Trading Gains in NASDAQ

+   [II.2.A. Gains from market making in NASDAQ securities, excluding II.2.A.1, gains from OTC trading in listed equities.]
+b   [IIa.2.B – (IIA.2.B, nonpublic only.) The fraction, b, of all gains not attributed to options or nonpublic IIA firms is attributed to NASDAQ trading gains.

where b = estimated fraction of public Part IIA firms' trading gains due to NASDAQ equity trading, assumed to be 0.50 in the calculations. Remainder is assumed to be gains from debt trading. The fraction, b, applies only to IIA firms because gains from debt trading are separately accounted for in the case of Part II firms.

CHAPTER 8

INSTITUTIONAL DESIGN FOR ELECTRONIC TRADING

Kevin McCabe
Stephen Rassenti
Vernon Smith

INTRODUCTION

In this chapter we study the role of experimental economics in the design of auction institutions for electronic trading. A large number of implementational questions are currently being asked in the field. Can we reduce price volatility without decreases in efficiency? What is the effect of market fragmentation? What is the "value added" role of the specialist? Should traders be allowed to see the book? Should we use "circuit breakers" to interrupt continuous trading? How should we start a market? How can we prevent people from colluding? What rules, if any, should be placed on program trading? How do we reduce the vulnerability of uninformed traders?

Historically, we know that the field does not wait for the "best" theoretical answers to such questions but proceeds with trial-and-error learning by doing. In this chapter we argue for the use of laboratory research as a complement to learning in the field. In section two following, we review the methodology used by experimental economists and the types of questions which can be studied. We make two observations. First, experimental methods are less expensive for asking "what if" types of questions. Second, through experimental controls we are able to make more informative measurements of performance. In the remainder of this section we show how experimental methods are used in specific research programs.

Economic theory tells us when incentive problems are likely to exist. Such theories are predicated on "ideal" conditions similar to the assumption of a "perfect vacuum" in physics. In practice, incentives operate in less than ideal environments leading to important empirical questions. When do the incentive problems suggested by theory become important for practice? Do they work as theory predicts? Why or why not? In the third section we show how laboratory experiments can be used to study a specific incentive problem, for instance, the incentive to trade off-floor. In the fourth section we show how laboratory experiments can be used as a "test bed" to measure the effect of new call market rules on incentives and performance.

In the final section, we conclude by indicating some of the broader issues raised by applied experimental research. First, we point out the need for the development of research programs which allow a methodical transition from "pure" laboratory experiments to "pure" field experiments. Second, we indicate some of the basic theoretical questions raised by experimental research.

EXPERIMENTAL ECONOMICS

A common view of the practice of science is that we use experiments to study nature. However, it is more to the point to say we experiment because we are curious. It seems that our curiosity never allows us to be convinced by anything less than direct experience. Whatever is the problem, we always want to test our solution against experience as we try to improve our solutions and our understanding of phenomena. But curiosity alone cannot be construed as science.

An important aspect of science is communication and the formation of a common experience base. Do we share a common understanding? We accept experimental evidence because, in principle, anyone could have run the experiment and made the same[1] observations. Similarly, we accept models of theories because, in principle, anyone can follow the rules of reasoning from assumptions to conclusions. Science does not accept, at least as common experience, unsubstantiated observations or unproven conjectures. The direct benefit of science for society is the invention of tools which allow us to extend our interaction with nature and each other, to improve our common understanding of phenomena. In this way we provide answers to the question, "Do you see what I see?"

An Experimental Framework

Adam Smith's claim, that a fundamental characteristic of people is their desire to truck, barter, and exchange, comes close to describing what most economists would consider a fundamental law of economic science. How can we use experiments to improve our understanding of this law? Smith (1982, 1989) describes a generic model for experimentation based on the descriptive framework of the "new" institutional economics.[2] This framework consists of three parts: an economic environment, a set of institutions, and a set of behavioral forces. We will apply this framework to the study of alternative exchange systems, in particular, electronic exchanges.

The Trading Environment

We say that a set of agents can gain by trading units of some object if there exists a price p' such that some agents would like to purchase units at that price, i.e., quantity demanded $D(p')$ is positive, and some agents would like to sell units at the same price, i.e., quantity supplied $S(p')$ is positive.[3] If the quantity supplied is fixed, i.e., $S(p) \equiv N_s$ for all $p \geq p_{\min}$, then we have a one-sided market.[4] (In securities markets these are new issues or primary markets). If the quantity supplied is variable, depending on price, then we have a two-sided market[5] (see Figure 8–1). (Secondary exchange markets in the case of securities).

In trading environments agents may know (or estimate) their own values from buying or selling units of a commodity but this information is private, i.e., they do not know this information for other agents. Agents observe messages (bids, asks, and quantities) from which they can try to infer other agents' valuations. However, in order to infer values, agents must have a model of the message-sending behavior of other agents. Since values are private, the experimenter in the field is at the same disadvantage, i.e., how to identify private values from message-sending behavior. A distinguishing characteristic of a laboratory economic experiment is the use of reward techniques which sharpen control for private values.

One way to control for private values is the induced value proce-

FIGURE 8–1
Example of Induced Supply and Demand Environment

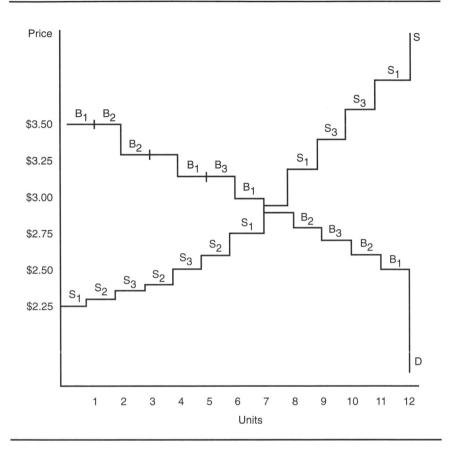

dure described by Smith (1976). This is done by creating an abstract commodity which has no direct value to subjects. Subjects are given a property right in the commodity in terms of resale or maximum willingness-to-pay schedules for buyers and unit cost or minimum willingness-to-accept schedules for sellers. These schedules are denominated in domestic currency, that is, U.S. dollars for experiments run in the United States. Units of the commodity are traded at prices denominated in the domestic currency, and profits are calculated and paid in cash to subject based on their trades. Consider the following example for a buyer and seller.

A buyer's resale value schedule may consists of the successive unit values ($3.50, $3.15, $3.00, $2.50). Now suppose in the course of trading our buyer buys his first unit at the price $3.15 and his second unit at the price $2.85. The profit from these trades is $3.50 − $3.15 = $0.35 for the first unit and $3.15 − $2.85 = $0.30 for the second unit, or a total profit of $0.35 + $0.30 = $0.65. If the redemption schedule has declining values, reflecting decreasing willingness-to-pay (or diminishing marginal return), then we have induced a downward sloping demand schedule for that subject. Formally, we let $d_i(k)$ be the redemption value of the kth unit to subject i, and we let $p_i(k)$ be the price subject i paid for the kth unit. Profit on the kth unit is given by $\pi_i(k) = d_i(k) − p_i(k)$. If subject i buys b_i units at the prices $p_i(1)$, $p_i(2)$, $p_i(3)$, ..., $p_i(b_i)$, then subject i's total profits are:

$$\pi_i(k) = \sum_{k=1}^{b_i} \pi_i(k) = \sum_{k=1}^{b_i} [d_i(k) − p_i(k)]. \tag{8.1}$$

A seller's cost schedule may consist of the successive unit costs ($2.25, $2.75, $3.20, $3.80). Now suppose in the course of trading our selling sells his first unit at $3.30, second unit at $3.15, and his third unit at $3.25. The profit from these trades is $3.30 − $2.25 = $1.05 on the first unit, $3.15 − $2.75 = $0.40 on the second unit, and $3.25 − $3.20 = $0.05 on the third unit, or a total profit of $1.05 + $0.40 + $0.05 = $1.50. If the unit cost schedule shows increasing unit costs, reflecting increasing willingness-to-accept (diminishing returns), we have induced an upward sloping supply schedule for that subject. Formally, we let $s_j(k)$ be the unit cost of the kth unit to seller j, and we let $p_j(k)$ be the price at which seller j sold unit k. Profit on the kth unit is given by $\pi_j(k) = p_j(k) − s_j(k)$. If subject j sells q_j units at the prices $p_j(1)$, $p_j(2)$, ..., $p_j(q_j)$, then subject j's total profits are given by:

$$\pi_i(k) = \sum_{k=1}^{q_j} \pi_i(k) = \sum_{k=1}^{q_j} [p_j(k) − s_j(k)]. \tag{8.2}$$

In order to assure that subjects have incentives in alignment with the induced values, certain assumptions are needed. We denote the subject's native indirect utility for money as $V_i(m_i, r)$ where m_i is i's holding of money and r is a vector of prices for real goods and services. Since the experiment converts subjects actions/messages into money, and actions are assumed not to be an argument of V_i the only influence the experiment has on a subject's incentives is through increases or decreases in m_i. Further note that a subject's preferences are assumed to not depend directly on other subject's actions or outcomes. We further assume that $\partial v_i / \partial m_i > 0$, i.e., subjects are nonsatiated in money.

A processing cost issue can be raised concerning the inducing procedure. If m_i is a subject's initial wealth then final wealth is given by $m_i + \pi_i$ where π_i is the money earned from trading in the experiment. This is an artifact of the attempt to gain control of preferences and necessitates three additional assumptions:

1. The cognitive cost of converting outcomes to domestic currency, money, is zero (no decision cost). See Smith and Walker (1993) for a model showing how maximizing decisions are affected by decision cost, and a survey of experimental evidence of how the effect of monetary rewards changes the trade-off between decision cost and deviations from standard theoretical predictions.

2. Subjects understand the instructions which explain this reward procedure.

3. Subjects believe that the actions and outcomes from the experiment cannot affect future earnings of money.

If we have $i = 1, \ldots, I$ buyers each with resale schedules $d_i = [d_i(1), d_i(2), \ldots, d_i(\bar{k})]$, then we can construct the aggregate demand schedule,

$$D(p) = \sum_{i=1}^{I} \#[d_i(k): d_i(k) \geq p \text{ for } k=1, \ldots, \bar{k}]. \qquad (8.3)$$

We can graph this schedule by sorting the aggregate set of redemption values, $\overset{I}{\underset{i=1}{U}} d_i$, from highest to lowest and plotting the sorted array. Figure 8–1 shows an example of an aggregate demand schedule with four buyers.

Similarly, if we have $j = 1, \ldots, J$ sellers, each with unit cost schedules $s_i = [s_i(1), s_i(2), \ldots, s_i(\bar{k})]$, then we can construct the aggregate supply schedule,

$$S(p) = \sum_{j=1}^{I} \#[s_j(k): s_j(k) \leq p \text{ for } k=1, \ldots, \bar{k}]. \qquad (8.4)$$

We can graph this schedule by sorting the aggregate set of unit costs, $\overset{J}{\underset{j=1}{U}} s_j$, from lowest to highest and plotting the sorted array. Figure 8–1 shows an example of an aggregate supply schedule with four sellers.

So far we have assumed subject have the role of buyer or seller. Alternatively we can consider a pure exchange model, where subjects are traders, by giving subjects a valuation schedule d_i and an endowment of abstract commodity w_i and money m_i. At the end of buying and selling the subject/trader has a final allocation q_i of the abstract commodity. If the prices $p_i(t)$ indicate the sale of a unit on the tth transaction, in which case $p_i(t)$ is negative, or the purchase of a unit on the tth transaction, in which case $p_i(t)$ is positive, then the subject/trader's profit is:

$$\pi_i(k) = \sum_{k-1}^{q_i} d_j(k) + \sum_{t-1}^{T} p_i(t). \tag{8.5}$$

The Trading Institution

The trading institution defines how subjects' actions/messages are translated into outcomes. From a systems perspective this is accomplished by specifying (1) initial states, (2) how actions/messages change internal institutional states, and (3) the set of terminal states/outcomes. An example of trading rules for a hand-run double auction follows:

R1 (Start and End Rule)   The auction starts at some point in time and lasts five minutes.

R2 (Initial State)   The initial state is zero contracts and the standing bid is zero while the standing ask is 999. The bid/ask support is [0, 999].

Table 8–1 shows a typical display of state information consisting of the book, a list of contracts, and the current time. Notice a contract, always for one unit, specifies the buyer, seller, and price. The book shows the order flow (bids and asks).

(Messages)   Once the auction begins, any message of the form

m_1 - buyer i bids x,

m_2 - seller j asks y,

m_3 - buyer i buys (accepts a standing ask),

m_4 - seller j sells (accepts a standing bid), is acceptable.

Note that the messages m_1 and m_2 affect the book by changing the standing bid or standing ask. The messages m_3 and m_4 affect contracts by making a new contract, i.e., a buy message forms a contract between that buyer and the seller with the standing ask at the asking price while a sell message makes a contract between that seller and the buyer with the standing bid at the buying price.

TABLE 8–1
Typical Information in a Double Dutch Auction

Panel A: Contracts

No.	Buyer	Seller	Price
1	3	7	$3.00
2	1	9	$2.70
3	4	5	$2.20

Panel B: Book

No.	Bid[a]	No.	Ask[b]
1	$2.00		
		6	$5.00
		5	$4.25
3	$2.30		

[a] Standing Ask = $2.30
[b] Standing Bid = $4.25

R4 (Improvement)   The message m_1 must specify a bid higher than the standing bid while the message m_2 must specify an ask lower than the standing ask.

Thus, the bids and asks are forced to monotonically converge toward each other.

R5 (Contract)   The message m_3 can be sent whenever a seller has the standing ask and the message m_4 can be sent whenever a buyer has the standing bid. Whenever a message m_3 or m4 is sent, contracts are updated and the standing bid is set to zero while the standing ask is set to 999. (An auction ends with a contract, starting a new auction.)

What Questions Can Experiments Address?

Given an environment and institution, theory predicts the likelihood of action/messages by specifying subject behavior. For example, if we assume that subjects maximize own profits; that subjects are price takers; and that behavior converges to a condition where quantity supplied equals quantity demanded, then we would predict the convergence of prices and quantities to a Walrasian equilibrium. Thus, it is possible to test (or select) between theories which contain well specified behavioral axioms.

Note that in this description of equilibrium we did not specify the trading institution. However, in order to test this theory, some institution must be used. For example, when the Double Auction is used experimentalists have found that a Walrasian equilibrium is good predictor for most (but not all) supply and demand environments. Thus, a second use of experiments is to compare observed behavior when the institution or environment is changed.

A third use of experiments is to evaluate policy proposals with respect to specific performance criteria. In these experiments the experimenter tries to identify salient aspects of the institution and environment which may interact with the proposal to produce unintended effects. The nature of these experiments is to isolate potential problems before implementation in order to improve debate and subsequent modification of such proposals through the provision of empirical contrapositive evidence.

A fourth use of laboratory experiments is as a "test bed" for auction design. The idea of a test bed is common in engineering, such as the use of wind tunnels in testing aerodynamic designs when accepted physical theories fall short of modeling the complex dynamics of interacting forces. Since auction design involves many complex behavioral forces, it seems natural to use the laboratory to test alternative auction rules. The advantages are twofold. First, the laboratory allows both control and replication, thus improving our ability to learn by doing. Second, failures in the laboratory are far less costly compared to failures in the field.

Efficiency as a Measure of Performance

Adam Smith's characterization of the desire to trade is measured in an experiment by the resulting gains from trade. Given the environment in Figure 8–1, consider a contract for one unit between buyer 1 and seller 2, where buyer 1 buys his first unit and seller 2 sells her second unit, at a price of $1.75. The trade is profitable for both buyer 1, who earns $2.25 − $1.75 = $0.50, and seller 2 show earns $1.75 − $1.50 = $0.25. The gains from trade is then computed as $0.50 + $0.25 = $0.75. Total gains from trade is then defined to be the sum of individual gains from trade. It is easy to show for a single market that total gains from trade is maximized at the competitive allocation. In Figure 8–1 this occurs when buyers 1, 2, and 3 each buy one unit; sellers 1, 2, and 3 each sell one unit; and buyer 4 buys two units, while seller 4 sells two units. This results in a total surplus of ($2.25 + $2.00 + $1.75 + $1.50 + $1.25) − ($0.75 + $0.75 + $0.75 + $1.00 + $1.00) = $4.50.

For any given set of observed trades in an experiment, we can then compare the realized gains from trade relative to the maximum gains from trade. For example, suppose buyers 1 and 2 each bought two units and sellers 1 and 2 each sold two units, actual gains from trade is ($2.25 + $0.50 + $2.00 + $0.75) − ($0.75 + $1.25 + $0.75 + $1.50) = $1.25. This comparison can now be summarized in terms of a measure of efficiency defined to be the percentage of the maximum gains from trade. In terms of our example, efficiency = ($1.25 / $4.50)100 = 27.8 percent. In comparing institutional treatments, experimental economists will often compare efficiencies as a measure of performance. If transfer payments are allowed and income effects are ignored, then an improvement in efficiency is coincidental with Pareto improvement, i.e., higher efficiency makes at least some people better off without making anyone worse off.

Efficiency measures the relative profitability of a trading institution for all traders, that is, buyers, sellers, and middlemen. Since efficiency is built up from individual measurements, it can also be used to make welfare comparisons, i.e., is one group made better off relative to another? For example, in the theoretical optimal auction literature the appropriate measure of performance is seller profits, since the problem is formulated as one of optimal design for the seller. In this chapter, we focus on optimal design for all agents.

An interesting example of the use of efficiency is in looking at the role of arbitragers. By finding new possibilities for gains from trade, arbitragers can increase efficiency. In the laboratory we can study arbitrage profits as one of the components of overall efficiency and examine to what extent competition drives arbitrage profits to zero.

An Example: Off-Floor Trading Experiments

In this section we review research on a specific incentive problem: the incentive for member traders to "free-ride" on an exchange's price discovery services by trading "off-floor." The incentive arises for two reasons. First, there is asymmetric information since the exchange cannot cost-effectively monitor off-floor trading by exchange members. Second, the exchange and member traders have a "goal conflict" in that members would like to minimize their individual transaction costs. The latter include the bid-ask spread and fees for exchange services. The experimental data also suggests that some block traders may go off-floor so that their positions are not made public. Thus, a buyer and a seller, well known to each other, agree on a trade price inside the standing bid-ask spread. In doing this, they lose the exchange's guarantee of every trade but reduce their own transactions costs.

There is little doubt that, socially, exchange firms reduce transactions costs by centralizing the meetings of potential buyers and seller (thus reducing search costs) and by providing timely opportunity cost information in the form of common information on the bid-ask spread and contract prices. By reducing both the search and transaction costs for individual traders the exchange provides a valuable service. At the same time published price information from such auctions provides a public good to all users, which reduces their negotiation cost if they should choose to trade privately.

Recent nonexperimental studies by Cohen, Conroy, and Maier (1985) and Mendelson (1987) suggests that off-floor trading, resulting in market fragmentation, can reduce market efficiency. These studies predict that off-floor trading will increase bid-ask spreads, thus raising negotiation costs and resulting in lost trades. The exchange loses both the direct commission on the off-floor trades as well as the commissions on lost trades. Society loses by the reduced value of the exchange's price data.

Laboratory experiments can be used to answer a number of different questions about off-floor trading. First, under what conditions does off-floor trading take place? As we have noted earlier, incentive problems are more likely to occur when there is a clearly perceived advantage to individuals in engaging in this behavior. Abstract models, which let us isolate and study potential incentive problems, are not necessarily good vehicles for predicting their occurrence. Here, experimentation and theory should be very complementary. Second, how badly does off-floor trading affect market performance? As a measurement issue this question is clearly empirical; however, it is hard to answer this question with field data where fundamentals, such as preferences, are unobservable. Third, how can we reduce off-floor trading? This is an institutional design question and, as such, is speculative. In this instance, theory suggest answers, laboratories study implementations with controlled measurement, and field experiments provide verification in less controlled settings. In the remainder of this section, we review the experiments by Campbell, LaMaster, Smith, and Van Boening (1991), hereinafter called CLSV.

In all of their experiments, CLSV use an updated Plato computerized double auction originally described by Williams (1980). Thus, "on-floor" trading was computerized. Off-floor trading was implemented by a seating arrangement such that potential partners were seated next to each other: each buyer was seated between two sellers and vice versa. These potential partners could make direct written offers through an experimenter intermediary. Once an off-floor offer was made it must be either accepted or rejected. Note that asymmetric information was implemented indirectly in that no penalty (above an implicit transaction cost) was put on off-floor traders.

An important characteristic of the double auction is the endogenous formation of the bid-ask spread. This is a natural consequence of the incentive to underreveal true values and costs as part of the negotiation process. The existence of such a spread is well documented in laboratory experiments with double auction and *occurs in the absence of a market specialist or broker/dealer.* Intuitively, the bid-ask spread reflects the range of prices which subjects believe are still open to negotiation. Exploring this intuition became an important part of the CLSV design.

In their first environment, CLSV used a static supply and demand environment with explicit transaction costs both on and off-floor. The transaction cost on floor was set higher than the transaction cost off-floor in order to reflect the addition of transaction costs for using the exchange. CLSV found strong support for the incentive to trade off-floor.

Given the ease with which off-floor trading was attained with explicit differences in costs, it was natural to ask if other incentives for off-floor trading exist. This is an important question for field study. Exchanges do penalize members for off-floor trading, but it is unclear whether costs trading off-floor are lower than costs for trading on floor. Its prohibition restricts the availability of data on the extent of off-floor trading.

In a follow-up set of experiments, CLSV switched to the stochastic supply and demand environment shown in Figure 8–2a. In this environment, subjects were randomly, and privately, assigned to a step on their

FIGURE 8–2a
Induced Supply and Demand Environment (CLSV Design)

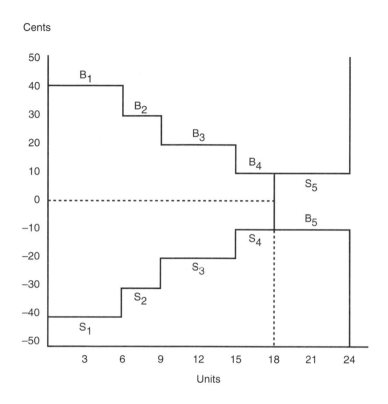

respective supply or demand schedule each period. The schedules were then either held constant across periods or uniformly shifted each period by a random constant (upward or downward) from the origin. This allowed one to assess the effect of uncertainty in the trading environment on the bid-ask spread. Note the existence of a 20 cent range which can accommodate prices at the equilibrium prediction of 18 units traded. This range is called the equilibrium tunnel. In Figure 8–2b, we plot the midpoint of the tunnel for each of the 15 periods of an auction session, under the random shift conditions.

Two points can be made about this design. First, the equilibrium price tunnel of 20 cents accommodates a relatively large bid-ask spread. Second, in the more uncertain environment, since values were privately

FIGURE 8–2b
**Midpoint of Equilibrium Price Tunnel for 15-Period Session with
CLSV Design**

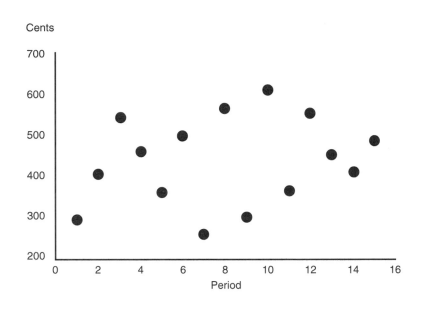

shifted, subjects' price experience in one period had little relation to prices in the next. CLSV conjectured that this uncertainty would result in a larger bid-ask spread compared with the constant equilibrium, since subjects would discover that a larger range of prices were potentially negotiable in the stochastic equilibrium environment.

In a number of baseline experiments (without off-floor trading) CLSV find that increased uncertainty in the environment increases price volatility within much larger bid-ask spreads. As an example, in Figure 8–3 we plot contract prices for a 15-period experiment with random shift conditions. In this plot, prices have been normalized each period to reflect a zero midpoint for the equilibrium tunnel. Note that contracts are often executed outside the equilibrium tunnel in a range almost four times as large. On the other hand, average prices, shown by the solid line, stay within the equilibrium price tunnel.

Given the results from their baseline experiments, CLSV conjectured that subjects would have an incentive to trade off-floor inside the

FIGURE 8–3
Contract Prices for Typical Double Auction Experiment with
CLSV Design

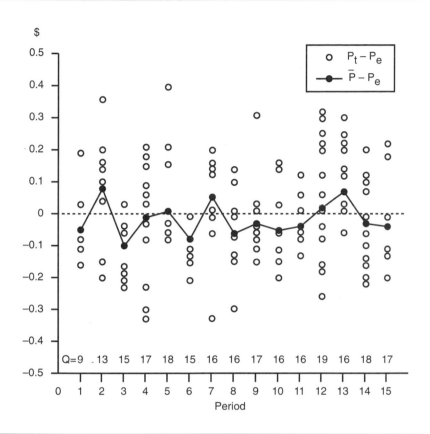

bid-ask spread. A problem for participants with trading on floor is the competition from their side of the market. This competition gives subjects an incentive to trade at unfavorable prices in order to ensure that they make a purchase or sale. By secretly trading off-floor, subjects reduce competition from their own side, allowing them to negotiate a price closer to the midpoint of the bid-ask range.

When off-floor trading was added to the stochastic supply and demand environment, subjects showed a strong desire to trade off-floor. Furthermore, off-floor trading increased with experienced subjects, i.e., subjects who had participated in a previous off-floor trading session.

While off-floor trading did decrease market efficiencies, the amount of decrease was not statistically insignificant. These experiments do document the empirical cost to exchanges caused by off-floor trading, but they provide only weak empirical evidence for a social cost.

The CLSV results suggest several directions for further research. First, experimentalists can examine alternative trading mechanisms (for example, uniform price "call" auctions) which undercut the incentive to trade off-floor inside the bid-ask spread. Second, by looking at other supply and demand environments and working with experienced subject, experimentalists may be able to document the social cost of market fragmentation. Third, experiments can be used to further explore the relationship between market uncertainty, subjective negotiation ranges, and the bid-ask spread. Fourth, experiments can be used to examine the process of negotiation in sanctioned dual settings such as the upstairs market on the NYSE. Readers will no doubt be able to add to this list.

Designing Alternative Call Markets

The main distinction between the continuous double auction and a call market is the number of parties simultaneously involved in a trade. In the double auction trade is bilateral. When a buyer or seller makes a bid or ask, they precommit to contract at the terms specified by their bid or ask. A bilateral trade occurs on condition that someone accepts the standing bid or ask for all or a part of the quantity specified. In a call market trade is simultaneous and multilateral. Again buyers and sellers precommit their willingness to buy and sell units at terms specified by their bid or ask. Similar to double auction, a multilateral trade is executed when some condition is met: for example, when a specified amount of time has passed.

There are certain advantages to multilateral trades as discussed by Schwartz (1988). These advantages are the potential for uniform pricing (i.e., no price discrimination for the traders in a multilateral contract); greater aggregation of willingness to buy and sell information is captured in prices; and, compared with the blind sealed-bid call auction, call markets are available which generate real-time feedback of information regarding the acceptance status of individual bids and offers. Feedback information allows traders to respond with new messages and thus reduce their price and execution uncertainty. A disadvantage is reduced immediacy of contracting. However, if there is a demand for such immediacy, a specialist, for a fee, could provide this service by taking the bid or ask position submitted by a trader before the call is completed.

In a research program started in 1987, we have used laboratory methods to study alternative call market implementations which eliminate some of the disadvantages of existing (sealed-bid) call markets while maintaining their advantages over continuous trading. This research is summarized in Table 8–2. Coincidental with our research has been the development of a similar interest in designing new call markets in the field. Based on our research, one of our preferred call market implementations is what we call the Uniform Price Double Auction (UPDA). A similar mechanism was developed independently and contemporaneously by Steven Wunsch and was implemented, based on our recommendations to the Arizona Corporation Commission by the Arizona Stock Exchange (AZX). This suggests that laboratory research in the study of call market design offers strong synergies with field implementations. In this example, learning in the laboratory closely paralleled similar learning in the field.

A Framework for Auction Design

The flowchart in Figure 8–4 captures many of the crucial design features of an auction. Implicit in this flowchart are (1) the availability of external state information such as the system clock and (2) the arrival of messages to a buffer, available for processing. Consistent with standard flowchart notation we use diamonds for decisions which affect the flow of the auction. Sometimes these decision blocks include processing such as the removal of an unacceptable message from the message buffer. Square blocks are used to indicate important processing tasks and display blocks are used to indicate messages which are sent back to agents.

A brief description of the flow of an auction follows (we refer the reader to the rules of the double auction R1–R5 on pages 127–128 for an example). All auctions start when some condition is met. This may be as simple as a starting time (see R1). Once an auction is started, internal state information (such as the book and the set of contracts) must be initialized (see R2). The auction then enters a loop in which it processes incoming messages from the buffer and takes appropriate actions. Note that their is also a rule which states when the auction is over.

Given that the auction is not over, several decisions must be made. Is there a message? If so, is the message acceptable? If so, does the

TABLE 8–2
Institutional Design

		Institution			
		Dynamic (Greedy)[a]		*Dynamic (Backtracking)*[b]	
Environment	*Static*	*Price from Floor*	*Price from Mechanism*	*Price from Floor*	*Price from Mechanism*
One-Sided Single Unit	Second Price (F/T)	English (F/T)	Dutch (F/T)		English Auction (F/T)
One-Sided Multiple Unit	Uniform Price Auction (F/T)	Candle or Country Auction (F/T)	Dutch Clock (H/T)	Vickrey Back-tracking (H/T)	
		Vickrey Matching (H/T)	English Clock (H/T)		
Two-Sided Multiple Unit	Sealed Bid/Offer (F/T)	Double Auction (F)	Double Dutch (H)	Uniform Price Double Auction (H/F)	Tatonne-ment (F)
			Dutch English (H)		
			Double English (H)		

[a] *Greedy* does not allow recontracting or retrading.
[b] *Backtracing* is with respect to recontracting of prices or allocations.
F=Institution appears in the field.
T=Game theoretic analysis exists for at least some environments.
H=Hybrid institution.

message cause us to change an internal state of the system? If so, do we inform participants that the state has changed? In addition to this cycle, we also check to see if a call should take place. Here we use the term more generically to indicate a condition which leads to a contract. This raises the following questions. Is there a contract pending? Is so, who

FIGURE 8–4
Flowchart for Auction Design

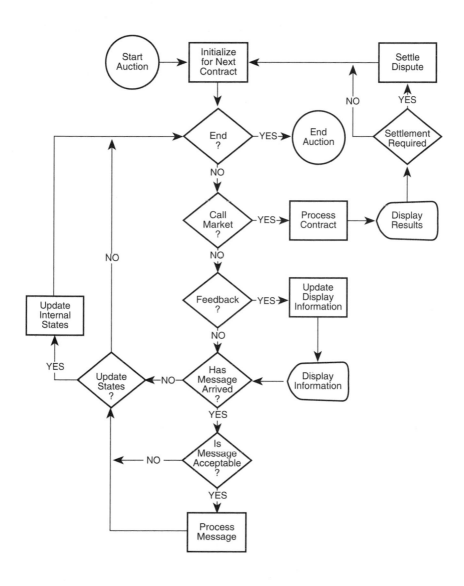

should we inform? Are there any disputes? If so, how should they be handled? A contract leads to an initialization of some state information (see R5), followed by a return to message processing.

By specifying the set of recognizable messages, the set of internal states, and explicit conditions for each decision block an auction is implemented. In this chapter we will examine the results for a number of different auctions which have been designed and examined in the laboratory. These auctions include the English Clock, Vickrey Matching, and Vickrey Backtracking for one-sided markets (subscription markets with fixed supply); and Double Dutch, Dutch English, Double English, Uniform Price Double Auction, and Tatonnement Auctions for two-sided supply and demand environments.

Research on One-Sided Call Markets

Given the exploratory nature of our research, we started where the theory was strongest: fixed supply, private values markets where each buyer desires at most one unit. Such markets have direct application to initial offerings of securities. For example, there is a great deal of current interest in the form of the proposed new Treasury bond auction.

A sealed-bid uniform price auction (where each individual is a buyer of at most one unit) gives subjects a dominant strategy incentive to reveal their true values. However, this dominant strategy is not obvious, and in studies by Cox, Smith, and Walker (1985), auction prices varied a great deal from prices predicted by the theory. Vickrey (1976) proposed a uniform price English (open outcry) auction that gives subjects feedback which ostensibly makes the dominant strategy feature of the auction more apparent. In Vickrey's (1976, p. 14) words,

> A Pareto optimal procedure is available, however, if all the items are auctioned simultaneously, with up to n bids permitted at any given level, the rule being that once n bids have been made equal to the highest bid, any further bid must be higher than this.

In McCabe, Rassenti, and Smith (1991b) (herein MRS1), we report experiments with ten buyers and four units of supply. Each experiment ran 22 auction periods. In each period, subject were each given a resale value which was drawn uniformly with replacement from the interval [0, 224]. This resale value was good for the redemption of one unit bought in the current period. In Figure 8–5, we show an illustrative demand

FIGURE 8–5
Supply and Demand for a One-Sided Market

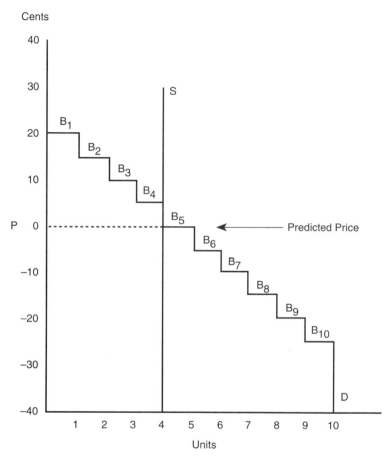

Notes

B_k is the value of a unit to buyer k.
P is the predicted price normalized to zero.

curve with equally spaced resale values. By Vickrey's rules, buyers have a dominant strategy to stay in the auction until the bidding exceeds their resale values. The theory predicts that the buyers with the four highest resale values (i.e., B_1 to B_4) will each buy a unit at a price P, equal to the fifth highest resale value.

We implemented Vickrey's proposal (which we call Vickrey

Matching) by requiring buyers to match the current bid. Once a bid had four buyers (the buyer who made the bid plus the three buyers who matched the bid), then a new higher bid was solicited. We found that Vickrey's auction was more efficient than the sealed-bid uniform price auction, but there was a tendency for overbidding from the floor, relative to the fifth highest value, which resulted in the sale of less than four units in some periods. This overbidding appeared to be due to subject impatience with the slow rate at which bids would sometimes rise. To correct this problem, we tested several different modifications.

In one modification, called Vickrey Backtracking, we allowed participants to lower the current bid as long as the revised bid was higher than any previous bid which had four buyers. We found that backtracking did prevent overbidding but almost doubled the average time to complete an auction as some subjects made considerable use of this option. We conjectured that our results could be due to our subjects' native time preferences. Some impatient subjects were more likely to overbid, while other less impatient subjects were more likely to backtrack. To test this conjecture, we designed a new auction which took control over price bids away from the participants.

In McCabe, Rassenti, and Smith (1991a) (herein MRS2), we report the results from experiments where we controlled the message space by using what we called an "English Clock" auction. In an English Clock auction, the price is set at a relatively low price, all buyers indicate whether they accept (are willing to buy) or not, and then price is incremented mechanically by an exogenous rule which is known to all bidders. At each clock price increase, buyers have the option to leave the auction. As soon as the number of buyers is less than or equal to the number of units sold, the auction is stopped and everyone remaining in the auction buys a unit at the penultimate clock price. Figure 8–6 plots price differences (between auction price and predicted price) for the Uniform Price and English Clock auctions. The English Clock auctions were more than 99 percent efficient and tracked predicted prices extremely well.

The results in MRS2 show that implementation questions remain after the (normal form) theory has been worked out. Vickrey's proposal is most closely implemented using the English Clock and not by the more obvious open outcry of prices from the floor. Different implementations use different extensive forms that are not necessarily equivalent. The ability of the English Clock to induce dominant strategy behavior

FIGURE 8–6
Price Differences for English Clock and Uniform Price Sealed-Bid Auctions

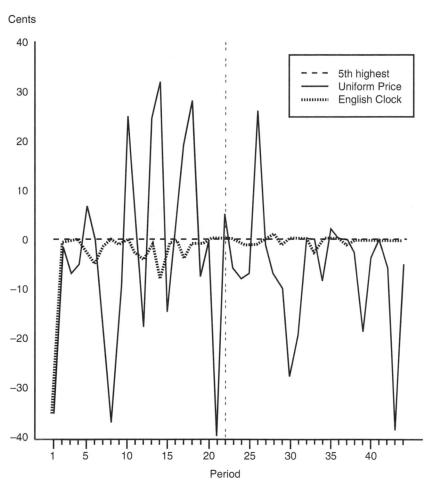

Notes

Periods 1–22 (Experiments EC1 and tb2dci1)
Periods 23–44 (Experiments EC2 and tb2dcgi1)

has led to its use in a number of other experimental studies, and it continues to be a very robust implementation.

Research on Two-Sided Call Markets

Our success with the English Clock auction led us to ask if a similar restriction of the message space in two-sided auctions would also improve performance. In McCabe, Rassenti, and Smith (1992a) (herein MRS3), we implemented three clock auctions: Double English (EE), Double Dutch (DD), and Dutch English (DE). All of these auctions implemented uniform price, multilateral trades, with feedback of information during the auction. We compared these auctions to the Plato DA using the CLSV random environment shown in Figure 8–2a. We found that EE, DD, and DE resulted in uniform prices similar to the average prices connected by the solid lines shown in Figure 8–3. This result supports the argument for order consolidation in determining market clearing prices by reducing volatility and providing "fair" (full information, uniform) pricing.

However, efficiency comparisons for the three call markets vary considerably. Computing average efficiencies across all periods of all experiments we find that EE was far less efficient (around 73 percent), while DE showed similar efficiencies to DA (around 87 percent), and DD outperformed DA with an average efficiency around 96 percent. These differences can be explained by looking at the differences in rules in the clock auctions.

In DD, our best performer, two Dutch price clocks are used. The buyers' clock starts with a very high (unfavorable) price and the sellers' clock starts with a very low (unfavorable) price. Initially, the buyers' clock is decremented by a fixed rule, and the sellers' clock is incremented by a fixed rule. Unlike the one-sided English Clock, in which price changes are exogenous, clock prices are synchronized with the order flow, as follows. The buyers' clock is decremented (while the sellers' clock is fixed), until a buyer signals his or her willingness to buy. At this point we have a unit of excess demand on the buyer side and the buyers' clock is stopped. Now the sellers' clock is incremented until a seller signals his or her willingness to sell. At this point we have a contract between a buyer and seller at a price to be determined somewhere between the two clock prices. The sellers' clock then continues to be incremented until we get a unit of excess supply. At this point, the sellers' clock is stopped, and the buyers' clock is restarted at the previous clock price. This process continues with the active clock switching whenever a unit of excess supply or demand is reached. The auction is over when the clocks meet and all the resulting contracts are consummated at the common indicated price.

Notice that in the DD pricing procedure the terms of trade improve for each side. At first, subjects may underreveal their values (by waiting) in order to keep their clocks running and get a better price. However, as the clocks move closer together, the incentive to underreveal is less. At some point participants are mainly interested in getting a trade, and we see lots of revelation of marginal units near the theoretical supply and demand cross.

In EE, our worst performer, two English price clocks are used. The buyers' clock starts with a very low (favorable) price, and the sellers' clock starts with a very high (favorable) price. At these prices buyers and sellers signal their respective demand and supply quantities. The buyers' clock is incremented by a fixed rule, and the sellers' clock is decremented by a fixed rule. Again, the clock prices are synchronized with the order flow, as follows. Suppose initially that demand exceeds supply. Then the buyers' clock is incremented (with the sellers' clock fixed). As the price increments, the price becomes less favorable, and buyers drop out. As soon as there are fewer buyers than sellers, the buyers' clock is stopped. Now the sellers' clock is decremented until there are fewer sellers than buyers. At this point, the sellers' clock is stopped, and the buyers' clock is restarted. This process continues with the active clock switching whenever there are fewer buyers or sellers. The auction is over when the clocks meet and all the units still in the auction trade at the common clock price.

Notice that incentives have changed relative to DD. In EE, participants must stop their clocks in order to maintain prices at more favorable terms. However, to stop their clocks, participants must reduce the number of units offered. Since the incentive to withhold units is greatest when the clocks are far apart, participants do this when they are least informed about eventual market prices and are, therefore, likely to remove units which would be profitable in equilibrium. Once a unit is removed, it cannot be reinstated; and, as a consequence, trading volume is decreased in our EE auctions.

In DE, only one price clock is used. This clock is initially set high, making it an unfavorable (Dutch) clock for buyers and a favorable (English) clock for sellers. Initially we expect to see zero units demanded and the maximum number of units supplied. Therefore, the clock price is decreased, and, as the clock is decremented, buyers offer more units and seller offer fewer. The auction is over when units demanded equals units supplied.

When we compare DD, DE, and EE, we find that efficiency is directly correlated with the convergence properties of revealed quantities. See Figure 8–7. In DD the revealed units of supply and demand strictly increase, while in DE the revealed units of demand strictly increase and the revealed units of supply strictly decrease; and, finally, in EE the revealed units of supply and demand both strictly decrease. (Hypothetically, we could interchange the two clocks in DE to get an English Dutch (ED) mechanism that converges from below, as indicated in Figure 8–7.) Thus, for our auction experiments, convergence from the extramarginal side (where units should not trade by the Walrasian model of competition) reduces efficiency.

DA is similar to DD, since the revealed units of supply and demand in *contracts* are increasing. Therefore, we conjecture that the differences in efficiency between DA and DD are due to the bid-ask dynamics. In DD the bid price is incorporated exogenously in the buyers' clock, while the ask price is incorporated in the sellers' clock. Thus, in DD, bids and asks move from less favorable to more favorable. By comparison, the improvement rule in DA requires bids and asks to move from more favorable to less favorable by those announcing quotations. As a consequence, DA is more likely to cause contracts which include extramarginal units and thus reduce efficiency.

A number of questions remain concerning the feasibility of DD in a field implementation. First, we can ask how robust is the synchronization of the clocks? In the field the clocks will be started by the auctioneer. In order to test the robustness of DD to the choice of starting prices, we always started our buyers' clock at 800 and our sellers' clock at 100. Given the random shifts in the environment (see Figure 8–2b), this meant that sometimes the buyers' clock was much closer to the predicted equilibrium, while at other times the sellers' clock was much closer. Our data suggested that DD was robust to these asymmetric—relative to the equilibrium price—starting clock prices. We have yet to test if DD is less robust when the induced supply and demand curves are themselves less symmetric than those shown in Figure 8–2a.

Two more questions relevant to field implementation are as follows:

FIGURE 8–7
Direction of Convergence of Prices and Revealed Quantities in DD, DE, and EE Auctions

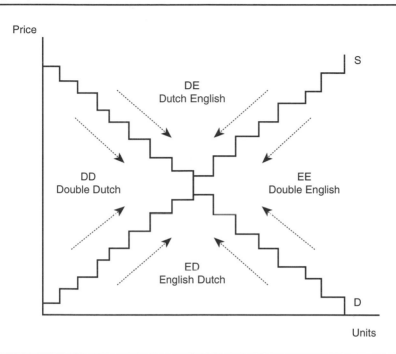

How would DD perform with traders, subjects who could both buy and sell? How would DD perform with limit orders, messages to reveal units of supply and demand when the clocks reach prespecified prices? These questions do not begin to exhaust the kinds of questions which can emerge when an auction is considered for field implementation.

The Interplay between Field and Laboratory

Tatonnement auctions have been used in the field as a form of call market in the London bullion market and the old Paris Bourse. In general a Tatonnement auction works as follows:

1. Set an initial price.
2. Solicit buy and sell orders at this price.
3. If the number of buy orders is higher than the number of sell order (excess demand), then raise the price and start at step 2 again.

4. If the number of buy orders is lower than the number of sell order (excess supply), then lower the price and start at step 2 again.

5. If the number of buy orders is equal to the number of sell orders (revealed supply equals revealed demand), then end the auction.

Joyce (1984) studied Tatonnement markets where buyers could buy at most one unit and sellers could sell at most one unit. Joyce found such markets to be highly efficient. This raised an important question. Since Tatonnement reveals units of supply and demand, similar to DE and Tatonnement backtracks with respect to price (based on excess orders), we would expect from our work with previous auctions that Tatonnement should have problems. Were Joyce's results due to his choice of environment or is Tatonnement an exception to the empirical pattern?

In a recent working paper by Bronfman, McCabe, Porter, Rassenti, and Smith (1992), we studied the performance of Tatonnement in an environment where subjects had multiple units (Figure 8–2a). We found that Tatonnement auctions are very sensitive to implementation rules. Of all the rules used to implement Tatonnement, we found that giving participants full information on the order flow and placing no restrictions on orders resulted in its best performance for our environments. However, the general Tatonnement has lower average efficiencies (around 85 percent) than DA, DD, DE, and UPDA, and much higher variances in both prices and efficiencies across trading periods. Furthermore, as in our results with Vickrey Backtracking, we found that Tatonnement tended to backtrack repeatedly, resulting in relatively long auctions.

Note that DE was found to be more efficient than a general Tatonnement and that DE is also a Tatonnement auction, but one which adjusts prices downward in response to excess supply. DE does not backtrack. However, the DE Tatonnement is much more restrictive than a general Tatonnement process, since in DE prices move in only one direction. In a general Tatonnement prices move in both directions, depending on excess demand or excess supply. As a consequence, our results for DE support the hypothesis that restricting the message space does improve the efficiency of call markets.

In some circumstances it is difficult to restrict bid-ask messages to the simple entry and exit decisions in our clock auctions. This led to a study of a Uniform Price Double Auction (UPDA), which allows the same messages as a regular DA. The results from this study are reported in McCabe, Rassenti, and Smith (1992b) (herein MRS4). Since then, the Arizona Stock Exchange (AZX) has opened trading with rules very similar to UPDA. When we become aware of this field application (by Steven Wunsch) three years ago, we extended our study to look at alternative implementations.

UPDA works as follows. After the auction begins, buyers and sellers submit bid and ask vectors. In our auctions each element in the vector submitted indicated a bid or ask for one unit. This was done for simplicity, since a block bid of 100 units at $190 could be interpreted as 100 single-unit bids at $190 (as long as the rules allow orders to be broken up). For example, a buyer may send the vector ($190, $175) indicating that he or she is willing to pay $190 for a first unit and $175 for a second unit. Once orders arrive they are aggregated into supply and demand schedules as indicated on pages 123–127 *(The Trading Environment)* of this chapter. From these supply and demand schedules, a tentative clearing price and allocation is made and displayed to participants (see MRS4 for the details of this computation). Participants who fail to trade units can now improve on their bids and asks until the market is closed.

Returning to the flowchart in Figure 8–4, we can indicate the types of rule changes we looked at. The decision to call (end) the market can be based on an exogenous rule (that is, the elapse of a certain amount of time, for example, one hour on the AZX) or an endogenous rule (when no new acceptable bid or ask arrives for a specified amount of time). The decision to update the state of the system (i.e., recompute the tentative multilateral trade) can be based on either of the following two rules. The "both sides" rule allows any participant to beat the terms (bids or asks) on his own side of the market or meet the terms of the other side of the market. Any new bid or ask vector which does this causes a recomputation of the tentative trade. The "other side" rule requires a participant to meet the other sides' terms to enter the cross (set of accepted bids and asks). We also looked at two feedback rules. Under limited information, the participant only learns if her own bids or asks have been tentatively accepted, while under full information participants see the complete order book as it evolves in real time.

We found that the best all-around performance was achieved with a fixed-time close, the other side update rule and a closed book. We get poorer performance from the both sides update rule. We observe that the both sides rule causes a large amount of competition from one's own side of the market resulting in slow convergence and lost trades. We also found that an open book using the other side rule encourages strategic behavior resulting in lost trades. However, when we used the both sides rule we found improvement by opening the book (the AZX rules).[6] A similar result was obtained in our general Tatonnement auctions. This suggests that when auction rules are performing relatively poorly due to lost trades, then opening the book and providing full information allows traders to better coordinate their trading efforts. The improvement from better coordination seems to outweigh the potential strategic consequences of full information. In conclusion, we found that UPDA can perform as well as DA in efficiency terms while reducing price variance.

Figure 8–8 summarizes the efficiency results for the six different two-sided auctions using the environment in Figure 8–2a. The poor results for Double English indicate the hazard of assuming that any adaptation of standard one-sided trading rules (such as English auctions) will achieve the desired results in two-sided exchange. This reduced efficiency may never be recognized as a problem in the field where efficiency cannot be directly measured. Since field institutions often evolve to satisfy "special" interests, resultant institutions may or may not be a Pareto improvement over precursors. Experimental economics can help us understand the consequences of subtle rule variations.

"Smart" Markets

Alfred North Whitehead once stated, "Civilization advances by extending the number of important operations which we can perform without thinking." While Whitehead was thinking about the advances in routine calculations in mathematics, his point is equally valid when we consider auctions. No better example of his aphorism can be found than in the study of "smart" computer-assisted auction markets.

In order to understand smart markets, we start with the following computational view of an auction. In the market environments described in this chapter, the demand schedule is given by the unit values $[v_1, \ldots, v_n]$, such that $v_{i+1} \leq v_i$ for all i, and the supply schedule is given by the unit costs $[c_1, \ldots, c_m]$, such that $c_j \leq c_{j+1}$ for all j. Competitive equilibrium is a price p^* and a quantity q^*, such that the return on each unit is nonnegative, i.e.,

   (i)   units bought satisfy $0 \leq v_i - p^*$, and
   (ii) units sold satisfy $0 \leq p^* - c_j$, and
   (iii) q^* is the highest index q, such that $c_p \leq v_q$.

FIGURE 8–8
Average Efficiency by Auction Type in Five-Period Intervals
(CLSV Design)

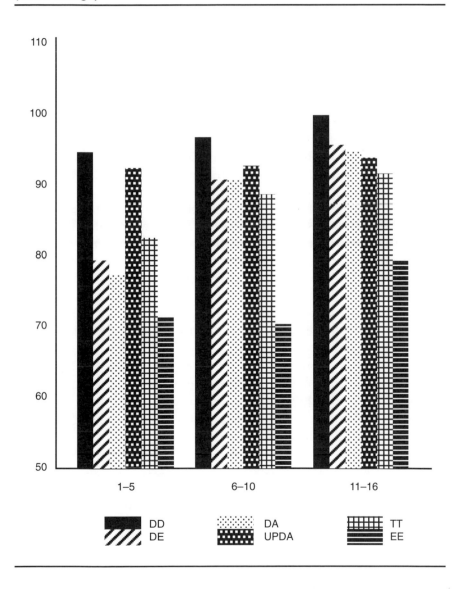

This competitive equilibrium allocation is a solution to the following linear program which maximizes total surplus subject to discreteness
constraints:

$$\max_{(b, s)} \quad \sum_{i=1}^{n} v_i \, b_i - \sum_{j=1}^{m} c_j \, s_j, \tag{8.6}$$

such that

$$\sum_{i=1}^{n} b_i \le \sum_{j=1}^{m} s_j$$

$0 \le b_i \le 1$, for $i = 1, \ldots, n$;
$0 \le s_j \le 1$, for $j = 1, \ldots, m$;
where $b = (b_1, \ldots, b_n)$; $s = (s_1, \ldots, s_m)$.

Given the structure of (8.6), if a solution exists, then there exists a
solution which satisfies the condition that b_i and s_j are either 0 or 1 for
all i, j. Thus, we know that we can maintain our indivisibility assumptions.

Notice that a solution (b^*, s^*) to (8.6) matches units of supply with
units of demand. One method to create such a matching is through
voluntary trading. However, such trading requires participants to agree
on price. In order to solve for the equilibrium price p^*, we can solve the
dual linear program:

$$\min_{(a, b, p)} \quad \sum_{i=1}^{n} a_i - \sum_{j=1}^{m} b_j, \tag{8.7}$$

such that
$v_i \le a_i + p$, for $i = 1, \ldots, n$;
$p - b_j \le c_j$, for $j = 1, \ldots, m$; and
p, a_i, b_j are all nonnegative.

In the dual problem, p is naturally interpreted as the market price, while
the a_i's and b_j's represent the unit profits of the buyers and sellers.

Given (8.7), we can view a market institution (such as DA, DD, DE,
UPDA, etc.) as a particular *decentralized numerical algorithm* for solving the dual pricing problem using sample information (gradients) solicited in the form of bids, asks, or unit quantity responses. Note that bids
and asks (public information) are surrogates for values and costs, which
are private information. A natural question only answerable in the labo-

ratory where private values and costs can be controlled is the following. In soliciting bids and asks as surrogates for the v_i and c_i and using this data to solve (8.7) [which we call the implemented solution to (8.7)], how well so we approximate the true solution to (8.7) with the true value and cost data, which are not observable in the field? This is the question that we seek to answer in the laboratory. A formal approach to this problem can be found in the optimal mechanism design literature in economics. One result in this literature which is of general interest is that every auction mechanism will be somewhat imperfect in implementing the true solution to (8.7).

With few exceptions, economists have ignored the inherent difficulty with market coordination in complex matching environments. This has led to the conventional viewpoint that allocation problems with only a few simple side constraints can be solved using decentralized markets, while allocation problems with many complex side constraints, such as power transmission and pipeline networks, require centralized regulation or ownership. However, it seems reasonably clear that no matter how complex is an allocation problem, it can always be broken into two parts: (1) the solicitation of value information and (2) solving an optimization problem. With advances in computer technology and numerical operations research techniques, we are able to perform part (2) for a vast range of problems. However, we have lagged behind in our ability to perform part (1)—to provide incentive-based input data for processing by operations research algorithms.

In 1987 we were funded by the Federal Energy Regulatory Commission to study market solutions to the deregulation of natural gas. This research is summarized in McCabe, Rassenti, and Smith (1989, 1990, 1991a, 1991b). The natural gas market can be characterized as a spatial network of wholesale buyers and wellhead producers who are connected by gas pipelines. Buyers submit location-specific demand schedules for delivered gas; suppliers submit location-specific supply schedules for produced gas; transporters submit link-specific supply schedules of pipeline capacity. The market optimization problem, with both physical and bid-ask constraints, can be characterized as a linear program, while bids and asks can be collected using some form of call auction. Feedback of information can now reflect the optimal allocation given the existing order flow allowing participants to adjust their messages given their local circumstances. This is one of many examples of a smart computer-assisted market.

SUMMARY AND CONCLUSIONS

Laboratory experiments provide institutional designers with two important tools. First, we can control the trading environment and institutional rules. Second, we can replicate these environments. Using these tools, we can better isolate the effects of different institutions, which define incentives, constraints, and information states, on individual behavior. Such a methodology then becomes a natural complement to the "learning by doing" approach to market design in the field.

In this chapter, we reviewed experimental research on two incentive problems. First, the incentive to trade off-floor, and, second, the incentive to provide private information to an organized exchange. The experiments which were conducted on these two problems typify experimental economics research.

In our review of experiments on off-floor trading we found strong empirical support for an incentive to trade off-floor. The incentive to trade off-floor comes not only from a desire to reduce commission costs but also from a desire to trade inside the standing bid-ask spread thereby allowing the two traders to share the gains normally paid to dealers as a transaction cost. This suggests that exchanges might concentrate on less costly trading mechanisms whose rules undercut the incentive of traders to make exchanges inside the dealer bid-ask spread.

In our review of experiments on call market design, we found strong empirical support for the efficiency of uniform-price call markets, such as English Clock, Double Dutch (DD), and Uniform Price Double Auction (UPDA), which provide market clearing efficiencies at least as high as Double Auction (DA). Since these auctions all allow traders to respond to precontract information feedback, these auctions reduce trader uncertainty. They also eliminate the bid-ask spread characteristic of continuous DA trading. This may provide one answer to the question of how to reduce incentives to bypass the exchange and trade off-floor.

Our results on two-sided call markets suggest that significant improvements can be made in such auctions by

1. providing information feedback to which participants can respond,
2. keeping the message space small, thus restricting the participants' responses,
3. making all messages by subjects potentially binding,
4. keeping the price formation rule as simple as possible, and
5. converging to the final allocation by strictly increasing revealed units of supply and demand.

NOTES

1. Of course, in practice we don't get the exact same observations, due to factors beyond our control. Instead, we use sampling theory to test the hypothesis that two sets of observations came from the same population.
2. See Reiter (1977) and Hurwicz (1973) for the theory of mechanism design and evaluation.
3. In this chapter, we start with derived (reduced form) concepts, such as supply and demand and nominal prices.
4. These markets are typical of situations where sellers must precommit to sell at market. Examples of such markets are estate auctions, the Dutch and Toronto flower markets, new subscriptions for capital, and the auctioning of Treasury securities.
5. Such markets are typified by the continuous trading markets of stock and commodity exchanges.
6. It is important to note that in our experiment, UPDA is being used as a price discovery process in which, as noted, certain rules do better than others. AZX opens at 4 p.m. EST, when the NYSE closes, and represents an after-market in which price discovery is not a significant function, although it could perform this in cases in which a major news event affects a certain stock immediately after the NYSE closes. Thus, any rule comparisons we have made in the laboratory with UPDA are not necessarily relevant to the AZX implementation.

REFERENCES

Bronfman, C., K. McCabe, D. Porter, S. Rassenti, and V. Smith. (1992). "Tatonnement Auctions: Theory and Behavior." University of Arizona working paper.

Campbell, J., S. LaMaster, V. Smith, and M. Van Boening. (1991). "Off-Floor Trading, Disintegration, and the Bid-Ask Spread in Experimental Markets," *Journal of Business,* 64: 495–522.

Cohen, K., R. Conroy, and S. Maier. (1985). "Order Flow and the Quality of the Markets," in Y. Amihud, T. Ho, and R. Schwartz (eds.), *Market Making and the Changing Structure of the Securities Industry.* Lexington, MA: Lexington Press.

Cox, J., B. Roberson, and V. Smith. (1982). "Theory and Behavior of Single Unit Auctions," in V. Smith (ed.), *Research in Experimental Economics,* 2nd edition. Greenwich, CT: JAI Press, pp. 1–43.

Cox, J., V. Smith, and J. Walker. (1985). "Expected Revenue in Discriminative and Uniform Price Sealed-Bid Auctions," in V. Smith (ed.), *Research in Experimental Economics,* 3rd edition. Greenwich, CT: JAI Press, pp. 183–232.

Hurwicz, Leonid. (1973). "The Design of Mechanisms for Resource Allocation," *American Economic Review,* 63: 1–30.

Joyce, Patrick. (1984). "The Walrasian Tatonnement Mechanism and Information," *Rand Journal of Economics,* 15: 416–25.

McCabe, K., S. Rassenti, and V. Smith. (1989). "Designing 'Smart' Computer Assisted Markets: An Experimental Auction for Gas Networks," *European Journal of Political Economy,* 5: 259–83.

McCabe, K., S. Rassenti, and V. Smith. (1990a). "Auction Design for Composite Goods: The Natural Gas Industry," *Journal of Economic Behavior and Organizations,* 14: 127–49.

McCabe, K., S. Rassenti, and V. Smith. (1990b). "Auction Institutional Design: Theory and Behavior of Simultaneous Multiple Unit Generalizations of Dutch and English Auctions," *American Economic Review,* 80: 1276–83.

McCabe, K., S. Rassenti, and V. Smith. (1991a). "Testing Vickrey's and Other Simultaneous Multiple Unit Versions of the English Auction," in R. M. Isaac (ed.), *Research in Experimental Economics*, 4th edition. Greenwich, CT: JAI Press, pp. 45–79.

McCabe, K., S. Rassenti, and V. Smith. (1991b). "Experimental Research on Deregulated Markets for Natural Gas Pipeline and Electric Power Transmission Networks," *Research in Law and Economics,* 13: 161–89.

McCabe, K., S. Rassenti, and V. Smith. (1991c). "Experimental Testing of 'Smart' Computer Assisted Markets," *Science,* 254: 534–38.

McCabe, K., S. Rassenti, and V. Smith. (1992a). "Designing Auction Institutions: Is Double Dutch the Best," *The Economic Journal,* 102: 9–23.

McCabe, K., S. Rassenti, and V. Smith. (1992b). "Designing a Uniform Price Double Auction: An Experimental Evaluation," in D. Friedman et al. (eds.), *The Double Auction Market: Theories and Evidence.* New York: Addison-Wesley, SFI Studies in the Sciences of Complexity, proceedings volume XV.

Mendelson, Haim. (1987). "Consolidation, Fragmentation, and Market Performance," *Journal of Financial and Quantitative Analysis,* 22: 189–207.

Reiter, Stanley. (1977). "Information and Performance in the (New)^2 Welfare Economics," *American Economic Review Proceedings,* 67: February, pp. 226–34.

Schwartz, Robert. (1988). *Equity Markets.* New York: Harper & Row.

Smith, Vernon L. (1976). "Experimental Economics: Induced Value Theory," *American Economics Review,* 66: 274–79.

Smith, Vernon L. (1982). "Microeconomic Systems as an Experimental Science," *American Economic Review,* 72: 923–55.

Smith, Vernon L. (1989). "Theory, Experiment and Economics," *Journal of Economic Perspectives,* 3: 152–69.

Smith, Vernon L., and James M. Walker. (1993). "Monetary Rewards and Decision Cost in Experimental Economics," *Economic Inquiry,* 31: 245–61.

Vickrey, William. (1976). "Auctions, Markets, and Optimal Allocation," in Y. Amihud (ed.), *Bidding and Auctioning for Procurement and Allocation.* New York University Press, pp. 13–20.

Williams, Arlington W. (1980). "Computerized Double Auction Markets: Some Initial Experimental Results," *Journal of Business,* 53: 235–58.

CHAPTER 9

ASSESSING ALTERNATIVE MARKET STRUCTURES USING SIMULATION MODELING

Bruce W. Weber

INTRODUCTION

The proliferation of information and communication technologies and growing intermarket competition for trading volume has led to many market design innovations. Some markets today operate as networks of linked trader workstations with on-screen price discovery and trade execution. Increasingly, market providers are considering combining periodic call markets and continuous trading, and dealer and auction features. We find that evaluating the impacts of new market designs and hybrid markets requires detailed representations of the trading mechanisms. These must take into account many of the complexities that are often abstracted out of analytical models. Maintaining tractability in equilibrium analysis often preprecludes capturing many actual operating details of a market. In addition, an ability to observe users' and market participants' interactions with different market structures is an innova-

Kalman J. Cohen of Duke University and Robert A. Schwartz of New York University are joint developers of the specialist-auction model and contributed numerous improvements to the work. Eric K. Clemons of The Wharton School provided many insights that are reflected in the paper into applying simulation modeling to the study of financial market structure. Nic Stuchfield, Director of Barclays de Zoete Wedd Securities, Ltd., was instrumental in developing the assumptions and the dealer strategies for the competing market maker model.

tive component of this research. We can expose market participants to the functioning of different trading mechanisms and measure responses to market design innovations.

By accommodating features of actual market mechanisms whose effects we are trying to study, simulation modeling can augment the results available from closed-form modeling. Well-designed simulations can provide insight into market design choices that may strongly influence transactional characteristics and performance. For instance, we can gauge the specialist's influence on market quality by including factors—for instance, strategically placed limit orders and orders of varying sizes—that have been abstracted out of other models for analytic convenience. Simulation has yielded useful results in other microstructure research, in particular for examining phenomena for which tractable solutions to analytical models are not possible. Cohen, Conroy, and Maier (1985) used simulation to analyze market quality under different sets of trading priority rules. They showed that systems that consolidate orders and ensure that trading priority is by an order's time of arrival in the market increase the quality of the market. Hakansson, Beja, and Kale (1985) studied the market effects of alternative price-setting and own-inventory trading policies for an NYSE-style specialist/dealer using simulation and found that pricing rules "independent of the specialist's inventories break down." Garbade (1978) investigated the implications of interdealer brokerage (IDB) operations in a competing dealer market with a simulation model and concluded that there are benefits to investors from IDBs through reduced dispersion of quotes and transaction prices closer to the best available in the market.

This chapter details models of several prevalent trading mechanisms and illustrates their use in interactive market simulations. The market structures are an intermediated auction market like that on the NYSE, a competing dealer market, like NASDAQ or London's SEAQ, and a single price call auction, such as AZX. A fourth market design can be examined by eliminating the specialist role in the first design. This is a disintermediated order matching market or consolidated limit order book (CLOB), similar to the CATS trading system in use on the Toronto Stock Exchange, the Paris Bourse, and several other stock markets. The next section describes the order flow assumptions which are common to the models. Later sections will detail the specific assumptions of the alternative market designs and illustrate the interactive simulations that have been developed.

COMPONENTS OF THE ORDER FLOW AND
INFORMATION MODEL

In the models, trading is in a single security and is the result of "machine-generated" order flow and programmed decision rules for market intermediaries such as dealers or a specialist. Investor orders are either market orders for immediate execution or are limit orders reflecting a willingness to trade only at a particular price or better. A trader using a limit order accepts some uncertainty in the execution of their order in return for a more advantageous price. In the interactive simulations, a user can observe the market process and enter orders or quotes. The user can take on one of several roles in a simulation, including an investor adding to or reducing a portfolio position, a day trader that speculates on short-term price movements, a competitive market maker, or a specialist. The model of external order flow makes assumptions about the arrival process of investors' orders, the placement strategies used, the occurrence of informational change, price volatility, and the proportions of market and limit orders.

Order Arrival Machine orders are generated stochastically from market supply and demand functions, which are assumed to result from the aggregate net demand schedules of investors. The order arrival rate functions are price-dependent, Poisson processes, which are positively and negatively sloped, respectively, in price (see Figure 9–1). The Poisson assumption was validated using time-stamped transactions data on stocks traded on the London Stock Exchange (Weber, 1991). A Poisson order arrival process with rate equal to λ orders per hour implies that interarrival times are exponentially distributed with mean interarrival time beta = $1/\lambda$. Kolmogorov-Smirnov goodness-of-fit tests failed to reject the null hypothesis of exponential interarrival in 17 of 22 sample periods at the .10 level of significance. We would expect to reject just over 2 cases due to random realizations. While the fit is not perfect and order arrivals exhibit more clustering than predicted by exponential interarrivals, the Poisson assumption appears sufficiently justified for capturing the typical behavior of the order arrival process.

The supply and demand structure follows those previously developed in the market microstructure literature (Garman, 1976; Mendelson, 1987), in which buy and sell arrival rates are step functions of the difference between the quoted price and the equilibrium value of the security. Garman termed the intersection of supply and demand functions a "sto-

FIGURE 9–1
Buy and Sell Order Arrival Rates

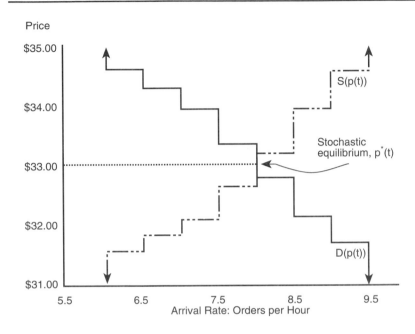

At market prices higher than p^*, the arrival rate of
sell orders will exceed the arrival rate of buy orders. The price response
to this demand imbalance will depend on the market design. The parameter $\lambda_t \, (p, p^*)$ is time subscripted and dependent on p^*, because the order
arrival rate is subject to change due to information events and momentum trading that are described in the next section. The parameter λ_t will
increase when market prices do not fully reflect information (that is,
prices away from p^*) or when an uninformed, protracted price swing (a
"run") is underway.

   Order Size   The order flow is generated by simulated traders who
are either potential buyers or seller, bidding for, or offering, between one
and 25 units of the security. This reflects a convenient normalization that
is consistent with the empirically observable range of order sizes. A unit
may represent, for instance, four round lots, or 400 shares. Beyond 25
units (10,000 shares), we assume the trade would be handled as a block
trade and negotiated outside the standard market design or arrive in the

market in smaller broken-up pieces. On the basis of its fit with empirical data from the New York Stock Exchange's TORQ (Trades, Orders, Reports, and Quotes) database, the Beta distribution was selected for order sizes in the simulation (See Figures 9–2 and 9–3). The TORQ database was constructed using quotes, transactions data, and orders that were handled by the SuperDOT system. The data cover 144 randomly chosen stocks traded on the NYSE. In the simulation, order sizes are distributed as a discrete linear transformation of a Beta (a, b) random variable, which is continuous and defined only on (0, 1). The two parameters, a and b, are set to correspond to the observed mean and variance of order size from the TORQ database. The Beta distribution is useful for modeling activity completion times and quantity demands that are bounded on a finite interval.

Order Placement Strategies   The machine-generated order flow consists of liquidity, informed, and momentum trading orders. The liquidity orders are either limited price orders or market (immediately executable) orders. Market orders execute on arrival, but have a maxi-

FIGURE 9–2
Empirical Order Size Distribution [a]

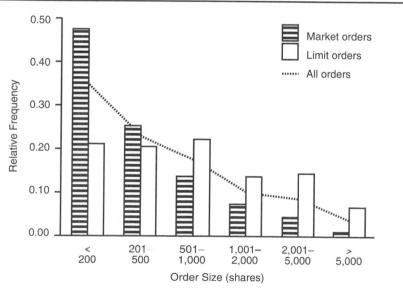

[a] From TORQ data system order data on 875,133 NYSE orders in 144 stocks between November 1990 and January 1991.

FIGURE 9–3
Simulation Order Sizes [a]

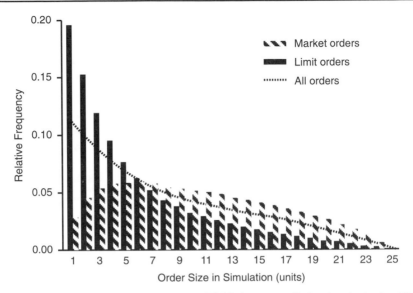

[a] From Beta distributions on [1, 25]. Based on TORQ data, mean limit order size is about 2.5 times mean market order size.

mum acceptable premium or discount to the current bid or offer. If the market order is large enough, its price impact (the need to hit successive lower priced bids or to lift higher priced offers) will exceed the acceptable discount or premium, and the remaining order quantity will become a limit order after partially executing against the limit order book. Order prices are generated by the discrete analog to a double triangular (or yawl) distribution (see Figure 9–4). The yawl distribution is consistent with optimizing behavior by investors derived by Cohen, Maier, Schwartz, and Whitcomb (CMSW, 1981). The relative size of the two triangles reflects the eagerness of investors to execute buy and sell orders. Because of the "gravitational pull" of the bid price for sellers and of the offer price for buyers (CMSW, 1981), the distribution has little probability mass just above the bid price for sell orders and just below the offer for buy orders. In Figure 9–4, the number after the decimal in the price on the vertical axis refers to eighths of a dollar. The mode of the distribution is one tick below the offer for sell orders and one tick greater than the bid for buy orders. Notice that wider spreads increase

FIGURE 9–4
Double Triangular Distribution of Sell Order Prices [a]

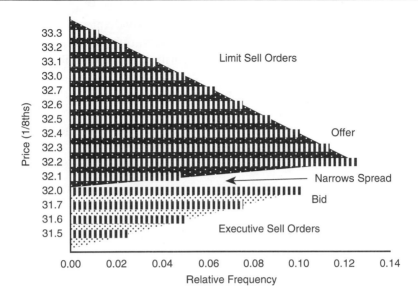

Price (1/8ths)

Price		
33.3		
33.2		
33.1	Limit Sell Orders	
33.0		
32.7		
32.6		
32.5		
32.4	Offer	
32.3		
32.2		
32.1	Narrows Spread	
32.0		
31.7	Bid	
31.6		
31.5	Executive Sell Orders	

0.00 0.02 0.04 0.06 0.08 0.10 0.12 0.14

Relative Frequency

[a] Prevailing bid price is $32 and offer is $32 3/8. About 70 percent of probability mass is above the bid price.

the likelihood of spread-narrowing limit orders. The order placement models are symmetric, so that the arrival rate of buy orders at the bid price and below is equal to that of sell orders at the offer and above. The three parameters of the double triangular distribution are (1) the relative height of the two triangles, (2) the maximum amount that a limit sell price will exceed the inside offer price, and (3) the largest acceptable discount (drop from the bid price) by an executable sell order for a quantity larger than that available at the bid. These parameters and probable prices of arriving limit orders were obtained in several interviews with NYSE specialists and floor trading staff.

Information Generation Idiosyncratic information events occur that change the share value, p^*, at which buying and selling order arrival rates are balanced. The time between information changes is assumed to be exponentially distributed with mean, μ. The memoryless property of the exponential distribution means that knowing the time elapsed since the last information change has no bearing on the time of the next change. Information arrival is assumed to be fairly infrequent relative to order arrivals.

Price Diffusion   When there is a change in information that will shift the "balance price," p^*, at which the arrival rate of buy orders equals the arrival rate of sell orders, an observation is made on a price diffusion model in which the natural logarithm of the equilibrium value evolves according to a continuous random walk without return drift. To assure nonnegative prices, the natural log of price is used, yielding a log-normal distribution for the equilibrium price. The white noise term, e_t, is normally distributed with variance linear in the time since the last observation. This is consistent with the price diffusion models used in the financial economics literature (Garbade and Silber, 1979; Cox and Rubinstein, 1985; Mendelson, 1987).

$$\ln p_t^* = \ln p_{t-T}^* + e_t \text{ where } e_t \sim N(0, T\sigma^2)$$

$$\Rightarrow p_t^* \sim LN(\ln p_{t-T}^*, T\sigma^2)$$

Notice that the price diffusion process implies that returns have the Martingale property. As a result, the natural logarithm of the current price is an unbiased estimator of the natural logarithm of any subsequent price:

$$E(\ln p_{t+T}^* \mid p_t^*) = \ln p_t^*$$

Information Effects   The model assumes that some market participants generating the machine order flow have access to information about a security's value (e.g., greater research into the company's prospects). The order flow consists of liquidity orders, noise orders, and informed orders. The arrival rates of informed orders depend on the market prices and the fundamental value of the security, p^*. If the bid and offer quotes straddle p^*, there is no informed order flow. When p^* is outside the bid-offer range, additional one-sided market orders will be generated according to a Poisson process. Thus, a bid quote greater than the full-information balance value, p_t^*, increases by a set percentage the arrival rate of sell market orders, so that sell order arrivals exceeds the rate of buy order arrivals. The excess supply of tenders to the market will on average cause prices to fall because additional orders can be expected to sell to the (high) bid quotes until they are depleted. This leads to a thinning of the book on one side and an adjustment of market prices to p^*. A parameter specifies the additional arrival rate of informed orders (when p^* diverges from the bid-ask quotes) as a percentage of the base arrival rate of liquidity orders.

Intermediaries in the markets (specialists and market makers) can only infer p^* from the book and their inventory positions. A growing long position, for instance, indicates that the market quotes may be too high and informed investors are profiting by selling at these prices. For instance, a limit order to sell 3 units at 32-⅞ will execute immediately if there is a bid of 32-⅞ or higher available for 3 or more units. The price diffusion process and the sensitivity of the buy and sell order arrival rates to deviations from the information implies that the intermediary/dealer's inventories will provide a noisy signal of the value, p^*. An increasing dealer position is denotative of quotes that are too high, relative to the equilibrium value. Building up large positions—price speculation by the intermediary—is likely to lead to losses and potential bankruptcy.

Runs and Reversals   Handa and Schwartz (1993) established that transaction-to-transaction prices for the 30 stocks in the Dow Jones industrial index in 1988 exhibit more runs, or extended unidirectional price changes, than is consistent with a random walk process. Runs can be followed by reversals, which are price movements in the opposite direction. Bid-ask bounce effects were removed, and clusters of five trades were examined. The clusters were flat 93 percent of the time (average price change 6.5 cents) and were runs or reversals as part of a protracted series 7 percent of the time. The average run size was 28.9 cents, and the average reversal size 30.4 cents or about 0.5 percent of the average share price. These protracted price series were found to introduce first-order positive autocorrelation in returns. This result is consistent with some investors buying on up trends and selling on down trends on the false belief that information has changed and a shift in share value has occurred.

To account for the evidence that market trades follow more run and reversal patterns than predicted by a white noise random process, *momentum trading* orders are included in the models. This is accomplished by changing the relative likelihood of buy and sell orders, which is normally unity, when the number of consecutive bid-side or ask-side trade prices in a row exceeds a given number, for instance, three. In actual markets, momentum trading could result from "chartists" looking at short-term price trends to infer informational change from consecutive one-sided trade activity. Momentum traders that identify successive buy trades may enter a buy order themselves hoping to buy low in the transition to a new, higher price level. For one parameter setting, if three bid-side trade prices occur in a row, then the arrival rate of sell market orders is increased 40 percent. The arrival rates of all other orders are held constant. This will result in more runs of price changes in the same direction than a stationary random process. Note that buying runs increase the chance that uninformed trading will drive the market offer below the stock's fundamental value, and a sell run may raise the bid above the fundamental value. Once the bid-ask quotes no longer straddle p^*, informed order flow will reverse the run by initiating an increased flow of market orders on the other side of the market.

SPECIfiC ASSUMPTIONS FOR THE MARKET DESIGN MODELS

Each of the market designs examined contains assumptions about the specific trading procedures applied.

Specialist-Auction Market

The specialist-auction market is based on a central market with a limit order book and a designated specialist intermediary. Limit orders execute against arriving market orders according to price and time priority. The specialist provides quotes when there are insufficient limit order on the book.

Order Book   The auction market is based on an order book containing public investors' orders ranked by price (in eighths of a dollar units) and time of arrival. The order book also contains the specialist/dealer's bid and ask quotes (B_s and A_s), which are set to be good for up to 10 units. The 10 units bid or offered by the specialist are not included in the displayed order quantity. Table 9–1 illustrates one possible state of the order book during the trading day. The current highest bids to buy are at \$32-⅞ for 5 units and the lowest offers to sell are at \$33-⅛ for 11 units.

Large orders can have "market impact" and can move prices up for

TABLE 9–1
Specialist-Auction Market Limit Order Book

| Bids | | Price | Offers | |
Orders	Quantity	(in eighths)	Orders	Quantity
		33.3	14	3
		33.2	5	1
		33.1	A_s 11	2
		33.0		
2	5	32.7		
1	5 B_s	32.6		
2	15	32.5		

buyers and force transactions prices down for larger sellers. In the market situation illustrated, a market order seller of 10 units on the NYSE would ordinarily receive a price of 32-¾ because the cumulative volume at the best bid is only five.[1] If the market sell order was for 16, it would also execute at 32-¾ because the specialist, who is bidding 32-¾, would participate as a buyer of 6 units. The functioning of the market for large orders is consistent with observed discounts for large sell orders and premiums for large buy orders.

Specialist Policies   In the simulation model, the specialist's trading policies comply with the rules imposed on actual NYSE specialists. The principal rule the specialist must observe is *affirmative obligation*, which is described in NYSE Rule 104.10(b):

> In connection with the maintenance of a fair and orderly market, it is commonly desirable that a member acting as specialist engage to a reasonable degree under existing circumstances, in dealing for his or her own account when lack of price continuity, lack of depth, or disparity between supply and demand exists or is reasonably to be anticipated.

Affirmative obligation requires the specialist to make bid and offer quotes when limit orders do not provide sufficient liquidity, adequate price continuity, or acceptably tight spreads. In our model, the specialist's portfolio is assumed to consist of a single stock, where Q_t is the number of shares held by the specialist immediately after a trade is completed at time t. The position at time t is summarized by the pair (c_t, v_t), where c_t is cash on hand and v_t is the value of the shares held. Let q_t

be the specialist's quantity of shares held (negative for net sales or "short" positions, and positive for net purchases or "long" positions) for the trade done at price P_t at time t:

$$\text{Share portfolio (no. of shares)} \quad Q_t = Q_{t-T} + q_t$$
$$\text{Cash (\$)} \quad c_t = c_{t-T} - q_t P_t$$
$$\text{Value of position (\$)} \quad v_t = Q_t p_t^m = Q_{t-T} p_t^m + q_t p_t^m$$

where p_t^m is the mark-to-market price, i.e., the bid price if Q_t is positive and the offer if Q_t is negative.

In the simulation, the specialist follows an inventory-driven policy to set bid and ask quotes. The quote adjustment rules are consistent with the profit-maximizing specialist policies derived by Conroy and Winkler (1981, 1986) and were verified by the NYSE specialists we interviewed. The specialist lowers his quotes after buying more stock when his position is excessively long and raises his quotes after selling stock when his position is excessively short. The position limit at which the specialist adjusts his or her quotes is a parameter in the model (see Figure 9–5). Assuming the limit is 25, when the specialist is long (or short) more than 25—representing 10,000 shares—quotes are revised one-eighth downward (or upward). Adjustments keep the quotes near the unobservable fundamental value, and diverging from this has the effect of increasing the absolute size of the specialist position. For a trading activity level similar to the NYSE average (80 transactions per day in the average listed stock), position limits of 10 to 30 units of the security provided realistic levels of specialist participation, and small positive profits on average.

The specialist's spread is set to a default value at the beginning of a simulation run according to the level of activity and volatility of fundamental value. The specialists' default spread is increased for lower order arrival rates and higher volatility of the stock's fundamental value. The specialist also adjusts quotes using private information on the state of the limit order book. A "thicker" limit order book on either the bid or offer side results in the specialist raising his bid or lowering his offer, thus narrowing the spread to compete with limit orders. A thinner book with fewer limit orders causes the specialist to widen his spread.

Input Parameters and Output Validation   Input settings can be calibrated to correspond to empirical output data. For example, special-

FIGURE 9–5
Initial Parameter Menu for Specialist-Auction Market

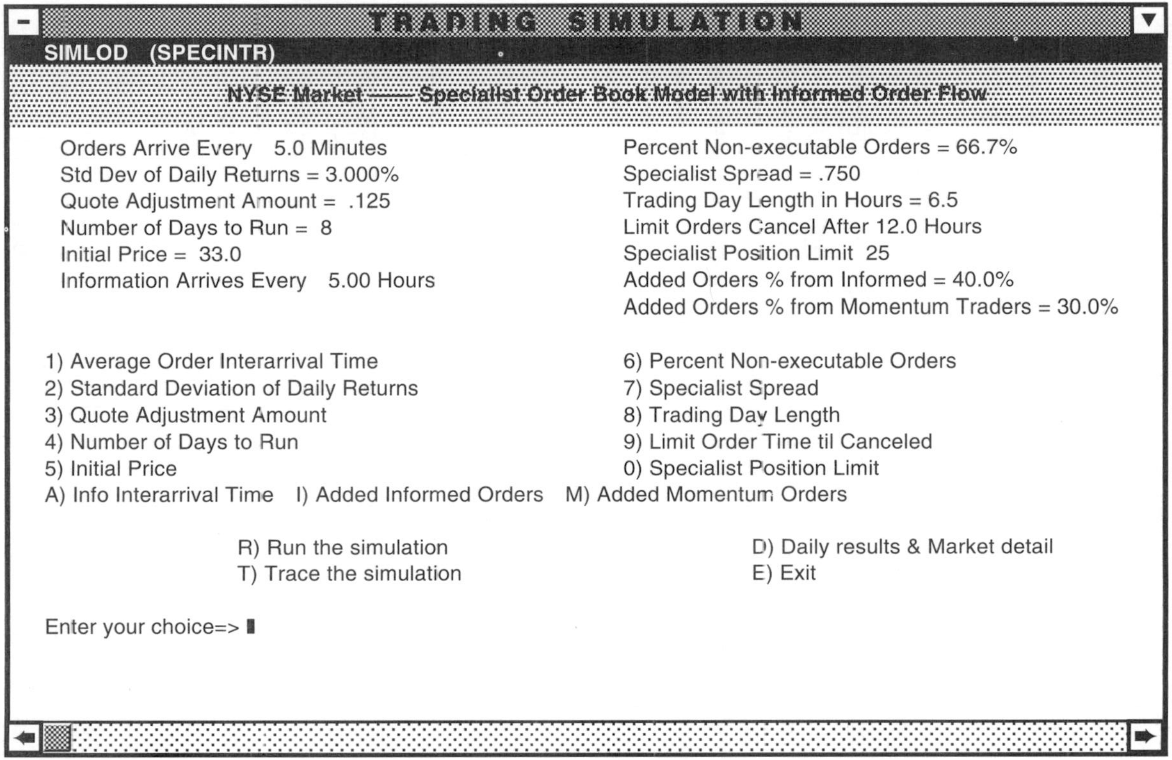

```
┌─┬─────────────────────────────────────────────────────────────────────┬─▶─┐
│ │                     T R A D I N G   S I M U L A T I O N             │   │
│ ├─────────────────────────────────────────────────────────────────────┤   │
│ │ SIMLOD  (SPECINTR)                                                  │   │
│ │                                                                     │   │
│ │     NYSE Market ——— Specialist Order Book Model with Informed Order Flow │   │
│ │                                                                     │   │
│ │ Orders Arrive Every  5.0 Minutes         Percent Non-executable Orders = 66.7% │
│ │ Std Dev of Daily Returns = 3.000%        Specialist Spread = .750    │   │
│ │ Quote Adjustment Amount = .125           Trading Day Length in Hours = 6.5 │
│ │ Number of Days to Run = 8                Limit Orders Cancel After 12.0 Hours │
│ │ Initial Price = 33.0                     Specialist Position Limit 25 │
│ │ Information Arrives Every  5.00 Hours     Added Orders % from Informed = 40.0% │
│ │                                          Added Orders % from Momentum Traders = 30.0% │
│ │                                                                     │   │
│ │ 1) Average Order Interarrival Time       6) Percent Non-executable Orders │
│ │ 2) Standard Deviation of Daily Returns   7) Specialist Spread        │   │
│ │ 3) Quote Adjustment Amount               8) Trading Day Length       │   │
│ │ 4) Number of Days to Run                 9) Limit Order Time til Canceled │
│ │ 5) Initial Price                         0) Specialist Position Limit │
│ │ A) Info Interarrival Time  I) Added Informed Orders  M) Added Momentum Orders │
│ │                                                                     │   │
│ │           R) Run the simulation                  D) Daily results & Market detail │
│ │           T) Trace the simulation                E) Exit            │   │
│ │                                                                     │   │
│ │ Enter your choice=> ▮                                               │   │
│ │                                                                     │   │
└─┴─────────────────────────────────────────────────────────────────────┴─▼─┘
```

ists' participation on the NYSE is about 19.2 percent of trading volume (NYSE *Fact Book*, 1992), and specialists' revenues were $437 million in 1992, including both commissions and trading gains. Dividing specialist trading revenue by specialists' aggregate volume provides an average measure of their trading margins or retained spread. A range of parameter settings lead to model output measures that are consistent with NYSE market measures. While not an explicit design goal, this emphasizes the fact that, for appropriate parameter settings, our model of order arrival and trading behaves like the actual market.

The specialist's position is private information available only to him. In the model, larger position limits led to specialist losses. Larger limits mean that quote revisions lag movement in the fundamental value of stock. Smaller position limits reduced the extent of specialist participation without contributing to profitability. After some study, the specialist's spread in the simulations is set according to the volatility and activity level of the stock and averages about 2 to 3 percent of the stock's price.

Interactive Simulations   The user version of the specialist-auction model shown in Figures 9–5 and 9–6 allows the user to act as a floor trader who will build and liquidate short-term positions or as a broker who is either building or reducing a position for an investor client. The objective is to earn trading profits or to acquire (at low cost) or reduce (at higher prices) a position in a given amount of time. The initial screen in Figure 9–5 provides the inputs values for a particular run of the model. The parameters are the average interarrival time for the Poisson order arrival process, the standard deviation of returns for the price diffusion process, the amount by which the specialist changes quotes (one-eighth here), the number of days the simulation will run, the initial security price in the model, the average interarrival time for changes to the security's fundamental value, the percentage of incoming order volume that are not immediately executable limit orders, the default spread of the specialist ($\frac{3}{4}$ here), the length of each day in the simulation (9:30 a.m.–4:00 p.m. here), the time that unexecuted limit orders will remain on the order book until canceled, the position limit of the specialist, and the additional informed orders as a percent of the liquidity order arrivals that will occur when the fundamental value, p^*, falls outside the bid and ask quotes.

The program can run in several modes. "Run the simulation" shows the current book on the left side of the screen, the last eight trade publi-

FIGURE 9–6

Specialist-Auction Market Screen with User Choice Menu at Bottom. (User is short 7 units and has a mark-to-market loss of 3.00)

```
                    T R A D I N G   S I M U L A T I O N

BIDS      PRICE    OFFERS |  DAY  2    TIME 10:37   MID 33.3125
          34.5    0     0 |
          34.4    0     0 |  PR   33.2  33.1  33.1  33.2  33.2  33.3  33.1  33.1
          34.3    0     0 |  QTY     3     2     7     3    20     1     1     5
          34.2    0     0 |  AT   1037  1027  1004   955   933  1552  1549  1547
          34.1    1     1 |  Run of  3 Bid-side trade prices in a row
          34.0    0     0 |  YOUR POSITION   –7 CASH   230.62 PROFIT   –3.00
          33.7   26     3 |
          33.6    0     0 |
          33.5    7     3 |
          33.4   19     4 |
        Sp 33.3   3     2 |
  1   4   33.2          |
  2  11   33.1          |
  2  11   33.0          |
  2  15   32.7          |
  4  18 Sp 32.6         |
  3  20   32.5          |
  2  13   32.4          |
  4  24   32.3          |
  2  11   32.2          |
  0   0   32.1          |   3 SOLD!  At Flashing Price
(B)uy limit. (S)ell limit. (L)ift offer. (H)it bid. (P)ause.  (C)ontinue  =>
```

cations, the state of any current runs, and the cash and profit. "Daily results & Market detail" adds a summary at the end of each day, and the (normally unobservable) specialist position and profit, and the fundamental value of the security. "Trace the simulation" lists each individual order arrival and details its execution or its positioning in the limit order book.

After the simulation has been launched, machine-generated orders arrive in the market and execute or go onto the order book. When in the interactive trace mode, as shown in Figure 9–6, each arriving order results in a message to the user at the bottom of the screen. The menu below the message gives the user several choices. A buy limit order enters a bid of a size specified by the user onto the book. A sell limit order results in an offer entry. Lifting the offer is a market purchase of a size specified by the user. If the quote is for adequate size, the trade will occur at the current ask quote. Hitting the bid is a market order to sell at the current bid quote. Market orders larger than the inside bid or offer will move up or down the book until the quantity is sufficient and execute at a single price (the final counterparty order's price).

Competing Dealer Market

A competing dealer market consists of market makers, each quoting continuous two-way prices and quantities, and a facility to display these quotes. The NASDAQ market and the government and corporate bond markets in the United States, and the London Stock Exchange (LSE) are competitive market maker structures. Competing dealers buy and sell securities at quoted prices. Their inventories buffer transient fluctuations in investors net demand for a security and smooth out what might otherwise be volatile changes in market prices. In general, dealers do not hold speculative long-term price positions in the securities they trade. They seek to maintain an essentially flat book (zero position in the security) and change their quoted prices in response to their inventory, the observable order flow, and other market maker actions. The model of competing market maker operations is based on the author's collaboration with the Director of Equities Trading of a London-based securities firm. The dealer market simulation has received an enthusiastic response in the firm where it is used as a training tool for their market makers to learn how to manage positions under a range of trading conditions.

In the competing dealer model, the order arrival process, information change, and order placement are unchanged from the specialist-auction model. In Figure 9–7 an initial price of £3.65 is used. Market structure features that are unique to the competitive market maker model are described below.

Market Components The competing dealer market is made up of a user-chosen number of dealers, a display to their competing quotes, and an interdealer broker screen display. Interdealer brokers (IDBs) operate in many dealer markets including the U.S. government bond market and the LSE market. IDBs provide an anonymous facility for dealers to display bid and offer quotes to each other, and to lay off unwanted positions. IDB quotes are generally not available to investors and are not continuous, meaning that at some times there may be no quotes on an IDB screen. In Figure 9–9, an IDB bid is available at £2.59. Different dealer markets also have different rules for trade publication. For instance, in the London Stock Exchange market, large size trades that are three times larger than Normal Market Size (NMS) are only published 90 minutes after the trade is reported. For instance, in Figure 9–9, the trade of size 16 at 13:10 is only publishable after 14:40. Also in Figure 9–9, the user has a small long position of 2 and a profit of 0.96.

Market Maker Quotes Each of the chosen number of dealers is assigned a spread, a market share, and a position limit. The NMS and publication limit parameters determine at what quantity trades are not reported. In Figure 9–8, trades larger than 15 units will not have their prices published on the user screen until 90 minutes have elapsed. Also in Figure 9–8, the attributes of seven dealers were specified. For this run, the user was Dealer 3 and appeared on the left of the market screen in Figure 9–9. The most recent trade events appear at the bottom of the screen and scroll upward. As a dealer, the user has a number of menu options available including moving his or her quotes up or down, narrowing or widening the spread, changing the frequency of program pauses for use input, lifting (buying) from another dealer, hitting (selling) to another dealer, and entering or changing an IDB quote.

When the mechanical dealers' positions increase beyond their position limits, they take a number of steps to reduce the risk and the size of the position. The first step taken once the position exceeds the position limit is to enter an IDB quote. For instance, if a dealer becomes short more than his limit, he will enter an IDB bid at a price between the screen bid and offer. If the position becomes larger than twice the position limit, the dealer will look for an IDB quote to trade against or raise

FIGURE 9–7
Initial Parameter Screen

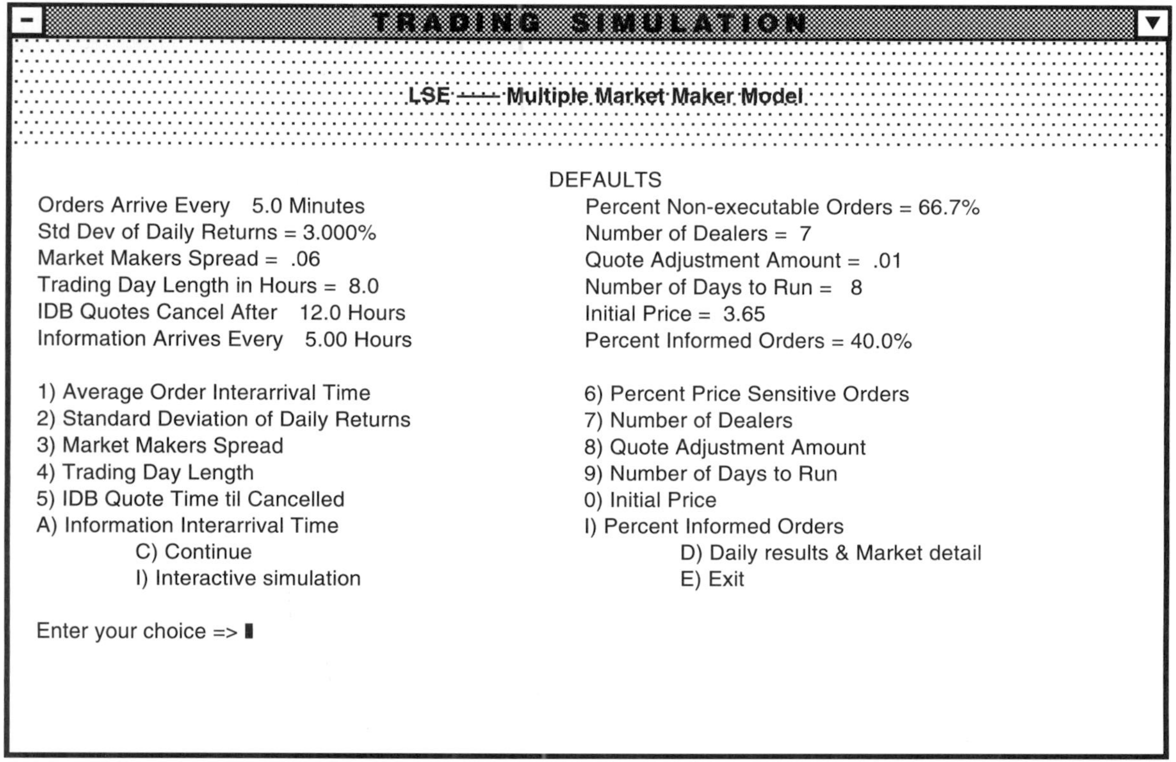

```
▬                                                                    ▶

                    T R A D I N G   S I M U L A T I O N

                    LSE: ───── Multiple Market Maker Model

                              DEFAULTS
                              Percent Non-executable Orders = 66.7%
                              Number of Dealers = 7
                              Quote Adjustment Amount = .01
                              Number of Days to Run =  8
                              Initial Price =  3.65
                              Percent Informed Orders = 40.0%

Orders Arrive Every   5.0 Minutes
Std Dev of Daily Returns = 3.000%
Market Makers Spread = .06
Trading Day Length in Hours =  8.0
IDB Quotes Cancel After   12.0 Hours
Information Arrives Every   5.00 Hours

1) Average Order Interarrival Time       6) Percent Price Sensitive Orders
2) Standard Deviation of Daily Returns   7) Number of Dealers
3) Market Makers Spread                  8) Quote Adjustment Amount
4) Trading Day Length                    9) Number of Days to Run
5) IDB Quote Time til Cancelled          0) Initial Price
A) Information Interarrival Time         I) Percent Informed Orders
        C) Continue                         D) Daily results & Market detail
        I) Interactive simulation           E) Exit

Enter your choice => ■
```

FIGURE 9–8
Second Parameter Screen Specifying Dealer Attributes

```
┌─┬──────────────────────────────────────────────────────────────┬─┐
│ │                    T R A D I N G   S I M U L A T I O N        │▶│
│─│··············································································
     LSE Market ——— Multiple Market Maker Model

                              DEALER DEFAULTS
Number of Dealers = 7    Normal Market Size(NMS) = 5   Publ'n Limit = 3 x NMS
Dealer    Spread       Pos'n Limit        Market Share
  1         .06            10                 24.3%
  2         .06             9                 19.3%
  3         .06             9                 14.3%
  4         .06             8                 14.3%
  5         .06             8                 14.3%
  6         .06             7                  9.3%
  7         .06             6                  4.3%
Dealer 3 will be monitored (or 0=> not interactive)

1) Spread               3) Market Share         5) Normal Market Size
2) Position Limit       4) Monitor Dealer       6) Publication Limit (x MNS)

              D) Rund and provide daily results     T) Trace the simulation
R) Run the simulation (final output only)
              E) Exit the simulation


Enter your choice => ■
```

FIGURE 9-9

Competing Dealer Screen at 3:40 p.m. on Sixth Day. (Left side lists market trade publications. Rights side is the user's trade blotter and position)

TRADING SIMULATION

3	1	2	4	5	6	7	Day 6	15:40	Buy	Sell	CP	Dlt	Time	Day
0-6	0-6	0-6	1-7	0-6	0-6	9-5	13@261	8:50	1		C	265	9:13	4
9-5	0-6	9-5	8-4	8-4	0-6	7-3	4@260	10:26	1		C	265	9:48	4
							18@263	9:10		-3	C	268	10:54	4
9-5	0-6	9-5	8-4	8-4	0-6	7-3	4@263	11:47	1		C	265	12:46	4
9-5	0-6	9-5	8-4	8-4	0-6	7-3	10@261	11:47	1		C	265	14:34	4
9-5	0-6	0-6	8-4	8-4	0-6	7-3	12@260	11:52	1		C	265	14:47	4
9-5	0-6	0-6	8-4	8-4	8-4	0-6	10@262	12:10	1		C	261	16:29	4
9-5	0-6	0-6	8-4	8-4	8-4	0-6	12@264	12:52	1		C	260	10:05	5
9-5	0-6	0-6	8-4	8-4	8-4	0-6	4@260	13:04	4		C	260	10:26	5
9-5	0-6	0-6	8-4	8-4	8-4	0-6	10@260	13:04	1		C	260	10:54	5
7-3	7-3	7-3	7-3	7-3	7-3	7-3	9@263	13:27		-10	MM	262	12:10	5
7-3	7-3	7-3	7-3	7-3	7-3	7-3	6@257	15:26		-1	C	263	13:07	5
7-3	7-3	7-3	7-3	7-3	7-3	7-3	10@259	15:26		-1	C	263	15:28	5
							20@263	15:03	1		C	257	15:40	5
7-3	7-3	7-3	7-3	7-3	7-3	7-3	13@263	8:46	1		C	257	10:51	6
							17@263	8:54	1		C	257	11:20	6
							16@263	13:10		-1	C	263	12:11	6
7-3	8-4	7-3	7-3	7-3	7-3	7-3	5@263	15:40		-16*	C	263	13:10	6

IDB: Bids 2.59   Offers   T : 35   V : 108 I :   2C :   -4.20   P : .96

7-3   804   8-4   8-4   8-4   8-4   8-4   8-4   Touch   2.58- 2.63   Trds 265   Vol 961

MIDSPREAD PRICE INCREASED, OTHER DEALERS RESPONDED, IT'S NOW 2.605

(Q)uotes, (S)pread, (P)auses, (L)ift, (H)it, (I)DB entry, (C)ontinue =>

or lower their quotes. If the position exceeds three times the limit, the dealer will initiate trades with other dealers to reduce the position.

Order Handling   Dealer markets generally do not maintain a limit order book, so incoming orders are market orders and are routed to a dealer according to the screen prices. If all of the dealers are making the best bid price, an incoming sell order will be allocated to a dealer on the basis of market share. A dealer with a 20 percent market share will have a one-fifth chance of getting the next order. If only some dealers are making the best price, the order will go to a dealer, based on the following algorithm: double the market shares of all dealers making the best quote and add to the market shares of the other dealers. The sum is used to normalize the adjusted market shares of the individual dealers. Market share is multiplied by two for dealers making the best quote and is unchanged for others. For instance, if there are four dealers and two of the four have 20 percent market shares and are making the best quote, and the other two dealers with 30 percent market shares are *not* making the best quote, then the probability that one of the dealers on the quote will get the trade is $2\times20/(2\times2\times20+2\times30) = 40/140 = 28.6\%$. The likelihood of one of the nonbest quote dealers receiving the order is $30/140 = 21.4\%$. The adjusted probabilities total to unity.

Adjusted market shares lead to smaller (but nonzero) probability of receiving a customer order when a dealer is not making the inside quote. This is consistent with the market practice of *preferencing* order flow, which results in the dealers not making the inside quotes nevertheless receiving orders. In an analysis of a sample of LSE trading from July 1989, the market maker(s) quoting the best, or inside, price for a stock received only 41.3 percent of the incoming trading orders, with the rest going to market makers quoting less attractive prices, but who were willing to match the best prices posted by their rivals.[2] The explanation often given for such preferencing of order flow is that established relationships between brokers and market makers, or investors and market makers, lead many orders to be directed not to the market quoting the best price, but to firms that have good reputations for trading in large size or matching or improving upon the best available quote.

Figure 9–10 provides the interactive user with a final report. In this three-day simulation, the user (bottom row) ended with a short position of 9, and a mark-to-market profit of 1.04.

FIGURE 9–10
End of Interactive Simulation in Competing Market Maker Model. (User was Dealer 3 at the bottom of the comparative performance table)

TRADING SIMULATION

Bid-Ask	Eq.P	Bal.P	Spread	%Price	%RTTC	AvgPChg
3.72- 3.77	3.84	.094	.0505	1.37%	.01%	.0179

IN 3 DAYS: NUMBER OF BUY ORDERS 149   NUMBER OF SELL ORDERS 150
OF 167 TOTAL TRADES THERE WERE 6 IDB TRADES AND 8 INTRAMKT TRADES
OF 526 TOTAL VOLUME 60 WAS IDB AND 60 INTRAMKT
AT TERMINATION BUY-SALE BALANCE VALUE WAS 3.84

MARKET MAKER SITUATION AT TERMINATION:

dlr.no	mkt.shr	pos.lmt	vol	no.trds	bid-ask	cash	invtry	profit
1	24.3%	10	87	40	3.72- 3.78	71.05	-19.00	-1.91
2	19.3%	9	133	35	3.71- 3.77	-10.37	3.00	1.15
4	14.3%	8	63	18	3.72- 3.78	56.28	-15.00	-1.32
5	14.3%	8	177	30	3.72- 3.78	28.59	-7.00	1.71
6	9.3%	7	72	15	3.72- 3.78	22.95	-6.00	-.09
7	4.3%	6	93	14	3.72- 3.78	-4.04	1.00	-.20
YOU 3	14.3%	9	141	31	3.72- 3.78	35.60	-9.00	1.04

FIGURE 9–11
Initial Parameter Screen for Single Price Call Auction

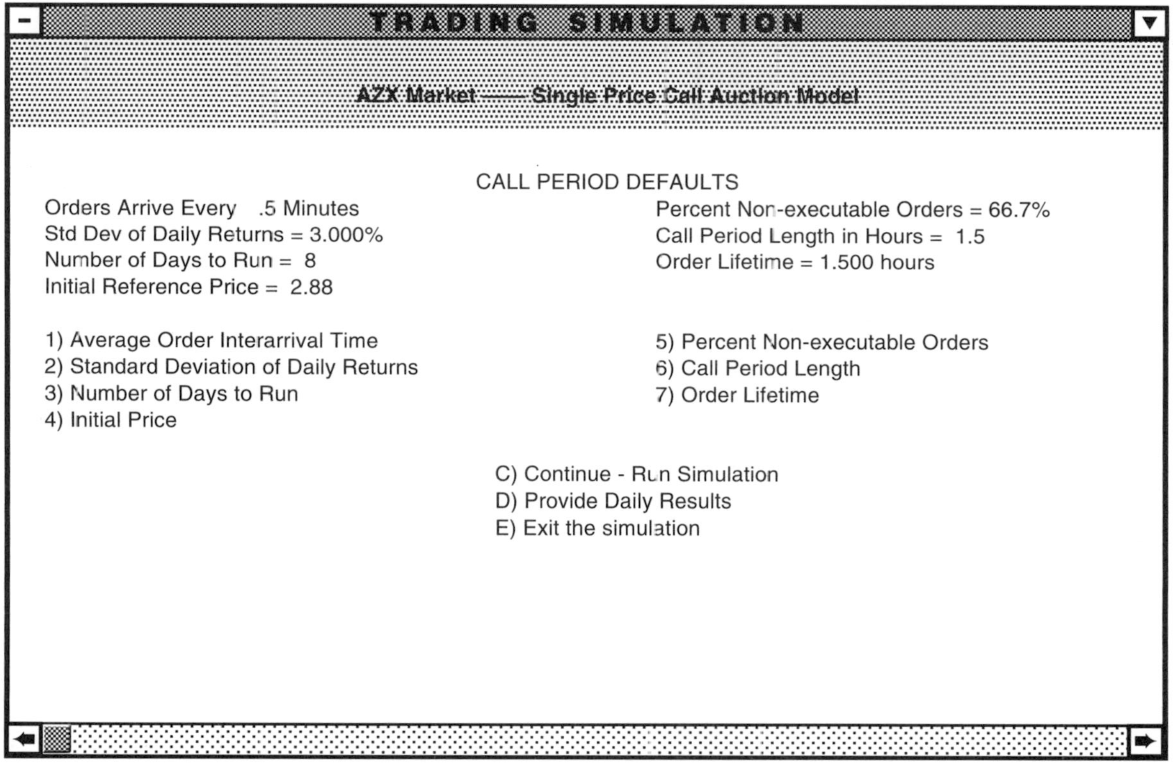

FIGURE 9–12
Single Price Call Auction with Minimize Absolute Imbalance Pricing Rule

TRADING SIMULATION

bid.count	bid.qty	price	imbal	offer.qty	offer.count	BAL_P: 2.75
16	61	2.86	119	180	40	
16	61	2.85	108	169	37	
16	61	2.84	107	168	36	
16	61	2.83	104	165	33	
18	69	2.82	67	136	29	
18	69	2.81	53	122	26	
18	69	2.80	47	116	22	
18	69	2.79	23	92	20	
20	71	2.78	4	75	17	
21	72	2.77	-15	57	16	
23	75	2.76	-19	56	15	
26	94	2.75	-38	56	15	
27	95	2.74	-39	56	15	
28	96	2.73	-40	56	15	
29	97	2.72	-41	56	15	
30	98	2.71	-42	56	15	
32	100	2.70	-44	56	15	

Day 2 At 17:35 the clearing price is 2.78 with an imbalance (sell-buy)
of 4 Shares purchased were 71 and shares sold were 75

Call Market

The call market is a single price batched order auction that takes place at specified times such as the beginning or end of the trading day (see Figure 9–11). The model is similar to the NYSE opening procedure and the proposed price discovery operation of the Arizona Stock Exchange (AZX) which receives buy and sell order between 4:00 p.m. and 5:30 p.m. to be matched. Currently, AXZ matches buy and sell orders at the NYSE closing price. In a crossing, buyers and seller trade at the same price. The inputs to the call auction model include the length of the call period, the additional order arrivals in the 90 minutes between the close of the continuous market and the call market, the variance in the fundamental value in the call period, the reference price from the close of the continuous market, and the limit and market order proportions.

The call market uses a pricing algorithm that finds the minimum imbalance between buying and selling volumes. For the clearing illustrated in Figure 9–12, a price of 2.78 was established and shares traded are 71 with offers for a quantity of 4 going unsold. Other possibilities are to select the price that maximizes the trading volume at the call (Cohen and Schwartz, 1989). In some circumstances, these will give different clearing prices.

CONCLUSIONS

We presented a model of order arrival, order placement, information change, and run and reversal momentum trading. This order flow model can be held constant across mechanisms to compare the response of alternative market structures to identical order flow. The chapter then detailed models of several prevalent trading mechanisms and illustrated their use in interactive market simulations. Because the design of a secondary market trading system is a principal determinant of its liquidity, we can benefit by applying simulation to examine the market quality impacts of market structure choices and various design features under *ceteris paribus* order flow conditions. Simulation allows us to build detailed representations of the trading mechanisms that take into account many features of actual market mechanisms whose effects we are trying to study and whose complexities are often abstracted out of closed-form models. The simulations also provide an interactive environment for users to make trading decisions and measure their performance in different market structures. We can expose market participants to the functioning of different trading mechanisms and measure responses to market design innovations.

The work has shortcomings. Left out are machine participant responses to market conditions. For instance, the proportions of market and limit orders could change over time or as a result of market conditions. Negotiation of inside-the-spread trading price is not treated in the models. Trades occur in the models at the best displayed quotes at the time of the order's arrival. In fact, price betterment occurs in most markets including the NYSE and the London Stock Exchange. The LSE itself noted in its Fall 1988 *Quality of Market Review* that "institutional investors have found it necessary to negotiate for the best deal." In a sample of LSE transactions data in nine stocks in July 1989, 44.5 percent of all trading volume was being done at prices *better* than the SEAQ *inside* quotes displayed at the time of the trade.[3] Finally, there may appear to be excessive discretion in choosing inputs to the models such as dealer spreads and percent of limit orders. Although the choice of inputs may seem arbitrary, this would also occur in parameterizing any closed-form model when some of the input parameters are unobservable.

NOTES

1. The trade execution rule reflects how some, but not all, continuous limit order book markets operate. An alternative trade execution rule used in other markets (e.g., the Singapore Stock Exchange) is to execute relatively large orders to two or more prices. For the example in Table 9–1, a market sell order of 10 units would trade 5 units at $32-⅞ and 5 units at $32-¾, for an average cost of $32-¹³⁄₁₆. The model can be modified to apply this trade rule and create an alternative market structure.
2. Clemons and Weber (1989) and data reported in Franks and Schaefer (1990).
3. Clemons and Weber (1989) and data reported in Franks and Schaefer (1990).

REFERENCES

Clemons, E., and B. Weber. (1989). "Market Quality in London: A Report to the Domestic Equities Market Committee." London Stock Exchange.

Clemons, E., and B. Weber. (1990). "London's Big Bang: A Case Study of

Information Technology, Competitive Impact, and Organizational Change," *Journal of Management Information Systems,* 6: 4 (Spring), 41–60.

Clemons, E., and B. Weber. (1991). "Evaluating the Prospects for Alternative Electronic Securities Markets," *12th Annual International Conference on Information Systems Proceedings.* New York, (December), pp. 53–63.

Cohen K., R. Conroy, and S. Maier. (1985). "Order Flow and the Quality of the Market," in Y. Amihud, T. Ho, and R. Schwartz (eds.), *Market Making and the Changing Structure of the Securities Industry.* Lexington, MA: Lexington Books, pp. 93–109.

Cohen, K., S. Maier, R. Schwartz, and D. Whitcomb. (1981). "Transaction Cost, Order Placement Strategy, and the Existence of the Bid-Ask Spread," *Journal of Political Economy,* 89: 287–305.

Cohen, K., and R. Schwartz. (1989). "An Electronic Call Market: Its Design and Desirability," in H. Lucas, Jr., and R. Schwartz (eds.), *The Challenge of Information Technology for the Securities Markets: Liquidity, Volatility, and Global Trading.* Homewood, IL: Dow Jones-Irwin.

Conroy, R., and R. Winkler. (1981). "Informational Differences between Limit and Market Orders for a Market Maker," *Journal of Financial and Quantitative Analysis,* 16: 5 (December), pp. 703–24.

Conroy, R., and R. Winkler. (1986). "Market Structure: The Specialist as Dealer and Broker," *Journal of Banking and Finance,* 10: pp. 21–36.

Cox, J., and M. Rubinstein. (1985). *Option Markets.* Englewood Cliffs, NJ: Prentice-Hall.

Franks, J., and S. Schaefer. (1990). "Large Trade Publication on the International Stock Exchange." London Business School, Institute of Finance and Accounting.

Garbade, K. (1978). "The Effect of Interdealer Brokerage on the Transactional Characteristics of Dealer Markets," *Journal of Business,* 51: 3, 477–98.

Garbade, K., and W. Silber. (1979). "Structural Organization of Secondary Markets: Clearing Frequency, Dealer Activity, and Liquidity Risk," *Journal of Finance,* 34: 3 (June), pp. 577–93.

Garman, M. (1976). "Market Microstructure," *Journal of Financial Economics,* 3: 257–75.

Hakansson, N., A. Beja, and J. Kale. (1985). "On the Feasibility of Automated Market Making by a Programmed Specialist," *Journal of Finance,* 40: 1 (March), pp. 1–20.

Handa, P., and R. Schwartz. (1993). "Dynamic Price Discovery." New York University working paper (May).

Mendelson, H. (1987). "Consolidation, Fragmentation, and Market Performance," *Journal of Financial and Quantitative Analysis,* 22: (June), pp. 189–207.

Schwartz, R. (1991). *Reshaping the Equity Markets: A Guide for the 1990s.* New York: Harper Business.

Weber, B. (1991). "Information Technology and Securities Markets: Feasibility and Desirability of Alternative Electronic Trading Systems," University of Pennsylvania unpublished dissertation.

Weber, B. (1994). "Transparency and Bypass in Electronic Financial Markets," *Proceedings,* HICSS-27.

PART TWO

REGULATORY CHALLENGES

CHAPTER 10

MARKET 2000: A WORK IN PROGRESS

Brandon Becker
Janet Angstadt

INTRODUCTION

The equity markets have changed dramatically over the last 20 years. New technology, new trading procedures, new products, new analytical pricing models, and a changing investor population have all led to a more diverse market. Moreover, it appears that these changes—indeed, the rate of change itself—will continue to accelerate in the future.

Both the organized equity markets and the broker/dealer community have responded to the new challenges with their characteristic innovation and flexibility. Indeed, in many respects, the equity markets today are stronger than ever before. These markets serve the needs of many classes of users with different expectations and demands. At the same

Mr. Becker is the Director of the Division of Market Regulation, U.S. Securities and Exchange Commission, and Ms. Angstadt is an attorney in the Office of Automation and International Markets, Division of Market Regulation. The Commission, as a matter of policy, disclaims responsibility for any private statement by any of its employees, and the views expressed herein are those of the authors and do not necessarily reflect the views of the Commission.

Ms. Angstadt is an associate with Schiff Hardin & Waite. Her contributions to this chapter occurred while she was a senior counsel in the Division of Market Regulation at the Commission. The views expressed herein are those of Ms. Angstadt only and do not necessarily reflect those of the Commission, members of the staff of the Commission, or of Schiff Hardin & Waite.

time, however, these evolving markets, intermediaries, and users have highlighted underlying tensions in the current equity market structure that, if left unexamined and unaddressed, may result in equity markets that are less efficient for investors and issuers alike. The challenge for the future is how to accommodate as many classes of users as possible in a fair field of competition without impairing investor protection or the maintenance of fair and orderly markets.

Congress, for example, has recognized the challenges facing the industry. Two years ago, Edward J. Markey, Chairman of the House Subcommittee on Telecommunications and Finance, inquired about the effects of new computerized trading systems and whether they were fragmenting the equity markets.[1] During the spring and summer of 1993, he held hearings on this and other market structure issues, such as payment for order flow and soft dollars.[2] Similarly, Congressman John Dingell, Chairman of the Committee on Energy and Commerce, has written about the practice of payment for order flow and other order-handling procedures.[3]

While responding to these concerns,[4] it became apparent to William H. Heyman, former Director of the Division of Market Regulation (Division), that these and other related issues needed to be addressed in a broader framework because of the various interrelationships among the issues. Accordingly, to help the Commission produce a forward-looking approach, Bill Heyman instructed the Division staff in late 1991 to organize a study of the U.S. equity markets. Former Chairman Richard C. Breeden agreed that such a study was necessary and, subsequently, announced the Division's Market 2000 study in December 1991.[5]

Scope of the Study

Because of the critical role the equity markets continue to play in raising capital and marshaling investors' savings, the Market 2000 study will focus on the structure of the U.S. equity markets and the regulatory environment in which they operate. In particular, the study will review the operation of the primary and regional exchanges, the over-the-counter (OTC) market (including NASDAQ and the third market), proprietary trading systems (PTS), nonintermediated trading, and trading in U.S. securities effected by U.S. broker/dealers in overseas markets.[6]

The study is not intended, however, to dictate what the structure of the equity markets should be in the year 2000. Indeed, because of the vibrant resilience of market forces, the Commission could not dictate market structure issues, even if it tried. Rather, market structure questions ultimately will be resolved in cities like Chicago, New York, London, and Tokyo—not Washington, D.C. Nevertheless, competition should not be skewed by antiquated regulation, unfair practices, or an inequitable allocation of self-regulatory costs. Moreover, such competition should not be at the expense of basic investor protection objectives.

Concept Release

To begin the study, the Division published a concept release in 1992 in which we outlined the scope and objectives of the study and discussed the primary issues.[7] Among the issues are (1) whether the equity markets are becoming fragmented so that price discovery is impaired, (2) whether our regulatory structure facilitates fair competition between markets and market participants, (3) whether practices such as payment for order flow and soft dollars represent competitive tools or abusive practices, (4) how PTSs should be regulated, (5) whether transparency— the extent to which quote and last-sale information is made publicly available on a real-time basis—is adequate in the equity markets, (6) whether there are lingering anachronisms in the regulatory structure that impede market development and efficiency, and (7) how all of these issues are affected by internationalization, the growth of institutional investors, derivative products, and advancements in trading technology.

NATIONAL MARKET SYSTEM HISTORY

The Commission has a long history of involvement in this area. Thirty years ago the Commission's *Special Study of the Securities Markets* included an examination of equity market issues.[8] In addition, over 20 years ago, the Commission undertook an in-depth examination of the equity markets and their regulatory structure.[9]

As a result of that review and the Congressional hearings which followed, the Commission recommended (and Congress adopted in 1975) amendments to the securities laws that directed the Commission to facilitate the creation of a National Market System (NMS). In part, the concept of a NMS was premised on the need for integrated market facilities when multiple markets trade the same securities. In 1975, Congress was concerned with, among other things, several specific problems, namely (1) the market fragmentation resulting from a market structure driven by fixed commission rates and comprising geographically separate markets trading the same security, (2) the institutionalization of the markets, and (3) barriers to competition among markets that existed at that time.

Congress did not define the NMS. Instead, Congress believed the NMS should evolve through the interplay of competitive forces as unnecessary regulatory restrictions were removed. Congress provided the Commission the needed flexibility and discretion to work out specific details. The Commission was expected, in those situations where competition was not sufficient, to use the powers granted to it to act promptly and effectively to ensure the NMS was put in place.

Congress set forth the goals for the NMS in section 11A of the Securities Exchange Act of 1934 (Exchange Act). These goals address many aspects of the securities markets including fair competition, economically efficient executions, availability of information, opportunities for best execution, and execution of customer orders without dealer intervention.[10]

The SEC and the securities industry have made a number of changes to meet these objectives, including the elimination of fixed commission rates,[11] partial removal of stock exchange off-board trading restrictions,[12] the development of the Consolidated Transaction Reporting System,[13] the Consolidated Quotation System,[14] the Intermarket Trading System (ITS),[15] and a last-sale reporting system for NASDAQ securities.[16]

CHANGES IN THE EQUITY MARKETS

The U.S. equity markets have developed dramatically in response to many forces, not the least of which are the advances in technology and intensified market competition, both domestically and globally.

Trading volume has grown tremendously, due in part to advances in technology. the average daily volume on the New York Stock Exchange (NYSE) 20 years ago was less than the volume that usually occurs in the first 20 minutes of trading today. Indeed, the average daily NYSE trading volume in 1992 of approximately 202.8 million shares would have been considered an extraordinary day in 1985. Trading volume also has grown in NASDAQ stocks. For example, ten years ago, the average daily trading volume in NASDAQ/NMS securities was approximately 17.4 million shares, while in 1992 the average daily trading volume was 162.2 million shares.

The investors have changed, too. The predominant trend of the last 20 years has been the growth in the size and diversity of the users of the equity markets. In 1975, American households held most equity assets, whereas today, institutions own over 50 percent of U.S. stocks. In addition, institutional investors dominate daily trading, accounting for an estimated 75 to 80 percent of the average daily volume on the NYSE. These entities are far larger than their counterparts of 20 years ago and utilize more sophisticated and powerful trading technology. As the equity markets well know, the institutional traders continue to demand more and more services from the markets they use.

The growth in pension funds and equity mutual funds has been particularly significant.[17] From 1975 to 1992, the amount of U.S. equities held by private and public pension plans grew from $132 billion to $1.3 trillion.[18] Indeed, the largest public pension fund today almost holds as many equity assets as all public pension funds combined in 1975.[19] Mutual funds, too, have become increasingly significant participants in the equity markets. Between 1975 and 1992, mutual funds' share of total U.S. equities more than doubled. Although the pace varies, investors continue to invest billions of dollars every month. According to the Investment Company Institute (ICI), investors poured an unprecedented $10.2 billion into stock funds in January 1993, surpassing the previous record of $9.9 billion set in November 1992.[20] In July 1993, investors added $18 billion to equity funds, with $8.7 billion constituting new investments in such funds.[21]

Derivative products today play a more significant role in our equity markets. In 1975, the only standardized equity derivative products in existence were call options on several stocks. Today, trading strategies involving these products significantly have altered the nature of the stock market and have facilitated the use of passive management or "indexation" strategies by large investors.[22]

There have been dramatic advances in securities trading technology. Both the markets and broker/dealers have increased their ability to quickly route orders and execute those orders. Technology also has made it possible for information (whether it be pricing information or news events) to be available instantaneously and to an increasingly wider audience. Twenty years ago, the NYSE's DOT System and the regional exchanges' automatic execution systems simply did not exist; now, along with similar systems of third market makers, they are the staple of small order executions. Further, the NASDAQ system, which began operations in 1971, is not the second largest stock market in the world. In addition, technology has made it possible to reduce risks in the clearing and settlement systems, as the Commission's recent decision to require a T+3 settlement cycle illustrates.[23] Technology has produced other changes. PTSs are taking advantage of computers to provide electronic executions. The trading desks of large broker/dealers—aided by advances in telecommunications, computer technology, and the introduction of derivatives—have become significant forces in the equity markets and now operate on a global basis.

Aside from the advancements of technology and the growth of institutional investors, the unfixing of commission rates in 1975 has had a profound effect on competition between markets. Commission rates have shrunk to pennies per share for institutional investors and the growth of discount brokers has widened brokerage choices for retail investors. Not least among the changes since 1975 has been the growth of third-party soft-dollar practices and payment for order flow.

OBJECTIVES OF THE MARKET 2000 STUDY

In light of these changes, the equity markets today have many classes of users with different expectations and demands.[24] The challenge for the NMS is to accommodate as many classes of users as possible without impairing investor protection, while continuing to provide reliable and efficient price discovery. To some degree, technological advances will facilitate this as existing markets are able to provide new and better services and products. In addition to technology, competition will ensure that markets are responsive to users, but that competition must exist under reasonable ground rules. Idiosyncrasies of the regulatory structure should not unfairly subsidize particular competitors.

Accordingly, we hope the Market 2000 study provides answers to two core questions of regulatory oversight of the equity markets. First, how should the Commission balance the goals of facilitating a fair field of competition between markets and preserving an efficient price discovery mechanism? Second, how should that balance be attained in a manner that results in fair and orderly markets while maintaining investor protection?

Aside from these two primary questions, another important objective will be to determine the proper role of the Commission in overseeing the continuing developments of the equity markets. There has been a widespread difference of opinion over the role the Commission has played in the development of the equity market structure. One viewpoint would have the Commission exercising *more initiative* in the process; the other that we should have *less government action* to alter, shape, or direct market forces. Whatever the merits of either view, market participants frequently have looked to the Commission to mediate the seemingly intractable market issues that continually arise.[25] Although it would be ideal if the Commission could minimize its referee role, it probably will not be able to shed this role entirely. Thus, it will be important for the Market 2000 study to produce a forward-looking plan for the Commission.

To date we have received 58 comment letters and a dozen academic papers. The commentators represent a wide range of interests, including (1) the primary exchanges and the National Association of Securities Dealers (NASD), (2) the regional exchanges, (3) pension funds and mutual funds, (4) a large trading firm, (5) a large discount broker, (6) several foreign markets, (7) academics, (8) and industry trade groups, such as the Securities Industry Association, Security Traders Association, National Specialists Association, and the Investment Company Institute. We have appreciated the diversity of comments on the study. In addition to analyzing the comment letters, the staff has collected data that should assist us in addressing the various issues.

THE COMMENT LETTERS

Generally, the commentators seem to argue that we have identified the right issues. While some may quibble about which particular issue should receive priority attention, there were few suggestions about new areas to be studied. Indeed, even though some commentators question the need for regulatory action at all on some issues, virtually all feel that a Commission response is needed, even if that response is an affirmative statement that the Commission will not address an issue.

Not surprisingly, there are a wide range of views regarding what the

Commission should do about the various issues. One common theme, however, was "What I'm doing is good and needs less regulation—what my competitor is doing is bad and needs more regulation." Clearly, in may of the letters, it has been necessary for the Division to separate the wheat from the chaff, and it may be hard for the Commission to avoid the referee role referred to earlier. Three issues which have divided the commentators demonstrate some of the questions we face: (1) payment for order flow, (2) order interaction (that is, order exposure), and (3) transparency. What follows is a discussion of these three issues in the context of a hypothetical trade.

Payment for Order Flow

Assume a broker/dealer has received a customer's order to buy a certain amount of XYZ stock. One of the first decisions a broker/dealer must make is where to route the order for execution. Without doubt, the broker/dealer must seek out the best execution for its customer's orders,[26] but, in doing so, a broker/dealer may be influenced by economic incentives to route an order to a particular market. For example, does the broker/dealer own a specialist firm that trades the stock; or, if XYZ is a NASDAQ stock, does the broker/dealer make a market in it? Is the broker/dealer receiving payment from a third market maker to route its small orders in XYZ? Does the broker/dealer have a reciprocal order flow arrangement with another firm whereby it will ship order flow in XYZ to the other firm? Is the order in XYZ large enough to need special handling? Has the customer insisted on a particular marketplace? Does the broker/dealer have an internal crossing system to match up customer orders in XYZ?

Many commentators have focused solely on the issue of payment for order flow. Payment arrangements typically involve market makers or exchange specialists compensating brokerage firms for directing customer orders to them. Commentators are deeply divided on the appropriateness of this practice. Supporters argue that payment for order flow increases competition and encourages innovation,[27] and, further, that firms routing their order flow regularly to a specific market or market maker are providing value that is very different from the value provided in routing a single order and that they should be compensated for that service.[28] Opponents argue that the practice interferes with the firms' obligation to provide best execution and that the benefits to the executing broker never flow back to the customer.[29] These are difficult issues of long-standing import.[30]

Partly in response to the comments to the Market 2000 study, the Commission recently proposed a disclosure scheme for payment for order flow practices.[31] The proposal aims to enhance disclosure of payment for order flow practices on customer confirmations, annual account statements, and account opening information. It defines payment for order flow to include all methods of compensating brokers for directing order flow.[32] Specifically, the Commission would require broker/dealers to include on the confirmation of each transaction whether payment was received and, if so, the amount of any monetary payment, discount, rebate, or reduction in fee received in connection with the transaction.[33] Disclosure regarding the firm's policies regarding payment practices also would be required in opening a new account and, on a yearly basis thereafter, on the annual account statement.[34]

Disclosure on both the confirmation ticket and the annual statement could provide a customer with the opportunity to make an informed choice as to whether he or she will do business with a particular broker.[35] Not all brokers accept payment for order flow, and customers, in reality, do have a choice. If they object to their broker accepting payment for order flow, they can take their business to another broker or negotiate a different commission structure.

While the Commission is proposing to require that all payment for order flow be disclosed to the investor, the Commission will consider alternative approaches to addressing payment for order flow and invites commentators to address alternative approaches. These alternatives include requiring that payment for order flow be passed through to customers, adopting a decimal-based system for the pricing and reporting of all securities of which transactions are reported on the consolidated tape, or banning the practice outright as inconsistent with the Act.

Order Interaction—Order Exposure

Once the broker/dealer has made the decision to route the order to a particular market center, another set of issues arises. If XYZ is a listed stock, will the market center merely execute the order at the best prevailing intermarket bid or offer, or will it try to provide a better execution? Will the order be exposed so other market centers can interact with it, or will it be internalized by a dealer at the first market center? If there are pre-existing limit orders at another market center, will the order trade ahead of those limit orders?

If the stock is a NASDAQ security, will the NASDAQ market maker display the order? If a limit order, will the market maker trade for its own account at superior prices until the order becomes a marketable limit order?[36] How will the customer know the answer to either question?[37]

The list of questions can go on and on. The important point is whether the NMS is a misnomer and whether what has arisen is a smorgasbord of competing markets and dealers, none of which interacts to any great extent with the other, but all of which price off the primary market. In the past, the Commission proposed a number of initiatives designed to promote order interaction such as a consolidated limit order book,[38] limit order information system (LOIS),[39] order exposure rules,[40] and a neutral order routing switch.[41] All of these have been criticized by various commentators, and the markets have instead competed on other terms. Do the developments in the market suggest that the Commission should revisit these proposals,[42] or should the Commission go the other way and remove all restrictions on competition between markets and market participants?

Transparency

After the trade in XYZ is completed, another series of questions arise as to how the trade will be reported. If it is executed on an exchange or over NASDAQ during regular trading hours, it will be reported to the tape within 90 seconds. Suppose the trade is executed after hours—will it ever reach the tape? Suppose it is faxed to the broker/dealer's foreign desk for execution—will it ever be reported to any tape?

These questions raise the issue of transparency. The term transparency is used to refer to the degree to which last-sale (price and volume) and quotation information is made publicly available on a real-time basis. In the United States, "real time" generally means within 90 seconds of the execution of a trade. Transparency promotes investor protection, encourages market liquidity, and fosters the efficiency of securities markets by facilitating price discovery and open competition, thus reducing the effects of fragmentation. In the end, because it enhances the efficiency of the market's price discovery function and liquidity, transparency contributes to the efficient allocation of scarce capital among competing demands for that capital.[43] Nevertheless, the growth of trading alternatives requires that the Commission revisit the existing transparency requirements.[44]

CONCLUSION

Market 2000 is a "modest" study. It is modest in that we know full well that our first responsibility as regulators is to do no harm. We are anxious to avoid fixing, in the name of investor protection or efficient markets, something which basically is not broken.[46] At the same time, we recognize that regulation inevitably sets the ground rules and that it is important that those rules be consistent with new market realities. Our hope is that, as a result of the continuing dialog with the industry and others, our markets will continue to grow and prosper.

NOTES

1. *See* letter from Edward J. Markey, Chairman, Subcommittee on Telecommunications and Finance, U.S. House of Representatives, to Richard C. Breeden, Chairman, SEC, dated May 16, 1991.
2. "Oversight Hearing on the Future of the Stock Market Focusing on the National Market System Before the Subcommittee on Telecommunications and Finance of the House Committee on Energy and Commerce," 103d Congress, 1st session (April 14, 1993); "Oversight Hearing on the Future of the Stock Market Focusing on Inducements for Order Flow Before the Subcommittee on Telecommunications and Finance of the House Committee on Energy and Commerce," 103d Congress, 1st session (May 13, 1993); "Oversight Hearing on the Future of the Stock Market Focusing on Proprietary Trading Systems Before the Subcommittee on Telecommunications and Finance of the House Committee on Energy and Commerce," 103d Congress, 1st session (May 26, 1993); and "Oversight Hearing on the Future of the Stock Market Focusing on Soft Dollar Practices Before the Subcommittee on Telecommunications and Finance of the House Committee on Energy and Commerce," 103d Congress, 1st session, (July 13, 1993).
3. See letter from John D. Dingell, Chairman, Committee on Energy and Commerce, U.S. House of Representatives, to Richard C. Breeden, Chairman, SEC, dated March 6, 1992.
4. See letter from Richard C. Breeden, Chairman, SEC, to the Hon. Edward J. Markey, Chairman, House of Representatives Subcommittee on Telecommunications and Finance, dated July 11, 1991 (enclosing memorandum from William H. Heyman, Director, Division of Market Regulation, to Richard C. Breeden, regarding Response

to letter from Chairman Markey concerning Computerized Trading Systems, dated July 3, 1991); letter from Richard C. Breeden, Chairman, SEC, to the Hon. John D. Dingell, Chairman, Committee on Energy and Commerce, U.S. House of Representatives, dated July 2, 1992.

5. See Richard C. Breeden, "Past Successes, Future Challenges," address before the Securities Industry Association (SIA) annual convention, December 5, 1991.

6. By focusing on equity markets, we do not intend to minimize the important role of derivative markets. Rather, the Commission already has produced numerous studies of the derivative markets and many other studies are on-going today. See, for example, Division, *Trading Analysis of November 15, 1991* (October 1992); Division, *Market Analysis of October 13 and 16, 1989* (December 1990); Division, *Trading Analysis of October 13 and 16, 1989* (May 1990); see generally, Chairman Richard C. Breeden, address before the International Swap Dealers Association annual meeting (March 11, 1993); Commissioner Richard Y. Roberts, "Secondary Market Disclosure and Swaps," address before the National Association of State Treasurers legislative conference (March 3, 1993); Commissioner J. Carter Beese, Jr., "The Future of the OTC Derivatives Market: Where Do We Go from Here?," address before the Risk Magazine/CATS Software symposium, (London, December 1, 1992); Commissioner Mary L. Schapiro, "The Growth of the Synthetic Derivative Market: Risks and Benefits," address before the National Options & Futures Society (November 13, 1991). Recently, there have been studies initiated by the Group of Thirty and the General Accounting Office to examine the growing use of OTC derivative products. See Consultative Group on International Economic and Monetary Affairs, Inc. (Group of Thirty), *Derivatives: Practices and Principles* (July 1993).

7. See Securities Exchange Act Release No. 30920 (July 14, 1992), 57 FR 32587 (July 22, 1992).

8. *Report of the Special Study of the Securities Markets of the Securities and Exchange Commission,* H.R. Doc. no. 95, 88th Congress, 1st session (1963).

9. See *Institutional Investor Study Report of the Securities and Exchange Commission,* H.R. Doc. no. 64, 92d Congress, 1st session, part 1 (1971); see also *Statement of the Securities and Exchange Commission on the Future of the Securities Markets* (1972), 37 FR 5286 (March 15, 1972); SEC, *Policy Statement on the Structure of a Central Market System* (March 29, 1973), as reprinted in (1973) Sec. Reg. & L. Rep. (BNA) no. 196 at D-1 (April 4, 1973); Securities Exchange Act Release no. 14416 (January 26, 1978), 43 FR 4354 (February 1, 1978) (status report on the development of a NMS); and Securities Exchange Act Release no. 15671 (March 22, 1979), 44 FR 20360 (April 4, 1979) (status report on the development of a NMS).

10. The findings and objectives contained in section 11A(a)(1) provide that:
    (1) new data processing and communications techniques create the opportunity for more efficient and effective market operations;
    (2) it is in the public interest and appropriate for the protection of investors and the maintenance of fair and orderly markets to assure
       (i) economically efficient of securities transactions;
       (ii) fair competition among brokers and dealers, among exchange markets, and between exchange markets and markets other than exchange markets;
       (iii) the availability to brokers, dealers, and investors of information with respect

to quotations for and transactions in securities;

(iv) the practicability of brokers executing investors' orders in the best market; and

(v) an opportunity, consistent with the provisions of clauses (i) and (iv) of this subparagraph, for investors' orders to be executed without the participation of a dealer; and

(3) the linking of all markets for qualified securities through communication and data processing facilities will foster efficiency, enhance competition, increase the information available to brokers, dealers, and investors, facilitate the offsetting of investors' orders, and contribute to best execution of such orders.

11. Rule 19b–3 phased out fixed commission rates and was adopted in January 1975. See Securities Exchange Act Release no. 11203 (January 23, 1975), 40 FR 7394 (February 20, 1975). The Congress codified the restrictions on fixed commission rates in section 6(e)(1) of the Exchange Act added by the Securities Acts Amendments of 1975 (1975 Amendments).

12. See Securities Exchange Act Release no. 16888 (June 11, 1980), 45 FR 41125 (June 18, 1980).

13. See Securities Exchange Act Release no. 9850 (November 8, 1972), 37 FR 24172 (November 15, 1972) (Rule 17a–15 adoption release) and Securities Exchange Act Release no. 16589 (February 19, 1980), 45 FR 12377 (February 26, 1980) (redesignation of Rule 17a–15 as Rule 11Aa3–1).

14. See Securities Exchange Act Release no. 14415 (January 26, 1978), 43 FR 4342 (February 1, 1978) (Rule 11Ac1–1 adoption release) and Securities Exchange Act Release no. 16518 (January 22, 1980), 45 FR 6521 (approval of Consolidated Quote Plan).

15. See Securities Exchange Act Release no. 18713 (May 6, 1982), 47 FR 20413 (May 12, 1982) (permanently approving ITS operations).

16. See Securities Exchange Act Release no. 30569 (April 10, 1992), 57 FR 13396 (April 16, 1992) (Commission order approving NASD rule change that requires NASD members to report to the NASD transactions in NASDAQ securities, with certain exceptions). See also note 31 below.

17. See Division, *The October 1987 Market Break,* chapter 3 (1988). For a detailed discussion of the growth of mutual funds, see Division of Investment Management, SEC, *Protecting Investors: A Half Century of Investment Company Regulation* (1992).

18. Securities Industry Association, *1993 Fact Book* (1993).

19. The value of equity securities held by state and local retirement funds in 1975 was $25.8 billion. See SEC, *Annual Report for 1976*, at p. 188. CalPERS has $22 billion invested in equities. See letter from DeWitt F. Bowman, Chief Investment Officer, California Public Employees Retirement System, to Jonathan G. Katz, Secretary, SEC, dated October 15, 1992.

20. See Jonathan Clements, "As Cash Flows to Stock Funds, Small Investors Sway Skeptics," *Wall Street Journal,* February 26, 1993, p. C1.

21. "Wall Street Stock Headed for a Fall," *The Reuters Asia-Pacific Business Report,* September 3, 1993 (available in Lexis, Nexis Library, international file). As of July 31, 1993, ICI estimated that equity mutual funds accounted for $595 billion out of the

$1.847 trillion invested in all mutual funds.

22. The growth in equity assets committed to passive management in the 1980s was tremendous. From 1980 to the end of 1991, the amount of passively managed U.S. equity assets grew from under $8 billion to $231 billion. During this period, the percentage of total assets indexed by the top 200 pension funds increased from 2.5 percent to 14.4 percent. See J. Lakonishok, A Shleifer, and R. Vishny, *The Structure and Performance of the Money Management Industry,* Brookings Papers: Microeconomics (1992).

23. See Securities Exchange Act Release no. 33023 (October 6, 1993) (adoption of Rule 15c6–1, establishing three business days, instead of five business days, as the standard settlement time frame for broker/dealer transactions).

24. See Lawrence Harris, "Consolidation, Fragmentation, Segmentation, and Regulation," *Financial Markets, Institutions, and Instruments,* December 1993, reprinted as chapter 18 of this volume. See also Hans R. Stoll, "Principles of Trading Market Structure," *Journal of Financial Services Review* 6 (1992), p. 75. In general, there is an increasing array of markets, dealers, and products available to trade equity securities. This veritable "menu" of markets and products is a result of meeting the demands of market participants. For example, some market participants value low impact and anonymity of their trades; others want to avoid dealer intervention. Other market participants need immediacy; others are more patient. Finally, retail broker/dealers want faster and cheaper execution; large trading desks seek profitable (or at least less costly) block positioning.

25. See generally David M. Schizer, "Benign Restraint: The SEC's Regulation of Execution Systems," *Yale Law Journal* 181 (1992), p. 1551.

26. See Securities Exchange Act Release no. 15671 (March 22, 1979), 44 FR 20380, 20383 n. 30 (April 4, 1979). See also Securities Exchange Act Release no. 32170 (April 23, 1986), 51 FR 16004 (April 30, 1986) (interpretative release concerning the scope of section 28(e) of the Exchange Act); *In re Kidder, Peabody & Co.,* 43 S.E.C. 911 (1968).

27. See, for example, letter from Joseph R. Hardiman, President, NASD, to Jonathan G. Katz, Secretary, SEC, dated November 20, 1992.

28. See letter from Frederick Moss and David Colker, Cincinnati Stock Exchange, to Jonathan Katz, Secretary, SEC, dated November 20, 1992.

29. See, for example, letters from James E. Buck, Senior Vice President and Secretary, NYSE, to Jonathan Katz, Secretary, SEC, dated November 24, 1992, from James R. Jones, Chairman and CEO, American Stock Exchange, to Jonathan Katz, Secretary, SEC, dated December 8, 1992; from David Humphreville and Caroline B. Austin, Co-chairs, National Specialists Association, to Jonathan Katz, Secretary, SEC, dated December 11, 1992.

30. Brandon Becker, address before the National Security Traders Association 55th Annual Convention (October 31, 1998). There have been many studies on the practice of payment for order flow. See Marshall E. Blume and Michael A. Goldstein, "Displayed and Effective Spreads by Market" (previously titled "Differences in Execution Prices Among the NYSE, the Regionals, and the NASD"), November 10, 1992; Charles Lee, "Market Integration and Price Execution for NYSE-Listed Securities," *Journal of Finance* 48 (July 1993), p. 1009. Congressional hearings on

this subject were held in May 1993. "Oversight Hearing on the Future of the Stock Market Focusing on Inducements for Order Flow Before the Subcommittee on Telecommunications and Finance of the House Committee on Energy and Commerce," 103d Congress, 1st session (May 13, 1993).

31. See Securities Exchange Act Release no. 33026 (October 6, 1993). Although the Commission preliminarily believes a disclosure approach will best address concerns regarding payment for order flow, the Commission has requested comment on various alternatives to that approach. These alternatives range from prohibiting payment for order flow to clarifying the method by which trades and quotes are reported.

32. Proposed Rule 10b–10(e)(9) would define the term payment for order flow to include all forms or arrangements compensating for directing order flow, such as monetary payments, research products or services, reciprocal agreements, clearing or other services; adjustment of a broker/dealer's unfavorabie trading errors; offers to participate as an underwriter in public offerings; stock loans and shared interest accrued thereon; and discounts and rebates, or any other reduction for or credit against any fee, expense or other financial obligation of a broker or dealer routing a customer order.

33. Disclosure would be required on transactions involving national market securities only.

34. The information required to be disclosed on new accounts and annual account statements would include the firm's policies regarding receipt of payment for order flow from any broker/dealer (including market makers), exchange members, or exchanges to which it routes customer's orders for execution; and information regarding the aggregate amount of monetary payments, discounts, rebates or reduction in fees received by the firm over the past year.

35. Disclosure of payment for a single order may not fairly or adequately communicate the nature of the arrangement since the market makers' order stream and the broker/dealer's ability to obtain such payment is based upon orders in the aggregate.

36. See *In re E. F. Hutton & Co.* (the Manning decision), Securities Exchange Act Release no. 25887 (July 6, 1988), 41 SEC Doc. 473, appeal filed, Hutton & Co. Inc. v. SEC, Dec. no. 88-1649 (D.C. Cir. September 2, 1988), (stipulation of dismissal filed January 11, 1989). The NASD has recently proposed a rule that would eliminate the Manning safe harbor. As proposed, the rule would prohibit dealers from trading ahead of customer limit orders in their market maker capacity. See file no. SR-NASD-95-58.

37. See generally Michael J. Simon and Robert Colby, "The National Market System for Over-the-Counter Stocks," *George Washington Law Review* 55 (1986), p. 17.

38. See Securities Exchange Act Release no. 12159 (March 2, 1976), 41 FR 19274 (May 11, 1976) (requesting comment on issues relating to the development of a consolidated limit order book).

39. LOIS was never implemented, even in its pilot form. See Securities Exchange Act Release no. 17194 (October 6, 1980), 45 FR 67494. See also Securities Exchange Act Release no. 15770 (April 26, 1979) (proposed rule providing protection for all displayed public limit orders against executions of inferior prices by requiring satisfaction of those orders at their limit prices); Securities Exchange Act Release no. 31344 (October 21, 1992), 57 FR 48581 (October 28, 1992) (withdrawal of proposed price protection rule).

40. See Securities Exchange Act Release no. 18738 (May 13, 1982), 47 FR 22376 (May

24, 1982) (proposing two alternative rules providing for increased exposure of orders in certain securities by requiring market makers or market centers to expose customer orders in certain securities to other markets before executing them internally); Securities Exchange Act Release no. 19372 (December 23, 1982), 47 FR 58287 (December 30, 1982) (proposed rule, in revised form, requiring exposure of customer orders in certain securities); Securities Exchange Act Release no. 20074 (August 12, 1983), 48 FR 38250 (August 23, 1983) (Deferral of proposed exposure rule in order to solicit comment on the trading experience of broker/dealers and investors with respect to securities eligible for off-board trading pursuant to Rule 19c–3).

41. Securities Exchange Act Release no. 15671 (March 22, 1979), 44 FR 20360 (status report on the development of a National Market System).

42. See GAO, "SEC Actions Needed to Address Market Fragmentation Issues" (1993); "Oversight Hearings on the Future of the Stock Market Focusing on the Results of a GAO Study on Market Fragmentation Before the Subcommittee on Telecommunications and Finance of the House Committee on Energy and Commerce," 103d Congress, 1st session (June 29, 1993).

43. See Brandon Becker, "Market Transparency," address before the Financial Times Conference on International Securities Markets: Limiting Market Risk (London, May 12, 1992). See also Brandon Becker et al., "Automated Securities Trading," *Journal of Financial Services* (1992), p. 327.

44. While the Market 2000 study will consider transparency in the context of equity securities, it may provide insight that may be relevant for the less transparent debt markets. Generally, transparency is present in the trading of listed stocks, OTC stocks, and standardized option, but the same level of transparency is not present in the trading of government securities or corporate high yield debt securities. See Division, "Staff Report on the Municipal Securities Markets" (1993), pp. 17–22. The NASD recently has proposed real-time transaction reporting in equity securities that are not subject to real-time reporting under existing provisions of the NASD rules. See Securities Exchange Act Release no. 31096 (January 6, 1993), 58 FR 4189 (January 13, 1993) (notice of filing of file no. SR-NASD-92-48).

45. With apologies, see Milton H. Cohen, "The National Market System—A Modest Proposal," *George Washington Law Review* 46 (1978), p. 743; see generally Jonathan Swift, *A Modest Proposal for Preventing the Children of Ireland from Being a Burden to Their Parents and Country* (1729).

46. Walter Werner, the first director of the Commission's Office of Policy Planning, wrote elegantly about this principle. See Walter Werner, "Adventure in the Social Control of Finance: The National Market System for Securities," *Columbia Law Review* 75 (1975), p. 1233; Walter Werner, "The SEC as a Market Regulator," *Virginia Law Review* 70 (1984), p. 755.

APPENDIX TO CHAPTER 10

MARKET 2000 REPORT
Introduction and Executive Summary

The U.S. equity markets are an important national asset. They enable the nation to raise capital, provide investment opportunities, and promote entrepreneurship. For 60 years, the Securities and Exchange Commission (Commission) has worked to ensure that equity and market regulation protects investors, aids capital raising, and keeps pace with the changing dynamics of the secondary markets. The Market 2000 study, prepared by the Commission's Division of Market Regulation (Division), is another step in this process.

Over 20 years ago, the Commission undertook a similar examination of the equity markets. Questions had arisen as to the fairness, competitiveness, and efficiency of U.S. markets. As a result of the Commission's examination, in 1975 Congress enacted legislation that provided a new framework for establishing a "national market system" (NMS) for the U.S. securities markets. It was expected that in the NMS, competition would generate the best prices, comprehensive disclosure of market information would foster best execution of customer orders, and broker/dealers would place the interests of their customers first. Subsequent action by the Commission and the markets to advance the NMS have made the U.S. markets the most efficient and liquid in the world.

Since 1975, the markets have changed dramatically in response to advances in technology, new product developments, and global economic expansion. These changes have led market participants once again to raise questions regarding whether the existing regulatory framework has kept pace with market developments. Specifically, Congress, investors, and the markets have raised concerns about possible market fragmentation, inadequate disclosure of market information, and uneven regulation among competitors.

In response to their concerns, the Division undertook the Market 2000 study to address these issues and ensure that the U.S. equity markets remain vibrant and efficient. The Division began the Market 2000 study in July 1992 with the issuance of a concept release on "the overall structure of equity market regulation." The Division gathered data on equity trading and analyzed the comment letters submitted in response to the concept release. In addition, the Commission published a proposed rule to increase disclosure of payment for order flow. Concurrent with the Market 2000 study, Congress held hearings in 1993 on many of the issues in the study, and the U.S. General Accounting Office (GAO) released a report on market structure.

The Division's basic finding is that today's equity markets are operating efficiently within existing regulatory structure. Record amounts of trading activity are processed smoothly and efficiently. The equity markets continue to perform effectively their primary function of raising capital for public corporations. Investors have a wide range of alternative trading mechanisms from which to select. Although trading of major U.S. equities has become dispersed among the various markets and participants, this development has not impaired market quality. Accordingly, the Division does not believe that a major revision of equity market regulation is needed. The Commission should, however, concentrate on the improvements that are needed to make the markets work better for investors and to make competition work better for the markets. The Division believes that improvements are possible in four areas.

The first area involves the *fair treatment of investors*. The broadest possible investor participation, both retail and institutional, is vital to the health of the market. If the market structure works to the disadvantage of customers, they ultimately will lose confidence in the integrity and fairness of the market. To protect customers, professionals should seek to secure the best prices for their customers and should disclose relationships that could interfere with the customers' interests. Market practices such as payment for order flow, soft dollar arrangements, and certain order handling procedures raise concern as to whether investors are being treated fairly.

Second, *market information* should be disclosed in a timely and comprehensive manner. Information on quotations, trading volume, and trading prices is essential to the effective operation of the markets. Selective or partial disclosure of information impairs the secondary market pricing mechanism, weakens the ability of markets to compete, and prevents customers from monitoring the quality of their executions. Although U.S. markets are the most transparent in the world, the markets should redouble their efforts to ensure that full market information is being comprehensively disclosed in a cost-effective manner.

Third, *fair competition* among markets and market participants should be promoted. Over the past several years a variety of new market participants have emerged. Proprietary trading systems (PTSs) have developed and over-the-counter (OTC) market making in listed stocks (third market making) has grown. Although competition among market participants for order flow is healthy and leads to better markets, some participants believe that the existing competitive field is not level because of different regulatory obligations imposed on their competitors. To promote fair competition as well as investor protection, the Commission must ensure that the regulatory responsibilities of the various market centers are rationally allocated without stifling the ability of alternative markets and service to emerge. In some instances, this goal will require more vigorous oversight of new trading systems. In other instances, this goal will justify different regulatory guidelines for the organized markets.

Fourth, *open market access* needs to be expanded. Restrictions on where the users of the markets can transact business limits the ability of competition to provide better markets and services. Several exchange rules and proposals act to restrict market access. These restrictions need to be examined to determine if they serve valid regulatory purposes.

The Division recommends specific action in each of these areas. The most significant recommendations involve Commission rule makings on payment for order flow and soft dollar practices; proposals to narrow spreads and expand transaction reporting; and increased oversight of automated trading systems and third market makers. In addition, the Division recommends action to improve order handling practices for securities quoted on the NASDAQ system and to improve the overall quality of the OTC market.

The Division believes that the recommendations in this report will address existing obstacles to enhancing investor protection and promoting fair competition. the study is not a final analysis; new issues inevitably will arise as the markets evolve. Indeed, the study is designed to encourage changes resulting from market evolution. The recommendations are intended to build on the strength of our markets—their fairness, competitiveness, and openness—and to make them even more attractive as a means of raising capital and providing investments in the future.

Study Organization

The study is organized as follows: In the first half of the Report, the Division reviews the current state of the equity markets and presents a framework for regulating these markets at this stage of their development. The framework is followed by specific recommendations in the four areas identified above. Next, seven studies discuss the issues and recommendations in more detail. Data used in the Division's analysis are presented in exhibits to the Report. Finally, several appendixes describe various features of the equity markets.

CHAPTER 11

THE MARKET FOR MARKETPLACES: REFLECTIONS ON MARKET 2000

Kenneth Lehn

INTRODUCTION

In July 1992, the Securities and Exchange Commission (SEC) issued a widely publicized concept release seeking comments on what role, if any, it should play in shaping the future structure of U.S. equity markets. After digesting the many comment letters it has received, the SEC is expected to release a final version of its Market 2000 study in early 1994. This study is likely to contain the SEC's recommendations for regulatory change.

The SEC explicitly states that its regulatory approach will be guided by the statutory objectives contained in the 1975 amendments to the federal securities laws. The amendments require the SEC to foster the development of a national market system that simultaneously achieves several goals, including the promotion of (1) "fair" competition among brokers, dealers, and exchanges, (2) efficient execution of securities transactions, (3) investor protection (for example, facilitating best trade execution), and (4) broad availability of trade and quote information. Interestingly, in the release the SEC also indicates that it will "explore whether those objectives should be modified" and states that it "is not trying to dictate what the structure of equity markets should look like in the year 2000."

The report raises a variety of related issues, but three are featured prominently. First, it asks for comments on whether the growth of new marketplaces for trading listed stocks represents healthy competition or an undesirable fragmentation of order flow. It also seeks comments on whether specific market practices, such as New York Stock Exchange (NYSE) Rule 390, retard competition. Second, the report asks whether the SEC should promote greater transparency (that is, real-time dissemination of trade and quote information) in equity markets. In particular, it expresses concern about the lack of transparency in some of the emerging new marketplaces. Third, the report asks for comments on the payment for order flow, a controversial practice in which market makers pay brokers for directing order flow to them. Does this practice enhance competition in equity markets and serve the interests of investors? Or does it represent free-riding that diminishes liquidity and harms investors?

COMPETITIVE ISSUES

During the past decade, there has been a substantial increase in the trading of NYSE stocks in marketplaces other than the NYSE. The proportion of trading volume (on the consolidated tape) in NYSE-listed stocks accounted for by the NYSE has declined from roughly 85 percent in the early 1980s to roughly 65 percent today. Concurrently, the proportion accounted for by regional exchanges has increased substantially, from approximately 10 percent to more than 20 percent. Trading of NYSE-listed securities also has increased in the over-the-counter (OCT) market, proprietary trading systems (PTSs), foreign markets (mostly London and Tokyo), and nonintermediated markets where investors trade directly with each other.

There is general agreement that the structural change in U.S. equity markets has been caused by two important factors: substantial advances in communications technology and the growing importance of institutional investors. The dramatic change in communications technology has greatly reduced the costs of "producing" trading services, and it has facilitated the entry of new competitors into this market. Many of the

NYSE's new competitors employ trading systems that are very different from the continuous auction market used by the NYSE (for example, the electronic single-price call auction used by the Arizona Stock Exchange). Many electronic-based trading systems have become possible in recent years because of advances in interactive communications technology.

Concurrent with the supply changes, the growing importance of institutional investors has affected the demand for trading services, as different types of institutions have different demands for these services. For example, if index funds have less demand for immediacy than other investors, they will be reluctant to pay for the immediacy provided in a continuous auction market. These investors might find an alternative trading system more appealing if it provides less immediacy and lower trading costs. Similarly, some investors may prefer to trade in price discovery markets, while others find passive pricing markets satisfactory. Hence, the increase in the trading of NYSE-listed stocks away from the NYSE represents product differentiation that has evolved to meet the changing demands of customers in the market for trading services.

In short, the substantial supply and demand changes in the "market for marketplaces" in recent years has resulted in a greater dispersion of order flow across a diverse group of market centers. The SEC release acknowledges these changes and describes the market as "highly competitive." However, it goes on to seek comment on several issues concerning the competitiveness of the market. First, has the dispersal of order flow fragmented markets to the point where it is impairing liquidity and price discovery in the primary markets? Second, does the highly competitive market for trading services impair the SEC's ability to achieve other goals laid out in the 1975 amendments? Third, notwithstanding that the industry is highly competitive, do certain market practices, such as NYSE Rule 390 (limiting NYSE members from effecting transactions in NYSE-listed stocks in the OTC market) inhibit competition?

Fragmentation

The NYSE and others argue that the increased dispersion of order flow potentially may impair liquidity and price discovery in equity markets. According to the argument, the dispersion of order flow reduces volume in the primary equity market, which is the price discovery market. The reduction in volume, it is argued, can impair liquidity, induce additional volatility in equity returns, and widen bid-ask spreads in the primary market. Furthermore, if a disproportionate amount of the trading volume in nonprimary markets is accounted for by less informed investors (for example, index funds), then spreads in the primary market may widen further to compensate specialists for the increased likelihood that they are trading against more informed investors.

The issue of fragmentation is highly relevant for exchanges and other enterprises which provide trading services, since they may wish to design rules and procedures that mitigate adverse effects of fragmentation on the quality of their services. However, as a public policy goal, it is not appropriate to impede competition in order to avert fragmentation, since there is little evidence that fragmentation through stifled competition is the loss of valuable experimentation with new ways of trading securities. The SEC generally seems to recognize this and raises the issue of fragmentation as a prospective, rather than a present, problem.

The SEC's concern about fragmentation is understandable, given the statutory goals laid out in the 1975 amendments. The amendments require the SEC to promote "economically efficient trade execution" and "best trade execution" for customers. These statutory goals may lead the SEC to err too far in the direction of mitigating fragmentation, since the prospect of the same security trading at different prices in different marketplaces would be politically embarrassing to the Commission.

As others have pointed out, regulatory agencies may have a tendency toward minimizing the likelihood of highly visible "mistakes," even if this behavior leads to inefficiencies. For example, the Food and Drug Administration (FDA) can commit two types of errors: delaying or withholding safe drugs from the market (Type I) and allowing unsafe drugs in the market (Type II). There are costs associated with avoiding both types of errors, and efficient rules will result in the lowest total costs. However, some have argued that the political costs associated with the commission of Type II errors are substantially greater than those associated with Type I errors, since the Type II errors are much more visible.[1] For example, the FDA incurred great political costs in the late 1950s when it approved a drug (thalidomide) which led to large numbers of birth defects. Some scholars argue that the political costs associated with Type II errors lead regulatory agencies to err on the side of minimizing Type II errors, even though doing so results in inefficiently large Type I errors.[2]

This theory of regulatory behavior is relevant to the fragmentation debate. Allowing the same security to occasionally trade at different prices in different marketplaces is analogous to the FDA allowing an unsafe drug on the market. Given the SEC's legislative mandate to foster efficient and best execution, it may be excessively averse to the risk that prices of the same security may occasionally differ across markets, even if arbitrage makes the differences short-lived.

The SEC's regulation of the equity options market is consistent with this hypothesis. In the late 1970s, there was a highly publicized case of the same equity option (the Bally option) trading at widely different prices in two different markets. In response to outcries that some customers did not receive best execution in their trades of the options, the SEC sanctioned an allocation system in which options exchanges received exclusive rights to trade individual equity options. Recently, the Commission has acted to restore competition to the equity options market on grounds that the allocation system insulates options exchanges from competition and leads to a widening of bid-ask spreads.[3] Furthermore, in cases where equity options have been allowed to trade experimentally in multiple markets, there is little evidence of market fragmentation. The allocation system seems to have generated few benefits and large costs. To a large extent, the inefficiencies were incurred in order to avoid isolated cases of customers receiving different prices for the same security in different markets.

Market Linkages

The development of the Intermarket Trading System (ITS) in equity markets mitigates the risk of the same stock trading at different prices in different markets. Indeed, the SEC describes the ITS as "an important addition to the National Market System," in part, because it reduces the risk that customers will not receive best execution and, in part, because it purportedly enhances the competitive position of regional exchanges vis-à-vis the primary market. The SEC release asks whether structural changes in the ITS are required and whether the linkages between markets should be enhanced with the advent of new trading systems.

Here, too, the SEC may have political incentives to err on the side of excessive linkage, given the goals laid out in the 1975 amendments. A common view of market linkages is that, in addition to promoting best execution, they promote competition between marketplaces. For example, the SEC release states that the ITS "permitted regional specialists to attract orders from other markets by providing superior quotations and facilitated their market making by enabling them to lay off their risk

positions more efficiently, and at a lower cost, through offsetting transactions on primary markets."

A weakness in the SEC's discussion of this issue and other issues
involving market competition is that it lacks a cogent working definition
of "competition." As Robert Bork points out in a classic book on antitrust policy, the ambiguity of the phrase "competition" has often "resulted in the fruitless discourse of men talking past each other."[4] Using
Bork's taxonomy of definitions of competition, the SEC adopts a definition of competition that refers to the promotion of rivalry, rather than an
economics-based definition which emphasizes efficiency. As Bork discusses, enhanced rivalry often leads to greater efficiency, but it can also
result in less efficient outcomes. As a result, the promotion of
intermarket rivalry per se should not be a public policy goal.

An example that is often used in the antitrust area is the case of
resale price maintenance, that is, the practice in which a manufacturer
requires retailers to sell its product at a specified retail price. One view is
that this practice is anticompetitive, since it diminishes price rivalry in
the retail market. An alternative view is that this type of price rivalry can
actually diminish economic efficiency.[5] This is more likely where a
manufacturer wants retailers to invest in the advertising and promotion
of its products. Without resale price maintenance or some other vertical
restraint, retailers (for example, department stores) would be reluctant to
incur costs associated with the promotion of products, since other retailers (for example, discount chains) could free-ride off their promotion.
Furthermore, the discount chains can undercut their prices charged by
the full-service department stores, since they haven't incurred the costs
of promotion). In this case, the promotion of price rivalry can work
contrary to economic efficiency.

Similarly, mandated market linkages may promote intermarket rivalry, but they also can diminish efficiency. In effect, the primary market, that is, the price discovery market, is analogous to the full-service
department store. Potentially, other marketplaces can free-ride off the
primary market's quotes and perhaps provide better quotes since they
have invested less in the facilities that are required for price discovery.
To the extent that linkages reduce the ability of primary markets to
capture the returns on their investments in price discovery, they have
less incentive to invest in price discovery.

This argument suggests that the SEC should be cautious before
expanding the scope of the Intermarket Trading System. Certainly, exchanges should be free to develop voluntary changes to the ITS, subject

to the normal antitrust constraints. However, the case for SEC-mandated changes in the structure and scope of these market linkages is weak.

NYSE Rule 390

The SEC also asks for comments on the competitive effects of certain rules adopted by self-regulatory organizations, such as NYSE Rule 390. Critics of Rule 390 often refer to the rule as anticompetitive, since it limits the ability of NYSE members to effect transactions off the exchange. Ronald Coase has commented on the tendency to view exchange rules as anticompetitive: "Economists observing the regulations of the exchanges often assume that they represent an attempt to exercise monopoly power and aim to restrain competition. They ignore or, at any rate, fail to emphasize an alternative explanation for these regulations: that they exist in order to reduce transaction costs and therefore to increase the volume of trade."[6] Exchange members may voluntarily agree to limit their behavior through rules like 390, in order to provide trading services at lower cost. Off-board trading restrictions can promote economic efficiency by mitigating possible problems associated with fragmented order flow.

A major distinction should be drawn between restraints on behavior that are purely anticompetitive and those that affect the efficiency with which services are produced. For example, if two exchanges agree to collude on the pricing of their transaction services, they would be placing restraints on each other without any beneficial effects on the costs of providing trading services. This type of price-fixing agreement is clearly anticompetitive and diminishes economic efficiency. However, exchange rules are "intrafirm" restraints that affect the efficiency with which the exchange provides transaction services. In competitive markets, it is hard to see how intrafirm restraints can harm efficiency. Given the SEC's characterization of the market for transaction services as "highly competitive," it would be wise to ignore calls for the abolition of Rule 390 on grounds that it is anticompetitive.

Regulatory Arbitrage

More fundamentally, the economic basis for the SEC's regulation of exchange rules is quite weak, since there is not obvious "market failure" in the design of these rules. Exchange rules are, effectively, matters of organizational design. Firms in competitive markets have strong incentives to adopt rules that cater to their customers, and those that do not will experience reductions in their value. This has become an especially relevant topic in recent years, since the exchanges now confront competition from proprietary trading systems, which are operated as private broker/dealer businesses and not as self-regulatory organizations. Hence, the proprietary trading systems face less onerous regulatory burdens than exchanges and have greater freedom to change their rules and procedures.

The SEC concept release asks for comments on whether the present system of regulation is equitable or whether self-regulatory organizations bear a disproportionate share of the regulatory burden. Setting the equity issue aside, there is a legitimate issue concerning "regulatory arbitrage." Do the fortunes of proprietary trading systems depend in part on the less burdensome regulatory treatment they receive relative to the NYSE and other self-regulatory organizations?

There are three ways of eliminating, or at least reducing, this disparity in regulation—(1) increase the regulation of proprietary trading systems, (2) decrease the regulation of exchanges, or (3) a combination of items (1) and (2). While there is an institutional bias in regulatory agencies to regulate more, not less, it would be foolhardy for the SEC to solve this problem simply by enhancing its regulation of proprietary trading systems, as it could do through proposed Rule 15c2–10. First, changes in technology are making it increasingly easy for foreign markets to develop if the costs of U.S. regulation become too high, and a proprietary trading system presumably could operate as easily abroad as it could in the United States.

Second, the dramatic technological changes of the past decade are generally inducing large firms to shed highly centralized, bureaucratic governance structures in favor of decentralized structures that can adopt more quickly to the rapid changes occurring in their marketplaces. This is especially true for enterprises operating in industries heavily dependent on telecommunications (for example, IBM, AT&T), where change is especially rapid. Since the provision of trading services is highly reliant on telecommunications, exchanges fall into this category. Yet, the bureaucratic rule-making process under which they operate is an impediment to technological experimentation in the market for transaction services. It would be refreshing to see the SEC give exchanges more autonomy in crafting rules and procedures, much as large companies have given more decision rights to lower-level employees who have greater access to timely information. This not only would mitigate any regulatory arbitrage that exists between exchanges and proprietary trading systems, but it might facilitate more experimentation, innovation, and the adoption of more efficient trading practices by exchanges.

TRANSPARENCY

The SEC concept release expresses concern about whether new ways of trading equity securities (for example, proprietary trading systems, after-hours trading) have diminished the transparency of U.S. equity markets. Implicit in the SEC's discussion is that more transparency is always preferred to less transparency, that is, transparency is a free good. According to the SEC's reasoning, greater transparency (1) facilitates investor protection by making it easier for customers to monitor brokers, (2) promotes liquidity and price discovery, and (3) reduces fragmentation. Given its premise that more transparency is better, the SEC asks for comments on various ways of enhancing transparency in U.S. equity markets.

Notwithstanding the advantages, there also are costs associated with greater transparency. As discussed above, mandatory disclosure of real-time trade and quote information erodes the property rights that marketplaces have to the information. Since the information is costly to produce, mandatory disclosure discourages marketplaces from making investments in facilities and trading systems that "produce" prices.

As Mulherin, Netter and Overdahl, and Bronfman and Overdahl recount,[7] the issue of transparency is not new. The advent of the telegraph in the 19th century made it easier for traders who were not members of organized exchanges to free-ride off quotations generated by the primary markets (i.e., the exchanges). Legal battles over the ownership right to quotes ensued, climaxing in a 1905 Supreme Court case in which Justice Oliver Wendell Holmes ruled that these rights belonged to exchanges. After the rights to quotations were defined, exchanges were free to sell these rights to vendors and other traders at freely negotiated prices.

The historical accounts provided by the two studies show that, even in the absence of regulation, market forces provide some level of transparency. Although a case for more disclosure can be made on grounds that the market for information provides inefficient levels of information (since information has attributes of a public good), the SEC fails to make this case.[8] Instead, it relies on assertions about the virtues of transparency, leaving one with the impression that more transparency is always better.

In addition to ignoring the possible effects of transparency on the incentives of exchanges to discover prices, the SEC release ignores the fact that traders often prefer to keep their trades anonymous. The release recognizes that some trading in U.S. stocks may occur in foreign, less transparent, markets simply because some traders want their transactions to remain anonymous. Similarly, some attribute the relative success of Instinet and other proprietary trading systems in the after-hours market to their opaqueness. According to the argument, many investors demand anonymity, and marketplaces able to respond to this demand capture increased order flow.

Rather than try to extend transparency to foreign and off-exchange markets, as the release suggests, the SEC should consider the possible adverse effects that greater transparency may have on liquidity, price discovery, and the international competitiveness of U.S. equity markets. If some traders are reluctant to disclose their trades, and migrate to less transparent markets, then strict transparency rules can reduce trading volume and liquidity in the regulated U.S. markets. Similarly, price discovery can be impaired if informed traders are dissuaded by transparency rules that can reduce the returns from their investments in information.[9]

PAYMENT FOR ORDER FLOW

The SEC release also asks for comment on the practice of payment for order flow. This practice has become especially controversial in recent years as market makers and regional specialists have increasingly paid retail brokers for order flow in exchange-listed stocks. Presumably, a large proportion of the increase in the regional exchanges' share of trading in NYSE-listed stocks is accounted for by this practice.

The SEC release raises two primary policy questions about the payment for order flow. First, does the practice harm investors? According to critics of the practice, investors receive poorer trade execution than they would if their trades were executed on the NYSE. Furthermore, sometimes it is asserted that the payments made to retail brokers are rarely passed on to their customers. Hence, critics argue that investors receive poor execution without receiving any reduction in brokerage fees.

Given the competitiveness of the retail brokerage industry, it is hard to imagine that the payment for order flow could systematically harm investors. If some retail brokers kept the rebates, other brokers could capture market share by passing some of the rebate on to their customers in the form of lower brokerage fees. One of the uncontroversial truths in economics is that competitive markets serve consumers well. Since the retail brokerage industry is highly competitive, it would be a mistake for the SEC to curtail the payment for order flow on investor protection grounds alone. Recently, the SEC proposed a relatively modest rule that would require retail brokers to disclose whether they receive payments for order flow. Although the benefits of this rule are likely to be quite small, the costs are also likely to be small.

The second major issue raised by the payment for order flow concerns the impact of the practice on some of the market structure issues discussed above. For example, some critics argue that the practice can impair liquidity in the primary market by fragmenting order flow. In and of itself, this argument does not justify regulatory intervention, for reasons discussed above. However, to the extent that some market makers and regional specialists free-ride off the quotes in the primary markets, then it is legitimate to question the effects that the practice has on the incentives of primary markets to invest in the discovery of prices. But rather than curtail the payment for order flow per se, perhaps the SEC should reconsider the extent to which present market linkages facilitate free-riding.[10]

CONCLUSION

The SEC would be wise to adopt an unobtrusive approach in it Market 2000 study. Most likely, technology will continue to change in dramatic ways over the next decade, and new ways of trading equity securities are likely to emerge. Since neither the SEC nor any other institution can possibly predict the substantial technological changes that are likely to occur between now and the year 2000, it would be unwise to lay down a regulatory blueprint that may impede innovation and experimentation with new trading structures. In addition, the SEC is encouraged to adopt a definition of competition that is based on economic efficiency and not other factors, such as the promotion of rivalry.

NOTES

1. For a good discussion of the Food and Drug Administration's behavior, see Paul J. Quirk, "Food and Drug Administration," in James Q. Wilson (ed.), *The Politics of Regulation*, Basic Books (1980), pp. 191–235.
2. See, for example, Milton and Rose Friedman, *Free to Choose*, Harcourt Brace Jovanovich (1980).
3. For evidence on bid-ask spreads in the equity options market, see Robert Neal, "Potential Competition and Actual Competition in Equity Options," *Journal of Finance* 42 (July 1987), pp. 511–37.
4. Robert H. Bork, *The Antitrust Paradox*, Basic Books (1978), p. 58.
5. For a discussion of the two views, see Richard Schmalansee and Robert Willig (eds.), *Handbook of Industrial Organization*, vol. I, Elsevier Science Publishers B.V. (1989).
6. R. H. Coase, *The Firm, the Market, and the Law*, University of Chicago Press (1988), p. 9.
7. J. Harold Mulherin, Jeffry M. Netter, and James A. Overdahl, "Prices Are Property: The Organization of Financial Exchanges from a Transaction Cost Perspective," *Journal of Law and Economics* (October 1991), pp. 591–644; and Corinne Bronfman and James A. Overdahl, "Would the Invisible Hand Produce Transparent Markets?," Commodity Futures Trading Commission, Division of Economic Analysis working paper no. 92–10 (June 1992).
8. Even the "public goods" argument is only a necessary, but not sufficient, condition for greater transparency.
9. For a critical discussion of transparency, see J. Harold Mulherin, "Market Transparency: Pros, Cons, and Property Rights," in Kenneth Lehn and Robert Kamphuis (eds.), *Modernizing U.S. Securities Regulations,* Irwin Professional Publishing (1993).
10. Robert Schwartz argues that the continuous auction market actually encourages this type of free-riding. See Robert A. Schwartz, "Competition and Efficiency," in Kenneth Lehn and Robert Kamphuis (eds.), *Modernizing U.S. Securities Regulations,* Irwin Professional Publishing (1993).

CHAPTER 12

TRADE AND QUOTE TRANSPARENCY: PRINCIPLES AND PROSPECTS FOR THE YEAR 2000

Joel Hasbrouck

Transparency refers to the clarity with which market participants (and the public at large) can perceive the process of securities trading. A market is opaque if buyer and seller negotiate in secret and disclose their trade to no one. All else remaining equal, a market becomes more transparent with prompt and comprehensive disclosure of the terms of actual transactions and quotes or orders (which represent potential transactions). The benefits of transparency are informational: individuals can make better economic decisions if they know how much their assets are worth. The obvious costs of transparency are operational (for example, the cost of running the transaction tape), but there are also significant informational costs as well. In security markets, information is arguably a more important factor than in the markets for most other goods and services in the economy. This underlies the importance of transparency for security markets.

In the United States, markets organized as exchanges (the stock and futures exchanges) began to require prompt reporting of trades long before the appearance of external regulation. The Securities Acts

Amendments of 1975 affirmed the value of this trade transparency. They also mandated the extension of transparency to quotes, the bids and offers that represent the prices at which new sell and buy orders can immediately be accommodated. Since the 1975 enactment, the preservation and enhancement of trade and quote transparency have become established principles of market regulation.

Until recently, however, U.S. equity markets have been consolidated, with the preponderance of trading in New York Stock Exchange-listed securities occurring on the NYSE itself. A consolidated market provides conditions supportive of transparency. Transparency is easier to monitor and enforce, and the incentives for evading it are lessened if there are few opportunities for trading away from the central market. We currently appear to be in the midst of a firmly established trend toward a fragmented market system, one in which trading takes place in separate sites. The Securities and Exchange Commission's Market 2000 study is intended as a broad analysis of equity market issues. The aim of this chapter is more circumscribed: an analysis of transparency and the particular stresses that fragmentation imposes on it.

It must be admitted at the outset that neither economic theory nor empirical analysis yields practical normative statements about the optimal level of transparency, even under a consolidated market. The problem is that the costs and benefits arise in large part from informational considerations, for which it is difficult to impute values. The economic perspective is still a useful one, however, because it places transparency in a framework that at least illuminates some of the trade-offs involved when designing regulations.

In considering trade and quote transparency, the former is (in the United States, at least) the less controversial. Transaction prices and volumes of equity trades are disseminated (generally within 90 seconds) to the electronic tape. This helps investors monitor their brokers' efforts because they can observe whether they received a price that was close to other trades that took place at nearby times. The published price is also useful to investors who are not actively looking to buy or sell because it allows them to measure the value of their holdings and thereby make better consumption and investment decisions.

Yet although transaction price reporting is as close to a Mom-and-apple-pie issue as we have in U.S. securities regulation, the economic rationale is not unambiguous. In analyzing transparency, a useful general principle is that the requirement of disclosure imposes a private cost on the parties who produced the information. On the London Stock Exchange, for example, large trades are routinely disclosed to the public only with a substantial delay (Schwartz, 1992). Large trades often arise when a broker acts as principal in taking the other side of a large customer order, hoping to work off the position by finding other (probably smaller) counterparties over time. Many U.K. participants believe that required public disclosure of the original block trade would alert the market to the presence of a large "overhang," making it more difficult for the dealer to lay off the position. This would, in turn, make the dealer more reluctant to accommodate the customer in the first place.[1]

This chain of events illustrates another economic truth about transparency. Mandated disclosure cannot be relied upon to act in a neutral fashion, simply rendering visible that which was formerly hidden. Disclosure may fundamentally change the incentives that govern individuals' economic behavior. This may lead to side effects, as in the case above, that make the market worse. Contemplation of rules must therefore attempt to take into account the responses of participants.

In the United States, however, no one has seriously proposed the abandoning of trade reporting requirements in equity markets. This suggests that the social value of a public price record outweighs the private costs imposed on transaction participants. But despite this apparent consensus, a fragmented market system is likely to place stress on trade reporting procedures. Since trade transparency imposes private costs, it is feasible only to the extent that it is enforceable across all markets and participants. It is relatively easy to enforce trade reporting in a central physical exchange because surveillance and monitoring are also centralized. Fragmentation complicates matters.

One stress point is competition from markets (such as London's) that do not require full trade disclosure. The LSE has a relatively small share of the total trading in U.S. equities. It has achieved, however, a substantial share of the trading in French and German equities, which trade in their home markets under conditions of greater transparency. There are many differences across these markets besides transaction disclosure requirements. Therefore, London's success does not measure the competitive value of weakened requirements. Nevertheless, there are good reasons for supposing that disclosure remains a potential competitive weapon.

A second strain arises from the practice of net-of-commission reporting. On the NYSE and regional exchanges, the published trade price is the one reported to the buyer and seller. The commissions paid to their brokers are not reported but serve to decrease the seller's net proceeds and increase the buyer's net cost. Trades that occur off the exchanges, on the National Association of Securities Dealers (NASD) National Market System (NMS), for example, may be reported net-of-commission. A dealer who is acting both as broker and principal for the trade has the option of reporting the total amount paid by the customer for a purchase order (with the commission added in) or the total amount received in a sale (with the commission subtracted out). This only affects reporting. The customer's net cash flow is unaffected.[2] The information in the transaction price record is corrupted, however, since it is impossible for outside observers to separate price and commission. This problem is at least significant enough that NASD brokers have warned academic researchers that it may lead to misinterpretation of the public price record.

A final problem arises from basket trades, groups of stocks traded at one collective price. Since the components of the basket are not priced, there is no way to calculate a value that might be inserted into the reporting stream for an individual stock. While it is in principle possible that basket trades might be used to hide trades in individual stocks, there is no evidence that this is currently occurring. The reporting problem is also mitigated by the fact that basket trades tend to be "passive" trades. That is, the prices are determined by the existing prices of the component securities. As such, these are not transactions that are likely to be particularly informative. However, if trading practices change, it is certainly well within the capabilities of reporting technology to communicate the number of shares of each stock comprising the basket, as well as the overall price.

Despite certain indeterminacies, the analysis of trade transparency in fragmented markets is positively straightforward compared to that of quote transparency. The first problem is definitional. What exactly constitutes a quote? One attribute of a quote is that it proposes a purchase or sale of a specified quantity at a specified price. But this feature also characterizes limit orders. A quote has the additional property that it has been communicated to at least one potential counterparty. But even this may be too broad, as it includes offers and counteroffers occurring in negotiation between two parties. As a practical matter, most markets consider a proposed transaction to constitute a quote when it has already achieved some breadth of exposure. At the NYSE, for example, a limit order to buy becomes a bid when the broker discloses it to the trading crowd (Hasbrouck, Sofianos, and Sosebee, 1993).

A related problem is that bids and offers are only meaningful in a continuous market. The notion of a quote in the usual sense is foreign to most market systems in which trading is batched to occur at a single time. A call market may disseminate an indicative price (a tentative market-clearing price), but this does not represent a price that is immediately available. So it would seem from the outset that certain market architectures must be exempt from quote transparency mandates.

The next difficulty is that the quotes disseminated by a market may not be universally available. One of the forces driving fragmentation is segmentation, whereby we see markets with distinctive characteristics that are tailored for particular trading styles or clienteles. Perhaps the best current example of this is the market provided by Madoff Securities for brokers who specialize in handling retail traders. Madoff executes small retail orders at prices which are as good or better than the best posted intermarket bid and offer. The chance that such an order is motivated by superior or (illegal) inside information is small. It is therefore inexpensive to provide liquidity to such a trade. Since Madoff rebates a small amount to the broker who routes a market order to the system, it has been suggested that the effective spread facing a retail market order is smaller than the posted intermarket spread. Yet this smaller spread cannot presently be publicly posted. One constraint is that the minimum tick size precludes small improvements in quotes. But a second constraint is that under present rules, the posted quote would be available not just to the retail order, but to anyone who cared to trade against it. This would presumably include larger, nonretail, better-informed parties.

Another example of quotes that depend on the identity of the counterparty arises in the NASDAQ Selectnet system. This is a screen-based market in which NMS dealers can post quotes that are visible only to each other and not to the trading public. The Selectnet quotes are generally reputed to be better than those posted for dissemination to the general public. It was argued that Madoff was able to present lower effective spreads for detail orders because of the presumed lower information content of these orders. It is more difficult to make this argument for a market like Selectnet in which professionals are trading against professionals. Perhaps for this reason, Selectnet has been criticized as a device for exploiting market power. In practice, it is difficult to distinguish this from price discrimination that has a competitive justification.

The foregoing illustrates how the nature of the quotes has evolved from a uniform marketwide price to a range of counterparty-specific available prices. I now return to the central question of transparency. That is, should markets be required to freely disseminate their quotes, even with the qualification that these quotes may not be available to all traders?

The general rule that disclosure imposes a cost on the producers of the information holds forcefully in the case of quote transparency. Whereas transaction price disclosure might impose costs on the buyer and seller, they can at least be presumed to have benefited from the trade. The transaction has been completed, and both parties were satisfied with the terms (at the time, at least). In contrast, a bid or offer is an advertisement, a solicitation of a potential trading power. An information cost incurred by the trader who posts the quote will be covered only in the event that the solicitation is successful and the trader actually finds a counterparty. The possibility that the quoting trader may not realize a beneficial outcome from the activity suggests that the case for requiring quote transparency is likely to be weaker than that for trade transparency. It also suggest that consensus in the trading community on the extent of quote transparency is likely to be more elusive.

Like trade transparency, quote transparency is unusual in most markets for goods and services. The distinction between an advertised or posted price (published quote) and the best available price is a common one in negotiated markets with unique goods such as used cars or real estate. In these markets, where it is the sellers who advertise, the posted prices are generally accepted as a starting point for negotiation. The sellers have some uncertainty about the value of the item, and they are seeking an indication from the market (the strength of response to the ad) that will help them judge this. A seller may try to convey that the posted price is the actual price ("asking $5,000 *firm*"). But this attempt at precommitment requires an accurate estimate of value and even then may not be completely credible. (Will the seller really walk away from a bid of $4,950?)

The information disclosure problem for the quote-setting vendor is exacerbated if the good is not unique. In this case, other sellers are offering an identical good and a publicized offer may only serve to assist them in setting their prices. A familiar example arises in the market for consumer electronics goods. It is common for stores to include in their ads the statement, "We will match (or beat) any advertised price." To the extent that this precommitment is accepted as credible, it will be impossible for a dealer to build market share by cutting posted prices. Under such circumstances, it is unlikely that a dealer's best price will be advertised. Instead, dealers attempt to establish reputations for low prices. Once in the store, a customer may encounter further price reductions ("unadvertised special," or "in-store only" prices).

Few goods in the economy are as homogeneous as stock shares, and few advertising vehicles are as rapid as the quote terminal. It is not, therefore, particularly surprising that the information disclosure problem for a quote-setter in an equity market is a particularly difficult one.

The preceding identified two situations in which quote disclosure was problematic, those characterized by negotiation and those where the quote-setter is open to price matching. In U.S. equities markets, a degree of negotiation has always occurred on the floor of a stock exchange, particularly when a broker is attempting to arrange for the purchase or sale of a large block. The negotiation process need not be transparent. On the NYSE, two brokers can exchange offers and counteroffers that are not considered quotes and are not disclosed to others. To actually consummate the transaction, however, a bid and offer must be established, and in this fashion the outcome of the negotiation is integrated into the instituted market procedure. Currently, the most important place of negotiation is probably the upstairs market, where terms of trade for large block orders are arranged. Quote transparency in this market is, and always has been, minimal. When a customer approaches an upstairs market maker with a proposed transaction, the market maker will contact only those whom he believes are likely potential counterparties. There is no public dissemination of a bid or offer. Instead, the quote is selectively disclosed in a sequential fashion to possible customers. While it is debatable whether fragmentation per se directly affects the negotiation process, the indirect effects are likely to be substantial.

These indirect effects of fragmentation arise chiefly from price matching. In a consolidated market, it is feasible to enforce time-priority rules which specify first-come, first-served at a particular price. With time priority, a seller who cuts her offering price may find this price matched by other sellers, but at least she will be first in line if any buyers arrive. In a fragmented market, a broker holding an order need not direct it to the market that displays the best quote. The order may be directed to a market with an inferior posted quote with the understanding that it will be executed at a price corresponding to the best posted quote. As in the consumer electronics example, a widespread policy of "we will match any advertised price" undercuts the incentive to display one's best price. In fact, a floor broker "working" an order on the floor of the NYSE must exercise considerable judgment in deciding the price and quantity that constitute his public bid or offer. It is obvious that it might not be in the customer's best interest for the best price and size of the order to be revealed. There is no justification, therefore, for an inflexible policy of mandatory disclosure for limit orders.

If fragmentation increases the likelihood of price matching, then we should expect quote transparency to decline. This may take the form of wider posted spreads as a consequence of potential quoters' refusal to post their best prices. It may also creep in via a gradual softening of the quotes. In this case, although the posted spread may remain narrow, the quantities posted for sale or purchase will decline to some nominal amount. Either way, the quotes will no longer be serving their present purpose as a public signal of the terms of a possible transaction. Instead, the quotes will serve to draw order flow to a market under conditions of price uncertainty, an uncertainty that will then be resolved by negotiation.

In summary, then, the future for market transparency in the United States appears mixed. While fragmentation will impose stresses on it, transaction transparency is likely to remain at a level close to what we currently enjoy. The incentives for avoiding trade reporting are largest for block-trade dealers, and these are adequately accommodated in the existing framework. Quote transparency, on the other hand, is already besieged and is likely to become more so. This decline should not be considered a perverse side-effect of fragmentation, however. It will reflect instead sensible economic behavior on the part of those competing in the market.

NOTES

1. As a matter of terminology, British commentators often draw a distinction between trade reporting and trade publication. A broker reports all trades to the London Stock Exchange. The exchange staff therefore have access to the trade record for purposes of regulation and monitoring. Trade publication refers to the public disclosure of the terms of trade, which is, as noted, less complete. Outside of the United Kingdom, trade reporting is generally used synonymously with trade publication.
2. Customers may not be indifferent to reporting practices if it affects the allocation of trading and commission income in their own accounting statements.

REFERENCES

Harris, L. E. (1992). "Consolidation, Fragmentation, and Regulation." University of Southern California working paper.

Hasbrouck, Joel. (1991). "Security Markets, Information, and Liquidity," *Finanz Market und Portfolio Management* (1990), vol. 4, no. 3. Reprinted in *Journal of Financial Practice and Education* (1991).

Hasbrouck, Joel, Deborah Sosebee, and George Sofianos. (1993). "Trades, Orders, Reports, and Quotes at the New York Stock Exchange." NYSE working paper.

Schwartz, Robert A. (1991). *Reshaping the Equity Markets: A Guide for the 1990s.* New York: HarperBusiness.

Shapiro, J. (1993). "Recent Competitive Developments in U.S. Equity Markets." NYSE working paper 93–02.

U.S. Securities and Exchange Commission. (1992). "U.S. Equity Market Structure Study." Release no. 34–30920.

CHAPTER 13

IN THE PUBLIC INTEREST? REASSESSING THE REGULATORY ROLE IN THE FINANCIAL MARKETS

Corinne M. Bronfman

INTRODUCTION

In contrast to the industry structure of the securities markets in 1975, the U.S. equity markets today include not only the primary and regional exchanges and the over-the-counter (OTC) market but also the third market (the trading of exchange-listed securities in the OTC market), proprietary trading systems for publicly held U.S. equities, the opportunity for nonintermediated trading in such securities, and trading in U.S. equity securities effected by U.S. broker/dealers on overseas markets. The U.S. Securities and Exchange Commission (SEC) has recognized that these alternatives raise questions about the regulatory environment in which the markets operate including the proper allocation of regulatory (including self-regulatory) responsibilities, whether there is a need for enhanced transparency and questions about best execution and market fragmentation. On July 14, 1992, the SEC published its "U.S. Equity Market Structure Study" (Market 2000) in the Federal Register, requesting public comment "with regard to the functioning and characteristics of the U.S. equity markets, as well as with respect to regulatory issues that arise from the structure of the marketplace." The SEC also suggested a need to determine "the proper role of the Commission in overseeing the continuing development of the equity markets," that is, whether more initiative or less governmental action is needed to alter, shape, or direct market forces.

An analogous reassessment of the regulatory role in the futures industry is also taking place. On August 8, 1993, the Commodity Futures Trading Commission (CFTC) published in the Federal Register a request for public comment on issues raised by petitions for exemptive relief from the Chicago Mercantile Exchange (CME) and the Chicago Board of Trade (CBOT). The Chicago exchanges have requested exemptions from the requirements of the Commodity Exchange Act (CEA) for certain exchange-traded futures and options contracts. As characterized by the CFTC, "The petitions of the Chicago exchanges contemplate a regime under which the exchanges would hold no federally enforceable self-regulatory responsibilities under the CEA or Commission regulations, with the requested exemptions premised primarily upon the nature of the participants in the relevant contracts." These requests for exemption were enabled by the Futures Trading Practices Act (FTPA) of 1992 which added new subsections (c) and (d) to section 4 of the CEA. New section 4(c)(1) authorizes the CFTC, by rule, regulation, or order, to exempt any agreement, contract or transaction, or class thereof, from the exchange-trading requirements of section 4(a) or any other requirement of the act (other than section 2(a)(1)(B) (which addresses questions of jurisdiction between the SEC and the CFTC). Specifically,

> In order to promote responsible economic or financial innovation and fair competition, the Commission, by rule, regulation, or order, after notice and opportunity for hearing, may (on its own initiative or on application of any person, including any board of trade designated as a contract market for transactions for future delivery in any commodity under section 5 of this act) exempt any agreement, contract, or transaction (or class thereof) that is otherwise subject to subsection (a) (including any person or class of persons offering, entering into, rendering advice or rendering other services with respect to, the agreement, contract, or transaction) either unconditionally or on stated terms of conditions or for stated periods and either retroactively or prospectively, or both, from any of the requirements of subsection (a), or from any other provision of this Act (except section 2(a)(1)(B)), if the Commission determines that the exemption would be consistent with the public interest.[1]

This exemptive authority implicitly requires that the CFTC reassess the appropriateness of its regulations and its oversight responsibilities for both regulated and unregulated markets. The authority is limited only by new section 4(c)(2), which provides that the Commission may not grant an exemption from the exchange-trading requirement of the act, unless, *inter alia,* the agreement, contract, or transaction being exempted will be entered into solely between "appropriate persons" as defined in new section 4(c)(3), subject to such limitations as may be deemed appropriate by the Commission, in the public interest.[2, 3]

The futures markets and securities market regulators are governed by very different statutes. For example, section 4 of the CEA and CFTC regulations require that transactions in commodity futures contracts and commodity option contracts, with narrowly defined exceptions, occur on or subject to the rules of contract markets designated by the CFTC. Section 4(a) of the act specifically provides, *inter alia,* that it is unlawful to enter into a commodity futures contract that is not made on or subject to the rules of a board of trade which has been designated by the Commission as a "contract market" for such commodity.[4] Thus, off-exchange negotiation of large institutional trades and the development of institutional trading systems are not allowed under the CEA.[5] And while the securities industry continues to argue points for and against New York Stock Exchange (NYSE) Rule 390, futures industry regulation continues to enforce centralized trading and to prohibit the off-exchange negotiation or execution of futures contracts. This statutory prohibition may have fueled the growth of the swap market. The concomitant legal uncertainty in which the swap market operated served as the impetus for the exemptive authority in the 1992 FTPA (the threat that these deals could not be rendered void by a ruling that they were illegal futures).

With their very different statutes, some of the thorniest issues on which the SEC must take some sort of a position (specifically, payment for order flow and issues concerning order exposure)[6] are not yet faced by the futures market regulators because of the strong regulatory prohibition of off-exchange trading. To some extent as well, the trading publics are different, with close to 97 percent of futures market volume representing institutional trades versus a far larger presence of retail traders in the securities markets. And yet, viewed more broadly, the SEC and the CFTC are confronting similar questions in assessing their regulatory roles: (1) competition, (2) equal regulation (the demand for a "level playing field") versus a reassessment of the level of regulation appropriate to different trading publics and/or different trading systems, and (3) the public interest. Rather than focusing on specific issues, this chapter reflects on these broader concerns.

THE PUBLIC INTEREST

Both the CEA, which describes the regulatory responsibilities of the CFTC, and the Security Exchange Act (SEA), which circumscribes the role of the SEC, stress the role of regulatory oversight as being in the "public interest." The CEA defines the "(n)ecessity for Regulation" in the futures industry (paragraph 1031, section 3) in terms of the *national* public interest.[7]

> Transactions in commodities involving the sale thereof for future delivery as commonly conducted on boards of trade and known as "futures" are affected with a *national public interest.*

In this context, the "public interest" is justified because

> the prices involved in such transactions are generally quoted and disseminated throughout the United States and in foreign countries as a basis for determining the prices to the producer and the consumer of commodities and the products and byproducts thereof and to facilitate the movements thereof in interstate commerce.... The Transactions and prices of commodities on such boards of trade are susceptible to excessive speculation and can be manipulated, controlled, cornered or squeezed to the detriment of the producer or the consumer and the persons handling commodities and the products and byproducts thereof in interstate commerce rendering regulation imperative for the protection of such commerce and the national public interest.

In the SEA and the Securities Act Amendments (SAA) of 1975, the term "public interest" is often linked with the phrase "for the protection of investors, and the maintenance of fair and orderly markets," as in section 11(a) dealing with the "Segregation and Limitation of Functions of Members, Brokers, and Dealers,"

> The Commission shall prescribe such rules and regulations as it deems necessary or appropriate *in the public interest or for the protection of investors....*

and in paragraph 1095 mandating the establishment of a National Market System.

> The Commission is directed, therefore having due regard for the *public interest, the protection of investors, and the maintenance of fair and orderly*

markets, to use its authority under this title to facilitate the establishment of a national market system for securities...

However, Congress also regarded the public interest as benefiting from a competitive environment. Thus, in section 249 of the Securities Acts Amendments of 1975, Congress sought to clarify the authority of the SEC "to take all necessary steps to bring such a national market system into existence.... The objective would be *to enhance competition* and to allow economic forces, interacting within a fair regulatory field, to arrive at appropriate variations in practices and services." Similarly, the "public interest," under section 4(c) of the CEA includes the "national public interest, as noted in the Act, the prevention of fraud and the preservation of the financial integrity of the markets, as well as *the promotion of responsible economic or financial innovation and fair competition.*"

One problem is that the goal of protection of investors and the goal of enabling competition are not entirely consistent. As the Ontario Securities Commission observed in its analysis of the issues surrounding Instinet Canada, Limited, a centralized market is a better structure for achieving price priority protection, secondary priority protection, the provision of public good type of service, regulatory oversight,[8] and fairness. And an industry structure that permits interdealer and intercenter competition is more successful in meeting the diverse needs of investors and traders. Arguably, intermarket competition should provide incentives for markets to develop rules or systems that guarantee that participants will not be exposed to trading abuses. Would greater competition among market centers reduce the necessity for regulatory oversight?

At the same time, there is concern that an increasingly fragmented order flow could reduce the accuracy of price discovery and market liquidity. Thus, although systems like POSIT, Instinet, and the Arizona Stock Exchange have attracted a relatively low percentage of total NYSE volume, the SEC must consider how it should react if one or another (or all collectively) were to capture a meaningful percentage of the order flow. Similarly, in the futures industry, the CFTC must consider the impact if every contract traded on the exchanges were redefined as a "professional market" with access limited to appropriate persons.

One argument that is often used to support the need for regulation is to ensure "fairness"; that is, for the regulatory authorities to serve as a referee among diverse interest groups. Underlying this role is a lack of belief that market forces will provide sufficient incentives for market centers to develop rules to guarantee the protection of investors or to enforce fairness. To some extent their doubts may be well founded in that the efficient solution may not be the same as the fair solution. This inconsistency underlies the debate surrounding the call for a "level playing field" considered in the next section.

IS A LEVEL PLAYING FIELD OPTIMAL?

Section 6(b)(1) of the 1934 Securities Exchange Act provides that the criteria for registration as a national securities exchange include a determination by the SEC that, among other things, an exchange has the organization and capacity to comply, and to enforce compliance by its members and persons associated therewith, with the provisions of the 1934 Act, the rules promulgated by the SEC under the 1934 Act, and the rules of the exchange. In addition, section 19(g)(1) of the Act requires that an exchange enforce compliance by its members and associated persons with such provisions.

The congressional legislation that created independent agencies to oversee the securities and the futures markets viewed the exchanges as quasi-governmental institutions. This role was stated explicitly for the securities markets in a report by the Committee on Banking, Housing, and Urban Affairs associated with the 1975 SAA:

> The Committee has found a common and serious misunderstanding of the nature and limits of the concept of self-regulation. ...self-regulation is thought to mean that the securities industry regulated itself and therefore is not regulated by the government. ...fails to recognize the essential and continuing role of the federal government. Industry regulation and governmental regulation are not alternatives, but complementary components of the self-regulatory process. ...The SEC is charged with supervising the exercise of this self-regulatory power. (p. 23)

This quasi-governmental role is crucial to the determination of the approach to the regulation of alternative trading systems; at what level of trading volume (or in the case of the futures industry, for what trading public) does the federal regulatory role become operational?

Proprietary Trading Systems

In a series of no-action letters, the SEC has permitted a number of proprietary trading systems (PTS) to operate without the self-regulatory responsibilities of the exchanges (by regarding them as broker/dealers or by granting a low-volume exemption). In discussing proposed Rule 15c2–10,[9] the Commission took the position that regulation of these systems as an exchange was not appropriate as (1) they operated on a for-profit basis, (2) no "exchange-type market participants, such market makers or floor brokers, were involved, (3) customers furnished all quotes and orders themselves, (4) the PTS are distinguishable in function from exchange markets in that their capacity to execute automatically is based on derivative pricing, and (5) although the opportunity to advertise buy or sell interest is provided, the systems have not evolved into interdealer quotation or transaction mechanisms in which participants enter two-sided quotations on a regular or continuous basis, thus ensuring a liquid market.

Proposed Rule 15c2–10 that defines an approach to the regulation of these systems states that some form of oversight is necessary as trading volume increases. Additionally, with the potential for these systems to operate internationally, the rule making is necessary to fulfill the terms of memoranda of understanding (MOU) with other regulatory authorities (such as MOU that agree that surveillance information can be obtained). Another justification for the proposed rule making is the presumption that at some level of trading volume it becomes appropriate for public investors to have notice and opportunity to comment on the systems themselves and changes to them.[10]

Application of the Exemptive Authority

The different regulatory status of PTS is in many ways analogous to the differences between exchanges and contract markets regulated by the CFTC under the CEA, and those markets which have been exempted from CFTC oversight. In the futures industry, the exemptive authority has thus far been applied in three instances: swaps, hybrids, and the energy market. In the cases of swaps and the energy market, the exemptions relied to a large extent on the status and resources of the participants, that is, that the participants were all "appropriate persons" as defined in the FTPA of 1992. The CBOT's request for exemption for regulation under the CEA is for a "Professional Trading Market" where the instrument will be offered or traded by only professional traders (not public customers except those with at least $10 million in assets).[11] The petition suggests that any instrument "that may otherwise be subject to regulation under the Act" could be offered through its professional trading market. The exemption "would afford OTC market users the price transparency, legal certainty, and reduced credit risk of exchange markets, *without the burden of general federal regulation.*" The exemption sought by the CME would encompass the rolling spot currency contracts in which the CME was designated by the Commission as a contract market on April 6 and on May 19, 1993. According to the exchange, "the contracts closely mirror common cash market instruments now traded in the over-the-counter market, provide many economic advantages over these instruments and, *if allowed to operate with regulatory parity,* would provide considerable benefits in terms of costs, price transparency, and counterparty credit exposure." The CME proposes to restrict trading in these instruments to appropriate persons to conform with the conditions under which the exemptive authority can be applied.

In its request for comment on the exemptions proposed by the Chicago exchanges, the CFTC asks whether its regulatory interest is diminished by the exclusion of small traders from the market. Although this premise is consistent with the exemptive authority's limitation to "appropriate persons," the Commission has requested comment on whether the fact that the petitions seek to exempt markets for which designation as a contract market has been sought and obtained requires a different analysis than that previously applied to exempt hybrids, swaps, and energy products which relied on the statement in the Conference report to the 1992 Act that the goal of ... the exemptive powers was "to give the Commission means of providing certainty and stability to existing and emerging markets so that financial innovation and market development can proceed in an effective and competitive manner." Do the underlying facts and circumstances of these exchange petitions support exemptive relief similar to that granted the swaps, hybrids, and energy contracts?

Both applications would have the Commission retain antifraud and antimanipulation authority. The Commission's ability to enforce these proscriptions is, however, in part dependent on reporting requirements. In particular, the large trader reporting system is the Commission's primary tool for monitoring market concentrations and the potential for corners, squeezes, and other forms of manipulation. If the Commission were to retain antifraud and antimanipulation authority, should reporting requirements continue to apply? Accurate books and records and reports of transactions and account equity not only enhance the Commission's ability to detect and prosecute fraud, but also enable customers to monitor the performance of their accounts and seek legal redress if necessary. In the FTPA of 1992, Congress emphasized the need for a reliable and detailed audit trail. Can the Commission grant an exemption from audit trail requirements? How would the Commission detect and prove wrongful conduct?

Efficiency as a Standard

Must competition emerge only from off-exchange trading? Is it only possible to lower the level of regulation for alternative trading systems and not on the established exchanges? In fact, from this author's experience at the CFTC, undoing an established rule is difficult. A recent example is the ongoing effort to modify CFTC Rule 1.35, which specifies, among other things, that each order sent by a futures commission merchant (FCM) to the floor must include the customer's account identification number.[12] These record-keeping requirements permit a customer's order to be traced at each stage of order processing and help to prevent the improper allocation of trades and other abuses. This requirement posed difficulties for institutional money managers trading in multiple markets or using certain trading strategies. The CME proposed modifying this requirement under certain circumstances for institutional accounts managed by Investment Advisers (IA) registered with the SEC. Under the modified rule, an IA could wait until late in the trading day to assign the account number *if the customer granted permission in advance.*

By allowing IAs to wait until close to the end of the day to designate which trade is for which customer, they can execute intermarket strategies more effectively (particularly because post-trade allocation of trades has been allowable in the securities industry for a number of years). By applying this modified rule only to accounts for institutional customers who agreed to it in advance, the fraud problem seems to be taken care of. Institutional customers should be able to monitor for fraud themselves, and if they do not think they can, they will not grant permission. In short, the proposal to modify Rule 1.35 appears to provide an opportunity for regulatory relief without jeopardizing customers. When the proposal was published for comment in the Federal Register, several commentators objected,[13] and attempts to satisfy these critics produced a rule that was virtually useless from the perspective of the industry.

It would seem appropriate for both on- and off-exchange markets that the level of regulation be guided by efficiency considerations rather than by fairness or public interest criteria that are more subjective. Albrecht, Bronfman, and Messenheimer (1993) define efficient regulation as the set of rules that fulfill the agency's mandate without imposing excessive costs. This is illustrated in Figure 13–1, which describes the impact of fraud on the demand for transaction services and, thus, the volume of trade.[14]

Customers' valuation of prospective fraud is modeled as a per-unit tax (T_f) on the price paid for transaction services, Q. Thus, the costs of fraud and benefits of regulation are both captured through the price mechanism. The total price paid by demanders of transaction services offered in the market is $P + T_f$. Whatever the particular source of prospective fraud, demanders pay more than the price officially posted in the markets by suppliers (P). This serves to shift the demand curve faced by suppliers from D to $D - T_f$. Instead of the honest amount of equilibrium transactions services Q_e, the lower volume level Q_f obtains in the presence of fraud.[15]

Regulation can reduce the probability of fraud and thus increase participation, but it also increases the costs of providing transaction services. For example, regulators may prescribe record-keeping rules that increase the probability of detecting fraud but at the same time increase the cost of providing immediacy. In Figure 13–1, regulation reduces the prospective valuation of fraud to T_t, but also increases the unit cost of providing Q by T_c. T_c is a per-unit taxlike cost imposed on suppliers. Since T_c is less than ($T_f - T_r$), Q will increase and consumer surplus will increase to the triangle $a(P + T_r)b_r$. The efficient level of regulation will differ depending on the shape of the demand and supply curves, that is, the structure of the market being regulated and the principal players. The point at which costs increase more rapidly than benefits will, therefore, not occur at the same point in all markets.

This difference in the cost benefit structures among market centers and trading publics suggests that arguments to "level the playing field" across different markets (by making the regulatory approach and magnitude consistent) are not arguments for efficiency.[16] The real issue is not that of "equal" regulation but that of "appropriate" regulation. Thus, if a system succeeds in lowering the regulatory burden through a trading technology that is less open to abuse, it will be more competitive. Similarly, if the system is restricted to a trading public that needs a lower level of regulatory oversight, the greater involvement of the regulators that is necessary for other trading publics should not be mandatory.[17]

FIGURE 13–1
The Impact of Fraud on the Demand for Transaction Services

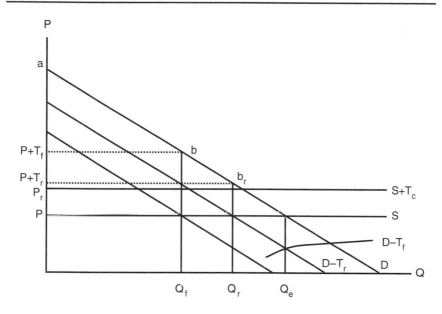

CONCLUSION

While the stated goals of regulation are hard to fault, its gross effects are often unpredictable and counter to the original intent (the law of unintended effects). For example, to fulfill the 1975 SAA, the SEC sought by various rulings to link all markets for qualified securities through communication and data processing facilities in order to "foster efficiency (and) enhance competition." Even the most cursory reading of many of the comment letters submitted to the SEC's Equity Market Structure Study shows that they exhibit almost complete unanimity in expressing the view that quote competition has not been achieved (including letters submitted by the U.S. exchanges, the NASD, institutional traders, Steve Wunsch, and academics who addressed the issue). Instead, the result has been "quote matching" where all systems guarantee to "match" the best price of any competitive market center.

Moreover, past regulatory rulings can also serve to perpetuate the status quo or to set up barriers for entry. A recent example is from the NYSE's comment letter to the SEC's Equity Market Structure Study.

The exchange came out in favor of maintaining the current level of transparency in the U.S. markets but was resistant to the integration of off-exchange trading systems into the disclosure facilities (the consolidated tape and the consolidated quote-reporting systems). "Unless the Commission subjects off-exchange systems and exchanges to the same substantive regulation, off-exchange systems should not have direct access to any NMS facility, including quotation and trade-reporting facilities." This attempt at exclusion is hardly benign, particularly when viewed in the light of NYSE Rule 410B. This rule seeks to reduce the incentives for member firms to route orders to the London market after the NYSE market close by requiring that any trades through NYSE members be reported on the consolidated tape, including any trades in foreign markets. Coupled with the NYSE position on transparency, this requirement has the effect of making it impossible for NYSE members to use the Arizona Stock Exchange because this nonintermediated market center with its once-a-day single price auction at 5 p.m. New York time would, thus, not be authorized to report its trades on the consolidated tape.[18] In a similar spirit, the CBOT proposed that transactions in any "professional market" must be cleared through a Commission-approved mutualized-risk clearing system which would give the established exchanges a good head start over any potential entrant.

As noted in the introduction, the statutes governing the oversight roles of the securities and futures markets regulators differ in important respects. Off-exchange trading of futures contracts is strictly prohibited under the CEA, whereas the development of alternative trading systems has been encouraged by SEC rulings consistent with the 1975 SAA. And yet, in 1993, both the SEC and the CFTC are facing similar questions. The CFTC has exempted the swap market from regulation under the CEA. In the securities markets, the SEC has exempted proprietary trading systems from the self-regulatory responsibilities of the established exchanges. The development of alternatives to centralized trading on the exchanges can be expected to continue. While academics and regulators are convinced of the benefits of centralized trading, the industry is increasingly moving away from standardized instruments towards unique customized contracts. A few things are clear from recent history:

1. The regulatory statute and its interpretation are important determinants of the ways the industry develops and the forms of competi-

tion. Markets generally find ways to approximate their desired evolution (often in spite of the statute). This does not mean, however, that the statute is benign. The costs of achieving a market solution may be higher than they would be otherwise (for example, the legal uncertainty under which the swap market operated until the exemptive authority was applied to these transactions retroactively and proscriptively in 1992).

2. The inevitability of unintended effects cannot be ignored. The exclusivity clause in the Commodity Exchange Act, for example, was intended to eliminate jurisdictional conflicts between the CFTC and the SEC; however, it was used by the futures exchanges to block competition from the securities industry. As discussed in note 18, the Chicago Futures exchanges were able to block the introduction of index participations by claiming that index partici- pations were futures and should be regulated by the CFTC, based on the "exclusivity clause" giving the CFTC exclusive jurisdiction over futures. And, as noted by Brandon Becker, director of the SEC's Division of Market Regulation, the comment letters received by the Commission had one repetitive theme, "What I'm doing is good and needs less regulation—what my competitor is doing is bad and needs more regulation."

Both the SEC and the CFTC have acknowledged the complexity of the issues they face in assessing their regulatory roles. This chapter has considered two issues in particular: (1) the definition of what is in the "public interest," and (2) the demand for a "level playing field." As the number of alternatives to the established exchanges increases, "letting the market decide" its preferred level of regulation and preferred trading environment should lead to an efficient solution to the practical and philosophical problems faced by the regulatory authorities. As noted by Brandon Becker, "(w)e recognize that regulation inevitably sets the ground rules, and that it is important that those rules be consistent with new market realities." The identification of these new realities underlies the efforts of both regulatory agencies.

NOTES

1. In this regard, the joint House–Senate Conference Report on the 1992 Act states that the "public interest" under section 4(c) includes the "national public interest noted in

the Act, the prevention of fraud and the preservation of the financial integrity of the markets, as well as the promotion of responsible economic or financial innovation and fair competition."

2. Section 4(c)(3) limits the class of "appropriate persons" to (A) a bank or trust company acting in an individual or fiduciary capacity; (B) a savings association; (C) an insurance company; (D) an investment company subject to regulation under the Investment Company Act of 1940; (E) a commodity pool formed or operated by a person subject to regulation under the CEA; (F) a corporation, partnership, proprietorship, organization, trust, or other business entity with a net worth exceeding $1,000,000 or total assets exceeding $5,000,000, or the obligations of which under the agreement, contract, or transaction are guaranteed or otherwise supported by a letter of credit, keepwell, support, or other agreement by any such entity or by an entity referred to in subparagraphs (A), (B), (C), (H), (I), or (K); (G) an employee benefit plan with assets exceeding $1,000,000 or whose investment decisions are made by a bank, trust company, insurance company, investment adviser registered under the Investment Advisers Act of 1940, or a commodity trading advisor subject to regulation under the CEA; (H) any government entity … or political subdivision thereof, or any multinational or supranational entity or any instrumentality, agency, or department of any of the foregoing; (I) a broker/dealer subject to regulation under the Securities Exchange Act of 1934 acting on its own behalf or on behalf of another appropriate person; (J) a futures commission merchant, floor broker, or floor trader subject to regulation under the CEA acting on its own behalf or on behalf of another appropriate person; (K) such other persons that the Commission determines to be appropriate in light of their financial or other qualifications, or the applicability of other appropriate regulatory protection.

3. In granting an exemption, the Commission must also determine that the agreement, contract, or transaction in question will not have a material adverse effect of the ability of the Commission or any contract market to discharge its regulatory or self-regulatory duties under the Act and that the exemption would be consistent with the public interest and the purposes of the Act.

4. This prohibition does not apply to futures contracts made on or subject to the rules of a foreign board of trade, exchange, or market. 7 U.S.C. 6(a).

5. Attempts to develop large order execution procedures consistent with the open and competitive requirements of the CEA have not succeeded. The most long-standing is LOX developed by the CME for the trading of the S&P 500 futures contract. It has done zero volume since its approval in 1991.

6. Payment arrangements typically involve market makers or exchange specialists compensating brokerage firms for directing customer orders to them. The issue of order exposure refers to the extent to which competing markets and dealers interact with each other (for example, the extent to which orders are internalized by dealers or exposed so that other market centers can compete).

7. The term "public interest" gained prominence in 19th century Supreme Court decisions that addressed the issue in the context of rulings that delineated bounds for regulation. Munn vs. Illinois (1877) was a landmark decision which set limits on property rights when the public interest was involved. At the time, virtually all of midwestern grain flowed through Chicago, the "gateway of commerce." Nine firms

owned all of Chicago's grain elevators and met periodically to fix storage rates. In 1871, the Illinois legislature passed a law fixing the rates the firms could charge. Munn and Scott, owners of one of the firms, ignored the law and were sued for failing to comply. Upholding the State of Illinois, Chief Justice Waite argued "…we find that when private property is affected with a public interest, it ceases to be juris private only…. Property does become clothed with a public interest when used in a manner to make it of public consequence, and affect the community at large. When, therefore, one devotes his property to a use in which the public has an interest, he, in effect, grants to the public an interest in that use, and must submit to be controlled by the public for the common good." See Zajac (1985).

8. For example, futures market regulation requires monitoring the positions of large traders. When the SEC proposed to institute a similar "Large Trader Reporting System," the securities industry pointed out, in a large number of comment letters, that because of the large number of possible execution facilities, it was virtually impossible for any broker to know the actual holdings of their clients. See comment letters in file number S7–24–91.

9. SEC File No. S7–13–89, Federal Register Vol. 54, No. 73, April 18, 1989. As reported in the *Securities Regulation and Law Report* 2/18/94, on February 14, 1994, the SEC withdrew its 1989 proposed rule 15c2-10 citing lapses of time, "subsequent developments," and the issuance of a recent rule proposal. Proposed rule 17a-23 calls for enhanced record keeping and reporting by sponsors of proprietary trading systems and other automated trading mechanisms.

10. The opportunity for public comment should perhaps be reduced for rule making by the established exchanges, at the same time that it is extended to cover some aspects of the alternative trading systems. In a June 1, 1994 meeting, the SEC proposed amendments to rule 19b–4 of the '34 Act and form 19b–4, governing the filing and review of proposed rule changed to SROs: (1) Filings of routine changes to order-entry or trading systems and other rule filings that do not significantly affect investor protection or impose significant burdens on competition would be able to become effective upon filing with the SEC; (2) Proposed reductions in certain annual filing requirements of SROs. The rule amendments would reduce or eliminate the annual filing requirement for certain information that is readily available through certain other means or is not useful enough to justify the burden the SROs to collect and file it annually.

11. Under the proposal, individuals who do not meet the net worth requirement would be able to participate indirectly in an exempt professional trading market through an interest in a commodity pool or other collective investment vehicle or through a discretionary trading system.

12. FCM's perform similar functions to brokers and the brokerage houses in the securities markets; they accept orders to trade futures on behalf of another party and accept funds to support the order (margin). They must be registered with the CFTC and must meet minimum financial standards.

13. See, for example, letter from George Painter, July 1, 1992. Concerns were also expressed by Congressmen John Dingell, Chairman of the House Committee on Energy and Commerce, and Edward Markey, Chairman of the House Subcommittee on Telecommunications and Finance, in a letter to the SEC and the CFTC, July 14, 1993.

14. The authors simplify the concerns of regulators by focusing on this single aspect of regulatory concern: fraud. More generally, financial market regulation addresses the issues of market integrity (efficiency and the level of systematic risk), financial integrity (margining, segregation of customer funds), and customer protection. The model can easily be extended to these other areas of regulatory concern.

15. The horizontal supply assumes that the exchange is operating at the appropriate scale for any realized fluctuations in the level of trading volume, that the average compensation received by liquidity providers is determined in a perfectly competitive environment resulting in zero economic profits, and that they are able to provide liquidity without hitting up against capacity constraints. Over very brief periods of time (intraday), the supply curve will be upward sloping. That is, a large order can only be filled after paying a premium (or selling at a discount). Over longer periods of time (year), the supply curve may be downward sloping; that is, the cost (and, thus, the price) of transacting is decreasing with trading volume. See chapter 8 in Schwartz (1991) for discussion and further references.

16. Stephen Schaefer (1992) reaches a similar conclusion in his analysis of capital requirements and arguments in support of "functional" regulation to ensure that banks and securities firms are regulated equally. He demonstrates that there may well be valid reasons for higher capital requirements on banks.

17. The fragmentation that results is another cost borne by the markets; presumably, the markets will determine the amount of fragmentation that trades off differential regulatory burdens for the increased cost of fragmentation.

18. The NYSE is, in no way, unique in its attempts to use regulation to serve to restrict competition. Another quite recent example (March 1989) was the introduction of Index Participations (IPs), financial instruments priced off an index of stocks, on the Philadelphia Stock Exchange, the American Stock Exchange, and the Chicago Board Options Exchange. In this instance, the Chicago Futures exchanges were able to block the innovation by claiming that IPs were futures and should be regulated by the CFTC, based on the "exclusivity clause" in the Commodity Exchange Act (which gave the CFTC exclusive jurisdiction over futures). The IPs stopped trading in September 1989. The new CFTC reauthorization legislation empowers the Commission to exempt hybrid products from its regulation. *Investment Dealers' Digest* (January 11, 1993) reports that the Philadelphia Stock Exchange is considering reviving IPs ("Index Participations May Rise from the New Product Graveyard," Hal Lux).

REFERENCES

Albrecht, William, Corinne Bronfman, and Harold Messenheimer. (1995). "Regulatory Regimes: The Interdependence of Rules and Regulatory Structure," in Andrew Lo (ed.), *The Industrial Organization and Regulation of the Securities Industry*. Chicago: University of Chicago Press.

Bronfman, Corinne. (1993). "If It Ain't Broke, Don't Regulate It," in Kenneth Lehn and Robert Kamphuis (eds.), *Modernizing U.S. Securities Regulation: Economic and Legal Perspectives*. Burr Ridge, IL: Business One Irwin.

Commodity Exchange Act of September 21, 1922, as amended by Act of October 23, 1974, September 30, 1978, January 11, 1983, and November 10, 1986.

Demsetz, Harold. (1991). "100 Years of Antitrust: Should We Celebrate?" Brent T. Upson Memorial Lecture, George Mason University School of Law, Law and Economics Center.

Lee, Reuben. (1992). "What Is an Exchange? A Discussion Paper." Capital Markets Forum, International Bar Association, London.

Schaefer, Stephen M. (1992). "Financial Regulation: The Contribution of the Theory of Finance," in John Fingleton (ed.), *The Internationalisation of Capital Markets and the Regulatory Response*. London: Graham & Trotman (Kluwer Academic Publishers, Boston).

Schwartz, Robert A. (1991). *Reshaping the Equity Market: A Guide for the 1990s*. New York: HarperBusiness. Reprinted Homewood, IL: Business One, Irwin (1993).

Securities Exchange Act and the Securities Acts Amendments.

Spulber, Daniel F. (1989). *Regulation and Markets*. The MIT Press.

U.S. Securities and Exchange Commission. (1992). Equity Market Structure Study, Release No. 34–30920, file no. S7–18–92.

Zajac, Edward. (1985). "Perceived Economic Justice: The Example of Public Utility Regulation," in H. Peyton Young (ed.), *Cost Allocation: Methods, Principles, Applications*. Elsevier Science Publishers.

CHAPTER 14

MARKET 2000: THE USER'S PERSPECTIVE

Harold S. Bradley

Investors Research Corporation (IRC), the investment manager for the Twentieth Century family of mutual funds, welcomes the opportunity to present views on how technology, competition, and regulation are reshaping the face of global equities trading. As a decidedly active, "growth stock" oriented, and nonquantitative money manager, IRC strongly advocates and utilizes many nontraditional trading systems which are under review by the SEC as part of its Market 2000 study.

Market 2000 addresses issues of philosophy and practice about which many market participants are deeply divided. The Congressional mandate of 18 years ago to move toward a National Market System has provoked a slow and painful process as many traditional service providers fight stubbornly to preserve practices that make markets less transparent, more inefficient and consequently more profitable for the middlemen. Such practices directly contribute to higher expenses for all investors, large and small.

The SEC's consideration of contentious issues such as market fragmentation, payment for order flow, soft dollar disclosure, NYSE Rule 390 and others show an agency beset with technology's abrupt and uncompromising intrusion into the once "clubby" atmosphere of exchange-centered markets. Technology compels the evolution of "exchanges" with specific physical locations, where all transactions require intermediation, to a "concept" of a central order-driven marketplace where buyers and sellers discover price efficiently and anonymously. We urge the SEC to affirm the "competitive correctness" of Private Trading Systems which, for the first time, afford investors instant access to a low-cost, highly *transparent* marketplace.

Recent changes by the major self-regulatory organizations at the NYSE, NASDAQ, and the London Stock Exchange suggest that the conventional exchange marketplace no longer supports a centralized price discovery function. In an effort to stem the flow of business to regional and offshore exchanges and automated systems, the NYSE has further eroded the central price discovery feature of the auction market and capitulated to a dealer community which demands still lower standards of transparency. New NYSE rules which allow straight customer-to-customer crosses of 25,000 shares or more without allowing stock on the specialist's book to participate—even though public orders on the book may have predated the "clean cross" by hours, days, or weeks—suggest that few investors have a compelling interest to display orders with the specialist. Furthermore, the recent practice of "flipping" in stocks by exchange floor brokers and specialists who are allowed to execute small orders in equal participation with large limit orders only then to "flip" the stock for ⅛ or ¼ reflects the desirability of a central limit order book where time and price of an order take precedence. Under current market structure, an investor assumes great risk in displaying either the quantity or price where he is willing to trade. Other investors are rewarded with this essential economic information which can then be used to consummate trades "upstairs."

Price discovery does not happen in a vacuum. At least one party in the process must indicate a price and quantity where stock can trade. Taking that "risk of price discovery" attracts contra-indications. Any system penalizing those willing to display a trading interest jeopardizes any process of real price discovery where the investor taking economic risk must have reasonable hope of economic reward.

NASDAQ has also moved to sharply constrict market transparency in its introduction of SelectNet, a private order-driven market modeled after the Inter-dealer Market (IDB) system in London. SelectNet offers a fee-based transaction system to registered market makers in NASDAQ stocks. This essentially agent-auction structure allows dealers to post orders at prices better than the "quoted" public market and restricts the availability of these "better than retail" prices to market makers only.

SelectNet has no place in a market where centralized price discovery is a goal. *If NASDAQ quotes represent the best public prices as the marketing literature indicates, then the ability to trade continually at prices "inside" the best quoted markets would be arbitraged away. The mere existence of a broker-only screen on SelectNet to post orders at prices "better" than the best public NASDAQ bids and offers makes a sham of the price discovery process in the public market.*

Much has been written about the economic processes that have led to wider public spreads in NASDAQ. One need only to examine a move to "private," nonpublic markets like SelectNet, London's IDB, and Germany's IBIS to understand that dealers have virtually no economic incentive to quote stocks in narrower spreads.

Established exchanges often fail to provide an efficient mechanism for buyers and sellers to meet anonymously and to negotiate price. The discovery process occurs only when the "advertiser" of a trading interest can be meaningfully rewarded for so doing. Open systems like the Arizona Stock Exchange (AZX), which establishes a "clearing" price through a call auction mechanism, and Instinet, which offers nonintermediated, continuous electronic trading, reward the providers of liquidity to the system with best prices and true markets.

At the very least, NASDAQ and the NYSE should have the foresight to supplement traditional continuous markets with a call market feature which allows investors nonintermediated, anonymous, computer-governed access to both open and close markets and, in the case of NASDAQ, to establish single opening and closing prices.

Transparency implies far more than a timely report of a trade to the tape. Transparency implies markets with unrestricted access, clear views of indications from buyers and sellers, and a central limit order book preference where aggressive pricing and time of order entry may be rewarded. Arcane trading rules now govern traditional central markets allowing investors to place "participate" market orders. No active decision making or price discovery takes place in the practice—participate orders free-ride on the passivity or aggressiveness of other investors. *An investor given this luxury deters other investors from "price setting" and chases them to alternative markets.*

An SEI Corporation evaluation of Twentieth Century funds trading costs shows that nontraditional systems have helped shareholders achieve low-cost access to true liquidity in both thinly capitalized, difficult to trade stocks and in the most highly capitalized household names.

The compilation and analysis of data related to trading costs defies simplistic approaches. the methodology used to compute such costs may fail to account for elusive opportunity costs attributed to "missed" trades, may allow a trader to "game" various standards (that is, volume weighted average price schemes), and may be so confusing as to render such analysis meaningless. However, SEI's methodology does allow for meaningful relative comparison of each broker's trading costs.

In Table 14–1, data from six-month trading periods from June 30, 1990, to December 31, 1992, are presented in the aggregate for all Twentieth Century funds. The table displays the simple mean of all dollars traded, average market capitalization, average volatility, and total trading costs as a percent of principal for both listed and NASDAQ stocks. The relative efficiency of all Private Trading Systems measured during this time significantly reduced the house average cost of trading.

The relatively high average market capitalization and lower volatility for trades executed on Instinet's Crossing Network and on the Arizona Stock Exchange would suggest that the contraparty may be index funds or other "large cap" passive or patient managers.

Stocks traded on the continuous electronic Instinet system, in stark contrast, exhibited much lower average market capitalization and much higher volatility than the IRC average. The average market capitalization of $4.25 billion for stocks traded on Instinet was less than half the $9.75 billion average capitalization for the house. Average trailing 90-day volatility of 45 percent for stocks traded on Instinet far exceeds the average 32 percent volatility for the complex and the 22 percent volatility which SEI pegs as the median for about 30 large managers in its database. *Low capitalization and high volatility would lead most financial theorists to expect that the intrinsic difficulty of the trades would carry high relative and absolute trading costs. Quite the opposite occurred.* Structural efficiencies of the Instinet system produced trading costs in NASDAQ securities equal to the house average cost for unlisted stocks and 13 percent to 39 percent lower than the firm's largest traditional NASDAQ market makers. Trading in listed stocks was 95 basis points cheaper on average than with traditional agents.

Alternative market systems are not spawned in response to structure that is either effective or efficient. Advances in technology have allowed economic theories on stock pricing to be tested. New methods for trading stocks have met the demand of new technology-intensive methods for selecting stocks and structuring portfolios. Quantitative firms have a

TABLE 14–1
SEI Corporation Study of Twentieth Century Trading Costs—
Six-Month Average Costs, June 30, 1990–December 31, 1992,
Impact of Commissions, and Market Impact (Nondollar
Weighted Mean of All Periods)

	Dollars Traded	*Average Market Cap*	*Average Vola-tility*	*Costs as % of Principal*	
				NASDAQ	*Listed*
TCI Funds Average	8,038,596,667	9.93	32	1.14	1.05
Broker #1	1,279,205,000	10.11	33	1.53	0.77
Broker #2	1,155,961,667	6.04	33	1.27	1.70
Broker #3	1,045,758,333	7.61	31	0.47	1.40
Broker #4	892,138,333	18.75	27	na	0.69
Instinet	746,441,667	4.63	44	1.14	0.10
Crossing Network	306,016,667	11.34	30	0.09	0.43
AZX	216,480,000	11.35	28	0.27	0.10
SEI Median for Industry			22%		

more "passive" interest in patiently buying and selling stocks that fit parameters and are easily substitutable. Index funds are challenged to maintain tight control over transaction costs as they attempt to emulate precisely the movements of various stock indexes. The convenience of single point pricing on either the AZX (which promotes price discovery and allows price improvement) and on Instinet's Crossing Network (at last-sale of the primary exchange) attracts many such investors.

As an active investor seeking liquidity in all venues, there have been no impediments to participation in such nontraditional structures. In fact, such systems derive strength from the nonintermediated access to investors that forums like the NYSE after-hours crossing session fail to deliver.

IRC's experience with Private Trading Systems indicates such systems offer: total anonymity, control over proprietary economic information as to one's trading style and intentions, assurances of the financial integrity of contra-parties, savings to shareholders in the form of lower commissions and sharply reduced market impact, almost instant electronic verification of trades, an impeccable audit trail, and true liquidity through enhanced standards of transparency.

Many large institutional investors subscribe to the view that access to a broker's capital for an "instant" trade is synonymous with "trading liquidity." The demand for immediacy grows because the communication of an investor's trading intentions are transmitted instantaneously to a host of intermediaries and potential adversaries in an inefficient market that serves often as an information sieve. A single phone call alerts literally dozens of individuals, including brokers with hundreds of accounts (where an indiscreet call to an investor with similar trading desires may prompt calls to still other brokers in the pursuit of still more "instant" liquidity), hedge funds, and other traders with short time horizons. This process quickly and dramatically raises the cost of doing business for the initiator of a transaction—pricing reflects innumerable opportunistic and conflicting interests. Markets with hundreds of broker/dealers, hundreds of institutional accounts and the attendant strong economic penalties attached to the disclosure of trading intentions by virtually any party means that the efficient meeting of buyers and sellers occurs with alarming infrequency in the marketplace.

Barriers to market competition and access arise from those whose traditional control of market structure is threatened. The NYSE has sacrificed many of the auction market's primary tenets to preserve market share over the short term and to avoid painful meaningful change. NASDAQ has introduced a "silent" private dealer market that excludes institutions and retail investors from its domain.

The London Stock Exchange does not compel reporting of trades to the tape for up to five days and the lack of transparency on most European bourses makes the United States appear as the standard bearer of efficient and open systems. Broker/dealers work both in the United States and abroad to internalize order flow and to preserve inefficiencies they may profitably exploit with effective principal market making.

One must examine seriously whether the concept of an exchange must be dramatically broadened beyond the scope of a single location or collection of dealers. There must be economic incentive and reward for dealers and customers to meet and trade in a centralized location—be it on computer or The Street. If the SEC supports the idea of a central limit order book, more efficient systems and continuing competition will ensue. However, the Commission cannot mandate what the most efficient structure will be—the market's investors will experiment and explore and ultimately determine the structure that provides the highest standard of shareholder protection and liquidity at the most affordable cost.

The birth of a new market structure may well be based on cooperative market making similar to the economic cooperatives forged in agricultural America. In agricultural coops, members receive direct economic inducement to do business because "excess" profits are repatriated to the members. In much the same way, evolution to a true National Market System will necessitate the promise of economic reward to potential members of any nontraditional marketplace.

All current Private Trading Systems are transaction fee based—demonstrating that investors will pay a fair premium for efficient access to markets. A new "cooperative exchange" could be comprised of members whose transaction charges fund regulatory overview and system development and whose profits are repatriated to members, thereby attracting and maintaining the widest constituent base. Firms which engage in investment banking or active individual company research could be compensated for the value of their work through a system of check-offs.

Traditional distinctions between money managers and broker/dealers have blurred in recent years, and the time may be right to redefine practices and responsibilities in the marketplace. Technology and broker "disintermediation" are companion terms. High profile traditional and nontraditional Wall Street firms such as Instinet, AZX, Jefferies, Fidelity, Morgan Stanley, First Boston, and others spend millions of dollars to develop more efficient internal order matching and processing mechanisms. One must conclude that institutional costs of doing business will decrease. Broker/dealers competing for "cheap" quantitative investor business and other passive commission flow will be faced with demands from active managers for lower commissions with no accompanying decrease in service expectations. Broker/dealers adapting technology to compete will likely cannibalize higher margin business which traditionally pays the bills.

As a result, expect to see more strategic alliances emerge like that between Bridge, AZX, and the Investment Technology Group. Do not be surprised to see Steve Wunsch and Instinet as major business partners in the developing trading infrastructure of emerging markets. And look to regional exchanges—imperiled by new trading systems—to radically challenge the entrenched infrastructure because the risks associated with change far outweigh the threat of extinction.

CHAPTER 15

COMMENTS ON MARKET FRAGMENTATION: THE USER'S PERSPECTIVE

Eric Fisher

Two years ago in preparation for their Market 2000 study, the SEC invited comments on a variety of issues related to equity markets, among which was the issue of what they called "market fragmentation." At the time I was impressed by the fact that their very use of the word fragmentation seemed to be a signal for the sort of comments they expected. Indeed, as I skimmed over their July 14, 1992, release, that impression grew. On page 27, for example I read:

> An important issue facing the market again is the extent to which *harmful equity market fragmentation* [my emphasis] has occurred, that is, fragmentation that impairs liquidity and price discovery, and whether it is possible (or even desirable) to prevent such fragmentation. The Division solicits comments on the extent of fragmentation that exists in the market today and the development of future trends toward or away from market fragmentation.

Was the SEC seriously asking for discourse on the question, "Why is market fragmentation bad?" Or even more forcefully, "Why is *harmful* market fragmentation bad?" Well, of course not! My first impression was wrong. Elsewhere in the release I found them asking, "Is 'fragmentation' simply another word for 'competition'?" The SEC was not begging for a particular answer, they were merely adopting common usage.

But I wish they hadn't. To fragment something is to break it, to ruin it. It's pejorative.

But even though the term fragmentation has somewhat unfortunate connotations, I would like to continue using it, if only to uncover an assumption which I believe is lurking behind its use—an assumption that needs discussing. I think a lot of people, when they talk about market fragmentation, are really assuming that somehow liquidity is fixed, that there is only a certain amount of it out there. It can't be created; it can only be "siphoned off," "fragmented," "destroyed," "consumed." I call this the pizza-pie theory of liquidity. There is only one pie, and you've just brought it home. There's no way to make it any bigger, but many ways to make it smaller: You could eat a slice; you could let some go to the dogs... Now, I think this assumption, this theory, is incorrect. Liquidity *can* be increased, as, for example, when the total cost of trading comes down. I believe our experience at CREF is proof of this. But before getting to that, I'd like to assume the worst. I'd like to assume that liquidity is, indeed, fixed and to address the question head on: "Is market fragmentation bad?"

To do this, I'd like to ask you to bear with me a bit while I tell a story. To set the stage, I'd like you to imagine a simple world where, to start with, all this fixed liquidity is only available in one market—an exchange where trading is continuous. Traders in this market are all investors or agents for other investor-traders, and I want to simplify their motivations by bunching them into two groups which I will characterize in a moment. The exchange itself has all the usual characteristics: market orders, booked limit orders, a "crowd" for price improvement, specialists for "orderly markets," and so forth. Now in such a market, conventional wisdom has it that the more orders and the more folks in the crowd, the "better" the price discovery. And the better the price discovery, the more efficiently scarce capital resources are allocated in the economy at large. In this world, the reason this happens is because investor-traders, armed with a forecast of what a firm's prospects are, form an opinion of what the price of its stock "ought" to be; they then compete with each other in an effort to buy at a price lower (or sell at a price higher) than what each one thinks is the "correct" price. Since all traders have a chance to accept a bid or lift an offer, when a stock finally trades, it means that its price is equal to what the consensus thinks it is worth. The fact that these traders base their forecasts on very different things is what makes the market, what causes trading to take place. But what is important, what I'd like to highlight is the notion that they trade based on forecasts, based on information, and that, because they are still around to trade, because they have survived, their past opinion as to what stocks were worth could not have been too far wrong. This leads directly to the presumption that their current forecasts aren't so bad either. Firms with the rosiest prospects thus experience a decrease in the cost of equity capital (the price of their stock goes up) and get to fund all their hot investment projects easily. So far in my story, only the folks who have opinions, those who make forecasts, end up doing the trading. It's as if Adam Smith's invisible hand had nailed a notice up on the exchange door, "If you don't know what it's worth, beat it!"

But these information-based traders, so the story goes, are not the only ones around. Some investor-traders simply want to cash in an investment or put cash to work across the board in a diversified basket of stocks. They are not trading based on information because they haven't any. They just want liquidity; they want to be price takers. In this regard they are clearly parasites—but not necessarily harmful parasites. They want the information-based traders, the big kids, to come up with a price, and then they want to trade at or near that price. But their attempts to do this are continually frustrated. They have noticed, for example, that whenever they try to buy in size, especially with a market order, the price typically rises when their trade is executed and then falls right back down to where it used to be. They simply can't convince other traders that their orders are informationless. There's just no mechanism.

And so this group, the liquidity-based traders, seek each other out and try to trade with each other. And because they haven't a clue as to what the price ought to be when their orders match, they use a price the big kids came up with (the close, the last sale, or the mean of the bid and offer). In doing this, they are simply doing what they always wanted to do: trade without market impact at prices which reflect consensus expectations.

Now, in this oversimplified market situation, is there any reason to suppose that this bit of fragmentation is harmful? What is wrong with letting the parasites do this? Has price discovery somehow been diminished? Has efficient capital formation been impaired? Is there some bit of information that we as a society have lost that should have been in the price but isn't, when liquidity-based orders are matched away from price discovery? In fact, might it not be just the opposite? Might it not actually be a good thing that these orders are siphoned off? After all, when they were part of the process, especially when they were large, they were disruptive and gave false signals.

Hold on a minute, you say, don't liquidity-based orders sometimes convey information? For example, responding to macroeconomic events at times, investors en masse either contribute or withdraw cash to or from mutual funds who, in turn, must place orders to either buy or sell stocks across the board? These orders convey information about investor sentiment—their expectations, their aversion to risk, and so forth. Yes, but at such times (the very times when there might be real information in liquidity-based orders) mutual funds and other large cash-flow-sensitive portfolios would typically all find themselves on the same side and their orders simply wouldn't match. They would try to match them up, but they wouldn't be able to, and their orders would spill over into the primary market, there to convey information and give the proper signals by being part of price discovery. So why not let what can be matched, be matched? Why not allow one slice of the pizza to be consumed privately, away from the party? Is there any harm in allowing—perhaps encouraging—this sort of fragmentation to exist?

But to get back to the story. What about the information-based traders? Presumably they are just as desirous of avoiding market impact as the liquidity-based traders. Wouldn't they want to participate in this matching system? And if they did, wouldn't this finally bring about what everyone has feared: impaired price discovery? Well, what might prevent them? Let's forget about devising rules and suppose that information-based traders are sufficiently innovative to find a way around them and that they do participate. Clearly, they can't all participate. They can't all become parasites, because then the host would die. Even if initially there was a headlong rush into the matching system in an effort to avoid market impact, some information-based traders, I daresay, would tarry in the primary market, if for no other reason than to place bids, make offers, and trade in minuscule size in an effort to "influence" the crossing price. And if some were doing it, others would follow suit. Soon, information-based traders would all be hard to work competing with each other to influence prices and, eventually, the process would look very much like what it is: vigorous, robust price discovery.

It is not hard to imagine that finally an equilibrium would be established for information-based orders in which the potential for loss arising from matching at an influenced price exactly offsets the potential for gain arising from avoiding market impact. Where this equilibrium would be, I don't know. But I doubt that it would harm price discovery. Price discovery is based on greed, and I don't see anything in this sort of order fragmentation which would diminish that.

One could also imagine the matching system evolving (regulations permitting, of course) into a single-price call auction market where prices were actually discovered. Information-based traders would probably demand this. They would demand a way of limiting their exposure to the vagaries of prices established (or perhaps influenced) elsewhere. The natural way to do this would be with a limit order book. Now, if that book were open (a feature information-based traders would probably find repugnant), liquidity-based traders would finally have a way of signaling their lack of information: they could place limit orders way in advance of the match and away from the last price as an invitation to let others decide or "discover" the price. If this sounds familiar, it is probably because you have heard of the Arizona Stock Exchange. Although now it is operating mainly as a matching system, the features are in place for it to evolve into a full-fledged auction where prices are actually discovered.

Perhaps I am belaboring a simple point which has already been made, namely, that it is not at all clear, even under the pizza-pie theory of liquidity, that order matching systems (parasitic and fragmenting though they may be) are bad. So let me end the story and move on to what is actually happened to the real world, where I think our experience at CREF demonstrates that these structures have been a positive good— and not just good for us, but for everyone.

For about seven years now we have been managing a $2.5 to $3 billion, low tracking error, high turnover portfolio using quantitative techniques. Turnover averaged about 80 percent per year, and experienced annualized tracking error was 37 basis points. The portfolio outperformed its benchmark in all but one of the seven years, averaging a modest annual 27 basis point advantage—all very unremarkable, except when you consider that the volume of trading was about 750 million shares valued at over $20 billion.

When we set it up, we were very worried about the impact of total transaction costs (commissions plus market impact) on relative performance. So we deliberately designed the algorithm to generate many more orders than we ever expected to execute. Our hope was that if we could be patient traders and find a way to wait for the other side, to be in a position of supplying liquidity rather than demanding it, we could minimize total transaction costs. A lot of our simulation work encouraged us to take this trading stance. We found, for example, that we didn't have to do all the turnover indicated by the various techniques we were looking at. There appeared to be diminishing marginal excess return to turnover, and it seemed to set in early on.

We started managing the portfolio at the beginning of 1987, doing all our trading on the desk in the traditional way. For the first five months, we just managed to hold our own over the benchmark we were using at the time, the S&P 500. All the gain we had hoped for was apparently eaten up in transaction costs. The algorithm itself (without transaction costs) performed in line with our historical simulations.

Now it was during this time that Instinet was developing their Crossing Network. At first we were not participants because of the risk of being taken out on one side or the other which would have necessitated trading aggressively in a costly fashion the next day, in order to make up any dollar imbalances. It was not until, largely at our prompting, that Instinet added a feature which allowed users to restrict the dollar value of matched buys to the dollar value of matched sells that we became heavy users. This feature made it possible for us to enter about 100 orders on each side without fear of large imbalances. With our orders and the fact that the balancing feature attracted other users, volume at Instinet started to take off.

For us, turnover increased but, because it was inexpensive (one cent per share at the close), excess return increased. But as the shares that we were able to cross on Instinet (and later match up on POSIT when it started up in the fall of 1987) went up, we increasingly found that the trades that came to us caused unwanted factor exposures to arise in the portfolio. In order to remove these, we had to go to the primary market—a clear example of orders going to the primary market because of activity in the alternative trading structures.

As I've already mentioned, over the seven-year period, we traded 750 million shares. Eighty percent of this was done on the matching systems at an average commission cost of 1.6 cents per share. In addition, we've estimated market impact costs by calculating the profit or loss off the close (for Instinet, it is the next day's close) for each share traded. For all matching system trading, this came to 0.7 cents per share, which puts total transaction costs at 2.3 cents per share, or a drain of about 11 basis points per year. For the remaining 20 percent of the trading, which was done in the primary market (principally the NYSE), total transaction costs were 9.1 cents per share (6 cents in commissions, 3.1 cents in estimated market impact). This also resulted in a drain on the portfolio of 11 basis points per year.

Over this period, if all transaction costs had been zero, we would have experienced an average annual excess return of about 50 basis points (that is, our actual excess return of about 27 basis points plus total transaction costs of about 22 basis points). If the matching systems had never come into being and we had been forced to trade in the traditional way, I estimate our total transactions costs would have averaged 53 basis points per year (9.1 cents per share for 100 percent of the trading, instead of just 20 percent), thus wiping out our entire gain. All of this means we probably would have abandoned, rather early on, the whole idea of attempting to add value by making slight bets on top of indexed positions using quantitative techniques. You just don't go for seven years losing money or merely staying flat.

New trading mechanisms can only break into our industry by offering their potential customers low tangible costs (in the form of low commissions) and the promise of minimal intangible costs (market impact). Whereas it is undeniable that at first their customers will have to come from somewhere else (they will fragment the customer base), in time the low costs will create new customers. With low costs, certain marginal techniques for adding portfolio value become feasible, whereas with the usual costs they are unthinkable. The process seems to create liquidity rather than fragmenting or destroying it. And insofar as we agree that the creation of liquidity—even liquidity away from price discovery—is desirable, then it behooves us to help create an environment where barriers to entry into our industry of new trading structures are as few as possible.

CHAPTER 16

MARKET 2000 PERSPECTIVES

Chris Hynes

Rather than describe the state of the markets in the year 2000, I would like to point out that the most important result of the Market 2000 study should be that the SEC is able to build a framework to allow the markets to develop in such a way as to meet the needs of the users, the investors. The current legislative framework within which the SEC must operate is rather aged and does not contemplate the changes in technology, variance in the size and differences in the strategies of asset managers, and globalization, just to name a few, that have occurred in the 60 years since the drafting of modern securities rules. Within this context, the SEC has done an outstanding job of encouraging competition and innovation in our complex system of markets.

While I believe that all investors should have the right to information equality, I do not believe that we must require each marketplace to guarantee all types of investors equal access to each marketplace, nor should individual markets be forced to protect orders priced on another market. Competition rewards and punishes markets that either do or do not properly serve their customers. Various classes of investors have different cost structures, and a certain degree of imperfection in limit protection may be overshadowed by the benefits of market segmentation.

Segmentation is the correct term to use to describe the use of different markets by investors having different execution styles or requirements. All too often, and sometimes quite conveniently, it is erroneously called fragmentation, which describes orders with similar execution characteristics which exist in different locations or on different exchanges. For example, the upstairs block-trading market is a market segment distinct from the exchange floor market. Upstairs trading of large orders has become an accepted part of our market structure for the past 25 years. Due to the number of competitors and the limited flow of information between them, the upstairs market is often fragmented as well, since a buy order at one firm cannot necessarily be crossed with a sell order at another. On the other hand, crossing networks provide another segment without any particular degree of fragmentation, since investors have essentially chosen a dominant network. Segmentation allows markets to maintain a reasonable amount of stability since orders not suited to them can be taken elsewhere for execution. In general, investors seem to be quite responsible when it comes to making segmentation and fragmentation decisions. They deliver the dominant share of auction market orders to the NYSE and a large share of crossing network volume to POSIT and evaluate new segments and competitors on their ability to offer a unique order flow without directly removing order flow from a competitive execution structure.

Payment for order flow is another issue that surfaces in the Market 2000 study and is the subject of rules proposed by the SEC. In looking at this issue, one should consider the viewpoint that payment for order flow does not necessarily corrupt those who receive the payment. In the block trading business, it is considered valuable for a dealer to find the other side of a trade, since there can be a considerable saving of market impact. Additionally, creating a rule restricting payment for order flow may discriminate against firms which have chosen to unbundle order collection and market making functions in favor of large, integrated firms.

A similar form-and-substance argument may be made when considering soft-dollar disclosure issues. We may want to be wary of proposals which force disclosure of certain types of research while exempting other types from disclosure. Full-service firms typically provide traditional, fundamental research on a "bundled" basis. Quantitative research, on the other hand, is often made available by nonbrokerage businesses on an unbundled basis. This leads to the explicit payment of soft dollars. If this practice requires disclosure, we may see data providers registering as brokers, further fragmenting order flow, incidentally, or we may find that the disclosure requirement merely stifles creativity and innovation.

Why should buyers be forced to file detailed reports on one type of research and not the other? They playing field would not be level.

The key to the success of the study is open discussion between market participants and the SEC concerning the future direction of the markets. We can then hope that the process will lead the SEC to an approach which will allow market structure to evolve freely in line with investor needs.

CHAPTER 17

NOTES ON PRIVATE INFORMATION AND THE ORGANIZATION OF SECURITIES MARKETS

Chester Spatt
Sanjay Srivastava

In these notes we explore the organization of security markets and the basis for restrictions on traders and the market maker(s) from the perspective of the theory of private information. The detailed organization of the market is important for understanding the costs of trading, investor and market maker order strategies, the sequencing of trades, and the evolution of prices and information in the market. Examining the rules underlying the microstructure of security markets also can enhance our understanding of the volatility of security returns and policy responses to the stock market crash of October 1987. Yet much of the focus of market microstructure theory has centered upon the Kyle (1985) and Glosten and Milgrom (1985) frameworks to emphasize the determination of transaction prices and quotations, while taking the form of the game as given. Our focus is in understanding the rules underlying the market and the implications for the market's dynamics.[1] For concreteness, much of our discussion will focus upon the New York Stock Exchange (NYSE) design.

The details of the market-making system are very important for understanding behavior in the marketplace. [Another recent treatment of market structure is given in Stoll (1992).] The choice of strategies by investors, the sequencing of trades, disruptions in the pattern of trade, and the rate of change in prices are determined by the form of market organization. The impact of the rules of the market-making system is illustrated by a variety of aspects of the crash of 1987. For example, the role of the specialist system on the New York Stock Exchange in stabilizing prices led to numerous trading suspensions (which meant that last transaction prices were often not indicative of fundamental or arbitrage valuation). The potential for arbitrage relations to pin down the relative pricing in the spot equity and futures markets was weakened not only by trading suspensions but also by the uptick rule governing short sales and restrictions on the use of the Designated Order Turnaround (DOT) System, limiting immediate execution in the equity markets.[2] At a general level, strategic order transmission by investors and traders, delegation and the agency relationship in trade execution, reputation and the long-term relationships of both firms and individuals, and adverse selection all have greatly influenced the overall design and operation of the market.

The NYSE specialist market has a variety of interesting features, many of which are not present in markets with competing market makers (such as the over-the-counter and open outcry markets). Among the more interesting types of rules in specialist markets (some of which also arise with competing market makers) are rules prescribing the sequencing of the execution of orders at a specified price, restricting market prices to a prespecified discrete set (for example, eighths or sixteenths), price continuity and stabilization rules that restrict the pricing of the specialist, restrictions on the acquisition of short positions on a price decline, the use of unscheduled closures, differences in rules by time of day (opening, closing, and intermediate trades) and trade size (block trades, round lots, and odd lots), and a no-trade restriction shortly after the transaction of a large block.

A specific motivation for a monopoly specialist is examined by Glosten (1989), who models the dependence of bid-ask spreads upon order size and shows that the monopoly specialist can find it optimal to subsidize large trades (at the expense of small ones) in order to maintain the informational dynamics and avoid the closing of the market.[3] This capability is a potential advantage of a monopoly market maker. Containing (regulating) the behavior of the monopoly specialist also can be useful for investors participating in the market. An alternative perspective is that restrictions on the monopoly market maker serve as a precommitment device to limit his ex post monopoly power and thereby attract order flow and increase the market maker's ex ante monopoly profit. This approach emphasizes alternative motivations for regulation of the behavior of the specialist and possible ways in which a monopoly specialist could be interpreted as part of an optimal trading mechanism in the presence of private information. This suggests interpretations of specialist regulation consistent with both the "public interest" theory of regulation and the "self-interested" theory of regulation.

Dynamic considerations are clearly important for understanding a number of the institutional features of observed security markets.[4] For example, the specialist is typically required to trade orders in the book at a fixed price in the sequence in which they were entered. Order priority rules that favor those who submit early limit orders increase the incentive of agents to reveal their private information. A rationale for providing traders higher priority for earlier limit orders is that the earlier revelation of private information is advantageous from an efficiency perspective. The discreteness of the price grid plays a role in this reasoning since the probability of a tied offer and the value of priority is much lower when the bids occur on a denser grid. The specialist cannot receive time priority (that is, he trades behind other investors) as his access to the market and resulting ability to cancel orders immediately prior to trades would confer a tremendous advantage if the specialist received time priority.[5]

While time priority applies to regular limit orders within the book, investors whose orders are being handled by floor traders can receive more favorable treatment as every individual trader at a post shares the order flow equally with the public book. In this sense the value of the time priority received by limit order investors is diluted. Of course, there is a delicate balance between providing sufficient time priority to attract the order flow of small investors in the book and providing reasonable access for the order flow of larger investors who find it unattractive to disclose their orders through the book. If such investors placed limit orders, they might be vulnerable to being picked off by informed traders, and they also would be reluctant to disclose their own orders. The dilution of time priority also is a consequence of the fragmentation of the market across competing market makers (for example, off the floor of the exchange) and especially the concentration of market orders in the order flow of the competing market makers.

One of the important characteristics of many security markets is that trading prices are restricted to a discrete grid (the grid can vary with the price of the stock). We suspect that among a broad class of mechanisms only a discrete price grid (in which the set of alternative posted prices do not reflect any of either the buyers' or sellers' private information) are locally robust to small perturbations in the prior beliefs. Restriction to a discrete price grid will exaggerate the observed movements in the bid-ask spread. Yet by restricting the domain of orders, the actual extent of adverse selection would be limited under a locally robust mechanism. Such conclusions would extend earlier work by Hagerty and Rogerson (1987), which analyzed those institutions that are robust across arbitrary prior beliefs. They established that among a broad class of mechanisms only a posted price system (in which the posted price does not reflect any of either the buyers' or sellers' private information) can satisfy simultaneously several basic restrictions on the mechanism's design. While the Hagerty and Rogerson (1987) analysis is cast in terms of abstract mechanisms, we anticipate that the approach of examining robust mechanisms will prove useful for understanding the extent to which these mechanisms can be interpreted as part of an optimal trading mechanism procedure in the presence of private information.[6] A relatively wide pricing grid also has the advantage of minimizing haggling and bargaining costs. Along other lines, a wide pricing grid results in a substantial incentive for investors to provide orders that will not be immediately executed but instead benefit from time priority.[7]

The New York Stock Exchange has continuity rules that discourage the market maker from altering the price too rapidly. For example, the specialists are graded on the frequency of their trades for which the price change from the prior trade does not exceed one eighth (in either direction) and must obtain the approval of a floor official when changing the price by a substantial amount. One advantage of such requirements is to prevent the specialist from exploiting sparsity in his book of limit orders to manipulate the book and move price by large amounts (that is, big price changes prevented) across the spread between buy and sell orders. The continuity rules would not be binding in the face of intervening orders in the limit order book because these would directly compete and thereby restrict the market maker's ability to set the price. The presence of a continuity restriction will reduce the market maker's ex post monopoly power by reducing the ability of the market maker to squeeze market orders and limit orders in his book, thereby influencing investor order strategy. Further, continuity rules can restrict the power of the market maker to exploit his informational advantage concerning the location of future limit orders. In fact, even the market maker may favor precommitment to a continuity rule because of the beneficial consequences of inducing investor order flow (absent the continuity rule investors may be too inclined to hold back their potential orders). If the rules of organization were designed by a specialist, then he might favor continuity requirements to encourage order flow (especially of highly profitable market orders). The same types of interpretations also can be offered about the specialist being evaluated on the frequency of his trades that are stabilizing. The stabilization requirements might reflect the collective desire of specialists to promote order flow by indicating to prospective buyers that they stand ready to provide liquidity when it is needed. In fact, an alternative interpretation is that the stabilization statistic proxies for the frequency of specialist trades buying at the ask and selling at the bid, an indirect measure of specialist profitability and trading across the spread. Interestingly, the decline in stabilizing trades in recent years has been accompanied by an increasing fraction of trades that satisfy the continuity standard.[8] This suggests that the stabilization statistic may not be a useful measure of performance but, instead, of the ability of the market maker to earn the bid-ask spread.

Preventing both investors and market makers from selling short, except on zero-plus ticks (so that the last price change is positive), precludes short selling on a declining price. Restrictions on the behavior of short sellers (who are relatively informed) prevent sales that would result in a decline from the previous price. Transactions costs are relatively higher on a short position than a long position because of the greater need to control the risk of default in the position. Portfolio theoretic considerations (for example, that aggregate holdings of each asset are positive in equilibrium) also suggest that relatively uninformed investors (liquidity traders) will be less likely to undertake a short position. Because of the high transactions costs and risks associated with selling short, it seems plausible that investors who have short positions are especially likely to be informed traders (e.g., as in Diamond and Verrecchia, 1987). In this sense restrictions on short sellers, such as arbitrageurs in the financial markets, can be interpreted to a great extent as restrictions on informed trading. Interestingly, investors are allowed to undertake short positions on the New York Stock Exchange if they are trading against the market (that is, if the most recent price change is positive) so that the rules of the market permit shorting when it stabilizes the market. Similarly, in exactly the states that the shorting is most likely to be driven by strong information (so that the investor is willing to bear the risk and costs of selling short despite an especially low price), the rules of the market restrict short sales. By restricting some of the informed selling, the market limits the degree of adverse selection and the informativeness of a price decline. Without the restriction on short sales after a down tick the market might dry up in the aftermath of a price decline. The extent of adverse selection might be considerable without a restriction to reduce the informativeness of a price decline. Though short sale restrictions limit market liquidity, they also reduce adverse selection and the possibility of a market break in the face of negative but not well-known information.

An interesting feature of the New York Stock Exchange is the role and importance of unscheduled market closures in individual securities (rather than having prices attempt to adjust immediately). These provide a safety valve in the event of pending news announcements or big order imbalances. This provides customers an opportunity to withdraw orders and equalizes somewhat the access to information. By controlling the adverse selection in this fashion, there is greater ex ante incentive to provide order flow. When the market is reopened there is considerable aggregation of information and volatility relative to reopenings after scheduled market closures.

A number of interesting issues arise regarding the book of limit orders. In particular, if the market maker has access to the book, then his strategy will be influenced by the information available to him from the book. As a result, investors have an incentive to conceal their demand in a small market, if the specialist controls the book. This raises the interesting question of whether it is optimal for the market maker to have access to the book of limit orders. Specialists on the NYSE routinely disclose the book to their customers (i.e., fellow members) who request the information, but they do not disseminate it electronically. Because the information is costly to obtain, the amount of disclosure is much more limited than if the book were disseminated electronically. The book information is valuable as judged both by the interest of investors in receiving it and the opposition of specialists to electronic dissemination (in part to avoid providing an edge to arbitrageurs).

The contrast in trading rules at different times of the day and for various order sizes can also be explored from the private information perspective. For example, it is well known that the market is thicker and more volatile at the open and close of the trading day (e.g., Admati and Pfleiderer, 1988; Harris, 1986; and Wood, McInish, and Ord, 1985). At the same time, the NYSE has different rules for determining the price at the open, close, and intermediate times of the trading day. Even the permissible strategies are somewhat different (for example, a "market on close" order is somewhat different than a market order during the trading day). Some of the differences in the design of the market at open and close (at which times a type of auction is conducted) compared to the remainder of the trading day explain or are caused by the differences in market thickness and price variability. There also are differences in trading rules as a function of order size (for example, small odd lots, round lots, and block trades). At one extreme the theoretical block trading literature (e.g., Seppi, 1990) emphasizes some of the special features of the block-trading mechanism, while at the opposite end of the spectrum odd-lot mechanisms are not sensitive to adverse selection and private information. Adverse selection considerations (which are much more important for larger orders) can explain the differences in design as well as trading suspensions in the public market and the exclusive use of private markets in some circumstances (especially when huge spreads would be inconsistent with the other rules of the public market).

NOTES

1. Our analysis of trading rules in these notes is informal and heuristic. An illustration of a formal mechanism design approach to selling financial assets is the modeling in Spatt and Srivastava (1991) of the efficiency of a posted price mechanism (with preplay communication) in a one-sided market.
2. Similarly, the NASDAQ was disrupted by the behavior of some dealers in closing the market.
3. A related motivation for a monopoly specialist is given in Leach and Madhavan (1993), where the specialist facilitates intertemporal price experimentation by subsidizing appropriate trades.
4. In fact, many of the specific aspects of the specialist system (for example, the uptick rule on short sales, the continuity rule, and order priority rules) are not well defined without several rounds of trading.
5. An interesting analysis of the adverse selection problem confronting limit order investors that is created by the market maker's option to compete with the limit order book is in Rock (1990).
6. We also wish to emphasize that our conjecture concerning the local robustness of mechanisms yielding only a discrete price grid is intended only to apply to settings in which the basic Hagerty and Rogerson (1987) posted price result obtains.

7. Related observations about the connection between time priority and discreteness are offered in Harris (1994).
8. The NYSE Fact Book (1992) provides aggregate annual statistics for the continuity and stabilization measures over time.

REFERENCES

Admati, A., and P. Pfleiderer. (1988). "A Theory of Intraday Trading Patterns: Volume and Price Variability," *Review of Financial Studies,* 1: 3–40.

Diamond, D., and R. Verrecchia. (1987). "Constraints on Short Selling and Asset Price Adjustment to Private Information," *Journal of Financial Economics,* 18: 277–311.

Glosten, L. (1989). "Insider Trading, Liquidity, and the Role of the Monopolist Specialist," *Journal of Business,* 62: 211–35.

Glosten, L., and P. Milgrom. (1985). "Bid, Ask, and Transactions Prices in a Specialist Market with Heterogeneously Informed Traders," *Journal of Financial Economics,* 14: 71–100.

Hagerty, K., and W. Rogerson. (1987). "Robust Trading Mechanisms," *Journal of Economic Theory,* 42: 94–107.

Harris, L. (1994). "Minimum Price Variations, Discrete Bid-Ask Spreads, and Quotation Sizes," *Review of Financial Studies,* 7: 149–78.

Harris, L. (1986). "A Transactional Data Study of Weekly and Intradaily Patterns in Stock Returns," *Journal of Financial Economics,* 16: 99–117.

Kyle, A. (1985). "Continuous Auctions and Insider Trading," *Econometrica,* 53: 1315–35.

Leach, C., and A. Madhavan. (1993). "Price Experimentation and Security Market Structure," *Review of Financial Studies,* 6: 375–404.

NYSE Fact Book. (1992).

Rock, K. (1990). "The Specialists' Order Book and Price Anomalies," Harvard Business School working paper.

Seppi, D. (1990). "Equilibrium Block Trading and Asymmetric Information," *Journal of Finance,* 45: 73–94.

Spatt, C., and S. Srivastava. (1991). "Preplay Communication, Participation Restrictions, and Efficiency in Initial Public Offering," *Review of Financial Studies,* 4: 709–26.

Stoll, H. (1992). "Principles of Trading Market Structure," *Journal of Financial Services Research,* 6:75–107.

Wood, R., T. McInish, and J. Ord. (1985). "An Investigation of Transactions Data for NYSE Stocks," *Journal of Finance,* 40: 723–39.

CHAPTER 18

CONSOLIDATION, FRAGMENTATION, SEGMENTATION, AND REGULATION

Lawrence Harris

INTRODUCTION

The growth of new trading systems raises concerns about how these systems affect security markets. In particular, some practitioners and regulators ask whether these systems fragment our markets, and, if they do, whether the fragmentation reduces market liquidity and price formation efficiency.[1] Responsible answers to these questions must explore exactly what is meant by market fragmentation, why it occurs, and what are the benefits and costs associated with market structure diversity.

This chapter describes the economic forces that cause markets to consolidate, to fragment, and to coalesce into a unified complex of di-

Reprinted with permission from *Financial Markets, Institutions, & Instruments.*

The author gratefully acknowledges partial financial support for this project from Jefferies and Co. The comments and opinions in this chapter are those of the author only and do not necessarily reflect those of the directors, officers, or staff of Jefferies and Co.

The author also gratefully acknowledge comments and suggestions given by Deborah Sosebee, David Leinweber, Jia Ye, and Partha Chatterjie, and participants in the December 1991 National Organization of Investment Professionals Conference.

verse segments.[2] Markets consolidate primarily because traders search for liquidity. Markets fragment because traders differ significantly in the types of trading problems that they confront. Traders therefore may support a variety of trading systems for trading the same fundamental asset. Fragmented markets coalesce into a unified complex of diverse segments when information freely flows between market segments and when some traders can trade in more than one segment. When these conditions are obtained, the market complex is best called a segmented market rather than a fragmented market. Difficult public policy problems arise in segmented markets because secondary precedence rules like time precedence are not enforced across market segments. If such rules are desirable, they must be implemented through government intervention.

Segmented securities markets are characterized by two types of competition: traders compete for best price within a given market structure, and market structures compete to serve diverse traders. Unfortunately, polices that would maximize the benefits from one type of competition can decrease the benefits obtained from the other type of competition. For example, if all trade in a given security were consolidated by regulation into the same market, it would be easy to find the best price for the security, but it would be difficult or impossible for innovative trading systems to develop and be adopted. Public policies therefore may need to balance the benefits obtained from these two types of competition.

The remainder of this chapter is organized as follows: The next section presents a short description of how technological forces have changed the security markets. The summary is not integral to the analysis and may be skipped. It does, however, present the technological context of the main points in the chapter. The economic analysis starts in the third section with a discussion of why markets consolidate. The fourth section examines the many reasons why markets fragment. The forces that reconsolidate fragmented markets into a segmented market are described in the fifth section. That section also discusses how payments for order flow may make it difficult to consolidate fragmented markets. The sixth section introduces some public policy problems related to externalities among various market segments. Finally, a summary and a list of open questions are provided in the final section.

TRADING SYSTEMS AND TECHNOLOGY

New trading systems have proliferated largely due to the growth in electronic communications and information processing technologies. Formerly, some prices (and occasionally a few quotations) were reported out of markets by horseback and ship. Later, they were reported by telegraph and telephone. Now, prices and continuous quotations are reported via dedicated communications systems run by computers. Formerly, all trading decisions were made by hand, and all trades were organized by hand. Now, computers commonly make and implement trading decisions while dedicated exchange, broker, and dealer computer systems organize trades automatically. This section briefly identifies the technological facilities that new trading systems are designed to exploit.[3]

Instantaneous communications technologies permit traders to see trading opportunities available to them far from where they sit and stand. Traders no longer need to stand on the floor of an exchange to know what is happening there. Traders sitting at a desk virtually anywhere in the world can now see opportunities wherever they occur.

These communications technologies also permit traders to act electronically upon any opportunity available to them. Electronic order routing systems allow traders to route their orders to whatever trading environment they believe will best serve their specific needs. They then can monitor the progress of their orders wherever they are sent.

Computing technologies now allow brokers and exchanges to implement trading systems that provide more service at lower cost. For example, crossing networks like POSIT and The Crossing Network match orders that formerly would have been matched by hand at greater cost. These computing technologies have also allowed applications to be developed that formerly would have been economically infeasible. The matching rules used by POSIT are based on a complex mathematical model that ensures that all traders are treated fairly subject to various constraints. No manual matching method can be implemented quickly enough to match trades as fairly as the current automated method.

Before electronic technologies grew to their present state of development, most trade was conducted at centralized regional exchanges. Professional traders wanted to belong to those exchanges because only by being present on the floors could they learn what market conditions and opportunities were available to them. Nonmembers traded through member-brokers because that was the only way they could access the central exchanges. Although no single market structure can simultaneously best serve the needs of every type of trader, all traders were willing to use the central exchanges because that was where the trading information was. Trading in some assets was fragmented across many regional exchanges because impatient traders could not (or would not) wait while their orders were sent, traded, and confirmed at distant exchanges. These traders paid high transaction costs to dealers who moved liquidity from market to market as demanded. The revenues these dealers made—essentially arbitrage profits—reflected the high cost of obtaining information and acting upon it across large distances.

Now that trading information is more widely disseminated, traders no longer need to go to central exchanges. They now go to whatever trading system best serves their specific needs, confident that prices in that market segment will reflect liquidity conditions in all other segments. New trading systems have proliferated as entrepreneurs, exchanges, brokers, and dealers compete to satisfy the liquidity demands of diverse traders.

MARKET CONSOLIDATION

Consolidation can be best understood by momentarily adopting a simple but highly unrealistic assumption. Assume that all traders and all trading problems that they face are identical. In particular, all traders trade for similar reasons; no traders are so large that they single-handedly can significantly affect market prices; all traders are equally patient (or impatient) to trade; all traders are equally creditworthy; and all traders pursue roughly the same investment strategies. Trader opinions about asset values need not—typically will not—be similar.

If this extreme assumption were true, all traders would want to trade in the same market in which all other traders trade. Traders can find the best terms for their trades (with minimum effort and time) when all other traders are in the same place. Traders would choose to trade in this market because liquidity would be higher there than anywhere else. Liquidity would be high because that is where traders would choose to expose their orders.

This circularity is known as the order flow externality. Traders who send their orders to a given market benefit all other traders who use that market. Each additional order increases system liquidity, which in turn attracts more orders.

The single market in which the identical traders would trade need not be organized in any central location. It can be organized within any communications network that allows traders to expose their orders universally and to act upon any exposed order. Electronic trading systems exist in part because electronic networks often provide cheaper and more efficient communications than face-to-face networks. A consolidated market is a market in which traders can universally expose their orders and in which traders can act upon any exposed order.

The identical traders' consolidated market would treat each trader equally. No one would receive any special preferences based on size, creditworthiness, or experience because (by assumption) no such differences would exist. All order precedences (which may, but not necessarily, include price, time, display, and/or size) would be strictly enforced regardless of how and where the trader accesses the market.

Occasionally a group of traders may want to create a new market based on a different set of trading rules or on a new technology. If the innovation lowers transaction costs or provides more service, all traders will join the new market, and the market will remain consolidated, albeit in a different form.[4] All traders will want to join the new market because all traders are assumed to be identical. If one trader decides that it is optimal for him to join, all other traders will arrive at the same conclusion.

It may be difficult to convince all traders to switch to the new market at the same time. If the new market structure is substantially better than the former, a small group of traders may start trading in the new market by themselves. Other traders will join the new market when they learn that it has greater liquidity and when they discover that the old market is losing liquidity as traders defect. If it is not optimal for a small set of traders to start trading in the new market system by themselves, the innovation will not be adopted until more traders demand it. An incumbent market structure therefore may survive even if other market structures could provide better service to traders if universally adopted. No trader wants to be the first trader in an innovative market.

Public Policy Implications

The role for public policy would be quite limited if all traders were identical. Good public policy would simply allow traders to choose for themselves the trading system that they prefer. Although the best market system would be a consolidated system, regulators do not need to impose one on identical traders. They will choose it for themselves.

Any regulatory efforts to impose a consolidated system risk choosing the wrong system and/or stifling innovation. Regulators would have to determine what market structure to use and when it should be changed. Should the consolidated system enforce time precedence like the NYSE? Futures markets generally do not. Should the consolidated system display all orders like the current CATS system in Toronto? Most trading systems do not. Should displayed orders have precedence over hidden orders as provided in the GLOBEX system and the Paris CAC? Some systems like POSIT do not even allow displayed orders. These differences in market structure are clearly significant. Serious losses to the public welfare could result if the wrong system were chosen.

When traders choose where they prefer to trade, the market structure that best serves their needs will be revealed through competition for their order flow. If traders choose to minimize their transaction costs, the revealed market structure will be the one that minimizes their trading costs.

Competition among market trading systems requires that markets be free to innovate in ways that may temporarily fragment existing consolidated market systems. Although the resulting fragmentation may disrupt the markets, the disruption will be transitory. Under the extreme identical traders assumption, the best market structure will eventually garner all the order flow.

Regulators can help ensure that the best market structure will eventually be revealed by helping disseminate reliable and unbiased information about competing market structures. Such information will make it easier for traders to switch to better trading systems as they become available. In particular, regulators should ensure that the public is adequately protected against fraudulent claims by would-be innovators.[5] Such regulation is necessary if the damage that unscrupulous individuals can do to the public welfare through misrepresentation would be greater than the damage they do to the reputations in the process.

MARKET FRAGMENTATION

Markets fragment because traders are not all identical and because the trading problems they face are not all identical. The same fundamental asset may simultaneously trade in different market structures because different structures better serve the needs of some traders than others. In this section, various differences among traders are examined and related to the different market structures that they prefer.

Unequal Access

By design or by historic accident, markets often deny some traders access to trading information or trading facilities that other traders have. For example, exchange members may have direct access to floor information and to trading opportunities that are unavailable to off-floor traders. The latter may only be able to trade by purchasing brokerage services from exchange members.

Many disadvantaged traders, especially large institutions and sophisticated individual investors, believe that they could execute their trades at lower cost and/or choose their trades more profitably if they had the same access to information and trading facilities that advantaged traders have. Disadvantaged traders naturally will favor market structures in which they have stronger and more equal roles. The resulting diversity in market structures is a competitive response to their disenfranchisement. Trading systems like Instinet, POSIT, and the Arizona Stock Exchange (formerly the Wunsch Single Price Auction) attract order flow, in part, because their users can trade without intermediation.

Exchanges argue that the obligations they impose on their members (affirmative obligations to provide services and negative obligations to refrain from competing with the public) make the relationship between their members and the public fair. This argument is valid to the extent that the disadvantaged traders value the services—typically liquidity provision—offered by exchange members. If the disadvantaged traders do not value these services as much as they value the privileges of membership, they will seek to become members. If denied access by the exchange or by law, they will seek and support market structures in which they have a more equal role.

Unequal Sizes

Traders differ in size. Some traders are so large that their orders can significantly move the market. Others are so small that their individual orders rarely have any impact on price.

Large Traders Large traders are reluctant to reveal their trading plans. They fear that if their orders were widely revealed before they arrange their trades, other traders would front-run them and thereby increase their trading costs. Large traders manage this risk by controlling the exposure of their orders. They prefer to expose their orders only to traders who commit to trading with them and, even then, only to the extent that their counterparts are willing to expose.

Executing large orders can be quite difficult (or expensive) in markets that widely display order flow information. If the orders are not exposed, finding contra-side interest is difficult. If the orders are exposed, they may be front-run. Large traders therefore prefer market structures that allow them to find parties willing to trade while minimizing the information that they must expose to find these parties.

On the floor of the NYSE, large orders are generally handled by floor brokers. The floor brokers only reveal their orders after identifying traders likely to be interested in trading, and then only to the extent that they believe the interested parties are willing to trade.

Try as they might, exchange floor brokers do not always manage order exposure perfectly. They may misjudge who might be interested in trading. They may misjudge the size that a trader is willing to take. They may inadvertently expose their orders by the way that they walk, talk, or otherwise present themselves. They may also deliberately reveal their orders to reward friends or to exchange favors with the traders with whom they must deal, shoulder-to-shoulder, every day of the year.

Large traders protect themselves against these risks by breaking their orders into parts. They then sequentially submit the parts to their broker as each part is filled. They may also submit the parts to different brokers.

The government bond trading system used by Cantor Fitzgerald is a market mechanism specifically designed to serve the needs of large traders. Traders confidentially indicate to the Cantor Fitzgerald broker that they are willing to trade at a given price. The broker then publishes the best bid and ask. When a trader indicates that he is willing to take a standing bid or offer, the taking trader and the standing trader then take turns revealing to the broker how much they want to trade. Increasing sizes are revealed until one of the two traders is no longer interested in increasing the size of trade. At that point, the broker executes the trade at the last agreed-upon size. All traders are able to see the agreed-upon size of the trade as it is growing, but no one except the two parties to the trade and the broker can see the negotiations. The system thus allows the two traders to see each other's orders only to the extent that they are willing to trade while ensuring that neither trader knows with whom they are trading. Some large traders are so sensitive about revealing size that they split their orders so that no one (but the broker) can confidently infer the full size of their orders. Occasionally, two such traders will unknowingly trade with each other two or more times in a row simply because neither trader is willing to let any other trader know the full size of their order.

The various electronic crossing networks provide the same service in a different form. These computerized trading systems take electronically transmitted orders and match them at a given price. The computers never reveal order size: they only reveal what matches have been made. Accordingly, all orders are only revealed to the extent that other parties are willing to trade.

Small Traders   Small traders like to expose their orders. They are not afraid of front-runners because front-running small orders is not generally profitable. Small traders expose their orders to attract other traders. Wide exposure allows small traders to fill their orders quickly at the best prices available.

Implications   Small and large traders prefer different market structures because they solve different trading problems. Large traders prefer to limit their order exposure. The display limitations they place on their orders make their trades difficult and expensive to arrange, but these limitations also decrease the probability that they will be front-run. Small traders prefer to expose their orders to minimize the costs of filling their orders. Diverse market structures exist because different-sized traders have different needs.

If all traders were required to trade in a single market that widely displays orders, large traders would be disadvantaged. They would respond by issuing smaller orders, waiting for them to execute, and then issuing more orders. This strategy would be expensive and could easily allow other traders to figure out what they are doing.

In contrast, if all traders were required to trade in a single market that does not reveal orders, small traders would be disadvantaged. It would be difficult for small traders to find each other in such a market. Small traders would be forced to trade with dealer specialists who would make markets that otherwise might be made in aggregate by small traders searching for the best price among all public orders. The NASD stock markets exemplify markets in which public orders are not widely revealed.

Asymmetric Information and Trader Motives

Different trading motives often cause traders to prefer various market structures. For example, some traders are well informed about fundamental asset values. These informed traders trade to profit from their information. They typically prefer market structures that do not reveal their identities when they trade. Otherwise, no one would want to trade with them. In contrast, other traders, by design or by chance, are relatively uninformed about asset values. They trade to invest savings for future uses or to obtain funds for current needs. Uninformed traders prefer market structures that allow them to expose their identities. They hope that by doing so, they can convince other traders that they are uninformed. This subsection shows how markets have responded to the needs of these two types of traders.

Well-informed and Uninformed Traders   Some traders expend significant resources to obtain information about fundamental asset values. Their research may include studies of firm activities, product markets, technologies, leadership, and the national economy. These informed traders then attempt to profit on this information through their trading.

Informed traders tend to make prices more informative. For example, if informed traders feel that the fundamental value of an asset is higher than the price at which they can buy it, they will attempt to buy the asset. Their purchases will raise the price of the asset so that it more closely reflects its underlying fundamental value. Informed traders profit when the information that they trade upon becomes well known (after they have traded) and if it is widely interpreted in the same way that they interpret it. If so, they will be able to sell the asset at a higher price. The profit that they make can then be used to fund further research. Their efforts benefit everyone: in our free market economy, prices are used to allocate scarce capital resources to the best managers and to the best projects. These allocation decisions are made best when prices are informative.

Market trading structures that reveal orders also tend to reveal informed traders' proprietary information before they can trade on it. This is especially true when the informed traders are well known. For example, Cargill is generally known to be well informed about wheat market fundamentals. When Cargill's trader is in the wheat futures pit, other traders will watch him to see what he is doing. If the Cargill trader wants to buy, no one will be willing to sell at current prices. They will figure that Cargill believes the fundamental value of wheat is higher than the current price. The exposure of Cargill's order therefore hurts Cargill. If forced to expose its orders, Cargill would spend less on research, wheat prices would be less informative of fundamental values, and resource allocation decisions would be less well made.

Cargill and other informed traders attempt to solve this problem by giving their orders to brokers to execute anonymously. This solution addresses the problem, but it does not completely eliminate it. If some orders are informative, traders will draw inference from the order flow even if they do not know its source. Informed traders therefore prefer to reveal their orders only to those with whom they are trading. As noted above, electronic trading systems easily can provide this facility.

In contrast, uninformed traders would like everyone to know that they are uninformed. They do not want other traders to erroneously assume that they are well informed. By convincing other traders that they are uninformed, they hope to obtain better prices than would otherwise be offered to them.

Sunshine traders are uninformed traders who try to convince other traders that they are uninformed by exposing their orders to everyone. Their strategy is based on the assumption that most informed traders would not expose their orders. Sunshine trading will be successful if sunshine traders are well known.

Markets fragment because some traders want to expose orders while other traders do not. If all orders were anonymous, informed trading would be more profitable. More traders would invest in fundamental information, and prices would more closely reflect fundamental values. Uninformed traders, however, would be worse off. They would seek market structures that allow them to demonstrate that they are uninformed.

The remainder of this subsection examines two specialized market structures that have grown largely to meet the needs of uninformed traders. Block trading markets serve the needs of large uninformed traders in individual securities. Index markets serve traders who do not want to trade firm-specific risk, in part, because they are unable or unwilling to compete effectively with informed traders.

Block Trading   Large uninformed traders cannot easily convince other traders that they are indeed uninformed. Most traders assume that large traders are well informed because well informed traders like to trade large orders. Moreover, since portfolio theory (and common sense) suggests that uninformed traders should hold diversified portfolios, uninformed traders generally would not be expected to trade large blocks in single issues. If an uninformed trader does want to trade a large block, there must be some special reason why. Most exchange traders, however, are unwilling to incur the expenses necessary to audit another trader's motives to find this reason.

Block brokers and dealers specialize in performing these audits. Block brokers audit their client's motives to ensure that they do not arrange trades that consistently hurt the other parties to the trade whom they also represent. Brokers who arrange trades that consistently hurt one side or the other find that traders are unwilling to trade through their intermediation. Block dealers audit their client's motives because they take the other side of the trade. They do not want to facilitate unprofitable trades.

Credible reasons that explain why uninformed traders would want to sell large blocks of stock are often related to bankruptcy liquidations or to divestments forced by social and/or legal responsibilities. Since very few reasons explain why uninformed traders would want to buy large blocks, block brokers and dealers do not often arrange large buyer-initiated trades.

Upstairs block markets exist, and, hence, markets fragment, because trading motive audits usually cannot be done on exchange floors. These audits are expensive and often require costly time-consuming research. Once obtained, however, the audit information is valuable. Upstairs block traders profit from this information (and therefore preserve their incentives to invest in it) by retaining exclusive use over it. They either broker the block transaction or facilitate it out of their own inventory. If the upstairs markets did not provide these services to large uninformed traders, block traders would not be able to organize liquidity as easily as they currently do, and block trading would be more expensive.[6]

Index Markets   The index markets represent another structural response to informed trading. Index markets allow uninformed traders to credibly demonstrate that they do not possess valuable firm-specific information.

Many traders believe that they cannot effectively gather good fundamental information about individual security values. They have found (or suspect) that they tend to lose to informed traders when they trade individual securities. They may lose directly by trading with informed traders, or they may lose indirectly by paying the high bid-ask spreads that dealers must demand to stay solvent if they often must unknowingly trade with informed traders.

To limit these losses while still holding equity positions, some traders have decided to hold and trade only portfolios of stocks designed to replicate broad indices like the S&P 500. This strategy ensures that their portfolio returns approximate the index returns. Such performance is better than that typically obtained by 75 percent of the actively managed institutional equity funds in any given quarter.

Specialized market structures, such as the index futures market and various list (program) trading systems, have developed to serve the special needs of index traders. These structures typically lower the costs of trading market risk.

Index futures are cheaper to trade than individual stocks because percentage bid-ask spreads are smaller in the futures market than in the cash stock market. Bid-ask spreads depend, in part, on the losses that market makers expect when they unknowingly trade with informed traders. If market makers expect that these losses will be large, they quote wide bid-ask spreads so that they can recover from uninformed traders what they lose to informed traders. Market makers in individual stocks are exposed to two types of informed traders. Those traders who specialize in firm-specific information and those traders who specialize in marketwide information. The latter are not generally regarded as a significant source of risk to the market maker because few traders— perhaps none—possess valuable private information about marketwide security values. Market makers in index futures charge lower spreads because they do not trade with informed traders who specialize in firm-specific information.[7]

List trading systems likewise lower trading costs for index traders. Index traders demonstrate by their use of large program trades that are not well informed with respect to the value of any one stock. The traders who take the other side of a program are therefore less concerned that the trade will lead to a loss, and they are therefore willing to offer better prices.[8] One reason that the POSIT trading system until recently did not accept orders for individual stocks (traders were required to submit lists with a minimum of five orders) was to discourage well informed traders in firm-specific risk from using the system. List trading systems also lower trading costs by lowering the physical costs of handling large lists. Systems like the Institutional Order Entry System (Bridge Information

Systems) and Quantex (Investment Technology Group, Inc.) allow traders to issue a single instruction that will apply to each stock in a list. These systems eliminate much repetitious work.

Unequal Patience

Some traders are more patient than other traders. Impatient traders want or need to establish their positions quickly. They demand liquidity and are generally willing to pay for it. They want someone to respond when they want to trade. Impatient traders pay bid-ask spreads and high commissions to increase the probability that they trade. Patient traders are in no hurry to trade. They are cost sensitive and are willing to wait for the market to come to them. They tend to supply liquidity. They offer liquidity through their limit orders and through the quotations of the floor brokers that represent them.

Some market structures serve the needs of impatient traders better than those of patient traders. The NASDAQ National Market System Small Order Execution System (SOES), for example, is a quote-based system that allows small, impatient traders to immediately trade whenever they want to. Users of this system, however, must pay bid-ask spreads (buy at the ask and sell at the bid) to the NASDAQ National Market System dealers. Since the National Market System does not provide a facility that allows public traders to place quotations, it does not serve the needs of patient traders. These traders instead prefer to use limit order systems at public exchanges or order-driven electronic trading systems such as Instinet, POSIT, The Crossing Network, and the Arizona Stock Exchange. These structures all allow patient traders to quote their interests and thereby to obtain lower transaction costs. None, however, guarantees that their orders will be executed.

All traders must decide whether they value execution certainty more than they value transaction cost savings. Those who value the former opt for market systems that provide execution certainty at the expense of transaction costs. Those who value transaction cost savings opt for market systems that provide lower transaction costs for executed trades, but lower certainty that orders will be executed.

Diverse market structures exist because no single trading system best serves the needs of both patient and impatient traders. Perhaps the best hybrid systems currently available are at the public exchanges. Exchange specialist dealers provide liquidity to all small impatient traders who demand it, but patient traders may submit limit orders that represent their interests. All traders, however, must expose their orders to the brokers and specialists who may then—by accident, design, or carelessness—further expose them. Many large traders prefer electronic trading systems that maintain complete order confidentiality.

Unequal Creditworthiness and Trustworthiness

Traders differ in their creditworthiness and their trustworthiness. Public traders in most developed countries generally assume that agreed-upon trades will settle. Trades actually only settle if traders both acknowledge and fulfill the terms of their agreement. When traders fail to do so, they impose costs upon those with whom they trade. In particular, since the ex post profitable side of a trade is usually prepared to settle, settlement failures usually hurt the party willing to settle.

Trustworthy and creditworthy traders therefore prefer to trade with each other and exclude their less worthy associates. When they cannot do so, they must somehow bear the costs that their less worthy associates impose upon them. Depending on the market, they may bear these costs directly when a deadbeat fails to settle properly with them, or they may bear them indirectly through their participation in a clearinghouse (effectively, an insurance pool) that guarantees performance. Markets fragment to exclude individuals who would impose costs upon others if allowed to trade. The excluded individuals may still trade, but they usually must trade through intermediaries who guarantee their trades, or they must trade with other similarly excluded traders. Exchanges, dealer networks, and clearinghouses impose financial and ethical standards upon their members to exclude traders who might impost unnecessary settlement costs upon others. Any universal trading system that would impose the same standards on all traders in effect would require the more creditworthy and more trustworthy traders to subsidize the less worthy traders.

MARKET SEGMENTATION: CONSOLIDATED FRAGMENTED MARKETS

The preceding discussions suggest that a trade-off may exist between the cost-reducing benefits of market consolidation and the service-enhancing benefits of market diversity. Within any given market structure, liquidity is greatest and transaction costs are lowest when all traders trade there.

All traders want all other traders to trade in the particular market structure that they prefer. But differences among traders cause them to prefer diverse market structures. Unfortunately, no single market best meets the service needs of all traders. Instead, a diversity of market structures now serves the various needs of different traders. The resulting fragmentation suggests that some of the cost-reducing benefits of market consolidation may be lost. In particular, concerns have been raised about whether fragmented markets lead to poor price formation and high transaction costs.

These concerns would be well founded if traders in the various market fragments did not know and respond to market conditions in the other fragments. If so, each fragment would constitute an isolated market in which price formation would take place independently of all other markets. The resulting array of prices would each depend on the supply and demand for liquidity only within each fragment. Prices would not efficiently incorporate all available information about fundamental asset values because information in one fragment, by assumption, would not be available to traders in any other fragment. Transaction costs would be high because liquidity demands in one fragment would not be met by liquidity supplies in another fragment. All liquidity demands would have to be satisfied separately within each fragment.

Information, Order Routing, and Arbitrage

Market diversity, however, does not necessarily imply inferior price formation and high transaction costs. The benefits of consolidation can be obtained in a fragmented market when information freely flows between market segments and when all traders do not have to trade in only one segment. These two conditions are sufficient to coalesce market fragments into a unified complex of diverse segments. They ensure that traders know what is happening in each market segment and that some traders will be able to act on that information should prices and/or liquidity conditions diverge.

Three mechanisms consolidate market segments: First, within each market segment, traders adjust their orders to reflect information that is revealed in all other segments. These adjustments cause prices to reflect the same information in all segments. Second, traders choose the market segment to which they send their orders. Traders who demand liquidity tend to use the segment that is currently most liquid. Traders who supply liquidity tend to use segments with the greatest current demands for liquidity. Trader order routing decisions thus balance the supply and demand for liquidity in all market segments so that liquidity will be comparable in all segments. Finally, arbitrageurs specialize in moving liquidity among market segments. They trade whenever prices in one segment fail to reflect prices in another segment. Arbitrageurs thereby ensure that asset prices are always approximately equal whenever and however the asset is traded.

The forces that consolidate market segments are quite robust. For example, even if some traders can only trade in a single market segment, the market will remain consolidated if other traders can freely route their orders to the various market segments. Under such conditions, if an order cannot move to its best market, the best market will be moved to the order. The arbitrageur who moves the liquidity, however, will have to be compensated.[9]

Markets can consolidate even if no coordinated mechanism like the Intermarket Trading System (ITS) routes orders from one market segment to another. Proprietary electronic routing systems that allow traders and brokers to select quickly the best markets for their orders make coordinated intermarket routing systems unnecessary. These routing systems can provide the same services that ITS was designed to provide.

Agency Problems, Payments for Order Flow, and Best Execution

The preceding discussion implicitly assumes that all traders act in their complete self-interest to seek the best price for their orders. This assumption may not hold, however, when traders use agents (brokers) to do their trading. Although brokers are generally expected to seek the best prices for their clients' orders, they may not always do so. If they do not, market fragmentation may reduce liquidity and make the price formation process less efficient.

The Agency Problem   Principal-agent problems arise when agents do not act as their principals would act if the latter had the same skills and information as the former. Brokers may spend fewer resources (time, effort, and investment in information systems) to find the best price that their trader-clients would want them to spend.[10]

Principal-agent problems typically occur when the agents' objectives differ from the principals' objectives. In the present context, the clients' objective is to obtain speedy, reliable, low-cost executions at the best possible price. The brokers' objective typically is to run a profitable business.

These two objectives do not necessarily conflict. In competitive markets, brokers can only remain in business if they satisfy their clients' objectives. Otherwise, their clients will switch to more responsive brokers.

The competitive markets solution to the agency problems stands on three assumptions. First, the brokers must want to remain in business. Brokers who do not seek new or repeat business may not value their reputations. Either through laziness, neglect, or calculated design, such brokers may be tempted to cut corners if they can do so. Second, switching among brokers must not be too costly. If switching is costly, clients may find it difficult to discipline lazy, neglectful, or untrustworthy brokers. Finally, clients must be able to observe, monitor, and measure their brokers' efforts at low cost. When clients cannot identify the service provided by their brokers, some brokers may be tempted to provide less service.

The first two assumptions generally well characterize the brokerage industry, but the last assumption is rarely true. Most brokers do value their reputations, and switching brokers is not very difficult. However, few brokerage clients—and probably no small clients—can observe, monitor, and measure their brokers' efforts at low cost. Given the high volatility of security prices, the general lack of real-time market information available to most brokerage clients, and the high cost of processing that information even when it is readily available, most clients cannot accurately determine whether their orders are well executed to not. Moreover, even if they could measure their brokers' performance, fairly evaluating that information is still more difficult. A fair evaluation would require that the clients compare the quality of service offered by at least a few different brokers.[11] Although a small industry exists to assist traders with these evaluations, such information is not generally available.[12]

Payments for Order Flow   A large controversy currently exists in the United States over payments for order flow. Some dealers pay brokers—typically one cent per share—for market orders sent to them. The mere existence of such payments suggests (but does not necessarily imply) a possible conflict of interest. Brokers are supposed to seek the best execution for their orders on behalf of their clients. If the dealers who buy their orders execute them at prices that are, on average, less favorable than those that can be obtained elsewhere, and, if no other differences in the quality of service provided can explain the differential, the brokers would appear to be in violation of their trust. However, if the execution prices are the same for comparable commissions or if the client receives other services such as faster and more reliable execution, then there may be no violation of trust.

Best Execution   The dealers who purchase order flow guarantee that they will execute market orders (with some size restrictions) at prices no worse than the best ITS quotations. Some dealers also display their orders in the ITS system to give other traders an opportunity to improve their prices, and some dealers also may match any printed price that is better than the ITS quotation.

The brokers who sell order flow claim they satisfy their fiduciary obligations to their clients by ensuring that they receive the best ITS quoted prices or better for their market orders. This argument requires three assumptions.

First, for a given order, the best ITS quotation must not be a quotation for a significantly larger or more difficult trade than that required to fill the order. Otherwise, a better price might be found for the smaller order or the easier-to-trade order. Although dealers are usually willing to quote tighter spreads for smaller sizes, they can only quote a single price and size on the ITS system. Primary market dealers often quote wide spreads for large size, but they will frequently fill small orders inside the spread. Order execution at the best ITS quoted spread can only be considered "best execution" for a given order if the quoted spread is appropriate for that order.

Second, the ITS system quotations must be meaningful. Market makers sometimes quote wider spreads than the spreads at which they actually are willing to trade many orders. This strategy allows them to discriminate among orders. They typically will not fill an order inside their quoted spreads if they believe that the order was issued by a well-informed trader. Order execution at the best ITS quoted spread should not be considered "best execution" if the quoted spread rarely represents the true market. Broker fiduciary responsibility presumably (unless otherwise agreed to by the client) requires that the broker search for the best price not only wherever it is posted but also wherever it is know to be found.

Third and last, there must be little chance that the order would cross with another market order if routed elsewhere. When two market orders cross each other, on average, both can be filled at the spread midpoint.[13] Order execution at the best ITS quoted spread should not be considered "best execution" if market orders frequently cross in some market segment.

This discussion overemphasizes the importance of price in the search for a definition of "best execution." The best price for an order cannot be defined without reference to the resources that must be spent to find that price. Patient traders who are willing to devote time and resources to search for the best price should typically get better prices than impatient traders who only want a quick, low-commission execution. Best execution thus also   depends on other service dimensions besides best price.

Summary and Economic Characterization   The order flows that are purchased by dealers typically are generated by small impatient public traders. As noted above, small traders cannot easily determine whether their brokers search well for the best price. However, they can (and do) audit the commissions that they pay their broker, and they can easily compare these commissions across brokers.

Payment for order flow probably occurs because small traders will not pay their brokers to search for the best price when they cannot audit the product of that search. Under such conditions, brokers are unlikely to search as diligently as they would if their clients could observe the product of their efforts. Small traders can, however, observe their brokerage commissions. Competition among brokers therefore tends to focus on commission reduction rather than execution price optimization. The payments for order flow made by dealers to brokers allow brokers to lower their commissions. The search for best price may suffer as a result, but the trade-off is accepted, given the costs of auditing execution efficiency.

The very fact that dealers are *able and willing* to purchase order flow suggests that the profits from filling these orders will more than cover the costs of purchasing them. At least four sources can account for these profits.

First, the dealers may fill the orders at prices that do not reflect the best prices at which the orders often could be filled, if a more patient search were conducted. For example, small orders may be traded at quoted spreads appropriate for large orders.

Second, order-purchasing dealers may be better able to discriminate among the orders than can other dealers. The order-purchasing dealers presumably will only trade with relatively uninformed traders. Other dealers, such as exchange specialists, may not have the legal discretion (or perhaps the competence) to discriminate among orders.

Third, the order-purchasing dealers may be better able to identify and access liquidity when they want to adjust their own inventories than can other dealers. For example, few regulatory restrictions limit the access of OTC dealers to the options market, but many such restrictions make it impractical for exchange dealers to use the options markets.

Finally, some order-purchasing dealers have automated trading systems that allow them to make market at lower costs than can other dealers. For example, the Madoff trading system takes orders, arranges trades, send out confirmations, and settles trades with no paperwork and no data-entry errors. Madoff's automated systems also allow him to identify and control the risks inherent in market making continuously and thereby reduce his dealing costs.

In competitive dealer markets, free entry and exit of firms will ensure that the payments for order flow reflect the above four sources of profit. Payment for order flow arrangements therefore represent the transformation of the brokerage market from a market for the provision of an unauditable service (search for bet price) to a market for the provision of a standard auditable service (very quick and reliable execution at low commissions).

In effect, the order-purchasing dealers become the subagents of the brokers' clients. The dealers purchase order flows from the brokers and execute them at standard prices. They then obtain the best execution possible for their own account when they trade (layoff) those portions of the order flow that cause them to be out of their desired inventory levels. As specialists in the provision and management of liquidity in a given issue, they presumably can identify and obtain liquidity more efficiently than can most brokers. The profits that they make on the difference between the standard prices they offer the broker and the costs of doing their layoffs are then rebated (in competitive markets) to the brokers who then rebate them (in competitive markets) to their clients. The clients thus obtain the benefits of the dealers' expertise at organizing, identifying, and accessing liquidity. In this framework, payment for order flow is simply another characteristic of a market organized to meet the needs of various service clienteles. The clientele in this case consists of impatient small traders who are unable to audit the price-searching services provided by their brokers.

Public Policy Concerns   Widespread payment for order flow may widen ITS bid-ask spreads. Payment for order flow results, in part, because some dealers can discriminate between easy (small and uninformed) orders and difficult (large and/or information motivated) orders. When these dealers take the easy orders, the remaining order flow, which typically is routed to the primary exchanges, is riskier and more difficult to execute. The removal of the easy orders will therefore cause spreads to widen in the primary exchange markets, and this may cause the ITS spreads to widen.

Since purchased order flows are often executed at the ITS quotations, the entire system represents a positive feedback process. Order flow purchases may lead to wider spreads which will make order flow purchases more profitable. In competition, the increased profitability of order flow purchases will increase the order flow purchase price. The increased profitability will also allow dealers to purchase less desirable order flows. Both activities may cause wider ITS spreads.

The circularity is attenuated by three processes: First, dealers narrow ITS spreads when they post quotations as they search for liquidity to do their layoffs. Second, dealers may continue to display market orders in the ITS system in an effort to improve price. Such dealers in effect provide an underwriting service. They guarantee the ITS price but may work the order to improve the price. Such dealers are actually dealer/brokers. Acting as dealers, they stop the orders (guarantee the prices) against their own account while acting as brokers they search for better prices. Finally, if the execution of market orders appears to be expensive and uncertain, public traders—even impatient ones—will switch from the use of market orders to limit orders. Since impatient traders tend to submit aggressively price limit orders, their orders will narrow the spreads.

EXTERNALITIES

The above analyses suggest that the segmentation of markets to satisfy the different service needs to diverse clienteles is generally beneficial. Such segmentation enhances the provision of liquidity to traders with varying needs. If information flows freely between market segments and if no serious agency problems are present, segmentation is unlikely to have any significant effects on price formation.

These conclusions, however, assume that activities in one market segment do not adversely affect market quality in another market segment. If, however, trading activities have external effects on other segments, segmentation may be harmful to the public welfare. This section considers both negative and positive externalities.

Negative externalities are activities taken in one market segment that adversely affect market quality in another market segment. Such activities may need to be regulated to prevent market deterioration through segmentation. The first subsection below considers the negative externalities that make it difficult to enforce secondary precedence rules.

Positive externalities are activities taken in one market segment that confer positive benefits on other markets. Since markets often are not directly rewarded for these activities, regulation may be needed to ensure that they are provided in a segmented market. The second subsection below examines market continuity rules and the enforcement of insider trading rules.

The External Effects of Secondary Precedence Rules

Market order precedence rules determine how buy and sell orders are matched. The primary precedence rule is price: order and quotations having the best price are generally given highest priority. Secondary precedence rules may be based on submission time, exchange membership, display instructions, and/or size.

The New York and American Stock Exchanges precedence rules give highest priority to orders and quotations with the best price. At a given price, public orders then have precedence over member quotations and orders. Within the set of public orders at a given price, the first-submitted orders generally have highest precedence.[14]

In contrast, in the NASD dealer markets, dealer quotations have precedence over public orders (dealers are not required to represent public limit orders); otherwise, price has precedence, and time precedence is not enforced. The GLOBEX and Paris CAC trading rules give precedence first to orders with the best price, then to displayed orders over undisplayed orders, and finally to orders ranked by submission time.

Precedence rule hierarchies affect the character of a market. Markets that give precedence to displayed orders over undisplayed orders tend to favor uninformed traders over informed traders. Markets that give precedence to size favor large traders over small traders. Markets that give precedence to dealers over public traders favor dealers (who presumably serve public traders). Markets that give precedence to time favor patient precommitted traders over impatient last-minute traders. These rules are neither uniformly good nor uniformly bad. They simply determine the character of the market.

Markets presumably choose their precedence rules (and all other trading rules, services, and fees) to serve best their members and/or desired clientele. Competition among markets for order flow represents, in part, a competition to determine what set of rules and trading systems best serves the different needs of the trading community. Traders generally benefit from this competition as exchanges and proprietary trading systems introduce service-enhancing and cost-reducing innovations.

Implications for Segmented Markets   Unregulated competition among markets may be harmful, however, if the competition prevents one market from effectively implementing what would otherwise be a beneficial set of trading rules. In particular, consider the problem of enforcing precedence rules.

Price priority tends to be self-enforcing. Traders always seek the best price, and they usually insist that their agents do so as well (if the search is not too expensive or time-consuming). Price priority will be enforced across a segmented market as long as traders know what trading opportunities are available in each segment and can act upon them. Segmented markets are consolidated by traders who search for the best price.

Secondary precedence rules, however, are not self-enforcing. When presented with several traders of equal creditworthiness and trustworthiness offering the same price, most traders are indifferent as to with whom they trade.[15] Markets must actively enforce secondary precedence rules such as time precedence because traders will not do so themselves.

Secondary precedence rules are difficult or impossible to enforce across market segments because markets do not have jurisdiction over each other. Government regulations do not require markets to cooperate with each other to obtain universal enforcement of secondary precedence rules, nor do markets voluntarily choose to cooperate. Cooperation in the enforcement of secondary precedence rules is generally disadvantageous to the weaker or smaller market. Traders who do not have precedence in one market (usually the larger or dominant market) often go to another market to obtain higher precedence at the same price. Markets also do not cooperate because the secondary precedence rules used in one market may conflict with the secondary precedence rules used in another market.

For example, time precedence is not uniformly enforced across all markets where exchange-listed stocks trade. Regional exchange dealers and over-the-counter dealers like Bernard Madoff routinely are willing to trade at the same bid or ask prices that are quoted at the New York and American Stock Exchanges, after the New York and American quotations are made. If these regional and OTC dealers can then attract market orders at these prices, they will trade ahead of the earlier quotation upon which they set their price.[16] If these market orders otherwise would have been sent to the primary exchange markets, these dealers disadvantage the exchange traders—dealers and public limit order traders—who stand behind the primary market quotations. Another trading activity that violates time precedence is trade crossing (matching) by brokers. Many brokers like to match trades internally for execution. Depending on the broker, these matches may be for small trades and/or for large block trades. Internal matching ensures that the broker can obtain two commissions for the trade instead of one. These brokers then execute the trade at a market where the trade can be executed without interference from an order book. This process, of course, hurts traders who place their orders in order books. In both examples, the failure to enforce time precedence universally makes placing an order in the limit order book less attractive.

A public policy problem therefore arises in a segmented market with respect to the enforcement of secondary precedence rules. If the rules are desirable, they must be implemented through government intervention. In particular, if the maintenance of a public limit order book subject to time precedence is desirable, it must be sheltered from competition that does not enforce time precedence.

Unfortunately, the desirability of secondary precedence rules is subject to opinion and disagreement. Reasonable economic arguments support both sides of the question. Moreover, since each of these rules tends to favor one type of trader over another, universal enforcement of a secondary precedence rule will benefit some traders at the expense of other traders. Finally, note that even if secondary precedence rules were deemed to be desirable, some hierarchical ranking would be needed to be made to ensure that rules in one market did not conflict with those in another.

The scope of this chapter does not permit a full discussion of the merits and demerits of secondary precedence rules. Two arguments, however, illustrate some of the many issues involved.

Secondary precedence rules are only meaningful if a minimum

price variation rules requires that all prices be expressed as a multiple of some minimum price variation. (The minimum price variation at the NYSE and the AMEX is usually one eighth of a dollar for stocks trading above one dollar.) If the minimum price variation is small, secondary precedence rules will not be economically significant because traders can cheaply obtain precedence through price priority.[17] Traders can always obtain precedence by offering a better price. The minimum price variation determines the cost of obtaining precedence through price priority.

It thus would appear that secondary precedence rules applied in conjunction with a significant minimum price variation reduce price competition by encouraging traders to queue their orders rather than to improve their price. This conclusion, however, does not necessarily hold in markets where orders are exposed. In such markets, traders willing to expose orders when protected by a significant minimum price variation may not be willing to expose if there were no minimum price variation. If they do not expose, the market may appear less liquid, and traders may send their orders elsewhere.

Time precedence, in conjunction with a significant minimum price variation, protects traders who expose their quotations and limit orders. By exposing their orders, these traders risk that other traders may act on this information to their disadvantage. In particular, some traders, called quote-matchers, may quote on the same side of the market when they see displayed orders. The quote-matcher tries to profit on the information revealed by the displayed orders or to profit simply from the free trading option provided by the displayed orders. In either event, quote-matchers attempt to get their orders—orders that would not have been submitted had the original orders not been displayed—filled ahead of the original orders. Time precedence and a large minimum price variation protect traders who display quotations by forcing quote-matchers to improve price significantly if they wish to acquire precedence.[18]

Without the protection of an effective time precedence rule, fewer traders will be willing to display orders. Those willing to display might only do so at prices less favorable, rather than more favorable, than those that would be observed with the rule. Bid-ask spread may increase, rather than tighten, and the displayed width and depth of the market may both worsen. These arguments may explain why over-the-counter dealers do not quote for much size and why spreads tend to be greater in OTC markets than in exchange markets. The OTC markets do not enforce time precedence among dealer quotations. These arguments are also raised by exchanges concerned about the loss of market share to regional exchange dealers and to OTC dealers.

Summary   In a segmented market, secondary precedence rules can only be enforced if all segments are required to coordinate enforcement of the same rules. Not all segments will want to do so, however. If such secondary precedence rules are desirable, they must be enforced through government regulation. The above arguments illustrate some of the difficult issues involved in the evaluation of secondary precedence rules. Given the problems and uncertainties that would be associated with regulatory solutions to the problem of universal enforcement of secondary precedence rules, it is not surprising that none has yet been imposed.[19]

Market Competition and Positive Service Externalities

Markets compete for order flow by offering services that they believe will be attractive to their clientele. The services that markets offer can be divided into two groups according to whether the benefits that they provide are private or public.

The first set of services includes services that benefit only the traders who use the market. Order routing systems and accounting systems are examples of such services. Usage of these private services is easy to measure. Markets can, if they desire, easily charge their traders to cover the costs of providing these private services. Because markets can measure and charge for these services, successful markets will provide as much service as is demanded by its users.

The second set of market services includes services that benefit all traders who trade the security, regardless of whether they trade the security in the market that offers these services. Exchange efforts to regulate market quality, such as the enforcement of continuity rules and insider trading rules, are examples of such public services. The usage of these services is difficult to measure. Since markets cannot charge everyone who benefits from them, it may be hard to markets to cover the costs of providing them. Markets in aggregate may therefore provide fewer of these services than they would if all trade in a given security took place in a single market. Several examples illustrate the problem:

The New York and American Stock Exchanges enforce continuity rules that require their specialists to provide liquidity at times when they otherwise might not be willing to trade. These exchanges presumably believe that the resulting improvement in market quality is attractive to their clientele. In particular, some argue that continuity increases investors' confidence and makes them more willing to invest in the security. These benefits (if they exist) are public goods since they are enjoyed by everyone who holds the security, regardless of where they trade.

The improvement in market quality, however, comes at some cost. Specialists must somehow be compensated for the losses that they expect when the continuity rule forces them into trades that they otherwise would not be willing to make. The compensation they receive is their unique franchise in their specialty. Specialists are expected to build up a financial reserve when trading during unstressed times so that they can finance their trading when demands are placed on continuity. If the system works properly, its effect is to transfer wealth from traders who trade when markets are not very volatile to traders who trade when the markets are volatile. Whether this is desirable public policy depends on how the continuity rule affects investor confidence and, hence, stock valuations.

Even if the objective is accepted, exchanges face two problems in obtaining it. First, exchanges must somehow ensure that the value of the continuity services rendered by the specialists is equal to the value of the unique franchises granted to them. This requirement is difficult to implement because both values are difficult to measure. Second, specialists must be able to make excess profits when not required to trade to provide continuity. Excess profits are not possible, however, if specialists must compete with dealers in other markets who are not subject to the same continuity rules. The other dealers will compete when trading appears profitable, but they will withdraw from trading at times when the exchange specialists must trade against their immediate interests to provide continuity. Competition among markets therefore makes it difficult for a market to provide a public good like continuity.

The regulation of insider trading and manipulative practices are other examples of activities that produce public goods. The desired effect of both activities is to increase investor confidence in the markets and to lower transaction costs for investors by decreasing the risk that they (or their dealer intermediaries) will be hurt when trading with traders who unfairly use the markets. These regulatory activities are expensive to provide. Exchanges fund them through fees that they charge the traders who use their markets. Since all traders benefit from these services, traders can avoid paying for them by patronizing markets where these services are not provided. Unregulated segmented markets therefore will provide fewer of these services in aggregate than would a single market that receives all the order flow. The problem is further exacerbated because these regulatory services are most valuable when all market segments coordinate their surveillance. The SEC currently requires all markets to coordinate the surveillance, but the proportion of the burden borne by the primary exchanges exceeds their market share. The SEC is the natural funder—and perhaps provider—of these services, but due to recent budgetary constraints, it has been trying to have the exchanges bear more of the burden.

CONCLUSION

Summary

Markets tend to consolidate because traders are attracted to each other. It is easier and cheaper to trade where other traders trade.

Markets fragment because traders and the trading problems that they solve differ. Different market structures serve some clienteles better than they serve others. When the benefits from differentiation to some clientele exceed the benefits from consolidation, markets tend to fragment.

Some traders are small and unconcerned about the price impacts of their trades while others are large and very concerned about front-running. Small traders tend to prefer market structures that widely expose their orders so that everyone can see and react to them. Large traders prefer market structures that allow them to control how and to whom their orders are exposed.

Some traders are well informed about fundamental security values and therefore very concerned about revealing their information while others are relatively uninformed and very concerned about minimizing transaction costs. The former prefer to trade in individual stocks while the latter often prefer to trade index portfolios.

Some traders are impatient to trade and therefore willing to pay for liquidity while others are patient and willing to wait for their price. The former prefer quote-driven markets while the latter prefer order-driven markets.

Some traders are trustworthy and creditworthy while others are less so. The former prefer to trade only with each other but the latter would like to do so as well.

Notwithstanding these differences, the benefits of consolidation are apparent to all users. Traders often trade in a market that would not seem best for them simply because that market has already attracted liquidity. Conversely, no market will attract and keep liquidity if it does not well serve a sizable clientele. Competition among market structures reveals which market structures best serve the various traders in our economy.

Fragmented markets tend to reconsolidate when information about market conditions within each segment is widely available to all traders. Traders then use this information to adjust their orders, reroute their orders, or issue new orders. As a result, prices and liquidity in each segment reflect information from all other segments. This chapter calls a reconsolidated fragmented market a segmented market.

Price formation does not take place in a single market segment only. Prices are determined only through the interactions of all traders in all market segments.

Traders naturally enforce price priority in a segmented market when they seek the best price for their orders. Secondary order precedence rules, such a time precedence, are not generally enforced in segmented markets. If such rules are valuable, they must be implemented through coordinated regulation.

Markets are less likely to regulate price continuity, insider trading, and manipulative behavior when markets are segmented. These activities benefit every trader in the market, but the exchanges can only charge those traders who trade in its segment. If such activities are valuable, they must be implemented through coordinated regulation.

Open Questions

This chapter identifies many economic forces that affect market structure. The main thesis suggests that no single structure is the best structure for all traders. Fragmentation into specialized clienteles will generally improve service (liquidity provision) without significantly affecting price formation if information freely flows among segments. However, some public policy objectives may be incompatible with unregulated competition. In particular, when trading or regulatory activities in one segment affect another segment, regulatory coordination may be required to obtain public policy objectives.

Such regulation necessarily will trade off the interests of diverse traders. This opens a number of unresolved public policy questions:

Are the externalities identified above significant? Is time precedence valuable? Is order exposure valuable? Is market surveillance valuable? If so, who should pay for it?

How do we trade off the interests of diverse traders? Should small individual traders be favored over large institutional traders? Should impatient traders be favored over patent traders? Should public traders be favored over member traders? Should informed traders be favored over uninformed traders?

Finally, even supposing that answers can be found to these questions, can they be implemented? Can domestic regulators regulate market structure in a world in which there is global competition to provide exchange services?

NOTES

1. These concerns motivate the Market 2000 study currently in progress at the Securities and Exchange Commission. See SEC Release no. 34-30920.
2. Several other papers also provide general discussions of these issues. These include Miller and Upton (1989), Stoll (1990), and Amihud and Mendelson (1991).
3. Extensive readings on the effects of technology on the securities markets can be found in books edited by Lucas and Schwartz (1989) and Wagner (1989).
4. The present value of the transaction cost savings plus the value of the additional services must be greater than any fixed costs of changing from one trading system to another, otherwise no one will change. The most important of these fixed costs include retraining traders to use new systems and reworking internal order routing systems to access the new system.
5. Newsletters within the private sector also can provide this service.
6. These perspectives on block trading are discussed in greater detail in Burdett and O'Hara (1987).
7. These and other perspectives on index trading are discussed in greater detail in Harris (1990a).
8. This argument assumes that the trade can be identified as being part of a program. The introduction of specialist electronic order book displays on the floor of the NYSE makes it more difficult for specialists to identify program trades. Formerly, program trades could be identified by the simultaneous printing of order cards or by observing runners delivering individual orders.
9. Arbitrage profits are a lower bound on the costs of holding fragmented markets together. When arbitrageurs freely compete with each other, their profits reflect only the costs of their doing business. Those costs include expenditures for building, maintaining, and operating systems to identify pricing disparities and act upon them.
10. The definition of the problem assumes that the clients would be willing to pay for the

unspent resources. If not, the agents are simply doing what the clients want, and no agency problem exists.

11. Goodness of execution also should depend on the commissions clients give to their brokers. Clients who pay large commissions presumably expect more services and better prices, on average, than clients who pay small commissions.

12. Able/Noser Corp., SEI Corp., the Plexus Group, and others provide transaction cost measurement services. Unfortunately, their methods differ, and the differences are a source of controversy. In general, transaction costs are best measured using methods that take into account the circumstances and motivations for each trade. Such methods are not widely available.

13. When the quoted spread is equal to the minimum price variation, the crossed order probably will be executed either at the bid or the ask. One of the orders will pay the spread while the other receives the spread so that on average, the two orders are filled with no market impact. The same result can be obtained with greater fairness (and unfortunately greater settlement costs) if half of the order size is traded at the bid and half is traded at the ask.

14. At the NYSE, matched crosses of 25,000 or more shares have precedence at a given price over other orders that might have arrived first.

15. Large traders may prefer to trade with other large traders because the cost of clearing their trades depends on the number of traders with whom they are matched. Such traders would favor a size precedence rule.

16. These dealers generally post ITS bids and offers one-eighth of a dollar outside the primary market quotes, although sometimes they post the same quotes or even better quotes than in the primary market. Some dealers guarantee at least the best ITS system quote to their clients who meet certain size restrictions. To their clients, this guarantee is, in effect, the dealer quote. Note also that many of these dealers also attempt to improve price for their clients.

17. In general, all but the last precedence rule in a precedence hierarchy must be based on discrete variables. Otherwise, no precedence levels deeper than the first continuous ranking variable would ever determine precedence. For example, suppose precedence were given to discrete prices expressed in eighths, followed by time submission in hundredths of a second, followed by size in shares. Size precedence would only determine precedence in the unlikely event that two orders arrived in the same hundredth of a second.

18. More detailed discussions of quote-matcher trading strategies and their effects on market liquidity appear in Harris (1990b) and Amihud and Mendelson (1991). Empirical analyses of their importance appear in Harris (1992).

19. The often proposed consolidated limit order book represents an attempt to obtain universal time precedence across all ITS-linked markets.

REFERENCES

Amihud, Yakov, and Haim Mendelson. (1991). "How (Not) to Integrate the European Capital Markets," in A Giovannini and C. Mayer (eds.), *European*

Financial Integration. Cambridge University Press.

Burdett, Ken, and Maureen O'Hara. (1987). "Building Blocks: An Introduction to Block Trading," *Journal of Banking and Finance,* 11.

Harris, Lawrence. (1990a). "The Economics of Cash Index Alternatives," *Journal of Futures Markets,* 10: 2 (April), 179–94.

Harris, Lawrence (1990b). "Liquidity, Trading Rules, and Electronic Trading Systems," New York University Salomon Center Monograph Series in Finance, monograph no. 1990–4.

Harris, Lawrence (1992). "Minimum Price Variations, Discrete Bid/Ask Spreads, and Quotation Transparency," University of Southern California working paper (June).

Lucas, Henry C., Jr., and Robert A. Schwartz (eds.). (1989). *The Challenge of Information Technology for the Securities Markets.* Homewood, IL: Dow Jones–Irwin.

Miller, Merton H., and Charles W. Upton. (1989). "Strategies for Capital Market Structure and Regulation." University of Chicago working paper.

Securities and Exchange Commission. (1992). "U.S. Equity Market Structure Study." Release no. 34–30920.

Stoll, Hans. (1990). "Principles of Trading Market Structure." Vanderbilt University, Owen Graduate School of Management working paper no. 90–31.

Wagner, Wayne (ed.) (1989). *The Complete Guide to Securities Transactions.* New York: John Wiley & Sons.

CHAPTER 19

BROTHER, CAN YOU SPARE A DIME? LET'S DECIMALIZE THE U.S. EQUITY MARKETS!

Junius W. Peake

VARIATIONS

Rule 62. Bids or offers in stocks above one dollar a share shall not be made at a less variation than ⅛ of a dollar per share; in stocks below one dollar but above ½ of one dollar per share, at a less variation than ¹⁄₁₆ of one dollar per share; in stocks below ½ of one dollar per share, at a less variation than ¹⁄₃₂ of one dollar per share…provided that the Exchange may fix variations of less than the above for bids and offers in specific issues or classes of securities.

—New York Stock Exchange Constitution and Rules

INTRODUCTION

Section 2 of the Securities and Exchange Act of 1934, as amended, contains these words:

For the reasons hereinafter enumerated, transaction in securities…are affected with a national public interest which makes it necessary…to…perfect the mechanisms of a national market system for securities…[1]

More than 18 years after that language was added to the law, the mechanisms of the national market system envisioned by the Congress have not yet been perfected. There are a number of structural deficiencies in the markets for equities now being examined by committees of the Congress as well as by the Securities and Exchange Commission (SEC or Commission). One issue which has not yet received a thorough scrutiny is the size of the minimum price variations permitted by exchange rules. Although there are some exceptions, the minimum price variation permitted between transactions in most equities is one-eighth of a dollar, or 12 ½ cents per share.[2]

The House Subcommittee on Telecommunications and Finance is conducting a series of hearings which are focused on certain problems and deficiencies in the structure of U.S. equity markets.[3] Concurrently, the staff of the SEC's Division of Market Regulation is also studying market structure issues and problems, with the objective of receiving suggestions to improve the U.S. equity markets for American and international investors.[4]

The report which will follow the completion of the SEC's study is scheduled to be released prior to the end of 1993 and, among its other conclusions and recommendations, will set forth the Division of Market Regulation's position on minimum price variations. It will address decimalization, even though the original announcement of the study did not mention this subject. According to the press report, the Commission's staff has been looking at decimalization since 1991.[5] However, the Commission's most recent past chairman, Richard Breeden, was quoted as being cool to the idea of decimal pricing.[6] The new SEC chairman, Arthur Levitt, has not yet taken a public position on the decimalization issue.

The origins of the practice of trading equities in price increments of one-eighth of a dollar have been lost in the wreaths of tobacco smoke which must have been pervasive in the taverns and inns of New York City, including the Tontine coffee house, where America's first organized financial market center, the New York Stock Exchange, was born. One theory suggests that setting minimum price variations at the one-eighth of a dollar level came about because of the practice of cutting the Spanish dollar into eight pieces or "bits." (Hence, of course, the origin of the slang term for our quarter-dollar coin, "two bits.")

An alternative theory (the one held by the author) is that competitors in an open outcry auction tend to "split the difference." When there is a bid of $21 and an offer at $22, for example, the next bid or offer may be made at $21 ½, thus splitting the $1 difference, followed by a counter halfway between the remaining difference, at $21 ¼ or $21 ¾, as the case may be, etc. The reason price splitting stopped at ⅛, rather than at ¹⁄₁₆ or ¼, is unknown, except that smaller increments were probably uneconomic for the professionals who made the trading rules.

Regardless of the origins of the practice, however, quoting and trading stocks in eighths of a dollar price increments has become almost endemic in the U.S. equities market. Improved trading technologies, together with lower, competitive commissions for stock trading, as well as a dramatic increase in institutional trading since 1975, the year the law was changed,[7] the development of index trading, in which the lowest possible transaction costs are most important, and the invention of so-phisticated derivative financial instruments, all have led some market participants and its overseers to ask: should the existing rules which prohibit finer gradations of pricing increments be eliminated?[8] This chapter argues they should and proposes that the minimum permitted price increment be reduced from the present standard 12 ½ cents per share to one cent, the smallest monetary unit in common use in the United States.

This chapter analyzes the arguments for and against moving to deci-mal-based pricing and concludes that such a shift would most likely result in reduced trading costs for investors and market makers, lead to an increase in trading volumes, reduce market volatility, and enhance overall market liquidity, while at the same time reducing or eliminating a number of trading practices which have been criticized by the Com-mission and the Congress, such as the paying of cash and noncash in-ducements for order flow by some market centers to attract orders from broker/dealers.[9]

BACKGROUND

In economists' terms, a "perfect" market for financial instruments would have, among its other wondrous features, no transaction costs. Needless to say, such a perfect financial market exists solely in the minds of those who dream of such structures. However, in the real world, investors seek to find and use markets which include, among their other attributes, the lowest possible costs of execution of their trades. That search is endless;

transaction costs will never be reduced to zero. Modern technology, however, provides many of the practical tools which offer greater efficiency in the trading process and lower transaction costs.

There is a constant economic battle waged between investors and the financial intermediaries which service them: broker/dealers and market centers (exchanges and over-the-counter trading system operators). Not surprisingly, intermediaries have a visceral aversion to being disintermediated. Just as bank tellers watched with dismay as many of their functions were replaced by electronic automated teller machines, so financial intermediaries fear what they believe to be the Armageddon of their industry as automation makes ever greater inroads.

There is a significant difference, however, between the policy making positions of bank tellers and financial intermediaries: Bank tellers have little or no influence in making bank operational policy; financial intermediaries own, control, and operate the facilities which their clients—investors—must use. Financial intermediaries make the trading rules; investors must use the systems in the way the rules require. At the present time, the minimum price variation, whether *de facto* or *de jure*, is one-eighth of a dollar. The operators of existing market centers almost unanimously oppose any change to smaller price increments.

For nearly two centuries, commissions charged for the execution of orders in stocks listed on exchanges were fixed by rule. After a great deal of study and controversy, Congress finally passed a law which forced commission rates to become fully competitive. That law, the Securities Acts Amendments of 1975,[10] focused most of the public's attention on the unfixing of the minimum commission rate structure. Fixed minimum commission rates had been one of the two major policy pillars on which the exchange stood and prospered for 183 years.[11]

The fixed minimum commission rates in force during the 1960s and early 1970s were very high when compared to those which are now being charged under competition. Whether or not a customer wanted any more service than a bare-bones execution, commissions were calculated at the same rate per 100 shares, whether the order executed was for 100, 1,000, or 10,000 shares. In other words, a 1,000 share order would have a commission charge 10 times greater than a 100 share order; a 10,000 share order would have a commission charge 100 times greater, and so forth.

In 1963, the Securities and Exchange Commission conducted a study which resulted in a 6,000-page report on the U.S. securities industry (the Special Study).[12] While a great deal of attention was given in the Special Study to the fixed commission rate structure of the NYSE, no mention can be found of the existence of the fixed minimum price variation rules of the exchanges. This omission should not have been surprising, however, since at that time fixed minimum commission rates, not fixed minimum price variations, were the focus of most of the debate.

> What are the qualities of a "good" trading market? It is sometimes said, in the law or elsewhere, that a market should be "fair," "honest," "free," "open," "efficient," "orderly," "continuous," "liquid" (or "fluid"), and perhaps other things.
>
> The act itself speaks only once of a "free and open market" when, in Section 15A(b)(7), it directs that the rules of registered national securities associations shall "remove impediments to and perfect the mechanism of a free and open [over-the-counter] market; * * *.[13]

The authors then provide their definitions of "free,"

> "Free" presumably implies that the forces of supply and demand should operate without the interjection of artificial factors. Insofar as the extraneous factors might be manipulative, the concept overlaps that of fairness. But "free," in its ultimate sense, may go further to exclude extraneous forces of a beneficent (i.e., stabilizing or market ordering) nature. In the latter sense, a completely "free" market would be one in which the spontaneous bids and offers of buyers and sellers would be permitted to affect prices regardless of the sharpness or duration of the resulting movements.[14]

While the reference to "free and open markets" in the statute is limited to over-the-counter stock trading, the legislation which mandated a national market system for securities did not limit that system to either exchange-listed or unlisted stocks. In fact, the legislation was drafted to include all types of securities subject to the Commission's oversight, but, to date, almost all of their attention has been focused on creating a national market system in equity securities alone.

Despite the statutory language, U.S. securities markets are by no means "free and open." There are many restrictive federal regulations, as well as exchange and NASD rules which prescribe in detail what can and cannot be done by investors and market intermediaries. Rule 62 of the New York Stock Exchange and its counterparts are good evidentiary examples of this.

A table[15] in the Special Study gives an idea of the level of fixed commissions which prevailed on the NYSE in 1963, the year of the study:

Table VI-cc-NYSE nonmember commission per round lot[16]

Price per share	$10	$25	$40	$50	$75	$100	$150
Commission							
Dollar amount	17	31.5	30	44	46.5	49	54
As % of principal	1.7	1.26	.975	.88	.62	.49	.36

Given the large size of the fixed commission rates, it is not surprising that the Special Study neglected to focus on size of the trading costs imposed on investors created by the imposition of a fixed minimum price variation of 12 ½ cents per share. According to the NYSE's data, the average stock price traded on their exchange was $47.53 in 1960 and $53.44 in 1965, while in 1975, the year the Securities Acts Amendments were passed, the average price of a share traded on the NYSE had declined sharply to $30.48.[17]

Today, however, competition has greatly reduced commission rates. Some "no brainer" institutional executions are done for as little as one cent per share.[18] However, commissions for institutional-sized orders are frequently higher, depending on the level of execution skill and/or other services required.[19]

It would be extremely rare today for commissions on institutional-sized transactions to equal—much less to exceed—the present fixed minimum price variation of 12 ½ cents per share, even if a charge for soft dollar services were included in the commission rate per share, a far cry from the fixed minimum rates in force during the 1960s.

Individual clients, as well, have benefited greatly from the unfixing of commissions. One discount brokerage firm,[20] Olde Discount, even advertises on television that they will execute some orders for more than 1,000 shares of stock without charging any commission for trade executions at all.[21] Other discount brokers advertise commission rates of far less than 10 cents per share. For example, Kennedy, Cabot & Co. has recently taken a series of full-page advertisements in *The New York Times*, in which they state they charge "2¢ per share commission to buy or to sell 5,000 shares and over, any price stock 2¢ per share," and "3¢ per share commission to buy or to sell 2,000 shares and over, any stock 3¢ per share."[22]

Technological innovations, especially the electronic telecommunication and trade execution facilities introduced during the last two decades, have reduced the cost of order entry, routing, and execution. Orders which used to require bespoke execution services are now commoditized. Many of the employees who are involved with order acceptance and processing functions are salaried, rather than on commission, further reducing execution costs. In short, it costs less to execute trades today than it did in 1963, 1973, or 1983.

It is unlikely that commissions can be reduced much further without significant structural changes being made to the trading mechanisms and/or changing the rules under which market centers operate. However, the rescission of one rule—the fixed minimum price variation rule— offers considerable promise of allowing further significant transaction cost reduction. It is now time to remove the last outdated remnant of the former fixed minimum commission rate structure which has for so long been so costly to investors and a barrier to more efficient markets: the fixed minimum price variation of 12 ½ cents per share.

Among the revisions made in the Securities Exchange Act by the 1975 legislation was a new section of the Securities Exchange Act of 1934, which ordered the SEC to "facilitate" the development of a "national market system" for securities trading.[23]

While the call for a national market system would be important for the operations of stock exchanges and the over-the-counter markets, the most visible effect of the legislation on investors was the requirement for total rescission of the fixed commission schedules charged for the execution of securities trades. Fixed minimum commissions were mandated for NYSE members under the Buttonwood Agreement, and established a cartel, two practices which are today prohibited by law.[24]

There is little or no question that the unfixing of securities commission rates since 1975 has had a beneficial effect for investors.[25] Trading volume is up substantially (see Figure 19–1).[26] Spreads between bids and offers are narrower on average, and, as shown above, commission rates are lower.

The two largest components of trade execution costs are commissions and market impact. Wayne Wagner postulates a total of four elements of cost associated with a trade: commission cost; [market] impact cost; timing cost; and opportunity cost.[27] He analyzed 54,000 institutional trades and determined that the average commission per share to be 5.6 cents, with lower commissions being charged by crossing net-

FIGURE 19–1
Annual Trading Volumes—New York Stock Exchange, 1970–1992

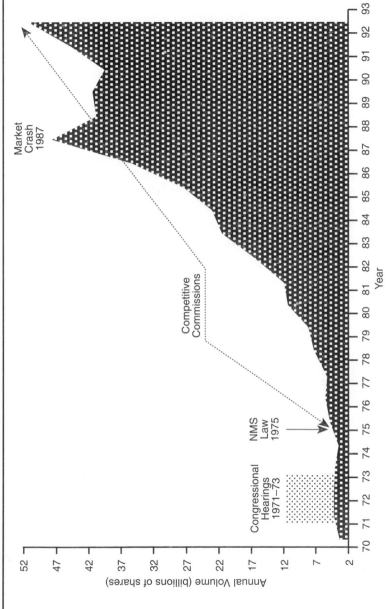

works,[28] and higher commissions being charged for trades "...that require execution skill or payment for research services."[29]

Wagner then estimates the costs of market impact for these transactions. He makes the point that, unlike commissions, which are shown as a separate line item on each confirmation sent to the customer, the size of market impact cannot be measured with precision. Wagner defines market impact as:

> ...the change in price between the time an order is presented to a broker and the actual execution. Thus it is the price change during the time the order is exposed to the market by the broker.[30]

For the 54,000 trades he analyzed, he estimates market impact cost to average 7 cents per share.[31] While it may be a coincidence that the average commission per share on these trades (5.6 cents), plus the market impact cost (7 cents) adds almost precisely to the 12 ½ cents which is the fixed minimum price variation permitted by NYSE Rule 62, it demonstrates that the minimum price variation approximates the combined total of the two major cost components of the execution of an institutional securities trade.

While it seems fairly certain that commission rates would remain constant if the minimum price variation were smaller than one-eighth, it also seems probable that market impact cost might well decrease. This logic holds because the minimum size of the market impact on any single order must be at least one-eighth of a point if there is a price change between the time the order is entered and executed. If, on the other hand, a minimum price variation were as small as one cent per share, market impact could be reduced by as much as one order of magnitude for some trades, less for others. Any reduction of market impact cost would inure to the benefit of investors and to market makers.

The size of the market impact is a function of market liquidity.[32] The greater the liquidity of the market in any security, the less market impact any single order should have. Thus, it is in the interest of all investors that the market should be structured to maximize liquidity.

The amount of potential savings to be realized by investors if market impact costs can be reduced is enormous. Total trading on all U.S. equity markets in 1992 exceeded 100 billion shares.[33] At that trading volume, if the market impact cost for both buyers and sellers could be diminished by just one-half cent per share (one cent total cost reduction for both parties), annual execution cost reductions would exceed $1 billion.

Professors Blume and Goldstein have written about what they call "effective spreads."[34] They demonstrate that the spreads displayed by market makers are often greater than the spread at which they are willing to trade. They write,

> If the displayed spread were always one eighth—the minimum spread for any stock with a price greater than one dollar, the effective spread would also be one eighth. Only when the displayed spread exceeds one eighth can the effective spread be smaller than the displayed spread.[35]

Taking Blume and Goldstein's findings to what would appear to be a logical conclusion, one could postulate that if the minimum price differential were further reduced from the 12 ½ cent per share minimum presently allowed, some dealers who would display a spread of one-eighth of a dollar might be willing to trade at prices between that spread.

BEST EXECUTION

One of the mandates given the Commission by the Congress in the 1975 legislation was to assure investors what has become to be known as "best execution."[36] Best execution, from the perspective of an investor, is to pay the least, if a buyer, and receive the most, if a seller. All else is pure sophistry. At the April 15th session of the Markey Hearings, Chairman William Donaldson of the NYSE made the following reply in response to a question from Chairman Markey:

> In a funny way, the idea of "best execution" is the worst execution. Best execution which is executed at either side of the market [at the bid or offer] is the worst execution. The best execution is a system which gives an opportunity for price improvement.

Chairman Donaldson is, of course, correct. If the quoted market is 20 bid, offered at 20 ¼, being able to trade between these two prices improves the execution for both buyer and seller. But suppose the fixed minimum price variation were one-quarter of a dollar, or 25 cents per share, rather that the present 12 ½ cents per share. It would be impossible to trade between the bid and offer at the eighth differential.[37]

With the fixed minimum price variation at 12 ½ cents per share, the same circumstances are extant, except it is impossible to trade at a spread smaller than 12 ½ cents. Why should investors—or market makers—be prohibited from trading at prices between the 12 ½ cent price increments? The only reasons are rules, customs, and traditions, none of which are embedded in stone.

Mr. Donaldson went on to note:

> And you can say that price improvement is just an eighth or a quarter [of a dollar]. Last year on the NYSE, we estimated that $500 million was saved by investors through 30 percent of their orders achieving price improvement between the bid and the ask.

If price improvement has that potential for investor savings with minimum price spreads at one-eighth, would it not be likely that substantial additional savings could be made if minimum spreads were reduced to one cent? With decimal pricing, best execution could become a certainty, rather than a concept, since the potential for price displacement by an order with a better price would force all orders through a central pricing mechanism to assure brokers' customers (and the brokers' regulators) that best execution was being attained. No longer would just matching a price at the narrowest eighth be sufficient; true price discovery and competition among buyers and sellers would be assured.

THE MAJOR STATED ARGUMENTS AGAINST DECIMALIZATION

As with all proposals for change, there are differences of opinion about whether or not the suggested change will be beneficial and, if beneficial, to whom: intermediaries or investors. Investors want the most efficient, liquid, cost-effective market possible. Financial intermediaries want a market just efficient enough to (a) attract as many investor orders as possible; and (b) structured in a manner which maximizes their own profits. These two objectives are not congruent. The provision of intermediation services has a monetary cost, and intermediaries want to maximize their revenues. Modern technology affords investors the opportunity for more efficient market structures which require less use of intermediation services. This dichotomy of economic interests results in widely disparate positions on the subject of decimalization.

Needless to say, those who provide the present level of intermediation services are not happy about the prospect of becoming disintermediated. However, intermediaries are fortunate: They own, control, and operate the markets' structural mechanisms, and, consequently, have a major role in determining what investors are allowed to do. Their economic power has enabled them to slow down the rate of change from older trading systems which require a strong dose of intermediation to newer ones in which investors would be able to trade with a lesser requirement for intermediation services. But at the end of the day, as always, those who oppose and resist technological advances will eventually be overwhelmed by their force. Ultimately, better systems will triumph, since the worst enemy of a good system is a better system.

This chapter advocates removal of the barriers to decimal pricing to enable investors to trade at lower costs. If this is to occur, however, the strong and organized opposition from many important players in the industry must be overcome. And, not surprisingly, those most vocal in their opposition to decimalization are the people who represent market centers which may be economically hurt by the change.

Following are the four principal arguments being made against decimalization:

1. There is no need for the change, since there has been no investor demand.[38]
2. It will cost several hundred million dollars to make the change.[39]
3. There will be a loss of market liquidity as a result of market maker defections.[40]
4. If the minimum price variation were one cent instead of 12 ½ cents, the time priority[41] of orders would be subverted, since a trader would merely have to improve the existing best price by a single penny (instead of 12 ½ cents) to move to the head of the order queue.[42]

RESPONSE TO ARGUMENT 1

There is no need for the change, since no investors have asked for it.

A supplier must have a service or product to sell before a demand can be created for it.[43] If it is impossible to obtain a narrower spread than 12 ½ cents, how could a customer demand such a service? But just because investors are not aware that spreads narrower than 12 ½ cents per share might be possible does not automatically mean that they would not want them if they were available.

After all, what buyer would prefer paying $20.125 per share for 100 shares if he or she could buy the same stock for $20.07, thus saving five and a half cents per share, or a total of $5.50 for the entire order? If one or more market centers can offer the service of executing trades at better prices because trading can be conducted with narrower spreads, investors will demand this improved service.

In addition, all business entities should want to be able to meet their customers' unstated demands, since being first to anticipate unstated needs provides a service supplier with a competitive advantage. Finding and meeting unstated customer needs is like finding an economic version of the Holy Grail. For example, so far as we are aware, there was no customer demand for Coca-Cola before it was created and offered for sale. While in no way necessary for human life or health, Coke now meets a formerly unknown demand which for centuries was unstated by the company's billions of consumers worldwide.

In addition, there *is* a public demand for decimalization. One investor, Jeffrey P. Ricker, has recently made known his demand for decimalization. In a letter of comment[44] on the SEC's Market 2000 study, Mr. Ricker made the following points:

> There are two components in the cost of trading a stock: brokerage commissions and "friction."
>
> For brokerage commissions, the only rule is that there are no rules. Thanks to May Day,[45] commissions are now only one-fifth of the 12 cents per share cost of trading an S&P 500 basket of stocks.[46] We're talking about 2 or 3 cents a share.
>
> The second cost component is called by a number of names, such as slippage, market impact, liquidity cost, and dealer spread... Friction is a direct result of the market structure, and here there are a lot of rules. Today, friction averages about ten cents a share when you trade an S&P 500 basket of stocks. With friction consuming about four-fifths of the cost of an equity trade, there is plenty of room for improvement.
>
> ...I think friction can be reduced from ten cents to a few cents per share... Furthermore, I predict trading volume will increase enough to make almost everyone else happy, too. With the right reforms, billion share days will become the routine.

Mr. Ricker goes on to write:

> The single most beneficial reform is decimal pricing for stocks. With decimal pricing and one cent price increments, or "ticks," friction is reduced, and you also resolve a lot of the concerns expressed by the Division [of Market Regulation] on the structure of the equity market.

Mr. Ricker continues:

> I believe decimal pricing is the single best reform we can make to the nation's equity markets. In addition to the obvious benefit of reduced friction, you also resolve some of the concerns expressed by the Division [of Market Regulation] on the structure of the stock market. For example, payment for order flow, fragmentation,[47] and internalization[48] are three problem areas resolved by decimal pricing.

He then makes a very important statement, dealing with the competition for order flow among the various market centers:

> In this "competition" there are no winners or loser, only ties. Because an extra eighth is a stiff price to pay to get inside the primary market quote, the nonprimary markets are seldom on the inside quote alone. Therefore, they do not appear to bear risk or contribute much to the price discovery process.
>
> Competition among the exchanges would be a lot more lively if stocks were priced in decimal. For an extra penny, an exchange could break a tie and have the inside market quote. More competition brings ITS closer to the original point of eliminating fragmentation. ITS becomes an arena instead of a cozy cartel.[49]

While Mr. Ricker is only one investor, the depth of thought and quality of his commentary should more than make up for the fact that his views have not yet been echoed by others. When the case for decimalization is finally presented and discussed, both individual and institutional investors will most likely add their voices to his. After all, investors of every stripe want to trade with the lowest possible transaction costs. The spread is a significant part of the transaction cost. Thus, narrower spreads mean lower costs. And narrower spreads are only possible when the existing minimum price differentials are reduced to cents.

RESPONSE TO ARGUMENT 2

Changing to decimals from eighths will require the
expenditure of huge sums of money.

At a recent House hearing which examined market structure, there was nearly universal skepticism toward the idea of shifting to decimal pricing, at least in the near future. In addition to William Donaldson of the New York Stock Exchange, who reiterated his argument that conversion costs would be inordinately high, the chief executives of the Boston,

Midwest (now Chicago), Philadelphia, and Pacific Stock Exchanges all raised objections to the prospect of decimalization anytime in the near future, although they all conceded that decimal pricing is probably inevitable. By contrast, Frederick Moss, the chief executive of the Cincinnati Stock Exchange, an all-electronic marketplace which has no trading floor, said his exchange would have no difficulty converting to decimals.[50]

There is also a certain sense of *"déjà vu* all over again" (to quote Yogi Berra) in listening to the argument that changes cannot be made because of their inordinate cost. When proposals were made in the late 1970s to build an electronic trading system known as a Composite Limit Order Book, or CLOB, which would consolidate all bids and offers from investors within each issue into an electronic centralized trading arena, the cost to do so became a stumbling block larger than the pyramid of Cheops.[51]

At the first NYU conference on market structure—at which Bob Schwartz, the chairman of this conference, was co-chair—the then Executive Vice President of the New York Stock Exchange, Francis J. Palamara, criticized the potential cost of a CLOB.[52]

> In costing out a prospective full CLOB, the Securities Industry Automation Corporation came up with a minimum price tag of $20 million and implementation time of three to six years.[53]

After continuing his criticisms, he concluded with his punch line:

> No matter how you look at it, $20 million plus is a lot of money.[54]

Contrast that statement with the recent testimony of the present chairman of the NYSE at the House hearings on market structure, referred to earlier, in which he stated that the NYSE had spent "more than $1 billion" over the past 15 years on automation of their market systems.[55] The automated systems introduced and operated by the NYSE do not yet include electronic execution capabilities for order in equities, such as those systems under discussion in 1978.

In addition, what might appropriately be called the "Chicken Little arguments" against market reform were constantly being made during the dozen years between the SEC's Special Study and the passage of the Securities Acts Amendments of 1975.[56] These arguments were filled with dire predictions about the calamity that inevitably would result for the securities industry if the then-existing NYSE minimum commission rate schedule was abolished. At a Senate hearing, such a prediction was made by the NYSE's executive vice president.[57] Other witnesses during those hearings and at parallel hearings being held by the House voiced similar concerns.

Finally, it is hard to believe that the NYSE, which has recently spent more than $1 billion on automation, would not have prepared for the possibility of a shift to decimals, especially when at least one unidentified senior exchange official said, referring to the potential for decimalization, "It doesn't take 20/20 vision to see [decimals] coming. I think it is inevitable."[58]

In fact, academic papers published by members of the exchange's in-house economics staff and their resident visiting academics from leading American universities demonstrate that the data records of trades and quotations carried within the NYSE systems contain prices in decimal format, carried out to five decimal places.[59] In short, while there will, of course, be some expense in shifting execution and quotation prices to cents from eighths, the size of that expense should be relatively small and nowhere near the astronomical sums suggested by NYSE officials.

In any case, the estimated cost of making such a conversion should already be known with some degree of precision, since the SEC in 1991 asked the Securities Industry Automation Corporation (SIAC), majority-owned by the NYSE and the sole vendor of services for the three major national market system components of the existing version of a national market system, to study the costs of making such a conversion.[60] While there has been no public report to date of the results of that study, it would not appear unreasonable to believe that it is completed.

RESPONSE TO ARGUMENT 3

Smaller minimum price differentials would cause (some) market makers to abandon their functions, thus reducing market liquidity.

The Securities Traders' Association (STA), a trade group for more than 7,000 market makers, came down against decimalization in one of the NASD's order execution systems. Representatives of the STA's board of governors were reported to have argued, "...decimal pricing also could reduce the spreads market makers receive in their trading activities...

adding that as the spreads narrowed, market making may no longer be economically feasible for some operations."[61]

Six months later, the president of the STA, John Watson III, was reported to have asserted that nobody on The Street would profit from such a move [decimalization].[62] The report went on to say,

> "The STA would oppose such a move," Watson said, adding that he perceived no apparent reason for replacing price quotations in dollars and fractions with quotations in dollars and cents. Responding to the argument that by narrowing spreads, the decimal quote system would benefit the investor, Watson said, "So would trading for nothing."
>
> "Everyone needs to make a fair profit," Watson said, adding that the cost of unraveling the present system would be prohibitive.

These arguments make no economic sense. Reducing the minimum price differential does not *require* market makers to reduce their spreads. These assertions are but another example of a Chicken Little argument, which has as its main objective: *If you scare 'em enough, maybe they'll go away.* The *market*, not market center operators, should determine the spread. History may be a useful guide in predicting the probable consequences of a change in regulations which has the potential for cost reduction. Although when fixed minimum commission rates were abolished in 1975, many people believed the rates would not decrease at all or would be reduced by only a small percentage. They came down dramatically. Competitive forces produced a far greater reduction in commissions than many believed were possible.

If bid-ask spreads for some securities are reduced below the present 12 1/2 cent minimums, they will be reduced solely because the market— instead of market center rules—have determined their size.

If some market makers leave the field and spreads remain at their present levels or are reduced, it will merely demonstrate that there were too many market makers in a business in which fewer were actually needed, just as some market makers went out of business or merged when the NASDAQ system's introduction in 1971 resulted in narrower spreads.[63]

If a consequence of minimum price variation reduction should be increased activity by investors functioning as *de facto* market makers, narrowing spreads by entering bids and/or offers at prices which better the existing quotations, this event should be loudly applauded by all, especially by the Commission and their congressional oversight committees, since the national market system legislation specifically called for "the opportunity for investors' order to be executed without the participation of a dealer."[64]

If the existing minimum price variations are made smaller, only three things can possibly happen:

1. Spreads (on average) will remain the same.
2. Spreads (on average) will be reduced.
3. Spreads (on average) will increase.

The first outcome is highly unlikely; the second, probable; the third also highly unlikely, since competitive forces will mitigate against this possibility.

However, some commentators have postulated that the market's overall liquidity will be reduced, even if the spreads narrow. The argument offered is that if spreads are reduced, market makers' profits will also be reduced, thus causing market makers to take smaller trading positions and thus reduce liquidity.

Narrower spreads will also reduce market makers' trading costs, since traders will be able to trade at those narrower spreads. Lower trading costs will increase trading volume, as has happened in the past. In short, the argument that liquidity will be reduced is assertion; no evidence has been offered to support the argument. Logic would appear to support the notion that an increase in liquidity will take place, since investors as well as market makers will be able to enjoy the lower trading costs that would automatically accompany narrower spreads.

RESPONSE TO ARGUMENT 4

A one-cent minimum price differential subverts time priority, since all a market maker (or investor) need do to improve an existing bid or offer is to increase a bid or lower an offer by one cent to gain price priority.

Perhaps it is well to state the obvious: A better price is a better price, regardless of whether it is better by one cent per share, five cents per share, or 12 ½ cents per share. Buyers want to pay the least possible; sellers want to receive the most money. For example, if, on average, investors can buy at $20.07 per share and sell at $20.07 per share, they are better off than if the buyers are limited to buying at $20.125 per share and the sellers to selling at $20.00 per share.

The hundreds of thousands of words which have filled recent SEC releases, congressional hearing testimony, and the financial stories about payment for order flow were focused on one number: one cent per share, paid by certain market centers for order flow directed to them. From all the attention paid to it, clearly one cent per share must be a significant sum of money in a financial transaction. Why else would members of Congress, SEC commissioners and staff, exchange and NASD CEOs, operators of proprietary trading systems, and a plethora of industry commentators, lawyers, and academics spend so much time on the subject?

One national financial reporter recently commented, "The subject of payment for order flow does not interest my editors any more because it seems to them like a 'victimless crime.'" The reporter is right. The one cent per share paid for order flow is not the real issue. The real issue is market fragmentation and the loss of market share by the traditional market centers, the exchanges.

With a 12 ½ cent minimum price variation, Bernard Madoff, operator of one of the new proprietary market centers, is able to pay one cent per share for much of his order flow and still perform his market making profitably. Because his firm's trading and trading support systems are very cost-effective, he is able to trade for a net spread of 10 ½ cents per share on a percentage of his orders and make a profit.

Under the one-eighth of a dollar minimum spread policy, it is relatively simple for Madoff to equal the prices being quoted in other market centers without adversely affecting the prices paid by the customers of his clients. On the other hand, if there were to be a reduction of the minimum price variation to one cent per share, dealing spreads might narrow to a level at which Madoff would no longer be able to offer a one cent per share cash inducement for order flow and remain profitable. With narrower spreads, customers would automatically receive the benefit of lower trading costs, rather than the brokers, who deliver their clients' order flow to firms like Madoff.

Professor Lawrence Harris of the University of Southern California makes a similar argument against reducing the fixed minimum price variation to one cent:

> Time precedence and a large minimum price variation protects traders who display [their quotations] by forcing quote-matchers to significantly improve price if they wish to acquire precedence.[65] (Words in brackets added.)

Harris opines that without the protection of a meaningful time priority rule (relatively large minimum price variations being the key ingredient):

...fewer traders will be willing to display orders. Those willing to display might only do so at prices less favorable, rather than more favorable, than those that would be observed with the rule [to reduce the size of price variations].[66] (Words in brackets added.)

Harris goes on to conclude:

Bid-ask spreads may increase, rather than tighten, and the displayed width and depth of the market may both worsen.[67]

Professor Harris speculates only that bid-ask spreads *may* increase. They may, of course, also decrease. If Professor Harris's speculation is correct, however, would not the stock exchanges be falling all over themselves to reduce the minimum price variation? Wider spreads and reduced depth would have the tendency to increase market makers' profits, while at the same time a position taken in favor of narrower price variations would give the public, regulators, and legislators the impression that the exchanges are altruists who argue positions which favor the interests of investors. The reason exchanges take the position against decimalization should be clear to all: the majority of the members they represent believe narrower spreads will reduce spreads, which would negatively impact market makers' profits.

Mr. Ricker makes a second argument which questions Professor Harris's conclusions, as follows:

A large [minimum] tick is totally unnecessary because there are ways to discover quote-matching other than raising the price.

Quote-matchers are common in the rough and tumble commodity pits that have small ticks. However, they don't get that common. Every so often someone aggressively bids for size, quote-matchers top the bid by a tick, and then the first bidder hits the matchers' bids while pulling his "aggressive" bid at the same time. The quote-matchers are tricked into supplying cheap liquidity.

The threat and occasional application of such discipline can control quote-matchers' activities to an economic equilibrium. In an efficient market the return to a quote-matching strategy should not be more than the return of any other strategy of comparable risk. (Word in brackets added.)

Ricker concludes his argument:

I believe a very small tick best encourages spread-narrowing limit orders. Legitimate or not, they all supply liquidity. Since quote-matching can be controlled by other means, there is no reason whatsoever to have a large tick.

In summary, the insidious eighth has until now been spared its due share of criticism. It is the largest single correctable source of friction in our nation's equity markets. If decimal pricing reduced bid-ask spreads by a nickel, investors would save $1.26 billion of costs per year on the Big Board alone. The most important benefits of decimal pricing are increased liquidity, less friction, and more efficient price discovery. In addition, decimal pricing helps resolve other problems in our equity markets, such as payment for order flow, fragmentation, internalization, and limit order precedence in cross trades, order matching, and quote matching.[68]

Professor Harris has written another paper in which he specifically addresses the minimum price variation, or "tick size."[69] Harris comes to the conclusion, based on his analysis of trade data that, if the minimum price differential were cut in half, to one sixteenth, the mean average spread for stocks would decrease by 38 percent for stocks trading below $10 (10.5 cents from 17 cents) and 21 percent for stocks selling above $40 per share (19.2 cents from 24.2 cents).[70]

Some financial intermediaries make arguments against decimalization which can best be described as schizophrenic. Many of these spend a great deal of effort and money railing against the practice of paying one cent per share for order flow, while at the same time arguing that reducing the fixed minimum price variation by 12 ½ times that amount will not accomplish anything useful for investors.[71] They claim that the third market dealers who execute orders in exchange-listed securities are depriving their customers of the one cent per share paid for order flow, as well as an occasional eighth of a point which could have been saved if the executions occurred on a primary exchange (read "their own exchange").[72] At the same time, the very same people argue against decimalization, which will probably save investors several cents per share on many trades, claiming that such an action might reduce liquidity and would be "too expensive" to implement.

In addition, these same people cite academic studies which claim to demonstrate that executions on the NYSE on average save investors money over time. An academic at the University of Michigan asserts that on the NYSE, "At a ¼ spread, a full 62 percent/(38 percent) of the NYSE /(NASD) trades execute between the best bid and ask prices. Clearly the best ITS quote is not capturing all the liquidity in the market."[73] Another study demonstrated that the Consolidated Quotation System, on which the SEC has relied to disseminate the best available prices, does not necessarily display all entered bids and offers, since specialists are allowed to conceal some of the bids and offers they receive from investors. As a result, there is little doubt that some reasonable percentage of orders can be executed at a price better than that shown with a quarter point spread.[74] If this is true, would not at least some orders entered when the spread is an eighth of a dollar, the existing minimum price variation, be executed at a price somewhere within that spread?

Professor Lee sets forth a table which shows the results of his calculations of "The Additional Cost of Buying."[75]

	Average by Shares	
Exchange	*1988*	*1989*
Boston	0.70	0.30
Cincinnati	−0.17	0.26
Midwest	−0.39	−0.18
Pacific	−0.21	0.25
Philadelphia	0.46	0.97
NASD	0.65	0.77
Instinet	0.01	1.03
All	−0.04	0.23

The NYSE apparently considers this price difference, which averages less than one-quarter of one cent per share, important, or presumably they would not have included the study in their submission to the Commission.[76] If 23/100ths of one cent is important, why isn't one cent—more than four times greater—even more important? After all, as noted above, a single one cent per share savings in total execution cost reduction (one-half cent for both buyer and seller), potential execution savings of more than $1 billion annually are possible.

In another study submitted to the Commission by the NYSE to support their case against cash payments for order flow, Professor Petersen and Fialkowski of the University of Chicago state in the abstract of their paper: "We find an average price improvement of 4.5 cents [per share] for a sample of retail orders. Inconsistent with a national market for equities, we find the expected price improvement is three cents higher on the NYSE when compared to the regional exchanges."[77] Again, the potential savings cited are far smaller than those which might be achieved if decimalization is introduced. We ask, "If 4.5 cents per share or 3 cents per share are significant amounts, why not 6.25 cents, the midpoint of an eighth point spread?" In another market, that for U.S. Treasuries, the Antitrust Division of the United States Department of

Justice is conducting an investigation into the minimum price variations used in trading Treasury securities. According to press reports of this investigation, a 1991 agreement among the primary government bond dealers restricts the minimum price variation to firms outside their group to 1/64th of a point, while they trade among themselves in smaller price increments.[78]

In short, if tiny price variations are so important to so many—academics, exchanges, investors, and the Department of Justice—why shouldn't a 12 ½ cent minimum price variation, the changing of which has the potential to save investors billions of dollars annually, not also be important?

The Unstated Arguments against Decimalization

Decimalization will lead to narrower spreads; narrower spreads will lead to disintermediation.

True. To the extent that investors can narrow spreads, there will be a greater likelihood that a buying investor's order will be able to be executed against a selling investor's order. In addition, greater competition in the market making and order execution businesses should lead to a reduction in the number of market centers trading the same securities—otherwise known as market fragmentation.

The greater the number of market centers acting as intermediaries, the greater the percentage of transactions which will require intermediation; the more centralized the trading, the less the intermediation.

Decimalization will result in reduced profits for market makers.

Probably not true. Narrower spreads will also result in lower trading costs for market makers; lower costs, in turn, should result in increased trading volumes. This combination—lower costs and increased volumes—may well lead to larger trading profits with lower risk, since a change to decimalization will reduce price volatility, because it will no longer be necessary for a stock's price to change by at least 12 ½ cents per share.

In addition, there would also be a greater chance of being able to better an existing bid and offer in a decimal environment (since there would then be 100 price increments within each dollar of price change). The market maker would be able to move to the front of an order queue more frequently than is possible today by raising a bid or lowering an offer by the small price increment of one cent. This would allow the market maker 92 more opportunities to cover a position, since there would be 100 prices between each full dollar of price change, rather than the eight allowed at present. This same opportunity would also, of course, be equally available for investors to reach the front of the order queue.

If a change to decimalization reduces profit margins to unacceptable levels for those who pay for order flow (whether that payment is in cash or otherwise), one of two things will happen: The firm will eventually discontinue using that stratagem, or return spreads to their former levels.

The operators of proprietary trading systems (PTS) do not have any exemptions from existing antitrust laws, as do the stock exchanges and the NASD, all of which are provided with a level of antitrust immunity because of the SEC's oversight of their rule making. An operator of a PTS does not have the advantage of a Rule 390, as does the NYSE, under which the NYSE can prevent its members from competing against them in trading listed securities.[79] Thus, the operator of a PTS must work for lower profit margins (should decimalization reduce his market making profits because spreads have been narrowed) or use some other methods to retain market share or attract new business.

On the other hand, as noted above, narrower spreads may also have the effect of reducing market makers' trading costs. If trading costs are reduced, they will also be reduced for investors, since the price at which trades made with a market maker on one side are billed at the market maker's net price (plus or minus a commission or markup). Reduced trading costs should lead to increased trading volumes, which may well restore market makers' overall profits to their former level (or even higher) as they receive smaller revenues on each trade, but increase trading volume.

WHY HAVEN'T THE CUSTOMERS BEEN MORE VOCAL?

While it is easy to understand why market intermediaries and the operators of market centers are fearful of the idea of shifting to cents from eighths of a dollar, it is more puzzling to understand why investors—

especially institutional investors—would not be arguing strenuously for that change to take place, since making the tick size smaller should reduce the cost of market impact and increase liquidity. Decimalization should be especially important for traders who use index trading strategies, since minimization of trading costs is crucial to their superior performance.

One answer is inertia. Inertia is very difficult to overcome. It requires great energy and cost to effect change. The idea of maintaining the *status quo* can be very seductive. Resisting proposals for changes is far easier than being their advocate. As was pointed out many centuries ago:

> There is nothing more difficult to take in hand, more perilous to conduct, or more uncertain in its success, than to take the lead in the introduction of a new order of things.[80]

Why haven't letters to the Commission and Congress advocating decimalization arrived from institutional investors, who trade in the largest volumes and would have the most to gain from lower transaction costs? While we are not certain, it may well be because most institutional investors rely on professional investment managers to represent their interests, to manage portfolios, and to handle the execution of their orders. One professional manager's performance is measured against the results achieved by its competitor—another investment manager who operates in the same market environment, in which minimum price variations are in eighths not cents. Thus, all the first manager has to do to look good is to beat or match his competitor. He does not have the option of trading in cents, while his competitor is stuck with eighths.

As a result, there is little or no incentive for investment managers (who, after all, are the ones who must deal with the market intermediaries on whom they are so dependent) to "rock the boat." Boat rockers usually pay a stiff economic penalty when they irritate those who believe a systemic change will impact them adversely. It would take a brave investment manager indeed to be the first to advocate decimal pricing when the intermediaries with whom he or she must deal on a daily basis think such a change is a bid idea.

Who, then, is left to support decimalization, other than academics? The answer should be the investors themselves. For example, the corporate executives, who are charged with the oversight of their pension funds,[81] and mutual fund plan sponsors, who sell billions of dollars worth of their stock to investors, should be in the forefront of those who demand a change to decimalization.[82]

Individual investors should also want to see a change to decimals. However, individual investors rarely write articulate letters to the SEC on the arcane subject of market microstructure. They do not do so because the existing market systems are complex, full of jargon, subject to complicated and lengthy rules not readily available to individual investors, and the confusing, strident arguments of the professionals who believe they will benefit from the maintenance of the *status quo*.

Mr. Ricker's letter to the Commission is a rare exception. The Commission, like most regulatory agencies, assumes that the market professionals have more expertise than retail commentators and that the former group's views should be given weight in a controversial issue. It is also difficult for a regulatory agency to take a position diametrically opposite from the professionals, regardless of how articulate or logical the argument made by a single investor—even if that argument is supported by a few academics, a consultant or two, and a former SEC Commissioner.

When there is a plethora of rhetoric—especially when there are warnings of potential catastrophe should the proposed change be made from the practitioners—it takes braver-than-average commissioners and staff members to be willing to swim against the tide (and poundage) of the paper that has been submitted. After all, although some few skeptics may not believe it, regulators have human reactions, too. And, as we were once told by a former chairman of the Commission, he did not want to leave office being remembered as the person who somehow damaged the U.S. equity markets.[83] In short, it is simpler to leave the *status quo* rather than to initiate change, even when that change removes anticompetitive exchange rules.

On the other hand, if a number of institutional and individual investors should decide to write to the Commission and the members of the House and Senate oversight committees, arguing that decimalization is in their economic interest, the Commission might well decide to take a harder look at a prompt move to decimalization.

THE POSSIBLE CONSEQUENCE OF DECIMALIZATION

There is no doubt that a former practitioner turned academic can be wrong. However, let us gaze into our crystal ball and attempt to predict which will most likely happen to the U.S. equity markets if the Commission requires that the rules of all national market system facilities, including ITS, CQS, and CTA be amended to permit bids, offers, quotations, and transaction reports to be entered and processed in decimal format:[84]

1. Investors—probably led by Mr. Ricker—will enter many of their orders priced in decimals, rather than eighths, in an attempt to reduce their trading costs.
2. All market centers, including primary and regional stock exchanges, will quickly be forced by competitive pressures to make decimal pricing the norm by amending their rules.
3. The practice of offering cash inducements for order flow will most probably vanish.
4. The amount and number of noncash inducements offered by market center operators for order flow will diminish and will eventually disappear.
5. There will be fewer market centers. Some will merge; the inefficient ones will vanish, as they should.
6. Spreads will narrow.
7. Trading volume will increase substantially.
8. Market liquidity will increase.
9. Price volatility will decrease.
10. The SEC will try to figure out how to modify the short sale uptick rule to accommodate the new minimum price variations, and their staff will, as usual, be able to write a proposed new regulation.[85]
11. While the standard minimum price differential will become one cent for a considerable time period, trades will continue to be made at the four odd half-cents, the vestigial remains of trading in eighths (12 ½ cents, 37 ½ cents, 62 ½ cents, and 87 ½ cents). Over time, however, these will disappear, unless the markets become so efficient that spreads narrow naturally to less than one cent, something which is unlikely to occur for the foreseeable future.
12. The opposition to a change to decimalization will quickly fade away, just as the arguments against fixed minimum commissions disappeared when the industry learned to adjust to a more competitive system.

We take considerable comfort in the probability that most, if not all, of these predictions will come true, if for no other reason than the fact that another paper presented at the 1978 NYU conference appears to have reach many of the same conclusions.

In "Assessing the Efficiency of Institutional Arrangements for a National Market System," a quartet of well-known academics, Cohen, Maier, Schwartz—yes, the selfsame Bob Schwartz who organized this conference—and Whitcomb, took a look at what might happen if the average spread was lowered. Writing about the transaction costs associated with the spread, they stated:

> Thus the spread (1)imposes a dollar cost when trades are made, (2) decreases the density of the limit order function which we have shown will increase variance, and (3) generates a further cost in terms of the utility not realized from continuous portfolio adjustments to changing prices and tastes. This analysis of the economic costs of the bid-ask spread is identical to that which we would use to show the economic costs of any other variable transaction cost—e.g., the stock transfer tax or commissions.[86]

The foursome then go on to note:

> Clearly the greater are transaction costs, the less will desired holdings change with price, and thus the less elastic will the effective demand to hold curve be relative to the latent demand curve.... Consider also the impact of trading costs on bid-ask spreads. ...[W]e have argued that, rather than being imposed by a specialist, the very existence of a bid-ask spread can be attributed to the cost of transacting. ...Thus the proposals by Black (1971),[87] Mendelson (1971),[88] and Mendelson et al. (1978)[89] for automation of the limit order book and trade execution system could potentially reduce transaction costs of entering limit orders and, hence, reduce variance and spreads.

CONCLUSION

It has been more than 18 years since the Congress ordered the SEC to "facilitate" the development of a national market system for securities. Important steps have been taken to reduce trading costs and make markets more efficient and liquid. Fixed commissions were eliminated. This one step alone led to increased market liquidity, lower transaction costs and the resultant higher trading volumes which are now the norm.

There are, however, a number of other structural problems which need to be addressed and resolved, including the increasing fragmentation of the U.S. equity makers, which adversely affects price discovery, increases investors' trading costs and makes market systems overly complex.

While these problems are being examined by the Commission and the Congress, one simple step may help greatly in moving the nation toward the national market system envisaged by the drafters of the legislation in the early 1970s. That single, simple step is to remove the final vestige of fixed commission rates: fixed minimum price variations, which act almost exactly as the long-banned fixed minimum commission rates did for so long.

No single market center need be forced to reduce its minimum price variation rules. All that needs be done to unleash the mighty engine of competition is for the Commission to mandate that the three major components of the existing system—ITS, CQS, and CTA—be able to accommodate bids, offers, trades, and report in decimals as well as in eighths of a dollar. Competition will be maximized, and the market will be improved. Once again, Adam Smith's "invisible hand" will do its wonderful work, and American (and international) investors will find we again have markets which have the lowest costs, and maximize efficiency and liquidity, ready to lead the global competition for financial services as we enter the third millennium.

ACKNOWLEDGMENTS

The author thanks his frequent collaborator, Professor Morris Mendelson of The Wharton School for his usual insightful comments and suggestions. He also thanks Dean William Duff and Professor James MacDonald of the University of Northern Colorado Business School for their reading of early draft and most helpful comments, as well as Ms. Alice Shuffler for her proofreading of this paper and for her transcription of a portion of the Markey Hearings. In addition, he thanks the students in his Financial Market Microstructure senior seminar for the notion that the economic effect of a fixed minimum price variation is identical to that of a fixed minimum commission. The members of the seminar are: G. Hefton, J. Hiltman, Jr., C. Howard, A. Kappeli, B. Laske, N. Molliconi, C. Pinson, D. Ryan, F. Spano, and J. Victory. All remaining errors are, of course, the sole responsibility of the author.

NOTES

1. U.S.C. 78b, sec. 2.
2. Rule 62 of the New York Stock Exchange (NYSE) is quoted at the start of this chapter. Other exchanges have similar rules on price variation. The National Association of Securities Dealers, which operates an electronic bulletin board system

which displays the current quotations of their registered market makers, known as NASDAQ (an acronym for National Association of Securities Dealers Automated Quotations), permits price variations of one-sixteenth for executions, but price reporting of executions is restricted to eighths.

3. "The Future of the Stock Markets," hearings conducted by the Subcommittee on Telecommunications and Finance of the House Committee on Interstate and Foreign Commerce, chaired by Congressman Edward Markey of Massachusetts. One of the main focuses of these hearings is the practice by some market centers of offering cash and noncash inducements for order flow. At the conclusion of the second hearing, on May 13, 1993, which was devoted exclusively to this practice, the subcommittee chairman offered four possible approaches to dealing with this matter: (a) banning the practice entirely, (b) requiring that the cash value of the inducements be passed on to the investors who entered the orders, (c) improving the disclosure of the practice to investors, or (d) moving to decimal pricing. (Decimal pricing would mean changing the permitted minimum price differentials between transactions to shift to the U.S. monetary units, rather than maintaining them at fractions. The smallest such unit is one cent.) Chairman Markey said, "As we're going along, this whole question as to whether or not moving to decimal pricing systems requires considerable attention by this subcommittee, which we are going to give." (The transcript of these will be published in a single volume as a House of Representatives committee print by the U.S. Government Printing Office after the series of hearings is completed. Citations from these hearings are hereinafter called the Markey Hearings.)

4. U.S. Equity Market Structure Study, Release no. 34-30920, July 14, 1992 (File no. S7-18-92).

5. See V. Zonana, "SEC Weighs Decimal Stock Pricing System," *The Los Angeles Times,* June 13, 1991, p. D-2. (Hereinafter Zonana article.)

6. Ibid.

7. D. Klein and A. Madhavan state, "In 1975, about 17 percent of the shares traded on the New York Stock Exchange were traded in blocks of 10,000 or more shares.... By 1988, block trading accounted for 55 percent of the NYSE share volume...." Almost all blocks of that size or larger are traded by institutional investors. ("The Upstairs Market for Large Block Transactions," The Wharton School, University of Pennsylvania working paper, September 1993.)

8. See, for example, S. Wunsch, "Response to post-hearing questions relating to the May 26, 1993, Telecommunications and Finance Subcommittee Hearing on the future of stock market proprietary trading systems," June 20, 1993 (hereinafter cited as the Wunsch Response). Mr. Wunsch's testimony and answers to questions can be found in the Markey Hearings.

9. See "Inducements for Order Flow: A Report to the Board of Governors, National Association of Securities Dealers," D. Ruder et al., 1991, as well as the Markey Hearings. In this chapter, the term "market center" includes registered and exempt stock exchanges, the over-the-counter NASDAQ system, and proprietary trading systems (PTS) which are operated by broker/dealers under the terms of no-action letters received from the Commission's staff.

10. Pub. L. No. 94-29, 89 Stat. 97 et seq.

11. The so-called "Buttonwood Agreement" which was signed by the 24 brokers who comprised the predecessor organization to the NYSE, called for a fixed minimum rate of commission to nonmembers. The fixed commission rate system lasted until its abolishment by this law.
12. *Report of Special Study of Securities Markets of the Securities and Exchange Commission,* U.S. Government Printing Office, Washington, DC, 1963.
13. Ibid., pp. 13–14.
14. Ibid., p. 14.
15. Special Study, part II, p. 323.
16. A "round lot" was then (and still is) 100 shares for all but a very few NYSE preferred stocks, which trade in 10-share units.
17. *New York Stock Exchange Fact Book 1984*, p. 82.
18. A "no brainer" is a trade which requires little or no market expertise and is executed routinely.
19. Many institutional orders are charged a larger commission than would be normal for providing execution services alone. In some cases, a portion of these commissions represent "soft dollar" payments to the executing brokers to compensate them for nonexecution-related services, such as the provision of research, quotation equipment, etc. Soft dollar payments were permitted under section 28(e) of the Securities Exchange Act, which was added by the Securities Acts Amendments of 1975. The propriety of continuing soft dollar payments is also being examined by the Commission's staff.
20. A discount broker offers bare bones execution and custodial services and does not give any investment advice. Discount brokers appeared immediately after the passage of the Securities Acts Amendments of 1975, and there are now many firms which offer such services.
21. To be sure, however, Olde must levy other charges and collect fees from some other sources to make such an offer and remain profitable. In addition to the 1,000-share minimum order size which can be executed without commissions, an investor must deposit securities and/or cash with a minimum value of at least $500,000.
22. *The New York Times*, September 15, 1993, p. A-18.
23. Securities Exchange Act, §11A(a)(2), printed in full in this chapter as Appendix A.
24. See, for example, J. Macey and D. Haddock, "Shirking at the SEC: The Failure of the National Market System," *University of Illinois Law Review* (1985), 315, in which they write, "The Buttonwood Agreement sounds much like a naked cartel arrangement, designed to reap profits for the signatories in excess of those necessary to keep them in the brokerage business."

    The Buttonwood Agreement is short. It was signed by the original 24 members. It reads:

    We, the subscribers, brokers for the purchase and sale of public stocks, do hereby solemnly promise and pledge ourselves to each other that we will not buy or sell from this date, for any person whatsoever, any kind of public stocks at a rate less than one-quarter of one percent commission on the specie value, and that we will give preference to each other in our negotiations.
25. Although the NYSE also had mandated fixed commissions on the trading of bonds listed on that exchange, this rule had long since been emasculated by the existence

of the Nine Bond Rule (formerly the 14 Bond Rule), which permitted negotiated commissions for bond orders for amounts which exceeded these sizes.

26. For example, in 1975 the total volume in equities on the NYSE was 4,839,400,000 shares. In 1992, comparable volume was more than ten times that amount: 51,825,700,000. (Source: *New York Stock Exchange Fact Book 1992.*)

27. W. Wagner, "Defining and Measuring Trading Costs," in *Execution Techniques, True Trading Costs, and the Microstructure of Markets,* Association for Investment Management and Research, Charlottesville, VA, 1993 (hereinafter, Wagner, 1993).

28. A crossing network is a proprietary trading system (PTS) which provides execution services, mainly to institutional investors. The best known are operated by Reuters (Instinet), the Jeffries Group (POSIT), the Arizona Stock Exchange, which is registered as an exempt exchange under the Securities Exchange Act's provisions.

29. Wagner, 1993.

30. Ibid.

31. Ibid.

32. In this chapter, a liquid market is defined as one with the capacity to execute a reasonable-sized order in a security without causing more than a minor price variation from the preceding sale price *in the absence of new information affecting the true value of the security.*

33. 1992 Annual Reports and Fact Books of the NYSE, NASD, and regional stock exchanges.

34. M. Blume and M. Goldstein, "Displayed and Effective Spreads by Market," Rodney L. White Center for Financial Research, The Wharton School, University of Pennsylvania, 1992, p. 6. This paper was used by the NYSE as a supporting document in their response to the SEC's invitation for comments on the Commission's Market 2000 study.

35. Ibid, pp. 6–7.

36. The exact language of the law is "...the practicability of brokers executing investors' orders in the best market."

37. There is one awkward technique which might be used. So-called "ginzy trading" is done when a portion of an order is executed at one price and the balance of the order at the next price differential. If, for example, one half of an order for 1,000 shares (500 shares) was executed at $20 per share and the remaining 500 shares executed at $20.125, the effective price per share would have been $20.0625. Ginzy trading is a term taken from the futures markets, where the practice is illegal, since in those markets no broker can execute a prearranged trade for a client.

38. See the Zonana article, in which William Donaldson, Chairmen of the NYSE is quoted as saying, "If there is a public demand, which I don't think there is, we would go for it [decimalization], but to change something just to change it is probably wasteful."

39. Ibid., "He [Chairman Donaldson] estimated that conversion to a decimal system would cost 'several hundred million dollars' in systems and other expenses."

40. See, for example, C. Torres and K. Salwen, "SEC Weighs Switch to Decimal

Stock Quotes," *The Wall Street Journal*, June 12, 1991, p. C-1, in which unnamed "Wall Street securities executives claim that a decimal system would make it more difficult to trade large blocks of stocks on U.S. exchanges. The 12.5 cent spread, they say, acts as a cushion, ensuring a minimum compensation to securities firms for the risk and cost of trading. They argue that the 'depth,' or size, of stock orders waiting to be traded in a market is as important as price."

 See also testimony of Nicholas Giordano and Leopold Korins at the Markey Hearings.

41. "Time priority" has been advocated by many who support centralization of order flow. "First come, first served" has been a traditional American idea of fairness. In a time priority system, bids and offers are queued within price by time of arrival at the trading arena. If three orders arrive to buy a stock at $20 per share, the first order entered would be executed first if a selling counterparty entered an offer of $20 or better. However, to establish time priority implies the existence of a single order queue, or centralization.

 No market center operator has yet advocated time priority across the entire U.S. equity market system (although some have established time priority rules within their own market center). The reason they have not done so is that implementing a time priority rule across all market centers subsumes a single trading arena per security, and no existing market center wishes to take the chance that it would not be able to be the survivor in such a competitive environment.

42. See, for example, J. Coffee, "Mysteries of the National Market System," New York Law Journal, January 23, 1992, in which he writes, "Trading stocks in terms of pennies also poses a serious public policy problem. If the minimum price variation were one cent, traders could circumvent the time precedence on limit orders at a given price by submitting a limit order under (or over) the existing limit orders by a penny and thereby obtain priority."

43. Say's Law, named for the French economist, Jean Baptiste Say, makes a similar proposition.

44. Letter from Jeffrey P. Ricker to the Securities and Exchange Commission, July 24, 1993, SEC File no. S7-18-92 (hereinafter the Ricker Letter).

45. "May Day" refers to May 1, 1975, the date the industry changed to negotiated commission rates.

46. A "basket" of stocks is a set of securities which actually make up the components representing a stock index, such as the Standard & Poor's 500 (S&P 500), or which serve as a proxy for the complete set. Many institutional and individual investors attempt to invest a portion or all of their equity portfolio in such stock baskets. Since the minimization of transaction costs becomes crucial in attempting to match the performance of such an index, these investors, known as "passive" traders, do their best to keep trading costs to the minimums.

47. A market is 'fragmented" if the same security trades in multiple market centers at the same time.

48. "Internalization," the subject of much discussion whenever market structure issues are raised, is the practice of a firm (usually a large brokerage firm with many retail clients) executing their clients' orders against each other, or against their own trading positions, without exposing the orders to a central pricing mechanism.

49. "ITS" stands for Intermarket Trading Systems, an SEC-approved component of their "national market system." ITS interconnects the specialists and market makers of the various market centers and permits these dealers to lay off their trading positions in other market centers without incurring large transaction costs.
50. The Markey Hearings.
51. During the years immediately following the passage of the 1975 Securities Acts Amendments, proposals were made to create a "Consolidated Limit Order Book," or CLOB, which would electronically collect and aggregate at each price differential all bids and offers for national market system qualified securities. Within such a system, best bid would always have the opportunity to meet best offer and, with each bid or offer, receive not only price priority but also time priority: best bid, first entered, could meet best offer, first entered.

    Since a CLOB would have had the effect of centralizing all bids and offers for each issue within a single electronic trading arena, the concept was anathema to the registered stock exchanges, especially the NYSE; and they mounted a concerted, successful lobby against the proposal. As an alternative, they persuaded the SEC to accept what is now known as the ITS system, or Intermarket Trading System, in which market makers can access each other's market centers when necessary.
52. F. Palamara, reprinted in E. Bloch and R. A. Schwartz (eds.), *Impending Changes for Securities Markets: What Role for the Exchanges?*, Greenwich, CT: JAI Press (1979), pp. 104–5.
53. Ibid.
54. Ibid.
55. See the Markey Hearings.
56. Chicken Little is a nursery story character who continuously predicts that the sky will fall.
57. See, for example, the testimony of Richard B. Howland, Executive Vice President of the New York Stock Exchange, at a hearing before the Subcommittee of Securities of the Senate Committee on Banking, Housing, and Urban Affairs, September 21, 1971, in which he summarized in his own words a report prepared for the NYSE by William McChesney Martin, as follows:
    1. For the millions of individual investors, there will be no negotiation.
    and
    3. Only in the case of very large investors, usually institutions, is there likely to be any negotiation.
    and finally
    4. Fully negotiable rates may cause a substantial concentration of the securities business in a few large firms.
    Securities Industry Study, Part I, U.S. GPO, 1971, p. 122.
58. C. Torres and K. Salwen, "SEC Weighs Switch To Decimal Stock Quotes," *The Wall Street Journal,* June 12, 1991, p. C-1 (hereinafter, Torres and Salwen).
59. See, for example, this quotation: "In the SELI files [the SELECT file], prices are given in dollars with five decimal places after the decimal point..." (J. Hasbrouck, "Using the TORQ Database," NYSE Research Paper Series, February 13, 1992, p. 30.)

60. Torres and Salwen.

61. *Securities Week,* January 28, 1991, p. 1.

62. *Securities Week,* June 17, 1991, p. 10.

63. At least one very large over-the-counter market making firm, considered by many to be the largest OTC market maker, the New York Hanseatic Corporation, went out of business rather soon after the NASDAQ system was introduced.

64. U.S.C. §78k 11A(a)(1)(C):

    The Congress finds that—

    It is in the public interest and appropriate for the protection of investors and the maintenance of fair and orderly markets to assure...

    > *(v) an opportunity...for investors' orders to be executed without the partici-pation of a dealer.*

65. L. Harris, "Consolidation, Fragmentation, Segmentation, and Regulation," in *Financial Markets, Institutions & Instruments,* December 1993. See also chapter 18, this volume.

66. Ibid.

67. Ibid.

68 The Ricker Letter.

69. L. Harris, "Minimum Price Variations, Discrete Bid-Ask Spreads and Quotation Size," June 1992, and forthcoming in *Review of Financial Studies.*

70. Ibid., p. 26.

71. Markey Hearings.

72. Ibid., especially the testimony of Richard Grasso, Executive Vice Chairman and Chief Operating Officer of the NYSE.

73. C. Lee, "Market Integration and Price Execution," University of Michigan, submitted as Appendix 1 of the NYSE's response to the Market 2000 study's invitation for comments.

74. See, for example, T. McInish and R. Wood, "Hidden Limit Orders on the New York Stock Exchange," in *The Competition for Order Flow and Market Efficiency,* Memphis State University, November 1992. Submitted as an attachment to the NASD's response to the SEC's Market 2000 study.

75. Professor Lee defines the number in his Table 5 as follows: "Table values represent the average additional cost of buying for off-Board trades, expressed in cents per share (negative values represent savings relative to the NYSE execution). The Lee and Ready (1991) algorithm is used to infer buy/sell directions. The price of each off-Board buy is compared to the price for adjacent NYSE buys of similar size. NYSE buys are considered adjacent if they occur within 2 minutes of the off-Board trade. The additional cost of buying is the difference between the off-Board trade price and the NYSE trade price (PrReg–PrNYSE). Sample size is 207,818 matched buy executions for 1988 and 332,121 matched buy executions for 1989."

76. See, for example, the testimony of Richard Grasso at the Markey Hearings.

77. M. Petersen and D. Fialkowski, "Price Improvements: Stocks on Sale," Center for Research in Security Prices, University of Chicago, 1992, submitted as Appendix 4 by the NYSE in their response to the SEC's Market 2000 study's request for comments.

78. M. Quint, "U.S. Investigates Pact on Bond Trade Prices," *The New York Times,* June 22, 1993, p. D-18.
79. Rule 390 of the NYSE, which they caption the "Market Responsibility Rule," prohibits the exchange's members from trading NYSE-listed securities as principal in most cases. However, NYSE members registered as specialists on the NYSE or regional exchanges do, of course, make principal trades in listed stocks.
80. Niccolo Machiavelli, *The Prince,* 1532, ch. 6.
81. Corporations should wish to maximize the returns on their pension fund investments, since for every dollar of increased return, there would be an additional dollar available for expansion or payment to their shareholders.
82. Many plan sponsors are also part of a financial institution which has as another of its divisions a broker/dealer which does not want to see spreads narrow.
83. Private conversation with the late William Casey.
84. While there would be no need for the Commission explicitly to require any market center to trade in decimals, it would be difficult (to say the very least) for it to continue trading in eighths if their competitors were trading at narrower spreads.
85. Our suggestion would be, "Abolish it." The uptick rule does not accomplish its stated objectives, is difficult to administer, and is not suitable for today's markets in which sophisticated derivative instruments are used to manage price risk.
86. At pp. 131–33 in E. Bloch and R. A. Schwartz (eds.), *Impending Changes for Securities Markets: What Role for the Exchanges?,* vol. 14 of *Contemporary Studies in Economic and Financial Analysis,* Greenwich, CT: JAI Press, 1979.
87. F. Black, "Toward a Fully Automated Stock Exchange," *Financial Analysts Journal,* 1971; part 1 in July-August and part 2 in November-December.
88. M. Mendelson, "From Automated Quotes to Automated Trading," NYU Graduate School of Business Administration, Institute of Finance *Bulletin* nos. 80–82, March 1972.
89. M. Mendelson, J. Peake, and R. Williams, Jr., "Toward a National Market System: The Peake-Mendelson-Williams Proposal for an Electronically Assisted Auction Market." This paper, which was a variation of the original proposal for an electronically-assisted auction market submitted to the National Market Advisory Board of the Commission in 1976, advocated a change to decimalization from fractional pricing.

APPENDIX A

NATIONAL MARKET SYSTEM LEGISLATION
SECURITIES EXCHANGE ACT

Sec. 11A(a)(1) The Congress finds that—

    (A) The securities markets are an important national asset which must be preserved and strengthened.

    (B) New data processing and communications techniques create the opportunity for more efficient and effective market operation.

    (C) It is in the public interest and appropriate for the protection of investors and the maintenance of fair and orderly markets to assure—

        (i) economically efficient execution of securities transactions;

        (ii) fair competition among brokers and dealers, among exchange markets and markets other than exchange markets;

        (iii) the availability to brokers, dealers, and investors of information with respect to quotations for and transactions in securities;

        (iv) the practicability of brokers executing investors' orders in the best market; and

        (v) an opportunity, consistent with the provisions of clauses (i) and (iv) of this subparagraph, for investors' orders to be executed without the participation of a dealer.

    (D) The linking of all markets for qualified securities through communication and data processing facilities will foster efficiency, enhance competition, increase the information available to brokers, dealers, and investors, facilitate the offsetting of investors' orders, and contribute to the best execution of such orders.

    (2) The Commission is directed, therefore, having due regard for the public interest, the protection of investors, and the maintenance of fair and orderly markets, to use its authority under this title to facilitate the establishment of a national market system for securities (which may include subsystems for particular types of securities with unique trading characteristics) in accordance with the findings and to carry out the objectives set forth in paragraph (1) of this subsection. The Commission, by rule, shall designate the securities or classes of securities qualified for trading in the national market system from among securities other than exempted securities. (Securities or classes of securities so designated hereinafter in this section referred to as "qualified securities.")

(3) The Commission is authorized in furtherance of the directive in paragraph (2) of this subsection—

   (A) to create one or more advisory committees pursuant to the Federal Advisory Committee Act (which shall be in addition to the National Market Advisory Board established pursuant to subsection (d) of this section) and to employ one or more outside experts.

   (B) by order, to authorize or require self-regulatory organizations to act jointly with respect to matters as to which they share authority under this title in planning, developing, operating, or regulating a national market system (or a subsystem thereof) or one or more facilities thereof; and

   (C) to conduct studies and make recommendations to the Congress from time to time as to the possible need for modifications of the scheme of self-regulation provided for in this title so as to adapt it to a national market system.

CHAPTER 20

MULTIMARKET TRADING: A SELF-REGULATORY PROPOSAL

Yakov Amihud
Haim Mendelson

INTRODUCTION

The proliferation of electronic trading and the resulting ability of traders to access multiple markets quickly and at low cost nullifies the concept of a "national market." In Europe, for example, traders in Milan can trade stocks of Italian companies in the Milan Stock Exchange where they are listed. Alternatively, they can trade the same stocks through London. The choice of a trading location is made by traders in real time and is beyond the company's control. While the company can select the market where it lists its stock, it cannot prevent the stock from being traded in another market. A similar phenomenon exists within the United States, where a stock listed on the New York Stock Exchange can be traded there, or in a regional market, or on the OTC market.

Yet, the trading location of a stock has a significant impact on its value. The reason is that the choice of a trading location affects the liquidity of the stock, which, in turn, has a substantial effect on its expected return and value. Thus, the firm's cost of capital is effectively determined by its trading location. Further, when a stock is traded in an additional market, the fragmentation of trading may reduce its liquidity, although this may be offset by the benefits of increased competition.

The question that arises is: Who should have the right to decide where the security trades? The listing decision is properly delegated to the firm's board of directors, which has a fiduciary duty to act so as to maximize the stock's value. Because the stock's value is an increasing function of its liquidity, other things being equal, the board has to choose the trading location that will maximize liquidity.[1] However, once a stock has been listed on an exchange, other exchanges and trading systems may elect to trade the stock without considering the impact on the stock's value, and without letting the firm whose stock's liquidity is ultimately at stake have any input to that decision.

In this chapter we propose that the company should have the right to determine where its stock will be traded. The determination of a trading location should be considered a property right of the company and should be protected by international law, just as the law protects other property rights of companies (and individuals), for example, in the area of registered trademarks, copyrights, and the like. We suggest that such a legal framework is more consistent with maximizing the liquidity of traded assets (and reducing corporate cost of capital) than current practices. It should certainly be enforced in domestic markets, such as the United States, where we observe a stock listed on one market (for example, on the New York Stock Exchange) being traded at the same time in regional markets, private electronic markets, and on the OTC. We propose that any market or trading system wishing to accommodate trading in a stock should be able to do so, but that it would be required to obtain the explicit consent of the issuing company. Thus, multiple market trading would be self-regulated by the firm whose cost of capital is at stake.

Below, we briefly review the effect of the liquidity of a company's financial claims on its value and on its cost of capital in the first section. In the second section, we review the effects of market fragmentation on the liquidity of traded assets. The third section presents our proposal.

LIQUIDITY AND ASSET PRICES

In Amihud and Mendelson (1986), we have shown, both theoretically and empirically, a positive relationship between transaction costs and average returns. Theoretically, we considered rational investors who take into account the costs of trading securities and found that, in equilibrium, assets with higher transaction costs yield higher rates of return because investors expect a compensation for their higher costs. This implies that higher transaction costs lower the value of a capital asset for any given cash flow that the asset generates.

We then estimated the relation between stock returns and their bid-ask spread (that is, the difference between the quoted buying price of the stock and its quoted selling price), which is a major component of the cost of transacting and used to proxy for illiquidity. The narrower the bid-ask spread, the more liquid the stock. The theory suggests that, other things being equal, the average return should increase as the spread increases, to compensate investors for bearing higher transaction costs. We tested this theoretical prediction by estimating the relation between the risk-adjusted average returns (in excess of the Treasury-bill rates) on NYSE stocks and their illiquidity, measured by their (percentage) bid-ask spread, over 20 years of data. Stock portfolios were grouped by their bid-ask spreads and by their systematic risk measure, *beta*. Then, we estimated the relation between the bid-ask spread and the portfolios' average returns (in excess of the Treasury-bill rate), controlling for systematic risk. The empirical results were consistent with the theoretical predictions: average returns are an increasing function of the bid-ask spread.

We found a similar relationship in the Treasury securities market. Treasury notes with less than six months to maturity are identical in their cash flow structure to Treasury bills with the same maturity, except that the notes are less liquid than bills. Our theory suggests that the notes should be priced lower than bills with the same maturity to compensate investors for their transaction costs. We found that this was, indeed, the case (Amihud and Mendelson, 1991a).

Thus, the firm's cost of capital is directly linked to the liquidity of its claims. A firm with given cash flows should always prefer that its claims be traded in a fashion that maximizes their liquidity.

In spite of the fact that liquidity affects the firm's cost of capital, except for the initial listing decision, the firm has very limited impact on decisions that will ultimately determine the liquidity of its claims. The decision on whether a stock will be quoted in units of eighths or sixteenths of a dollar or in cents has a paramount effect on the stock's liquidity—yet the firm has no control over that decision. The firm cannot negotiate what specific trading system its stock will trade in, where exactly it will trade, or in what order (on exchanges such as the Milan

Stock Exchange or the Tel Aviv Stock Exchange, where the order of trading makes a difference). This is because the decision to trade in a stock can be made by an exchange or trading system almost unilaterally, unless the firm actually requests listing (and is willing to pay for it).

Multiple market trading of listed stocks is a case in point. Research findings show that trading a stock in multiple markets has an unpredictable impact on liquidity. In particular, fragmentation of trading may cause a decline in liquidity, and this effect is currently beyond the company's control. This issue is briefly reviewed in the following section.

EXAMPLE OF A DETERMINANT OF LIQUIDITY: MULTIMARKET TRADING

The effects of multiple market trading on liquidity are uncertain. On the one hand, intuition suggests that competition between markets should foster innovation and reduce trading costs just as it does in traditional product and service markets. One the other hand, financial markets are markets in information, and information has many special features that set it apart from tangible goods as well as services. In particular, multiple market trading involves the risks of market fragmentation.

A market is fragmented if the results of order executions obtained in it are different from the results that would have been obtained in a central, single auction market. The central auction market is a proper benchmark because it is the market structure that maximizes overall surplus for any *given* set of orders.[2] Thus, other things being equal, order flow consolidation should lead to a superior market structure. On the other hand, intermarket competition may well bring down execution costs and create further incentives for innovation. It follows that multiple market trading involves a trade-off between the risks of fragmentation and the benefits of intermarket competition.

Both the costs of fragmentation and the benefits of intermarket competition have been evaluated in a number of studies [see a survey and analysis in Amihud and Mendelson (1991b)]. The conclusion is that the effect of multimarket trading on liquidity may go either way, depending on particular circumstances. To cite some evidence, Neal (1987) found that the bid-ask spreads were narrower on options that traded in more than one options market compared to similar options traded on a single market. Pagano and Roell (1990) found for French stocks traded in London that when the Paris Bourse opens, the spread in London declines and then increases again after the Bourse closes.

On the other hand, Pagano and Roell (1991) found for Italian stocks traded in London that their bid-ask spread *widens* when the Milan Stock Exchange is open and that the difference is highly significant. The widening of the spread could result from fragmentation of trading which reduces liquidity.

Thus, the effect of multimarket trading is not uniform in all cases, and the direction of the net effect is unsettled: the costs of fragmentation may or may not exceed the benefits of competition, and the result depends on the particular circumstances.

Liquidity is dependent on the availability of limit orders or quotes with narrow bid-ask spreads. One way in which multiple market trading can hamper liquidity is through quote-matching and the associated violation of secondary priority rules[3] across markets. When a market maker takes the risk of making a public quote or placing a limit order in the limit order book, he is essentially giving the market an option to buy or sell the stock at a fixed price over some limited time interval. The limit order or quote may attract either liquidity-motivated traders or traders with superior information (insiders). In the former case, execution occurs at a price that is favorable to the market maker. In the latter, the insiders will hit the quote and exercise the option only if this is favorable to them, to the detriment of the market maker. The market maker takes the risk of offering his quote in the hope that with enough liquidity-motivated trades, the bid-ask spread will compensate him for the losses to traders with superior information.

Market makers may be tempted to delay placing limit orders (or quotes) in the system and may try to negotiate with traders as they (or their orders) arrive at the market in an attempt to receive favorable executions and reduce the risk inherent in limit orders or quotes. When all market makers try to do this, the result is no limit orders (quotes) and no liquidity. Secondary priority rules, in particular those concerning *time* priority, provide the market maker an incentive to place orders in the system. In spite of the risk of placing orders early, there is the potential reward of being able to trade first. On balance, more limit orders and quotes will be placed for longer periods of time in a market that supports time priority. Thus, time priority enhances liquidity.

The ability of investors to trade a stock in a number of markets or trading systems breaks time priority, because such priority rules can be enforced only *within* a given market. Thus, market makers and investors may avoid the risks of placing limit orders or quotes and match the quotes in another market. The quote-matcher effectively takes a free ride on the market maker who generated the quote and on investors who place limit orders. However, this phenomenon clearly reduces the incentives to provide public limit orders or quotes in the first place. The result if that *if time priority rules are not enforced across markets, liquidity suffers.*

In Amihud and Mendelson (1990, 1991b), we proposed a scheme that enforces secondary priority rules across markets in a regional setting such as the European community or the options markets in the United States. However, the global enforcement of such schemes beyond well-defined market areas such as the European community is difficult, given that there is no international body regulating stock exchanges and trading systems. Further, the proliferation of nonexchange trading systems makes enforcement virtually impossible. In the section that follows, we propose an alternative scheme that places the regulatory decision where it properly belongs—in the hands of the issuing firm.

A SELF-REGULATORY PROPOSAL

The previous section established that fragmentation of trading in a security between markets may be harmful because it reduces liquidity, and, as a result, it increases the required return on the security. Investors are indifferent to this effect because they are fairly compensated for the lower liquidity on the security. Market makers have an incentive to trade in a security listed for trading in another market if such trading is profitable for them. In particular, the markets that accommodate trading in securities listed in other markets enjoy the revenues from this trading.

However, the issuing company (and the economy as a whole) could suffer from having its securities traded in other markets in addition to the market(s) where it chose to list them for trading. If the fragmentation of trading reduces liquidity, corporate cost of capital increases, and this would make the firm forgo investment projects.[4]

As shown in the preceding section, there are two conflicting effects: competition between markets increases liquidity, whereas the negative effects of fragmentation reduce liquidity. It is hard to imagine that regulators will be able to determine in each case whether multimarket trading is beneficial, liquiditywise.

We propose regulation that will endow the issuing company with the property rights over its securities in the sense that only the company can determine where its securities will be traded. It will be illegal for any market to enable trading in the securities of any firm without the consent of the company.

This type of regulation is not different, for example, from current laws that entitle a company to own its registered trademarks and brand names and forbids their use without an explicit authorization by the company that owns the trademark. This is governed by international law. Similarly, we propose that international law will protect the company against having its securities traded in any market without the company's consent.

The violation of this rule—trading part of the company's securities in a market where the company does not wish them traded—will hurt the overall liquidity of the company's securities and will hurt all securities holders who trade in the market (or markets) where the company permits its securities to be traded. This will constitute an activity by which some self-serving securities traders inflict a loss on all securities holders. Thus, in the interest of all securities holders, it should be the company that decides where its claims will be allowed to trade.

The objective of the company is to maximize its value. Liquidity is a major factor in determining the company's value, as explained in the first section above. The proposed scheme subjects securities markets and trading systems to this objective. The company will pursue only those trading arrangements that enhance the liquidity of its traded securities.[5] We expect that different companies will make different decisions whether to allow multimarket trading, according to their estimates of the effects of their decisions on their liquidity and value. Regulators will not be encumbered with the right to make decisions whether allowing multimarket trading if beneficial. Rather, the decision rights will shift to the company, whose value is at stake. Our proposal is thus radically different from the suggestion[6] that the regulatory authorities will confine listings to a single market, without giving the company the option to trade in multiple markets, and assuming that the cost of fragmentation is necessarily greater than the benefits of competition. We suggest that companies can decide these matters on their own.

Our proposed regulation will realign the incentives and actions of exchanges and trading systems with their proper role in the economy, that is, to provide liquidity to the issuing companies in a way which they view as beneficial to them. Because exchanges and trading systems attempt to attract trading volume, we often observe a "race to the bottom"—the relaxation of trading rules in an attempt to induce traders and market makers to switch to a new market or remain with an established market. Currently, regulators have no proper solution to this problem: if they enforce the higher standards on the exchanges they regulate, volume will move away; if they don't, they will be abrogating their responsibility to the public at large. By relaxing their trading rules to attract order flow, markets effectively take a free ride on the well-regulated markets. In the long run, all markets end up relaxing their standards and liquidity often suffers. The increasing loss of transparency and delayed reporting of large block transactions is a recent example.

In section above, we have discussed the role of time priority in providing liquidity, immediacy, and information. The self-regulatory scheme proposed here will lead to a *homemade enforcement* of cross-market time priority, if it is valuable to the issuing firm. Suppose two markets enter an agreement to establish a cross-market time priority system, while other markets do not join this arrangement. Then, companies will be more willing to allow the trading of their securities in these two markets and disallow it in other markets which are not cooperating in enforcing the cross-market time priority. In this way, companies' self-interests will be better aligned with those of the exchanges and trading systems.

Another benefit from our proposed regulation is that it will provide securities markets with strong incentives to implement efficient trading systems that will attract companies to allow their securities to be traded in them.

CONCLUSIONS

In this chapter, we attend to the problem of cross-market regulation. The fact that trading in a company's securities may take place in any market and using any trading mechanism affects the liquidity of these securities and, thus, their values. However, the company that issues these securities has no effect on the trading mechanism. Although the company may list its securities for trading in one market, the securities may be subsequently traded elsewhere. The effect of multimarket trading on the liquidity and values of securities is uncertain. In some cases, it can be beneficial; whereas, in others it can be detrimental. Competition between markets may lead to more efficient provision of market-making services and greater liquidity, but it could also cause fragmentation of the order flow which may have undesired effects on liquidity and volatility.

We propose a legal framework where the company will decide where its securities should be allowed to trade. This framework has a built-in ability to monitor the quality of markets, reward efficient markets that implement rules and trading mechanisms that increase liquidity, and penalize inefficient or illiquid markets. It will thus guarantee that the company will be able to control the liquidity of its securities to the extent that this is beneficial to the company. Most importantly, if the issuing company considers multimarket trading beneficial it will allow it; whereas, if it has detrimental effects because of fragmentation, it will forbid it. Thus, our proposed regulation will provide a homemade solution to the problem of cross-market regulation.

NOTES

1. When other things are not equal, for example, when there are differences in exchange fees, the board has the right to make the appropriate trade-offs.
2. The effects of market fragmentation on traders' surplus, volatility, and the informativeness of asset prices are analyzed in detail in Mendelson (1987). See Schwartz (1991) on exchange rules regarding order consolidation and on fragmentation.
3. On the secondary priority rules in securities markets, see Amihud and Mendelson (1990, 1991b), and Schwartz (1991).
4. We are not considering here general equilibrium consequences. Clearly, if the demand for investment in the entire economy decreases, the prices of capital assets and investment goods and services will adjust. Our analysis is, however, from the viewpoint of the marginal firm that may have the trading in its securities fragmented.
5. It is possible that the company will agree to allow its securities to trade in a fashion that reduces their liquidity if it is properly compensated for the loss of liquidity. This will occur, however, only if the overall value of the firm increases as the result of such an arrangement.
6. See, for example, the proposal by Junius Peake to the Securities and Exchange Commission regarding the Market 2000 project.

REFERENCES

Amihud, Yakov, and Haim Mendelson. (1986). "Asset Pricing and the Bid-Ask Spread," *Journal of Financial Economics,* 17: (December), pp. 223–49.

Amihud, Yakov, and Haim Mendelson. (1990). "Option Markets Integration." Paper submitted to the SEC.

Amihud, Yakov, and Haim Mendelson. (1991a). "Liquidity, Maturity, and the Yields on U.S. Treasury Securities," *Journal of Finance,* 46: (September), pp. 1411–25.

Amihud, Yakov, and Haim Mendelson. (1991b). "How (Not) to Integrate the European Capital Markets," in A. Giovannini and C. Mayer (eds.), *European Financial Integration.* Cambridge University Press.

Mendelson, Haim. (1987). "Consolidation, Fragmentation, and Market Performance," *Journal of Financial and Quantitative Analysis,* 22: (June), pp. 189–207.

Neal, Robert. (1987). "Potential Competition and Actual Competition in Equity Options," *Journal of Finance,* 42: (September), pp. 511–31.

Pagano, Marco, and Ailsa Roell. (1990). "Stock Markets," *Economic Policy,* April, pp. 63–115.

Pagano, Marco, and Ailsa Roell. (1991). "Dually-Traded Italian Equities: London vs. Milan." Mimeograph.

Schwartz, Robert A. (1991). *Reshaping the Equity Markets: A Guide for the 1990s.* New York: HarperBusiness. Reprinted by Homewood, IL: Business One Irwin (1993).

CHAPTER 21

CHICAGO MERCANTILE EXCHANGE: A MODEL FOR FEDERAL FINANCIAL REGULATION

presented by
Edward H. Fleischman

The Federal Government is more complex than it needs to be. Often, many different agencies deal with the same issue, and individuals, businesses, communities, and states find it impossible to have their problems addressed. Departments and agencies are already consolidating and simplifying their operations, and the Administration will seek to rationalize and streamline functions Government-wide.

—President Clinton
A Vision of Change for America

PRINCIPLES

The operation of open and competitive domestic and international markets for financial products and services has in recent years driven traditionally distinct financial market participants and financial marketplaces, both in the United States and worldwide, to imitate and to duplicate each other's functions. The federal financial regulatory structure has failed to adapt to these market changes as U.S. financial services have changed dramatically and international competition has increased exponentially.

In resisting adaptation to the changing realities of the financial markets, the existing regulatory structure has undermined its own effectiveness. In many contexts it has become counterproductive to desirable economic activity. Rather than providing conditions for market changes and innovations to occur with maximum systemic safety, it has tended to stifle competition and innovation.

Further, the existing regulatory structure, by relying on institutional rather than functional regulation, has magnified regulatory costs by replicating regulatory activities in multiple agencies.

The Chicago Mercantile Exchange believes that now is the time to propose a new regulatory structure, which:

- Should be consolidated in a single cabinet-level department within the executive branch of the government so that regulatory policies can be coordinated across financial products, services, and markets, and so that the regulators and the Administration can be held accountable for the success or failure of their policies.
- Should be organized along modified functional lines so that financial products, services, and markets delivering similar benefits and risks can be subjected to equivalent regulation and so that economic competition, rather than jurisdictional barriers or differences in supervision, can determine which products, services, and markets succeed in the marketplace.
- Should be structured to encourage innovation in domestic financial activities and adaptation in international markets so that financial products, services, and markets can continue to evolve in response to presently foreseeable and still-unperceived developments and challenges.

The model presented in this chapter is designed to realize those principles and, in doing so, to reduce the cost of parallel efforts in different agencies. Changes in substantive law will be important as well, but structural change is required to achieve greater flexibility, responsiveness, cost-effectiveness, and efficiency in federal financial regulation.

To quote from the 1986 House Subcommittee chairman's report entitled "Restructuring Financial Markets: The Major Policy Issues":

> There is a unifying theme in the extensive body of law and regulation governing U.S. financial institutions: *recognition of the financial system's*

economic role. Unless the system as a whole facilitates the transformation of financial capital into economic activity and growth, other objectives and strategies—including those that protect customers—will be ineffective.

THE MODEL

Figure 21–1 is a schematic portrayal of the model. For purposes of comparison, see Figure 21–2, which is a schematic of the current federal financial regulatory system.

The agencies consolidated in the model are the Office of the Comptroller of the Currency (OCC), Office of Thrift Supervision (OTS), the Federal Deposit Insurance Corporation (FDIC), the Commodity Futures Trading Commission (CFTC), the Securities and Exchange Commission (SEC), the Securities Investor Protection Corporation (SIPC), and the Pension Benefit Guaranty Corporation (PBGC). Bank and bank holding company regulatory functions of the Federal Reserve Board and ERISA regulatory functions of the Department of Labor are also included in the consolidation. The model extends functional federal regulation to depository institutions and insurance institutions to the extent that they perform functions equivalent to the functions of other federally regulated participants in financial markets. The model changes the prevalent pattern of concurrent federal/state jurisdiction only in narrowly specified way, and welcomes increased state involvement in the consumer protection arena.

Description

Consolidate Agencies in Cabinet-level Department
All the federal financial regulatory agencies other than the Federal Reserve System (OCC, OTS, FDIC, CFTC, SEC, SIPC, and PBGC) would be brought within the new department. In addition, the bank and bank holding company regulatory responsibilities of the Federal Reserve and the ERISA regulatory responsibility of the Labor Department would also be consolidated.

> *Explanation:*   The new department will be responsible for developing and implementing policy for the regulation of all financial markets and products in the United States. The success of

FIGURE 21–1
Schematic Portrayal of the Proposed Federal Financial Regulatory Service

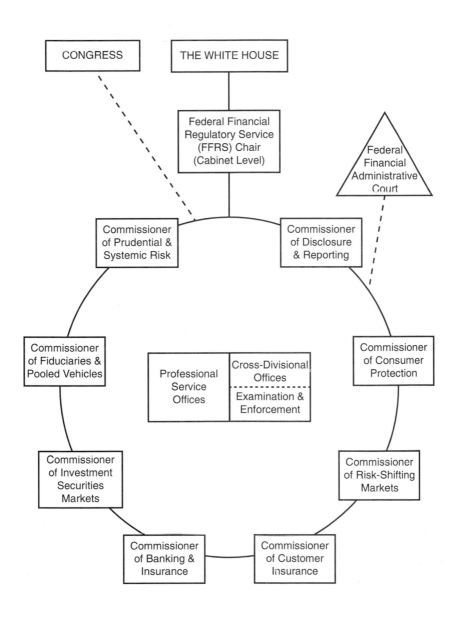

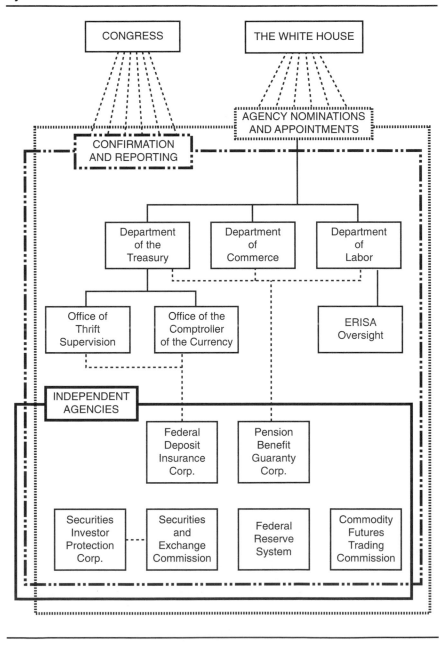

FIGURE 21–2
Schematic Diagram of Current Federal Financial Regulatory System

that financial policy requires vigorous and healthy financial institutions and financial markets. Consolidation of financial regulation in the executive branch will link financial regulation to overall financial policy and will clarify the accountability of the President (the nation's elected Chief Executive) and his appointees for the success or failure of the regulatory policies governing financial institutions and financial markets.

Federal Financial Regulatory Service

The financial regulatory functions would be structured in a single Federal Financial Regulatory Service (FFRS), operationally autonomous but subject to policy direction by the cabinet-level chairman. The FFRS would be headed by the chairman and a board of eight commissioners, each appointed by the President and confirmed by the Senate. Each of the commissioners would be individually responsible for a specified operating division of the FFRS. The chairman would be the administrative chief executive of the FFRS and would report directly to the President of the United States. On rule making and all other matters not delegated to divisional determination or reserved to the chairman, the commissioners would act together as a board.

> ***Explanation:*** The board of commissioners will provide the mechanism that has to date been lacking for coordination of financial regulatory policies that cross markets, functions, and industries. The appointment of individual commissioners with specified operating responsibilities will nevertheless introduce a degree of regulatory friction that impedes overregulation and encourages competition and innovation in financial services and markets. The chairman of the FFRS will be first among equals in development of regulatory policy and will be responsible for liaison with other executive branch agencies and with the Congress and for all administrative and support functions necessary to the operation of the FFRS.

Operating Divisions

The FFRS would have eight divisions addressed to specified functional operations:

1. ***Division of Prudential and Systemic Risk.***   Responsible for capi-

tal adequacy and the various other "safety and soundness" or "financial responsibility" requirements applicable in different ways to all regulated financial institutions and all regulated financial market participants and their affiliates. Responsible also for regulation of clearance and settlement of market transactions, for regulation of transfer of evidences of ownership of traded instruments, and for resolution of other systemic risk issues. This division would deal with the prudential risk incurred by individual institutions and individual market participants and would also deal with systemic risk in and across the financial markets.

Explanation: The crucial concerns across all financial markets and services are capital adequacy, the management of exposure to institutional, intermediary and counterparty risk, and the identification and reduction of systemic risks. Different roles in the financial markets will elicit different criteria for capital adequacy, but, whatever the formula deemed applicable to participants in a particular market, that formula requires cross-market perspective for equivalent applicability. This division will interact with the Federal Reserve Board in its role as the nation's lender of last resort.

2. ***Division of Disclosure and Reporting.*** Responsible for an integrated disclosure/distribution system for all public companies and for other entities seeking public financing. Responsible also for specialized disclosure and reporting systems mandated under federal law for specialized entities like ERISA plans. Distributions of domestic and foreign securities "registered" in the integrated system will be automatically qualified under all state regimes. Accounting policy applicable to all market participants would be supervised by this division.

Explanation: A general disclosure and reporting system is required that will promote capital flow both to private enterprise and to governmental use and will facilitate secondary market trading. Comparability and continuity of issuer-oriented disclosure, respect for home country standards, and ease of integrated distribution procedures will be the fundamentals of the system. General-purpose accounting, prescribed in this disclosure context, will be the starting point for capital adequacy formulas.

3. *Division of Fiduciaries and Pooled Vehicles.* Responsible for all varieties of pooled funds and for adviser/managers directing the deployment of "other people's money," whether on an individual or pooled basis.

   Explanation: Mutual funds, closed-end investment companies, commodity pools, bank commingled and collective trusts, insurance company separate accounts serving multiple clients, and trusts under ERISA plans are all essentially similar vehicles that require substantively equivalent regulation. Since the fiduciary functions of these investment funds' advisers/managers are qualitatively different from those of their market professionals, the administration of their specialized disclosure, professional competence and conflict-of-interest standards will be best conducted in the same division that regulates the funds themselves.

4. *Division of Investment Securities Markets.* Responsible for all trading in fungible non-offset instruments (debt and equity securities and other traditional and nontraditional securities other than options), for the stock exchanges, for the National Association of Securities Dealers (NASD), and for the professional entities (and their associated persons) registered in those markets. Responsible also for trading in other instruments commonly known as securities.

   Explanation: Developments in the creation of derivative and hybrid instruments, development in screen-based trading, and the general trends in financial market evolution are inevitably interweaving the markets for investment securities and the markets for risk-shifting instruments that overlie financial assets and obligations. The Divisions of Investment Securities Markets and of Risk-Shifting Markets (described above and below) may therefore fuse over time. Nevertheless, the economic constraints and implications of zero-sum markets (such as the futures and options markets) are qualitatively different from those of net-long markets (such as the stock markets) and are better served, at least for the intermediate future, by separate, competitive but policy-coordinated regulation.

5. *Division of Risk-Shifting Markets* Responsible for all trading in standardized offset instruments (whether overlying financial assets

or obligations, foreign exchange, or agricultural or mineral commodities), for the futures and options exchanges, for the National Futures Association (NFA), and for the professional entities (and their associated persons) registered in those markets. Responsible also (to the extent they are regulated) for forward and other tailored credit-risk-determined instruments (for example, interest rate and currency swaps) overlying financial assets or obligations.

6. *Division of Banking and Insurance.*   Responsible for administration of federal statutory provisions (not assigned elsewhere in FFRS) applicable to depository institutions, insurance companies, their affiliates, and their associated persons.

   Explanation: Banks and insurance companies are both financial market intermediaries and financial market participants. Provision of financial products and services by banks and insurance companies will elicit regulation that is substantively equivalent to the regulation applicable to competitive product and service providers. Much of that regulation (including most of the existing bank regulatory functions) will be conducted by other FFRS divisions. For example, primary responsibility for capital adequacy will be assigned to the Division of Prudential and Systemic Risk, and examination authority will be assigned to the cross-divisional Office of Examinations. There will still remain for this division a number of federally regulated matters, including the chartering of national banks, federal savings and loan associations and Edge Act companies, the regulation of bank holding companies, the determination of bank merger applications and foreign bank applications, and the oversight of specialized bank and insurance company conflict-of-interests policies. Bank holding company supervision will be moved to the FFRS because it is no longer necessary to the implementation of monetary policy by the Federal Reserve Board and because its goals need to be coordinated with overall financial regulatory policy. This division may have no insurance company regulatory role if there are no federal requirements applicable to insurance companies that are not covered by other FFRS divisions.

7. *Division of Customer Insurance.*   Responsible for FDIC, SIPC, and PBGC receivership and insurance functions, with delegated power to declare failures in circumstances authorized by the board.

Explanation: The federal insurance function, so necessary today, is likely to be replaced by less costly private solutions over
time. Until then, the insurers need to be able to protect the interests of their funds and the back-up ultimately provided by tax-
payers. Accountability is strengthened by keeping the insurance
functions within the single financial agency structure.

8. *Division of Consumer Protection.*   Responsible (along with the
   states) for the vast variety of retail-customer-directed sales practice
   protections across the spectrum of financial services. These include
   lending disclosure, deposit disclosure, disclosure by securities and
   commodities brokers to their retail clients, antidiscrimination laws,
   community reinvestment policies, privacy of information, and so
   forth.

   Explanation: Combining in the FFRS all consumer protections arising under federal financial regulatory programs links
   responsibility for consumer protection to responsibility for systemic safety, promotion of competition, and maintenance of the
   vitality of financial markets, and provides substantively equivalent protections for purchasers of competitive products across
   markets. This division will develop enhanced coordination with
   state consumer protection agencies in the various financial markets.

Professional Services and Cross-Divisional Functions

In addition to its operating divisions, the FFRS would have several units
that render professional advice or perform cross-divisional functions and
are responsible to the commissioners as a board, including:

1. *Offices of Chief Economist, Chief Accountant, and General
   Counsel.*   Responsible for advising the board on economic, accounting, and legal issues of general or cross-divisional applicability.

   Explanation: Professional impartiality in economic, accounting, and legal analysis and in translation of that analysis into
   policy advice to the board will be of urgent importance to the
   FFRS as the consolidated federal financial regulator and to all
   financial market participants. Direct responsibility by the professional service offices to the commissioners as a board will rein-

force the paramount importance to be accorded to the public interest in their professional determinations. In the accounting arena, the oversight relationship with the Financial Accounting Standards Board (FASB) will be continued.

2. ***Office of Examinations.***   Responsible for the conduct of coordinated examinations, fulfilling the regulatory need for inspection without imposing repetitive business interruptions on market participants due to separate examinations by different regulators.

   Explanation: Access for regulatory examination is an essential prerequisite for effective regulation of financial market participants, but duplicative examinations impose an onerous cost on those examined. Each operating division will prescribe what it needs to be examined, but this office will bring consistency to the conduct of consolidated examinations on behalf of all divisions.

3. ***Office of Enforcement.***   Responsible for investigation and prosecution of alleged violations of legal requirements. The substantive recommendation of violative conduct would require the concurrence of each affected division and, unless otherwise determined, board approval would be required to prosecute.

   Explanation: Effective enforcement is crucial to effective financial regulation. Still, substantive policy will be made by the FFRS through rule making by the Board and through rule interpretation by day-to-day regulators rather than through prosecution. When enforcement is necessary, however, consistency as well as promptness and effectiveness of investigation and prosecution will be achieved via this office.

Self-Regulatory Organizations

Under FFRS oversight, direct market governance would be delegated to the stock, futures, and options exchanges. Similarly, direct supervision of risk-shifting market professionals would continue to be delegated to the NFA, and direct supervision of investment market professionals would be delegated to the NASD (separated from its present NASDAQ governance), in each case in coordination with the states.

   Explanation: The repeated legislative determination to rely, in the securities and futures markets, on self-regulation for market governance and for day-to-day supervision of market professionals has proven to be insightful and generally successful at low systemic cost. Reliance on Self-Regulatory Organizations (SROs) should be continued and expanded where appropriate elsewhere in the federally regulated financial arena.

Adjudication

A separate Article 1 Federal Financial Administrative Court would be created to hear and decide all FFRS non-Article III civil enforcement proceedings brought by the Office of Enforcement upon authorization by the commissioners as a board. Appeal from the decisions in those cases would be to the appellate division of that Administrative Court and then to the Article III Courts of Appeals.

> *Explanation:* Both fairness and the appearance of fairness in regulatory prosecutions call for a separation between those who "indict" (in this case, the commissioners of the FFRS authorizing prosecution for alleged regulatory violations) and those who judge the appeal from the initial adjudicatory decision on that indictment.

SUMMARY

All human institutions need to be restructured from time to time. The framework for the current system dates to the 1930s. In the last 20 years, U.S. financial services have changed, grown, and been challenged dramatically in a global competitive environment. Regulation has not kept pace and, indeed, has been an impediment to efficiency, growth, and competitiveness. The time to rationalize and restructure the federal financial regulatory agencies is now so that we may position our financial services industry for the 21st century. This chapter presents a model for doing so—prudently, flexibly, efficiently, and "with recognition of the financial system's economic role."

PART THREE

GLOBAL CHALLENGES

CHAPTER 22

CONTEMPORARY EQUITY MARKETS

William H. Donaldson

THE RISE OF GLOBAL EQUITY MARKETS

Today, equity markets are global. In 1992 there was $2.34 trillion worth of international purchases and sales of equity, compared with about $11 trillion worth of domestic purchases and sales. This equates to approximately one dollar of international equity trading for every five dollars of domestic activity. This international activity is driven by at least three forces:

- Telecommunications costs and transaction costs continue to fall, making cross-border trading more economical.
- Increased supply of equities. This has been fueled, in part, by the large number of recent privatizations.
- Increased demand by institutions and individual investors for international diversification.

With both supply and demand increasing and a key component of transaction costs dropping, what problems remain?

The Challenge of Global Markets

One of the biggest challenges facing all of us is the search for ways to keep national securities regulation in harmony with the realities of this new, global marketplace. The NYSE is taking the initiative in shaping the transition to this growing global market.

Let us start with the fact that nation states still set the policies for securities markets. They provide the regulatory framework of rules within which we all operate. But horizons of both issuers and investors are no longer limited by national borders. National governments must begin to create a framework to regulate an increasingly global securities industry.

In today's world, it is commonplace for world-class companies to seek listings in all major markets. For example, we just celebrated the listing of our first German company, Daimler-Benz. Daimler was already listed in Germany, London, Vienna, Paris, and Tokyo, and is seeking a listing in Shanghai. Today's commonplace trade might be Nippon Life buying Daimler-Benz shares in Frankfurt or New York.

The NYSE has been working to resolve the regulatory impasse that exists in the United States, to make it easier for U.S. equities markets to list non-U.S. companies. There are two reasons:

First, American investors need convenient, efficient access to a much broader spectrum of foreign stocks without sacrificing regulatory safeguards. Although that is changing rapidly, they still cannot buy most of these securities in our regulated markets, whether it be NASDAQ, the regional exchanges, or the New York Stock Exchange.

Second, Americans are now underinvested in non-U.S. securities. In short, supply is not keeping up with demand. If investors choose to trade foreign equities on NASD's bulletin board market, they have to be satisfied with a maximum of two quotes a day, wide price spreads, and no last-sale reporting. Not what one would expect, particularly with top-tier, world-class companies. If institutional or individual investors go through several intermediaries to reach a foreign market where the shares are traded, they encounter fewer safeguards, wider spreads, and diminished disclosure. Charges, including spreads, can run eight to ten times what it would cost to purchase the security in our auction market environment.

Is There a Better Way to Meet Investors' Needs?

In the target universe of some 3,000 non-U.S. companies we follow, 2,000 companies now meet our quantitative standards for a listing on the New York Stock Exchange. The cream—the top 10 percent—average about 20 times the size of our average American prospect. At issue is the SEC requirement that the accounts of non-U.S. companies must meet

U.S. generally accepted accounting principles, or GAAP, in order to be eligible for listing on U.S. markets.

We would like to see the requirement made more flexible. I want to be clear on this point: In calling for flexibility, we are not talking about lowering accounting standards for listing on American markets. Rather, we are urging more emphasis on finding ways to present the information American investors need to make informed investment decisions that do not make it necessary for the non-U.S. company to reconstitute its accounts totally.

There are many different approaches to solving the problem. Clearly the harmonization of world accounting standards and the development of international standards of disclosure is the preferred route, but only if focus can be brought to what is now a fractionated, uncoordinated effort. This will require a concerted effort by regulators from the industrialized nations, working with counterparts from the legal and accounting professions. It must be an effort that is driven by a sense of urgency and a set of timetables and deadlines. Delay increasingly deprives U.S. investors of the transparency and safeguards of our regulated markets.

The competitive danger, of course, is that if we don't act promptly, trading will continue developing in non-U.S. markets and U.S. financial market superiority will erode. That would be a tragedy. Trading patterns for global trading will have been so deeply engraved that there will be no way of changing them. Just think of trying to get Chicago's futures and options business to move to New York or getting London's Eurobond market to come here. America has the largest, most diversified share owner based in the world—51 million individual investors and over 10,000 institutional investors. The NYSE, which is much larger than any foreign or domestic competitor, is the natural meeting place for world-class companies and global investors. It remains for our government policy makers to reorient their thinking, just as investors and market professionals have, to embrace the reality of the oncoming surge in global trading. This is our future.

What About the Present?

How is the NYSE itself doing in the current transitional stage leading to this competitive, global market? Readers of the financial press might wonder why the New York Stock Exchange is still around. A rather common theme in the journalism of the 1970s was the decline of the NYSE. "The last days of the club," boomed the title of one book about the exchange by a well-known journalist-author. Or how about the 1973 headline in *The New York Times* asking, "Are Exchanges Obsolete?" in which the author basically said, "Well, yes." For the 1990s, there is a newer book on the same theme, *Revolution on Wall Street: The Rise and Decline of the NYSE.* I suppose the NYSE has been proclaimed on its way to extinction even more times than Mark Twain read about his demise. It hasn't happened because during the 201 years we've been around there has been a constant adaptation to change, and, for the most part, those adjustments have been designed with the end customer—the investor—in mind.

How Is This 201-Year-Old Business Doing?

The NYSE is enjoying back-to-back record years by almost every important measure. New listings so far this year are running ahead of last year's record pace of 244. The 163 IPOs listed on the exchange so far in 1993 have raised over \$35 billion, about 80 percent of all equity IPO funds raised in the United States in that period. Our listing of non-U.S. companies is expected to be close to double last year's total, with companies coming from all over the globe, including many newly privatized enterprises. We now have a total of 144 foreign companies listed on the NYSE, 27 of which were added this year. Of particular interest is Daimler-Benz, which on October 5 became the first German company to list on the New York Stock Exchange.

We are benefiting from the trend back to equity from debt built up in the 1980s. By year end, U.S. equities markets will have recouped about one-third of the \$500 billion of equity lost through mergers and leveraged buyouts from 1980 through 1990. NYSE's trading volume is averaging just over 260 million shares per day, beating last year's all-time high by 30 percent. Trading in non-U.S. issues is up 50 percent and our 83 percent share of the overall market in trading NYSE-listed stocks is also an increase over last year. Eighty-six percent of the total value of all publicly traded equity securities in the United States is listed on the New York Stock Exchange. So, our numbers are good, and we will be working to keep them good over the long haul.

Our goal has been to make the New York Stock Exchange as efficient as possible and to turn that efficiency to competitive advantage in two ways: by lowering fees, and by using the savings to step up the pace of our technological advances. We are also working to make the NYSE a very entrepreneurial organization with an even more aggressive, competitive, customer-service orientation. Although we are working for change, we have not forgotten that our mission is to maintain an orderly market for investors—not just big investors or small ones—but all investors. We believe that is what gives us much greater liquidity than other markets and encourages investor diversity in the price discovery process.

Some Issues and Opportunities Deserving Closer Attention

To carry out our mission, we have to make a strong case to our regulators, the SEC and Congress. We must make sure that they carry out the legislative mandate spelled out in the 1975 Amendments. That Congressional mandate was, and I quote, "to design a national market system in such a way that public investors in those securities receive the benefits and protection associated with auction-type trading." That time, Congress got it right!

Here we see the relationship between regulation and competition, domestic and international. In this country we have the unique strength of two major market systems operating side-by-side, each filling a vital need: The over-the-counter dealer market for companies that do not meet the quantitative requirements for NYSE listing and, therefore, need dealers to provide liquidity; and the NYSE agency auction market for more widely held and more actively traded stocks that do not require a dealer to provide liquidity.

Problems arise, however, when there is an active effort to divert trading in liquid, exchange-listed stocks into other markets without the price competition of an auction. Customers' orders may be diverted to the over-the-counter markets or to proprietary markets, or they may be internalized. Regardless of why that diversion is taking place—perhaps a broker is being paid to divert orders—the question that should be asked is this: "Whose interest is being served, and is the customer getting the best possible price?" The issue is not regulation to restrict competition. Quite the contrary. The issue is regulation to require maximum competitive interaction of orders in an environment of fairness and fiduciary responsibility to the customers' interests.

In the international arena, London's dealer orientation is understandable.

I fully understand the rationale behind London's recent decision to delay reporting of large trades for up to a week. The idea is to protect dealers in return for the risk they take in maintaining markets in the stocks involved. Here in the United States, however, given the unique interface of the 51 million individual investors and 10,000 institutional investors mentioned above, I fear the consequences of any policies that bolster dealer profits in the short term and damage investor confidence in the long term. I believe it can be truthfully said that what is good for investors long term is also good for dealers. We will remain a strong voice on this matter.

But we won't stop there. We will continue to tear the costs out of our system, and we will continue to add to our technology base. We are currently accelerating the pace of our technological development to keep capacity, among other things, well ahead of the growth curve. We are working to reduce transaction turnaround time even further and to improve the flow of information into, and away from, the point of sale.

As an established, but nevertheless creative, market, we want some leeway to innovate. We see no reason, for instance, why we could not create embryonic extensions of our market that are not harmful to the auction and that would meet special needs of new customers, including passive investors. While we are talking about special services to customers, we must think about the needs of global investors, including the overseas investor. We trade shares of many non-U.S. companies in the form of ADRs which trade in U.S. dollars. However, the day may come when we add the capability of trading a given company's equity in several currencies, and there is nothing to stop us from fractionating our seats in a way that spreads our trading capabilities over 20 or 24 hours.

CONCLUSION

To conclude, I feel that there is a sense of urgency about harmonizing international regulations to facilitate global trading and stimulate the right kind of competition. I am excited about the opportunities ahead for all of us in this industry.

Intelligent people can disagree about issues and solutions, but I believe in the strength and the importance of U.S. capital markets and our equity trading mechanisms. My goals, and those of the organization I represent, are to enhance that strength.

CHAPTER 23

TWO SEC RULES IN AN ERA OF GLOBAL EQUITIES TRADING

William C. Freund

A decade or two ago, any paper on globalized equity trading would have started out discussing statistics to prove the accelerating growth of world trading in equities. Today, we can skip the academic ritual and begin by accepting the fact of a rapid trend toward global equity trading, a trend which will continue to gather momentum.[1]

I begin therefore with the thesis of this chapter, namely, that the world of international equity trading holds significant implications for government regulators. Two such implications appear to be most important at the present time:

- Cross-country listings of equities must bend to listing standards of the major international markets rather than to the preference of domestic regulators. The Securities and Exchange Commission (SEC) may effectively throttle U.S. competitiveness in international equities trading by persisting in its imposition of domestic rules on transnational companies.
- Trade reporting on exchanges must recognize the reality of global institutional trading in a setting of competitive trading markets.

CROSS-COUNTRY LISTINGS

International companies seeking to list outside their borders must, generally, abide by the domestic rules of foreign exchanges and their governments. In Europe, the economic community is attempting to tear down the separate walls of regulation though these have, by no means, been eliminated. Indeed, a convergence of regulations speeds more intense competition among exchanges. As *The Economist* noted, "Competition through diversity has encourage European exchanges to cut out the red tape that protected their members from outside competition, to embrace electronics, and to adapt themselves to the wishes of investors and issuers."[2]

International competition among stock exchanges rests fundamentally on the ability of exchanges to attract foreign global issues. A supermarket cannot enter into competition with other stores unless its shelves are filled with merchandise to buy. Stock exchanges carry stock listings as their merchandise in trade.

The Securities and Exchange Commission has been responsible for a dearth of foreign transnational listings on the NYSE and has curtailed the ability of the NYSE to engage in effective international competition in the trading of large foreign companies. The SEC has acknowledged the fact that most foreign-based international companies avoid listing in the United States because it requires abiding by two sets of accounting rules, one reflecting domestic practice, the other SEC requirements.[3]

The greatest roadblock to transnational listings on the NYSE is the SEC requirement that companies reconcile their financial statements to United States GAAP (generally accepted accounting principles) standards. There is an intellectual arrogance in maintaining that GAAP rules, as enforced by the SEC, are the best in the world and must be followed in U.S. markets. For example, the SEC finds unacceptable German rules that allow companies to plow back earnings into so-called "blind reserves." German companies argue that their investors have benefited from accounting practices that average out earnings over years, moderating earnings volatility, and focusing management attention on longer-run earnings performance criteria.

Many observers have noted that "if the bourses and their governments stay stuck behind national boundaries, business will simply bypass them."[4] The SEC's contention that it must safeguard U.S. investors is a mirage in the modern world of low-cost, high-speed communications. A former SEC commissioner noted, "Many SEC rules are arbitrary and were written in an era when U.S. securities markets could exist in splendid isolation."[5] He continued, "The fact is that U.S. citizens buy foreign stocks anyway; they just do so on foreign exchanges and at greater cost than if those foreign securities could be bought here."

Even more fundamental is the question whether SEC disclosure rules make for a more efficient market than exists without these rules in other leading foreign stock exchanges.

A number of scholars have examined this issue in a variety of ways.[6] Most recently, Professors William Baumol of New York University and Burton Malkiel of Princeton evaluated the efficiency of European and Pacific Rim stock exchanges by testing whether professional investors had any advantage over the performance of broad stock market indexes. If stock prices reflected most everything known about a company, that is, if foreign disclosure of accounting and other information was adequate, the uninformed investor placing her money in the averages would perform as well as the experts. Between 1982 and 1991, professionally managed portfolios did not outperform broad stock market averages on any persistent basis. There are now about a dozen studies which confirm that the risk-adjusted performance of professional investors matches the market averages, attesting to the efficiency of European and Pacific Rim markets.

Messrs. Baumol and Malkiel concluded that "Taken as a whole, the evidence supports the view that markets for the shares of non-U.S. companies appear to be as efficient as those for U.S. firms. Publicly available information seems to be incorporated quite rapidly into shares prices in all markets. Thus, informed investors can expect that the shares of non-U.S. companies are reasonably priced in relation to those of other firms. If this is the case, there is good reason to doubt that investors would benefit at all from any additional disclosure."[7]

SEC rules requiring foreign firms to reconcile their domestic financial reports with U.S. GAAP may actually be counterproductive by reducing investor mastery of the pertinent facts and by lulling them into a false sense of confidence.[8] The result may be to mislead rather than inform investors. Indeed, studies have found that home country accounting standards practiced abroad have, in many instances, provided more rather than less information than restatements to appease U.S. GAAP requirements.[9]

Investor protection requires a recognition that international companies operate in a variety of environments, reflecting differing business, legal, and regulatory practices. "For these reasons, international accountants generally warn that mechanically translating—or quantitatively reconciling—foreign accounting data to U.S. GAAP will often convey an illusion of comparability that does not exist. To understand a foreign company's financial position, one must ultimately come to terms with the home-country's accounting standards.[10]

Under the guidance of the International Accounting Standards Committee, efforts are under way to develop greater international accounting uniformity. But even more important in achieving greater uniformity in accounting disclosures is the pressure coming from increasingly powerful institutional investors. These investors have been more effective than the SEC in prying loose meaningful financial data from global companies.

A recent *International Herald Tribune* article carried the headline, "Swiss Companies Lift the Veil and Equities Like the Light." It noted that "adherence to international accounting standards and full disclosure of revenues, profits, and losses are becoming the norm rather than the exception for Swiss companies, say analysts, who note that the reforms have been prompted by investors. Indeed, the fabled Swiss shroud of secrecy that cloaked balance sheets for decades suddenly seemed less exotic...when shareholders started demanding an accounting of what was being discussed in board rooms across the country."[11]

The experience of the United States with "unregistered" issuers is highly pertinent here. In the private placement and Rule 144A markets, where unregistered securities may be sold, investors routinely demand and receive the same information as they do in registered issues. The reason is that, without full disclosure, securities would be discounted in the market and the cost of capital would rise.[12]

The final argument against SEC intransigence in recognizing foreign financial reporting is that the purported protection of American investors is a victory of theory over practice. Since the SEC's regulatory arm does not reach beyond national borders, U.S. investors trading abroad are denied all SEC regulatory safeguards. They are also denied the lower transactions costs and greater liquidity generally available in U.S. markets.[13]

The SEC has shown little give on the issue of foreign listings so far. Indeed, the SEC's determination to impose its will on foreign corporations was evident when the German firm, Daimler-Benz, agreed to adhere substantially to U.S. accounting standards. The SEC chief economist declared at the time that "the brave move by Daimler-Benz...makes it more likely that fair play will be the rule of this growing world game."[14] But other giant international firms are apt to be slow in following the Daimler lead; only where their need to raise capital in the

United States is very intense are they likely to submit to the SEC's regulatory jurisdiction. To the extent that we lose foreign listings and trading to other markets, we lose an international market where we retain a decisive competitive advantage.

It is interesting to note that when Daimler-Benz agreed with the SEC to flow through to their profit and loss statement some $2.5 billion of reserves, the stock did not budge on the Frankfurt Stock Exchange. Apparently, in their own way, investors already knew of the presence of these reserves.

"There is no question," notes a former SEC chief economist, "that the SEC understands the threat to the Big Board, which almost certainly will become a second-rate exchange unless it can trade the major international stocks."[15]

The Big Board has proposed a number of safeguards to alert the investing public to any differences in accounting procedures. Under the NYSE's proposals, the sole exception to the GAAP reporting rules would be for about 200 world-class foreign issuers, companies with revenues of at least $5 billion for the most recent fiscal year, a market capitalization in excess of $2 billion, and an average weekly trading volume outside the United States of at least $1 million or 200,000 shares. For these large, highly visible companies, the SEC would accept independently audited home-country financial statements as long as these included a written explanation of the material differences between home-country accounting practices and U.S. GAAP.[16]

To protect U.S. investors further, the NYSE has suggested that transactions in world-class foreign company shares be listed in a separate table or at least identified with an asterisk or other appropriate symbol to alert investors to different disclosure standards.[17]

It is time for the SEC to acknowledge that we cannot force transnational companies to march to the beat of our regulators. If they continue to close their eyes to the growing reality of world equity trading, they will strangle U.S. markets and do irreversible harm to the United States as the world's dominant financial center. SEC rules have been driving listings and trading abroad.[18]

TRANSNATIONAL LIQUIDITY AND BLOCK TRADING

Another set of rules tends to undermine the competitiveness of U.S. investment markets. The problem is SEC and exchange rules on reporting completed equity transactions, or what is often referred to as rules regarding market "transparency." U.S. practice has been to publish the price and volume of completed trades on a "real time" basis on computer screens around the world.

The major benefit of immediate disclosure of trade information is that it will allow investors to judge the fairness of their own executions and the momentum of stock prices.

But there are new realities to consider. Retail trades constitute a diminishing share of overall trading. Most transactions are now done by institutions in trades of 10,000 shares or more. Such block trading accounts for more than half of the total compared with only 16 percent in 1975. The giant trades of pension funds, mutual funds, and insurance companies are not generally matched on the floor of the NYSE but require advance marketing and frequent positioning by institutional brokerage firms. To complete block trades, brokers must, at times, be willing to commit their own capital to the purchase of securities, acting as dealers until another institution can be found to buy all or part of the block. By intermediating as dealers, these firms provide depth and liquidity to the equity markets.

Dealers are hesitant to disclose their transactions on a real-time basis. They do not want the world to know the inventory position they have acquired and the price they paid for it. Indeed, they may be reluctant to commit their capital in the first place if they are required to make immediate disclosure of price and volume details. Full and immediate disclosure of large block trades may encourage speculative trading against the dealers' inventories. Stephen Wells, chief economist of the London Exchange, put it more bluntly when he wrote that it "seems impossible for market makers to trade profitably in large size if everyone can see their hand."[19]

Sir Andrew Hugh Smith, chairman of the London Exchange, explained that it ended its real-time reporting of large trades in 1991 because "market makers became unwilling to commit their capital. They quoted firm prices for only small quantities of stock. With their capital commitments removed, liquidity fell. Market efficiency suffered, especially for major institutional investors who consider liquidity the most attractive characteristic of a market place."[20] The result, according to Chairman Smith, was a rise in the cost of corporate capital.

It is no wonder that many U.S. block trades are reported in London which provides an escape from SEC reporting rules and shields market makers from the large-trade reporting obligations for at least 90 minutes. In a world where capital is mobile, it becomes easy to circumvent national regulations.[21]

The 90-minute rule for reporting large blocks in London is intended to provide sufficient time for dealers to unwind their positions. But discussions are under way to grant even longer delays.[22]

It is sometimes argued that, unlike the London Exchange, the NYSE is an order-driven market where buy and sell orders are directly matched on the floor. That does happen to some extent. But large institutional orders in the United States, much as in London, involves dealers acting as principals in facilitating block transactions.

The SEC argues that one of the pillars of strength of U.S. markets is its transparency.[23] That is true, of course, to some extent. But the fact remains that instant dissemination of trade information on large blocks tends to inhibit liquidity. It has been proposed that instead of driving large dealer trades abroad, the SEC allow U.S. dealers the option of reporting trades above a certain size, say 100,000 shares, with a delay of up to 90 minutes. Perhaps a U.S. exchange or several exchanges could conduct an experiment permitting delayed reporting during certain hours of the day.[24]

London investors do not seem to have been harmed by their large trade reporting system. As long as bids and offers are available on a real-time basis, as they are in London, the investor knows the price at which he can deal. "There is a difference between conveying details on the price at which trades are made and conveying information about the portfolio of dealers."[25]

No aspect of regulation is an absolute good. What matters is the efficiency of markets. Large trades, negotiated upstairs, simply are different in their negotiation and placement with final investors than smaller trades consummated directly on an exchange. Immediate reporting of dealer trades can provide false information since such trades often reflect temporary market conditions which can generate volatility unrelated to fundamentals. In a sense, large block positions are trades in the process of unwinding rather than completed transactions. Once dealer positions have been unwound, "once the danger of exposing the position is passed then the fact that a significant stake has changed hands is potentially interesting information, and there is no reason why it should not be available to the market. This approximates to the actual transparency regime on other markets where the fact that a trade has taken place is only made public when the stock has passed out of the market to an investor."[26]

SEC rules need regular review to determine their impact on the efficiency and competitiveness of U.S. securities markets. Such a review is presently under way in the SEC's so-called Market 2000 study. The two issues discussed above need resolution—the sooner the better.

NOTES

1. Anyone who still needs convincing might consult the quarterly *Foreign Activity* report of the Securities Industry Association (120 Broadway, New York, NY 10271). The report for April 1993 covers the full year 1992 when U.S. investors acquired a record $51.5 billion of foreign bonds and stocks, up from 1991's $47 billion. Net purchases of foreign equities alone totaled $32.1 billion in 1992. This compares with $11 billion in net purchases of U.S. securities by foreign investors. Gross equity purchases were, of course, many times as large, totaling $4111 billion for U.S. investors in 1992 and $273 billion for foreign purchasers of U.S. stocks.
2. *The Economist,* June 19, 1993.
3. The SEC clearly recognizes that "the American rules are the reason German companies have avoided American capital markets." (Susan Woodward, chief economist, SEC, in *The New York Times,* May 30, 1993.) Indeed, not just German, but French, Swiss, and other companies as well. Fortunately, Canadian and British companies have accounting conventions similar to U.S. practices so that fewer such companies have avoided U.S. listings.
4. *The Economist,* February 1, 1992.
5. Philip R. Lochner, Jr., *Wall Street Journal,* November 16, 1992.
6. Show-Mao Chen, "U.S. Financial Reporting Requirements for Private Foreign Issuers: Policy Implications of Recent Empirical Studies," New York Stock Exchange working paper 92–06, January 5, 1992.

   Gabriel Hawawani, "European Equity Markets: A Review of the Evidence on Price Behavior and Efficiency," in G. Hawawani and P. A. Michael (eds.), *European Equity Markets.* New York: Garland, 1984.

   Franklin Edwards, "Listing of Foreign Securities on U.S. Exchanges," in K. Lehn and R. Kamphuis, Jr. (eds.), *Modernizing U.S. Securities Regulation: Economic and Legal Perspectives.* Homewood, IL: Business One Irwin, 1993.

   Robert E. Cumby and Jack D. Glen, "Evaluating the Performance of International Mutual Funds," *The Journal of Finance,* June 1990, pp. 497–522.

   Donald R. Lassard, "The Implications of Market Efficiency for U.S. Disclosure by Non-U.S. World Class Issuers," M.I.T., Sloan School of Management unpublished manuscript, September 24, 1990.
7. William J. Baumol and Burton G. Malkiel, "Redundant Regulation of Foreign Security Trading and U.S. Competitiveness," in K. Lehn and R. Kamphuis, Jr. (eds.), *Modernizing U.S. Securities Regulation: Economic and Legal Perspectives.* Homewood, IL: Business One Irwin, 1993, p. 46.

8. Ibid., p. 38.
9. Show-Mao Chen, "U.S. Financial Reporting Requirements for Private Foreign Issuers: Policy Implications of Recent Empirical Studies," New York Stock Exchange working paper 92–06, January 5, 1992.

   Gary K. Meek, "U.S. Securities Market Response to Alternate Disclosure on Non-U.S. Multinational Corporations," *The Accounting Review,* April 1983, pp. 394–402.

   Peter F. Pope and William P. Rees, "International Differences in GAAP and the Price of Earnings," presented at the 1991 annual meeting of the American Accounting Association, Nashville, TN, August 1991.
10. James L. Cochrane, "Assessing and Evaluating the Current Directions of Transnational Listings," New York Stock Exchange working paper 93–03, June 29, 1993.
11. *International Herald Tribune,* July 31, 1993, p. 14.
12. James L. Cochrane, "Assessing and Evaluating the Current Directions of Transnational Listings," New York Stock Exchange working paper 93–03, June 29, 1993, p. 11.
13. Institutional investors, in particular, are apt to buy their transnational companies in overseas markets. Individual investors are more apt to buy through the illiquid over-the-counter market pink sheets where quotation spreads are especially punishing. (Cochrane, op. cit., p. 13.)
14. Susan Woodward, *The New York Times,* May 30, 1993.
15. Gregg Jarrett, *Wall Street Journal,* June 19, 1992.
16. Cochrane, op. cit., p. 10.
17. It has been argued that U.S. companies might pressure the SEC to permit them to adopt different accounting reports. As long as GAAP is the accounting norm in this country, however, such companies would have to reincorporate abroad to qualify.
18. In 1992, the NYSE listed 120 foreign companies, compared to 599 for London, 594 for Germany, 240 for Zurich, and 222 for Paris.
19. London Stock Exchange *Quarterly*, spring 1993.
20. Unpublished speech by Chairman Smith to the Workshop of the International Federation of Stock Exchanges, Toronto, June 22, 1992.
21. OpEd article, William C. Freund, *Wall Street Journal*, September 2, 1992.
22. *Financial Times,* May 27, 1993.
23. Speech by Brandon Becker, Deputy Director, Division of Market Regulation, SEC, before the *Financial Times* conference on International Securities Markets, London, May 12, 1992.
24. Freund, op. cit.
25. Ibid.
26. London Stock Exchange *Quarterly,* spring 1993.

CHAPTER 24

TOMORROW'S EQUITY MARKETS: PROBLEMS AND OPPORTUNITIES

Rolf-E. Breuer

INTRODUCTION

In the 1990s, capital markets will be shaped largely by an upturn in equity business. Shares are becoming much more popular as an investment and financing instrument. This is due, among other things, to the current worldwide trend towards privatization of state companies, now particularly widespread in European countries with widening budget deficits. The second main factor is that many companies in Europe and elsewhere are inadequately capitalized for future investments. Combined with low interest rates, this will help popularize shares as an investment medium regardless of whether a small investor buys them directly or via a mutual fund.

The 1990s will also be a decade of derivative instruments. It has to be borne in mind, however, that each new wave of innovative products is reducing transparency on the increasingly complex financial markets. This affects, above all, the private, nonprofessional, and less-informed investor, who is therefore increasingly turning to professional asset managers.

International legal and administrative standards are required to boost the transparency of the markets and facilitate access to international financial capital.

GLOBAL DEVELOPMENTS

Growing Influence of Institutional Investors

Private asset formation is rising steadily in line with growing income above all in the western industrial countries. Since the population is also aging and state-backed pension schemes can no longer maintain the standard of living achieved during a person's working life, the role of private provisioning is gaining importance. Since these assets are mainly entrusted to institutionals, this group's influence on the financial markets will grow correspondingly. The institutionals aim to provide "global" services to their customers and greater international diversification of their portfolios. This will tend to accelerate financial globalization.

Accounting Geared More Strongly to International Standards

Increasing public-sector recourse to national capital markets has made some local markets too tight for private borrowers. They therefore have to depend even more heavily on access to international sources of investment capital. To implement that policy those companies must occasionally adjust their accounting methods to the guidelines which apply in the placement country. For German companies, this can mean having to draw up financial statements not only to meet German accounting practice, but also foreign regulations.

Stronger Focus on Anglo-Saxon Compliance Guidelines

Drawing international investment capital into a country requires reasonable transparency of national financial markets, an element of which are internationally recognized compliance guidelines and anti-insider dealing laws. In Germany, the second bill to foster the financial markets due to be passed soon will result in new legal regulations drawing on Anglo-Saxon usage and in the creation of a securities watchdog agency. Thus, international standards will also be established in Germany.

Electronic Trading Making Further Inroads in Stock Trading

One thing must be made clear: The trend toward electronic trading will continue, not least because that is the way the customer wants it. He wants to be able to have access to the market irrespective of his location. The advantages of computerized trading are improved market transparency (better information), higher liquidity, lower transaction costs, and quicker, more reliable, and thus more efficient settlement.

EUROPE IN THE YEAR 2000

European Stock Exchange: A Decentralized, Electronic Approach

Despite the existence of Eurobonds and Euroequities, local markets continue to dominate in Europe. It is still too early to speak of a European capital market, but we will mark great progress in this direction by the end of the decade. But the idea of a central European stock exchange—London financial market strategists picture a concept such as "SEAQ international"—is facing off against the decentralized approach, such as the upcoming cooperation between the DTB and MATIF. This scheme aims to link strengthening national markets through a Europe-wide network. But even with the Europeanization of capital markets, it would be sensible not to underrate the regional—or national—element. In order to gather adequate data about local conditions major European-scale investors have to turn to the nationals since a consultant in Frankfurt, for example, will always have better knowledge of local developments than, say, his colleague in London. naturally, the reverse is also true. In addition, a decentralized approach would have the advantage that competition between the national stock exchanges would result in the survival of the most efficient trading and settlement form.

National stock exchanges in Europe can only be linked through electronic networks. The implementation of an actual European floor-based exchange is no realistic proposition. Common information systems are conceivable shorter term, but common trading and settlement systems only longer term. Blue chips and government bonds could be the main elements of European trading, but the listing requirements would have to be standardized (the major objective of the Eurolist project). If the stock exchanges become computerized or if a dual system (including regional trading floors) emerges, remains to be seen. The investor will be the one who makes the final decision. DTB, IBIS, and Boss Cube represent important stages toward full computerization and centralization in Germany.

National (Tax) Regulations Need to Be Harmonized

There seems to be little chance that national securities regulations and accounting rules will be harmonized across the board in the foreseeable future. However, the national tax regulations, particularly the treatment of investment income, must be harmonized as rapidly as possible.

European Monetary Union: More Uncertainties

Events in the EMS from September 1992 until the fluctuation bands were widened this past August mean a major setback in the EMU project. But the goal remains as important as ever. The transition to a single European currency will give liquidity, market breadth, and market depth a major boost. The launch of a common currency is a big step toward a European capital market and will entail further harmonization—either through the market place or through EC rules. However, whether and when currency union will be achieved in currently very uncertain. The wording of the Maastricht Treaty notwithstanding, EMU is not a futures transaction with an agreed settlement date either in 1997 or 1999, but an option whose exercise has become increasingly dubious of late.

Privatizations in Eastern Europe Enhance Significance of Western Europe as a Financial Center

The economic transition and privatization of former state property are giving rise to new capital markets in eastern Europe. However, progress will be slow, the further east the slower it will be. Until the capital markets have developed to western standards, capital will be made available above all by tapping the west European financial markets. This gives especially Germany the opportunity to heighten its attractiveness as a financial center.

CONSEQUENCES FOR MARKET PARTICIPANTS

Intermediaries

In general, the need for intermediaries could be lessened as advances in electronic technology make direct access to the market increasingly feasible. Moreover, there will be an increasing demand for high-quality research and sound, customer-oriented (that is, individual) investment advice. As competition increases among the national financial markets, value-added service will become more and more important.

One potential hazard feared by the intermediaries is the trend of market players to transact their securities deals directly as the importance of the computer grows. A further trend is the increasing number of after-hours transactions (over-the-counter business). OTC business has the disadvantage of being riskier. The participants must bear not only the market risk, but also the credit risk of the contracting party.

Issuers

From the standpoint of major issuers, it will no longer be sensible, or necessary, to have listings on Several European stock exchanges, as electronic networks become more widespread. Different accounting rules are often an obstacle to listing in other markets, especially New York. Extensive mutual recognition of national rules is therefore desirable as far as companies are concerned. Otherwise, they have to draw up additional financial statements to satisfy foreign laws—a case in point is Daimler-Benz's listing in New York.

It may be interesting to note that Germany's banks are also changing their accounting methods in order to increase their transparency. This is basically to accommodate the new EC law. Deutsche Bank is still a step ahead of the other German banks in this respect since—even going beyond the EC regulations—it voluntarily publishes a profit figure not only in its annual report, but also in its interim report. I realize that this is only a small step toward the Anglo-Saxon accounting method. German accounting laws and practice still differ greatly from that system. The underlying principle of Anglo-Saxon accounting, that is, maximum transparency in the interest of the shareholder, is perfectly logical; but a reasonable case can also be made for German accounting practice, which is based first and foremost on the principle of caution and is geared above all to the interests of the creditor. That is why the requirements imposed by the SEC on foreign companies wishing to list in the United States go too far for some German companies. It should be noted that U.S. companies are allowed to list in Europe without being compelled to adjust their accounting methods. In my view, therefore, listing procedures should be designed to accelerate mutual recognition of national accounting rules internationally.

In any case, as in the United States, the increasing influence of institutional investors will probably result in greater corporate disclosure in Europe. Large, financially strong institutional investors will exert pressure on capital-seeking companies. This makes it all the more important for the companies themselves to worry about good relations with their shareholders. Even though maintaining good investor relations still does not receive proper attention in Germany, progress has been made in recent years. Meanwhile, most larger companies have set up investor-relations departments; very often, however, the lack of tradition means that information policy is virtually limited to the usual press releases.

Investors

Private investors are increasingly refraining from participating directly in securities trading, opting instead for institutional investors who offer professional asset management. As a rule, the latter glean information more quickly than private investors, thanks to their direct involvement in market activities.

Therefore, in the coming years the financial markets will continue to be separated into a wholesale market and a retail market. The small investors must therefore check which investment policy he should pursue in the future and how he can best protect his own interests. Even if more and more private investors do select investment funds, they will still have to make certain decisions independently—for instance, decide which fund to buy into. There are virtually no more global players in the field. Instead, the funds tend to concentrate either on special areas—for example, particular countries (or country groups) such as

Asia—or on certain sectors, or even specific financial instruments.

DEMANDS ON INTERNATIONAL fiNANCIAL MARKETS

Stronger Demands on the Innovative Power of the Stock Markets

In view of the increasing significance of OTC trading and the growing competition from off-the-exchange markets, the stock exchanges must work harder to enhance their product range, by ensuring market transparency, high liquidity, low transaction costs, and efficient settlement. Only the stock exchange can guarantee fair pricing.

Centralizing Financial Markets at National Level

The increasing globalization of the financial markets requires either centralization to form large national stock exchanges or the introduction of a unified price-fixing system like in the United States. European countries, in particular, are still lagging in this respect. Concentration on one stock exchange is the only way to achieve sufficient market depth and liquidity; that, in turn, should reduce transaction costs.

Regional Stock Exchanges as Niche Suppliers

The regional stock exchanges could adopt the function of niche suppliers in a national framework. They would then act as financial intermediaries between local investors and regional small caps. Smaller companies would thus be encouraged to go public; the anonymity between issuer and investor would be reduced, and this could help to make the share more attractive as a financial instrument.

Stronger Integration of the Stock Exchanges in a Common Financial Center

Local stock exchanges must become more strongly integrated within the individual countries and the large regions. Deutsche Börse AG was created in Germany to this end. It unites the crash and futures markets and provides an umbrella for processing information and settlement. What is till missing is common clearing. Positions in various markets can then be netted, and settlement will become more efficient.

Closer Coordination of National Watchdog Agencies

As financial markets become more global, the need for closer coordination between national supervisory agencies also rises. The deregulation of financial centers and above all the growing significance of off-shore centers make it easier for globally active investors to circumvent national regulations. In addition, the continuing development of financial products enables capital market players to side-step legal restrictions in their domestic market. New products, however, are often linked with new risks. The agencies must therefore continuously observe developments in the markets and be informed about changes so they can properly assess the inherent risks. This in turn means personnel must be well trained and, naturally, also be able to recognize breaches of market rules.

Comprehensive Clearing an Advantage

There will be no global equity markets. Instead of harmonization and centralization, cooperative solutions will dominate at international level. For reasons of efficiency, however, a comprehensive clearing facility would be an advantage. Setting up a European clearinghouse would be a major contribution in this sphere.

CONCLUSIONS

Globalization Will Not Eliminate Geographical Factors

The idea that geographical factors could lose their meaning is erroneous. The largest liquidity pool can be found—with a few exceptions such as foreign exchange, U.S. Treasuries, "global bonds," and shares of some multinational companies—in the respective domestic market. This is not expected to change, at least for the time being. Therefore, no "global equity market' will emerge in the sense that trading concentrates on one "world stock exchange." Thus, the national financial Markets will not become (fully) harmonized either.

The Concept of the Global Player is False

Owing to the dominance of domestic markets, being an "all-around sup-plier" in all the important regions of the world is a strategy unlikely to succeed in the coming years. The concept of the global player is unreal-istic for cost reasons alone. Especially for banks, all business is local.

National Economic Policy Approaches in Competition

The increasing competition among the financial markets also pits differ-ent economic policy makers against each other and squares off the eco-nomic frameworks shaping activities in the financial markets. Economic policy must ensure through an adequate (legal, tax, and monetary) framework that the attractiveness of equity investments is strengthened, and with it the attractiveness of the domestic financial market. Currently, this is all the more important since sufficient capital must be made available for the privatizations of state enterprises now planned in sev-eral western countries.

CHAPTER 25

FINANCIAL MARKET AUTOMATION AND THE INVESTMENT SERVICES DIRECTIVE

Ian Domowitz

INTRODUCTION

The Investment Services Directive (ISD) is a proposed structure for the regulation of financial services in the European Community. Although initially aimed at providing some standardization of rules governing the provision of investment services, the range of the ISD now seems to encompass the regulation and control of the financial markets within which such investment services organizations operate. This distinction itself has been the subject of much debate and provides only a small indication of the complexity of both the issues and the political process surrounding the formulation and approval of the directive.

The purpose of this chapter is to examine two issues that arise from considering the directive to be a basis for the regulation of trading markets, namely market transparency and market fragmentation. Loosely speaking, the London view is one of limited transparency in the sense of transactions information and competitive, possibly fragmented, markets, while Paris favors complete transparency and a market concentration requirement. There are already large literatures in existence that deal with these topics in general terms. The contribution of this chapter is an evaluation of the issues in terms of the current and forthcoming level of automation that characterizes the European securities trading markets.

The growth of automation in trading market structure has been explosive over the last few years, and it is impossible to ignore this fact in policy issues relevant to the ISD. There are at least 21 markets in Europe employing automated trade execution as an essential part of operations, and several of these are completely automated.[1] Another level of automation not involving automated trade execution also is relevant, namely, the computerization of the information dissemination process characterizing the modern dealer market operating in London. Both levels of automation have implications for the transparency and fragmentation of markets. Automated market structures have the capacity to tremendously increase the former, especially in the case of auction markets. The effect of automation on the latter is equivocal, because technology allows fragmentation, while providing a potential cure for its negative externalities at the same time.

Transparency and fragmentation are leading issues in the debate over the form of the ISD. The economic reason for this is the large potential impact of restrictions on these characteristics of market structure on the two basic functions of the market mechanism: the provision of liquidity and the price discovery process. Liquidity is multidimensional and, as a consequence, is both conceptually slippery and difficult to quantify. One general definition is the capacity to quickly execute orders near the last-sale price in the absence of news affecting the underlying asset's value. As such, liquidity is closely aligned with any idea of market quality. Price discovery is the process through which market value is established. It is rather obvious that, at some point in the trading process, such a price must exist in order for transactions to take place. Financial markets produce prices; prices constitute an economic good like any other. Different market structures provide different mechanisms for price production. Regulation and control of markets such as that envisioned under the ISD have implications for the quality of this production process.

It will be important to distinguish between two concepts of liquidity, both in understanding the ISD debate and in assessing the influence of alternative ways of automating financial market structure. The first might be termed insider liquidity, which is the liquidity provided by dealers or market makers, while outsider liquidity is that provided by investors, institutional or otherwise. Insider liquidity is provided to the investor with whom the dealer trades. There is no doubt that this form of liquidity provision is important to the functioning of the market. It is precisely this notion of liquidity, also called immediacy, that is emphasized by the London side of debates over the form of the ISD. It is a service to the market that can be rewarded in part by concessions to dealers in the form of reduced levels of disclosure requirements and increases in fragmentation that both lead to dealer profits. On the other hand, the market is expected to produce outsider liquidity as a major part of its basic function. Outsider liquidity is provided when one investor's position in a security is sold to another investor, regardless of whether the financial intermediation of a dealer is involved. Outsider liquidity is enhanced by high levels of transparency and greater market concentration, in some form. It is, at least implicitly, the emphasis of the Paris side of the debate, where the market is oriented more toward the direct interaction of investors through an auction market, rather than through dealers.

Transparency is the extent to which trading information is made available after each discrete market event. Two types of transparency must be considered in evaluating both the ISD debate and the degree to which market automation influences the policy issues. The first might be thought of as ex ante transparency, that is, information available before the trade that enables the trade to take place. Interpreted strictly, all that is needed for complete ex ante transparency is the information required to resolve transaction price uncertainty: firm quotations for each possible size of trade. Under this interpretation, the price of the last sale is not required for complete transparency. Further, transparency in this sense does not require that transactions take place in a centralized exchange in an environment automated with respect to the flow of information on price and size quotations. In addition to transaction price uncertainty, however, there is uncertainty about future prices. Transaction prices and sizes can offer considerable information in this regard. Ex post transparency is defined as the immediate publication of such data after each trade. Although most discussions of public market information group the ex ante and ex post concepts together as defining "full" transparency, they are substantially different with respect to their policy implications concerning the form and level of automation of the market. Debates over the ISD have at least implicitly recognized the distinction, however, with London claiming that ex post transparency is both sufficient for price discovery, while ex post transparency contributes to a lessening of liquidity in the market.

The ISD debate on market consolidation has focused on listing requirements to be imposed in order for a market to operate as an "organized" exchange. Arguments over listing requirements are essentially disputes over the extent of fragmentation to be allowed in the overall market. Proponents of complete consolidation argue that fragmentation lowers liquidity and degrades the process of price discovery. The opposing view is that competition is healthy, forcing quality provision of exchange-related services, and outweighing any negative externalities associated with multiple markets. There is a broad spectrum of degrees of fragmentation and how such fragmentation is achieved in practical terms. In order to aggregate the concept and discuss issues with respect to liquidity provision and market automation, fragmentation is defined in this chapter in terms of the degree to which orders in distinct submarkets are allowed to interact for the provision of outsider liquidity. Viewed in this way, automation serves to encourage fragmentation by lowering the costs of implementing competitive market structures, across which orders do not interact directly. On the other hand, automation of information dissemination helps to mitigate some of the negative externalities with respect to liquidity provision, and the automation of order routing and execution may in principle serve to consolidate seemingly disparate segments of the same market. The prescription generally espoused by proponents of automated markets as a cure for fragmentation, the so-called consolidated limit order book, is argued to be inappropriate in the context of the ISD, however. An alternative proposal is made for submarket linkages that has some theoretical advantages with respect to the improvement of market quality and is enabled by an increased level of market automation.

The chapter begins in the following section with a breakdown of types of market automation useful for characterizing advances in both dealer and auction markets. Given the emphasis on the ISD, examples are taken from the London and Paris markets. The links between transparency, liquidity, and automation are explored in the third section. Ex ante and ex post transparency are related to both insider and outsider liquidity considerations. The available empirical evidence on movements from opaque to transparent dealership markets and on comparisons between opaque dealerships and transparent automated auctions is reviewed. Fragmentation is discussed in the fourth section, by first detailing the spectrum of fragmentation possibilities and then providing a useful overall definition in terms of order interaction. The extent to which automation encourages fragmentation and ameliorates its effects is examined, and the latter is related to the fragmentation underlying the market for securities traded both in London and in Paris. Some remarks on automation and access restrictions proposed under the ISD conclude the chapter.

DEALERSHIP MARKETS, AUCTION MARKETS, AND AUTOMATION

Automation of a trading market can include computerization of order routing, information dissemination, and trade execution. The order routing system of the market mechanism brings buyers and sellers together so that they can trade.[2] Automated order routing has vastly changed the markets in which it exists, by introducing both new types of investors and new ways of trading.[3] The same can be said for computerized information systems, which allow the transmission of real-time market information to a much larger group of market participants than was previously possible. The set of information potentially immediately available to such participants is broader as well.[4] Automated trade execution systems are basically mathematical algorithms that enable trade matching without the person-to-person contact afforded by traditional trading floors or telephone networks. Messages between traders are transmitted through the order routing and information transmission mechanisms, which are then processed into trades according to a programmed set of rules that determine transactions prices and quantity allocations among traders active in the market.[5]

The purpose of this section is to describe both dealership and auction market structures in the context of these forms of automation. Given the emphasis on the ISD, examples are taken from the London and Paris equity markets.

Dealership Markets

The automation of the information dissemination process has formed the basis of the modern dealership markets. In an electronic dealership market, dealers or market makers quote prices at which they are willing to trade up to a specified size by displaying these quotes on computer screens. Order routing and trade execution typically are not automated, except for small order processing, which is discussed below. Instead, an investor transmits an order by telephone to a dealer, who executes the order at the prevailing dealer's quote.

There are three important points with respect to this trading mechanism. First, the market structure dictates that the basic function of providing outsider liquidity cannot be accomplished without insider liquidity. All transactions are done through the dealers, and orders from two outside investors cannot cross directly. There is no public limit order exposure. In fact, there is no consolidated limit order book. Second, each public order is transacted by a single dealer. Any such dealer does not know the price and size of the orders executed by other dealers until these are reported and displayed on the screens. Finally, and closely related to the second point, regulatory authorities control the speed at which transaction prices and quantities are made available to other dealers and the public via the information network. The market technology, on the other hand, allows for virtually instantaneous publication of all such information to market participants.

A leading example of the electronic dealership market is London's Stock Exchange, in which the centerpiece is the London Stock Exchange Automated Quotation (SEAQ) system.[6] The SEAQ system is relatively new, having been introduced in late 1986, accompanied by sweeping rule changes with respect to exchange operation and regulation. Foreign stocks are traded on SEAQ International, and London has the most extensive listing of foreign securities in the world, as well as the most foreign members.

Information transmission is automated through TOPIC, a data view system, and quotation and transactions data is available in machine-readable form over a separate system, CRS-Lynx. As noted above, order routing is not automated in general, except for very small size orders. Orders are transmitted to dealers by telephone. There is no limit order facility, and any retail customer limit orders are held by the broker until execution is possible at the limit price.

The number of dealers operating in London increased dramatically after the introduction of SEAQ and changes in exchange rules governing allowable dealer operations. Huang and Stoll (1991) report that 28 dealers were in the market in 1990, trading a volume of about $663,000 million in 1989. On the other hand, competition in the most liquid securities is concentrated among only eight dealers.

Auction Markets

An automated continuous auction embodies the computerization of order routing, information dissemination, and trade execution.[8] Traders submit "messages" through terminals to a central computer. These messages consist of various kinds of order information, as well as personal identifiers. The design of the automated market consists of two types of rules. The first stipulates what part of these messages are shown to other traders on the system.[9] The second set of rules dictates the means by which orders are translated into trades.[10] Typically, orders are written to an "electronic order book," in a sequence determined by such rules. Transactions occur when the price of the best offer to buy is equal to or greater than the best offer to sell, or sometimes when a trader accepts a quote for a certain size observed on the screen by touching a button. Roughly 70 percent of all automated trade execution systems currently in use are of this general design.

Unlike electronic dealership markets, automated auctions offer the possibility of the creation of outsider liquidity without market maker intervention, that is, without the provision of insider liquidity.[11] Orders from any trader are exposed to the entire market, not just to a single dealer. The act of crossing two orders, a market order with a limit order or two limit orders, or of accepting a bid on the screen creates outside liquidity directly. On the other hand, market making services can be introduced in such a market by the continuous posting of bid-ask quotes at different prices for different sizes by the market maker. Market making services also can be supported through a "request for quote" feature on the system. If a market order to buy arrives, for example, and there is not outsider liquidity in the form of sell orders on the book, the system signals designated market makers, who then post a quote for the size of the order. The incoming market order is executed against the best such quote.

One of the most advanced examples of the automated auction market for equities is the Paris CAC (Cotation Asistee en Continu). Introduced in 1986, all Paris-listed stocks were traded on the system by the end of 1989. Order routing and execution are automatic. Brokers route orders from terminals. They can execute against a standing bid or offer on the CAC electronic book or submit a new limit order at an alternative price. Partially filled orders remain on the book until executed or canceled. Market orders, i.e., orders to execute at the best bid or offer, are converted to priced limit orders and executed against the standing order in the book. The book prioritizes orders in terms of price and time. Orders that reach the exchange before the opening of continuous trading are processed through an automated batch auction and executed at a single price determined by maximizing trading volume at the opening.

Since 1988, transactions must be handled by firms known as a Société de Bourse (SB). Individual investors do not have direct access to the system. There currently are 45 SBs in operation, and some are at least partially owned by foreign firms. An SB is a dual-capacity dealer, allowed to execute retail customer orders and to trade on its own account. In this sense, an SB is no different from a London dealer.

Dollar volume of trading is sharply lower than that observed on SEAQ. Huang and Stoll (1991) report a volume of $122,720 million in 1989. Volume in foreign shares is even lower in comparison to the London market. Roughly 21 percent of London's dollar volume in 1989 was in foreign securities, as opposed to a little over 4 percent on CAC.

Free Trading Options and the Dealership/Auction Distinction

Electronic auction markets typically support both ex ante and immediate ex post transparency for traders on the system. More will be said about this in the following section. The important thing to note here concerning ex ante transparency is that quotes are necessarily firm for the size submitted with each price. Once a price-quantity pair is transmitted to the market, the computer will automatically make the trade in the presence of a contraside order that is eligible. A trader must explicitly cancel an order to avoid this possibility.

This problem is not limited to automated auctions and is an issue in any screen-based trading environment. In dealership markets, dealers place the analog of limit orders by posting a bid and an ask price. Traders operating in an auction market place limit orders on the book. Any such quote or order furnishes the market with a so-called "free trading option." The option to hit the bid or lift the offer has value if information arrives while the quote is still in effect that motivates an outsider to trade at that price for a sure profit.

In an auction market, dealers are given this free option, since it is outsider liquidity that is being placed on the book. In the dealership market, insider liquidity is advertised through the posted quotes, and the outside investor has the option.

The problem is thought to be more acute for the outside investor in the automated auction market. Although automated execution can reduce the option value by speeding execution and cancellation of orders, public investors are generally slower to adjust their limit orders. As dealer markets become more automated with respect to order routing, the speed advantage of a dealer is reduced relative to the outside investor. Dealers respond to this threat of increasing the risk of cashing in on the free option offered by their quotes by resisting additional automation, by reducing the size at which they quote firm prices, by increasing the magnitude of the bid-ask spread, or by simply refusing to honor the quote in a losing situation.[12]

Electronic Markets and Small vs. Large Order Handling

This discussion of the importance of free trading options for liquidity provision suggests that orders of different sizes might be treated differently in both electronic dealer and auction environments. This is indeed the case.

In dealership markets, small orders pose little threat to the dealer. The processing of small orders in dealership markets often exhibits automation of both the order routing and trade execution functions. This frees up the dealer to handle larger volumes of orders of more significant size. Public customer market orders of limited size are routinely channeled into a small order execution system. Orders are executed against the dealer offering the best price quoted in the system. For such small orders, trading is essentially anonymous and price negotiation is precluded.[13] In London, this system is called SAEF (SEAQ Automated Execution Facility). It is possible for a customer to route orders to a single dealer on SAEF, a practice called preferencing. Preferenced orders must still execute at the best quote in the market, whether or not the preferenced dealer is offering the best quote. Preferencing provides some individual disincentive with respect to aiding price discovery by the posting of better quotes. A dealer without substantial preferencing arrangements has less incentive to offer a better quote, since the order flow at his or her quote will go to a preferenced dealer. Proponents of preferencing arrangements argue that preferencing provides a way of rewarding dealers who establish and maintain a reputation for good executions overall, in the case of orders executed in an anonymous market for small sizes.[14]

In automated auctions, traders have a natural aversion to leaving large orders on the public limit order book. Huang and Stoll (1991) note that requiring the trading of large blocks of stock on CAC is thought to have been responsible for the loss of volume to London. In response, blocks have been negotiated off CAC since 1989 by "upstairs" traders and then passed through the system for execution at the negotiated price. The procedure does provide additional outsider liquidity with respect to regular orders on the limit order book, however, since limit orders on the CAC book are cleared against the block at their limit price.

The fact that off-system negotiation for large blocks was introduced into the Paris procedure has been argued to be proof that an automated auction is not sufficiently flexible to handle institutional investor needs. Revealed preference indicates that this is certainly so for CAC, but alternative designs for the handling of large orders in otherwise fully automated auctions are possible. In the Swiss SOFFEX system, for example, a special limit order book (the block board) exists. Blocks may be automatically executed, subject to special rules regarding price that make it more difficult to "pick off" a large order under unfavorable market conditions. In addition, traders wishing to negotiate the price or quantity of a block may do so within the system, following which the blocks are exposed to the regular limit order book and then executed against each other at the negotiated price. This procedure facilitates market making (and, hence, insider liquidity) for large trades within the automated auction system. It provides the flexibility that CAC lacks without taking the trade out of the system. Such designs would also encourage investor placement of larger orders in the system, providing direct outsider liquidity for blocks.

AUTOMATION, TRANSPARENCY, AND LIQUIDITY

Transparency is the extent to which trading information is made available after each discrete market event. Complete transparency might be defined as the immediate publication of all prices and sizes of trades, together with firm quotations for each possible size of trade. Automation has made complete transparency possible and, one might think, desirable.[15] Ex ante transparency and ex post transparency have different policy implications, however, and it is important to distinguish between them. They will be discussed in turn, followed by some available evidence on the effect of increased levels of ex post transparency, in particular, on market liquidity.

Ex Ante Transparency

Ex ante transparency resolves transaction price uncertainty. Complete ex ante transparency consists of firm quotes for all possible sizes of transaction. The definition also might include disclosure of the party posting the quote, but if a complete schedule of quotes exists and quotes truly are firm, such information may be considered superfluous.[16] On the other hand, even in the presence of firm quotes but lacking a complete schedule, identity serves to build reputation, for example, for being willing to trade larger quantities than advertised at prices not much different than the posted quotes.

In an electronic dealership market, it is the automation of the information dissemination process that enables ex ante transparency. Quote dissemination by dealers advertises the extent of the insider liquidity in the market, indicated by the magnitude of the bid-ask spread, the quantities available at the quotes, and the number of dealers in the market actively posting quotes. Although dealers typically do not publish complete schedules, dealer identity is revealed.[17] Dealers that fail to honor their advertised quotes can be identified by outside participants over time; similarly, those who are willing to deal at larger sizes at much the same price quoted for smaller quantity also can become known. Ex ante transparency in the dealership market provides no direct indication of the extent of outsider liquidity, however. This could be inferred only if the influence of individual dealer's retail order flow on the dealer bid-ask spread were known with some certainty.

London dealers restrict the extent of ex ante transparency in the face of the free option problem inherent in a screen-based dealership market. Stoll (1992) notes that London regulators have even limited the requirement that dealers honor their quotes vis-à-vis other dealers. Pagano and Roell (1990a) report that data gathered in July 1989 indicate firm quotes by London dealers up to a dollar volume of approximately $275,000. This amounts to share volumes of between 500 and 10,000 shares, depending on the stock in their sample.

In a computerized auction, ex ante transparency is provided by the combination of automated information dissemination and order routing systems. There are essentially three possible components to ex ante transparency for such auctions. First, since traders send orders to the electronic order book, the entire book, with aggregate quantity at each price, could be shown to the market. This provides a price-quantity schedule for both buy and sell orders, and is a direct indication of the extent of outsider liquidity available to the market. Second, display of the book could be restricted to show only the best bid and offer, with aggregate quantity available at those prices. In this case, outsider liquidity is known only for the best prices outstanding in the market, and the true depth of the market is not observable. Finally, all bids and offers, or just the best bid and offer, could be displayed in a disaggregated format that identified the traders submitting the orders.[18]

There is one further possibility with respect to restricting ex ante transparency that is sometimes implemented for automated auctions. Harris (1990) argues that traders who supply liquidity, but are concerned over the free option value of their orders, should be encourage to supply such liquidity by allowing them to hide the full size of the order. If this is permitted by the system design, ex ante transparency is not complete, and the full extent of outsider liquidity is not known to the market. The argument is essentially correct, however, and there is an intuitively plausible trade-off between complete ex ante transparency and the provision of outsider liquidity due to the free option problem in limit order systems. Systems that allow such a trade-off almost invariably impose some cost on the hiding of the size of an order, in terms of the execution priority of the order. In other words, such a cost imposes some additional execution risk in return for nondisclosure.[19]

Such hidden orders are allowed on CAC. They retain price priority but do not have time priority relative to orders shown to the market. They are revealed only when executed. There are two levels of ex ante transparency. The best bid and offer, with size, is reported to the public on a network called CHRONOVAL. The second level reveals real-time information about the order book including the price and quantity bid and offered at each price. This information is transmitted over TOPVAL and is available only to brokers. Data are currently unavailable to judge the depth of the book in terms of the size offered at the best bid and offers, say, in order to get some idea of the size of firm quotes compared with the London market.

Ex Post Transparency

Resolution of transactions price uncertainty is only one component in the decision to undertake a trade. There also is uncertainty about the future price of the security. The publication of transaction price and quantity data provides information in this regard. Complete ex post transparency here will mean the immediate publication of all transaction price and size information after a trade takes place, including the time of the trade.

The automation of the information dissemination process in both dealership and auction markets makes complete ex ante transparency feasible. In the latter case, it is simply an output of the automated trade execution mechanism, and such information can be displayed on the screen within a second of any transaction. Computerized record keeping allows the transmission of post-trade information within short periods of time in dealership environments, albeit not within a single second.[20]

There are several ways in which complete ex post transparency can be relaxed. The time of the transaction might not be reported, for example. Data transmission could be delayed until the position in question was "unwound," that is, disposed of to another investor. Information can include only aggregate volumes traded during some time frame, with only the range of prices observed over that time. Finally, one might discriminate between information concerning transactions made through a centralized market and those carried out off-exchange. The latter has implications for the issue of market fragmentation and will be discussed in the next section. All of these alternatives have been proposed over time in negotiations over the form of the ISD.[21]

Although such delays could be programmed into an automated auction, such markets typically exhibit full ex post transparency. Given that normal size transactions are subject to immediate publication, it also is difficult to delay information with respect to blocks in most automated auction structures. The reason for this lies in the details of the institutional structure of the market. In particular, large blocks that either are negotiated off-exchange or somewhere else within the system typically are exposed to the regular limit order book as part of the execution process. This implies that the price of the block, although not the full size, could be intuited from limit order book activity that is part of screen information.

Ex post transparency limitations also have effects in dealership markets that depend on aspects of market structure not directly tied to information transmission. London's SEAQ often is compared to NASDAQ, which affords relatively complete ex post transparency. On NASDAQ, transactions in so-called upper-tier stocks, accounting for roughly 90 percent of market value, prices and volumes of trades are published within 90 seconds. For lower-tier stocks, prices also are reported immediately, with volume published the next day. The argument is that, if NASDAQ dealers can profitably exist in that environment, so can SEAQ dealers. Franks and Schaefer (1990) report, however, that a greater proportion of trades on NASDAQ are matched; that is, dealers sometimes do not complete a transaction until a counterparty has been found, thereby delaying price reporting. In other words, insider liquidity is not threatened by trade publication, because the dealer retains the potentially valuable price and size information until after outsider liquidity has been found and the exposed position is cleared. Insider liquidity is less, however, under a system permitting such matched trades, since the investor initiating the transaction may not obtain immediacy from the dealer unless outsider liquidity is already present.

There are two possible conclusions that can be reached in this regard. The first is that complete ex post transparency has had the effect of reducing insider liquidity on NASDAQ by encouraging such matching of trades. There is less ex ante transparency on SEAQ, accompanied by less matching, and it might be said that insider liquidity on SEAQ is, therefore, greater. On the other hand, NASDAQ is considered a successful dealership market, one of generally high quality with respect to liquidity provision. This suggests the second conclusion, namely that increasing transparency and thereby reducing insider liquidity by some amount does not necessarily lead to a market with decreased outsider liquidity. Since it is the latter that is the function of the market, not the former, increased transparency does not drive dealers out of business to the extent that the market fails with respect to performing its basic function of quality price discovery. If this statement is taken seriously, it may also be conjectured that a dealership market, possibly opaque, may not necessarily be preferred to an automated auction market in which ex post transparency is part of the design. We now turn to some evidence on both these points.

**Transparent Auctions, Opaque Dealerships, and
Market Quality**

There is little empirical evidence available on the relationship between ex post transparency and market quality and on differences in quality in comparing dealer and auction markets. Fortunately, two studies exist that help cast some light on the following issues important to the ISD debate. First, does a transition from limited disclosure to ex post transparency improve market quality in a dealership market for which all other aspects of market structure remain the same? This question is relevant in considering the effect of a complete ex post transparency requirement in the ISD on London's market. Second, are there differences in market quality between an ex post opaque dealership market and a transparent automated auction market that are identifiable and could influence the choice as to which market attracts trades over the long run? The answer to this question is relevant in considering the long-run viability of the Paris automated market in the face of an ISD agreement that limits ex post transparency in favor of the London dealership structure.

Seguin (1991) considers the movement from ex post opacity to ex post transparency in a dealership environment. He examines the properties of transactions returns and bid-ask spreads for 2,639 stocks that obtained listing on the U.S. National Market System (NMS) between April 1982 and September 19987. Designed under the auspices of the NASD, the only basic difference between NMS and NASDAQ is immediate ex post transparency. In other words, the principal effect of moving from the old NASDAQ system to NMS is the real-time reporting of transactions prices and volumes; ex ante transparency and other aspects of the market structure were unchanged.

Although several theories suggest a positive correlation between increased information and the volatility of stock returns, Schwartz (1988) argues that information enhances the price discovery process, resulting in a stabilization of price movements. Generally speaking, such stability might be considered beneficial and a sign of market quality. In particular, volatility per trade is considered a measure of market depth, which, in turn, is one of the dimensions of liquidity.[22] Seguin (1991) does find that the increased information associated with ex post transparency decreases transaction returns volatility by a statistically and economically significant 8 to 10 percent, on average. Further, this decline is evident in an immediate and permanent fall in market volatility over the first seven days of NMS listing for a stock, that is, once transactions information is reported on a real-time basis.

The bid-ask spread is another of the few quantifiable indications of market liquidity, and small spreads indicate a tighter and higher quality market. Theoretical work suggests that spreads are comprised of three components: a pure transactions cost, and inventory effect, and dealer compensation for trading against traders with potentially superior information.[23] With respect to the last, introduction of ex post transparency could have two opposing effects. Dealers lose control over potentially valuable information, decreasing their advantage over investors and thus leading to a widening of the spread in order to provide themselves with some extra protection. This is essentially the London view. On the other hand, if the introduction of ex post transparency helps to identify informational trading more easily, dealers' potential losses to informed trades is reduced, and the spread should narrow.

It is the last possibility that seems to be born out in the data. Seguin finds that the magnitude of the spread falls by a statistically significant 3.5 percent, on average, following the introduction of last-trade reporting. Although Seguin does not provide any data on an increase in trade matching before the dealer consummates a trade and reports, it is clear from the volatility and spread results that ex post transparency does not jeopardize outsider liquidity by these measures, even if insider liquidity may be reduced somewhat. Further, ex post transparency did not drive the NASDAQ dealers out of business and cause a collapse of market quality, a possibility stressed by the London view.

Pagano and Roell (1990a, 1990b) examine the bid-ask spread as the measure of market liquidity for 16 stocks traded both on the Paris CAC and on London's SEAQ International. The data were gathered over part of July 1989 and time-stamped in such a way as to provide a perfect match by time of day. The comparison is, therefore, between the transparent automated auction and the more opaque dealership market, controlling for time and security type.

The first measure considered was the bid-ask spread applicable to trades for relatively small quantities. Using all the matched observations, Pagano and Roell find that the spread, as a percentage of stock price, was 1.52 percent on SEAQ versus 0.41 percent on CAC. To the extent that the spread measures market liquidity, the automated auction clearly provides the more liquid market.

The same qualitative comparisons are obtained for large orders, defined as the maximum size for which the SEAQ quotes were firm. Not only were the CAC spreads smaller than those on SEAQ, the spread for large transactions on CAC was not observed to be much bigger than those computed for small orders. These results suggest that CAC offers

greater liquidity than SEAQ International even for traders placing relatively large orders.[24]

AUTOMATION, CONCENTRATION, AND FRAGMENTATION

With respect to the ISD, the idea of "concentration" entails the potential
requirement that all trades should be executed on a "regulated" or "organized" market. The definition of such a market has itself been a point of
contention in ISD debates. On the surface, the definitional argument
concerns listing requirements. The Paris view is one of restricting the
definition of regulated markets to include only those that admit securities
for listing. London suggests any market should be allowed to operate
under the definition, so long as such a market has adequate rules for
determining which securities trade therein, despite the fact that they may
not be listed on a central exchange. SEAQ International would be an
organized market under this interpretation, but not according to the definition suggested by Paris.[25]

Listing requirements may have advantages in terms of exchange
oversight and monitoring of traded companies, and it has been argued
that reduced listing requirements would impose costs on expanding the
scope of a market.[26] Liquidity benefits of exchange listing also may be
traced to its role in forcing centralization of the provision of trading
market services and consolidation of orders. Attention is focused here on
this notion of centralization and the influence of the automation of market structure on the fragmentation of the trading market.

The Fragmentation Spectrum

On the most general level, there are two forms of market fragmentation.[27] Internal fragmentation occurs when all orders within a single
market are not allowed to interact with one another. This could occur,
for example, when block trades are negotiated off-exchange, and orders
on the regular limit order book eligible for a trade at the block price are
not executed against the block. It also may happen if exchange rules
allow a member to execute both sides of a trade without exposing either
the bid or offer to other orders previously transmitted to the exchange.

Spatial fragmentation refers to the trading of a security in more than one market. To the extent that the same stocks are traded on CAC and SEAQ International, the market for these stocks may be considered to be spatially fragmented.

Spatially fragmented markets also can be internally fragmented. In 1989, for example, Paris brokers were allowed to trade as principals outside the CAC system. In particular, the brokers are no longer required to route small orders through CAC. The new rules also allowed off-exchange negotiation of block orders.

This suggests an entire spectrum of fragmentation possibilities. A complete lack of fragmentation might be accomplished through the use of a consolidated limit order book with a requirement that all orders must interact by passing through the book. This would enforce both price and time priority for all orders. Different markets might exist for the trading of the same security, each with its own order book and possibly linked by communications channels. Time priority for orders may well be sacrificed under such a design, and even price priority is not assured without an order routing capability across markets and regulatory intervention. Each such market may be additionally fragmented by allowing in-house execution services by brokers and off-market proprietary trading systems. It would now be possible that the best quotes are not visible marketwide, increasing the likelihood that orders are not given the best pricing. Proponents of the consolidation of markets stress such potential negatives and view the overall result of fragmentation as a loss of liquidity. The other side of the debate favors the benefits of increased competition for the provision of exchange services with respect to lower costs and innovation in the supply of services to the investor.

The breadth of the spectrum of fragmentation suggests that yet another definition is required in order to usefully aggregate the concept and discuss the policy implications in the context of automation. It is tempting to define fragmentation as the inability of an order to trade with another order at the best available price in the overall market for the security. This would cover both spatial and internal fragmentation. It is not sufficient in the sense that a consolidated market under this definition could still suffer with respect to the liquidity provision required to produce the best prices. In particular, a satellite market could be established that executed trades at the prices offered in the primary market. Since the satellite market does not produce prices, it may operate at lower cost, allowing it to compete with respect to trade execution services. The primary market, therefore, may suffer a decline in outsider liquidity, which results in the degradation of the quality of price information.[28]

Stoll (1992) defines fragmentation as the inability of an order in one market to trade with an order (for the same security) in another market. This obviously applies to spatial fragmentation. It is easily extended to cover internal fragmentation by expanding the concept of "market" to include the submarkets provided by brokers' in-house execution and proprietary execution services. This broader definition is adopted as the basis for the discussion which follows. It equates complete market consolidation with maximization of outsider liquidity for the purpose of price discovery, for any given size of market.

Automation as a Cause of Fragmentation

The automation of exchange-related services can help fragment the market in the sense defined above. This is particularly true of the automation of information dissemination. In order for a secondary market to compete successfully with the primary market, it must be true that the quotes and transactions prices on the secondary be no worse than those offered on the primary exchange. This can be assured by monitoring quotation and price information on a continuous basis in both markets. Automation of information dissemination makes such monitoring a relatively easy task, removing one barrier to the competition for exchange services that can lead to market fragmentation.

In fact, free-riding on the quotes of the primary exchange is a means by which a potential secondary market can solve the pricing problem. Automation permits the direct appropriation of quotes from the primary exchange. The secondary market may then operate at lower cost relative to the primary, since it does not bear the burden of the production of price information. This diversion of order flow to the lower-cost producer of the transaction service, now the secondary market, may result in the inability for orders in all markets to interact with one another. This diversion of outsider liquidity away from the primary market may result in a decline of the quality of price information, leading to a deterioration of the price discovery process in the overall market for a security. Dealers on SEAQ International are thought to free-ride on CAC quotes produced by outsider liquidity demanders and suppliers.

Automation of the order routing and execution functions also may contribute to fragmentation by lowering the costs of exchange-services provision by secondary markets. Automated order routing and execution provides a relatively low-cost means of allowing brokers to divert orders toward a secondary market, in which an order can be executed against the quote offered by the primary market. Automated execution also makes in-house limit order files combined with a mechanism for automated execution of orders against such files. All such procedures fragment the market in the sense that they do not interact with order flow into the primary market.

Automation of all functions permits secondary markets to arise in the form of proprietary for-profit exchanges. There is a variety of such systems in London, for example, including BEST, BZW TRADE, and the IDB system, a wholesale market open only to dealers.[29] Such systems either execute automatically against primary market quotes or allow execution against direct outsider liquidity provided to the proprietary system in the form of independent quotes or other indications of trading interest.

Automation as a Cure for Fragmentation

Automated information dissemination systems cannot eliminate fragmentation as it has been defined here. Automated order routing and possibly automated execution must play key roles in this regard. Information systems do help mitigate some of the potentially harmful effects of fragmentation, however. In particular, reporting requirements that are enabled by such systems allow the entire market to have access to price and volume information, improving the price discovery process to the extent that ex post transparency is important. This has been recognized in London, for example. Executions on proprietary systems there re reported to the London Stock Exchange and displayed on TOPIC.[30]

Automation also may mitigate fragmentation effects simply by expanding the overall scope of the market. The automation of information flows and order routing introduces the possibility of new trading technologies and attracts new types of players to the market. It is possible that volume in the primary market could expand to the point that sufficient outsider liquidity exists for quality price discovery there, despite the existence of secondary markets that free-ride on the primary's quotes.

An expansion of automated order routing could allow the interaction between orders executed in-house by brokers and those on the primary exchange. Each limit order received by a firm can be listed on the in-house electronic book and simultaneously transmitted to the primary market's limit order book as a good-till-canceled order. Incoming market orders are executed against the best price available either in-house or on the exchange, within-house execution occurring when the in-house price is as good as the primary market. When executed on one book an order is automatically canceled on the other.[31] It should be noted, however, that such a solution cannot currently be applied in London, which lacks consolidated limit order book facilities for any size of order. On the other hand, it could easily be implemented in Paris, eliminating internal fragmentation with respect to the market for small orders, in particular.

The same basic idea for linking in-house systems to the central exchange can in principle be applied to the linkage of spatially distinct markets. The end result of such a line of thought is the existence of a consolidated limit order book with linkages to all markets, with execution by automated means, as proposed, for example, by Peake, Mendelson, and Williams (1979). Such a market lacks fragmentation completely, given the definition employed here.

Unfortunately, this idea has no current relevance to the ISD debate in its current form, unless one views the harmonization of financial services as encompassing the complete standardization of trading market structure. This is too sweeping a perspective, both politically and from the competitive point of view. Establishing any kind of consolidated limit order facility for the London dealers moves that market closer to an auction structure and, therefore, does not command any widespread support.

One alternative does suggest itself, based on the discussion of in-house system linkages with a centralized market. London dealers could be viewed as operating such individual execution services. Automation would allow the dealers to send retail orders, perhaps only of limited size, to CAC on a good-till-canceled basis. Execution would occur through the dealer or through CAC, depending on whether the dealer could offer the better price, given incoming order flow to the dealer. Further, London dealers could post their own quotes on CAC, allowing CAC order flow to interact with London retail flow indirectly through the dealers' supply of insider liquidity. This elaboration of the dual-entry brokerage system suggested by Cohen, Maier, Schwartz, and Whitcomb (1982) allows a certain amount of fragmentation to continue to exist, but not necessarily at the expense of market quality relative to that achieved in a consolidated market. Of course, such a mechanism will not exist without government intervention in the interest of consolidation, unless the London dealers find it especially profitable. It is difficult to reach any firm conclusion with respect to the latter. It would not be sufficient to simply establish a linkage that executes an in-house (to the dealer) order whenever the dealer quote is better than CAC and a market order arrives either in-house or on CAC. In this case, each dealer maintains an in-house book only and does not transmit orders to CAC. The dealer must, therefore, continue to buy and sell shares from inventory in order to provide the execution service. This idea is similar to the single-entry system considered by Cohen, Maier, Schwartz, and Whitcomb (1982), who argue that such a trading regime would exhibit larger bid-ask spreads and greater price volatility than a consolidated market.

CONCLUDING REMARKS

This chapter has attempted to assess the role of financial market automation in considering certain policy issues underlying the ISD. In many ways, automation is responsible for raising issues of transparency and fragmentation in the first place, by making both feasible in ways that were impossible even a decade ago.

Financial market automation is relevant to ISD proposals in at least one other respect, that of access to markets. Three issues have been raised. The first concerns whether credit institutions should have direct access to exchanges. This point is independent of any automation considerations. The second relates to restrictions on the number of members that should be allowed on any given exchange, while the third involves access to a domestic market from a foreign country.

The last point is crucial to SEAQ International, whose growth will depend on precisely such access. Automation of information dissemination and order routing make it possible, that is, such access can be implemented by means of an electronic trading system. It poses another dimension in which fragmentation may be abetted by automation, especially if an electronic trading system in one country is permitted to trade stocks listed in another country. In that case, fragmentation can occur, even if trading is concentrated on "organized" markets, as suggested by Paris.

Automation also makes possible virtually unlimited access to markets in terms of the number of participants. Trading floors have essential space limitations, but for all practical purposes, computers do not. Limitations on the number of seats on an electronic exchange simply establishes domestic monopoly power over the provision of exchange-related services. It does not contribute to outsider liquidity. Further, it is not at all clear that insider liquidity is somehow enhanced by restricting the access of traders providing competition with respect to liquidity provision.

NOTES

1. See Domowitz (1993a). This count includes three markets operating in Spain, Belgium, and Austria, which are not surveyed therein.
2. In addition to routing orders from investor to investor, investor to market maker, and market maker to market maker, the order routing system also provides trade information for the purpose of clearance and settlement, as well as to market participants for trade confirmation.
3. For example, the immediacy introduced by computerized routing has introduced trading strategies generically known as program trading. The rapid feedback to investors results in the development of new risk management strategies, permitting the direct entry of pension fund investors, for example, into the market. See Dewan (1990) for an overview of automation with respect to order routing.
4. Data potentially available to market participants in real-time includes, but is not restricted to,
   • the price and size of the latest trade;
   • the best bid and offer prices, and quantities available at those prices;
   • all prices, and size available at them, outstanding in the market;
   • trader identification for each quote;
   • counterparty identification for each trade;
   • sales and volume record of each trading session;
   • relevant information from other markets.
5. See Domowitz (1993a) for an overview of automated trade execution systems currently in operation.
6. Several systems constitute the overall London market, but SEAQ is the most important. The other leading example is the NASDAQ system operating in the United States.
7. The London Stock Exchange estimates that these market makers are responsible for more than 85 percent of trades in the 160 or so stocks that are most actively traded.
8. Auction markets for equities certainly existed long before any thought of automation. In a continuous double auction, bids and offers are submitted continuously over time.

Transactions also occur on a continuous basis, as bids and offers are accepted by some mechanism, such as using hand signals on a trading floor. In a periodic auction, bids and offers are submitted over some period and executed together at a single price and single point in time. The price is calculated by maximizing the total volume traded over possible transactions prices. Discussion will be limited to continuous auctions, since the periodic auction has largely been abandoned in Europe. It should be noted, however, that most continuous auctions are opened with some form of periodic auction. See Domowitz and Wang (1993) for a comparative analysis of the automated versions of the two institutions with respect to pricing, volume, and volatility characteristics.

9. For example, many automated auctions are anonymous, in that the personal identifiers are not shown to other traders. On some systems, a trader can dictate how much of the order size is displayed. Unpriced market orders are not allowed on some systems. A variety of other restrictions on allowable messages exist; see Domowitz (1993a).

10. Such rules are called execution priority rules. For example, first priority is given to the best price. There must be some way to resolve ties at a given price, however. Some designs enforce a first-in, first-out rule, i.e., time priority. Sharing rules or priority given to certain types of orders or even order size also exist in practice. See Domowitz (1993a) for a classification of execution rules currently in use.

11. In principle, it is feasible within this market structure to allow investors to trade directly with each other, bypassing "professional" traders or brokers completely. In practice, this happens only on systems not operated by, or regulated as, exchanges.

12. Stoll (1992) indeed reports that London regulators have limited the requirement that dealers honor their quotes vis-à-vis other dealers.

13. Such small order execution systems also can operate as an adjunct to auction markets. See Domowitz (1990) for examples and descriptions of such systems for both dealership and auction markets.

14. It should be noted, however, that the increased automation of order routing in such a small order execution system can impose an increase in the likelihood of capitalizing on the free option offered by the dealer quotes. This is happening in the United States on the Small Order Execution System (SOES) of NASDAQ, which is much like SAEF. In that case, some firms are providing retail customers with terminals to trade on SOES, who monitor dealer quotes and execute trades against those dealers who are slow to adjust posted quotations. Such customers now are called "SOES bandits," reflecting the dealers' view of the situation.

15. On a theoretical basis, desirability will depend on the type of information that defines transparency, the type of market structure, and the size of the overall market. Madhaven (1992), for example, defines transparency as the disclosure of order imbalance information. In an auction setting, he finds that it is possible for increases in such information to exacerbate market volatility and even result in market failure. On the other hand, if the market is sufficiently large, disclosure of imbalance information leads to increases in market liquidity and decreases in volatility.

16. This is not necessarily true in the automation of the interbank foreign exchange market, where credit risk plays a major role. Automated foreign exchange dealer markets such as Dealing 2000-2, Minex, and EBS screen automatically for counterparty risk, however.

17. Exceptions include the automated interbank foreign exchange dealer markets, which enforce anonymity.
18. Automated auction systems differ widely with respect to which such set of information is provided. See Domowitz (1993c) for an analysis of asymmetries of such information across classes of investors.
19. In particular, several systems will execute undisplayed orders after orders which are displayed that have equal standing in the electronic book with respect to price and some secondary priority such as time.
20. On the U.S. NASDAQ system, for example, trade information is published within 90 seconds.
21. The proposal that was negotiated and tentatively agreed to as of July 2, 1992, involves the following: After three hours, the share price of a particular position must be quoted at the highest and lowest level that it reached during the first two hours of that three-hour period. This will occur every 20 minutes. The procedure, therefore, involves a one-hour delay after the expiration of the period covered by the price. Additionally, the weighted average of the share price will be calculated over each six-hour period and published two hours after the six-hour period expires. There is a loophole, even for this limited version of ex post transparency. These obligations may be suspended by national market regulators in the case of "very large" transactions or "illiquid" transactions, or even in "very small" markets, where to publish such information may run the risk of revealing a trader's identity, all term in quotes remaining undefined. See USEC Brussels communiqué DAN 402-040742 to the U.S. Secretary of State and Department of Treasury, dated July 2, 1992.
22. See Domowitz (1993b) and the references therein.
23. See, for example, Ho and Stoll (1983) and Stoll (1989).
24. These comparisons are the relevant ones in consideration of market quality in the sense of outsider liquidity and price discovery. They do not imply, however, that trading should move immediately to CAC. Pagano and Roell report that commissions in London for large orders are only slightly lower than in Paris, but that estimates exist that roughly half of non-U.K. stock deals are transacted without a commission charge. If no commission is charged, the cost of trading in London, i.e., commission plus bid-ask spread, slightly outweighs the spread differential in favor of the CAC. It also is not clear that traders of large orders enjoy the same amount of immediacy on CAC as they do on SEAQ, but there is no clear evidence on this point. Neither of these caveats is really relevant for the small size comparisons, however.
25. There is an obvious way to interpret this definitional dispute in terms of regulatory constraints to competition favoring a particular party. The Paris definition would force a reorganization of SEAQ International should the ISD adopt it, possibly hampering its current viability. From another perspective, off-exchange trading is much less developed on the Continent than in the United Kingdom. It follows that London traders would enjoy at least a short-run competitive advantage if they could conduct off-exchange business freely throughout the European Community.
26. These considerations are beyond the scope of this chapter. See Smith (1991) for some discussion and references.
27. A third category, temporal fragmentation, is sometimes cited. This might be defined as trading in a security taking place over a long period of time and is a piece of

arguments in favor of single-price periodic auctions.

28. The argument here is essentially one of network externalities. Such externalities exist in an environment in which the best transactions are achieved in a market in which other orders are present. See, for example, Huang and Stoll (1991) on this point.

29. In fact, quotes posted in the IDB system need not be the same as those posted in SEAQ by the same dealers and are permitted to be better than the SEAQ quotes. Although arguments are made that dealers should have the ability to dispose of large inventory positions quickly, it is not at all clear why such favorable prices should not be available to outside investors. In other words, there is no clear rationale for the existence of such a wholesale market for dealers, given that outsider liquidity is, if anything, adversely affected. See Domowitz (1993a) for descriptions of BEST and BZW TRADE.

30. See Huang and Stoll (1991).

31. This is basically the dual-entry brokerage system described by Cohen, Maier, Schwartz, and Whitcomb (1982). The effect of this type of system is to allow some orders to be executed ahead of others with respect to time priority, which still is considered a negative aspect of fragmentation. On the other hand, these authors show that under the dual-entry system, overall market performance may not suffer relative to a fully consolidated market.

REFERENCES

Cohen, K. J., S. F. Maier, R. A. Schwartz, and D. K. Whitcomb. (1982). "An Analysis of the Economic Justification for Consolidation in a Secondary Security Market," *Journal of Banking and Finance,* 6: 117–36.

Dewan, R. M. (1990). "Order Routing: A Technological and Economic Perspective," in D. R. Segal (ed.), *Innovation and Technology in the Markets.* Chicago: Probus Publishing.

Domowitz, I. (1990). "The Mechanics of Automated Trade Execution Systems," *Journal of Financial Intermediation,* 1: 167–94.

Domowitz, I. (1993a). "A Taxonomy of Automated Trade Execution Systems," *Journal of International Money and Finance,* forthcoming.

Domowitz, I. (1993b). "Equally Open and Competitive: Regulatory Approval of Automated Trade Execution in the Futures Market," *Journal of Futures Markets,* 13: 93–113.

Domowitz, I. (1993c). "Automating the Price Discovery Process: Some International Comparisons and Regulatory Implications," *Journal of Financial Services Research,* 6: 305–26.

Domowitz, I., and J. Wang. (1993). "Auctions as Algorithms: Computerized Trade Execution and Price Discovery," *Journal of Economic Dynamics and Control,* forthcoming.

Franks, J. R., and S. M. Schaefer. (1990). "Large Trade Publication on the International Stock Exchange." London Business School manuscript.

Harris, L. E. (1990). "Liquidity, Trading Rules, and Electronic Trading Systems." New York University Salomon Center monograph no. 1990–4.

Ho, T., and H. R. Stoll. (1983). "The Dynamics of Dealer Markets under Competition," *Journal of Finance,* 38: 1053–74.

Huang, R. D., and H. R. Stoll. (1991). "Major World Equity Markets: Current Structure and Prospects for Change." New York University Salomon Center monograph no. 1991–3.

Madhaven, A. (1992). "Security Prices and Market Transparency." University of Pennsylvania, Rodney L. White Center for Financial Research working paper no. 1–92.

Miller, M. H., and C. W. Upton. (1989). "Strategies for Capital Market Structure and Regulation." University of Chicago manuscript.

Pagano, M., and A. Roell (1990a). "Shifting Gears: An Economic Evaluation of the Reform of the Paris Bourse." London School of Economics discussion paper no. 103.

Pagano, M., and A. Roell. (1990b). "Stock Markets," *Economic Policy,* 10: 65–106.

Peake, J. W., M. Mendelson, and R. T. Williams. (1979). "Toward a Modern Exchange: The Peake-Mendelson-Williams Proposal for an Electronically Assisted Auction Market," in E. Bloch and R. A. Schwartz (eds.), *Impending Changes for Securities Markets: What Role for the Exchanges?* Greenwich, CT: JAI Press.

Schwartz, R. A. (1988). *Equity Markets: Structure, Trading and Performance.* New York: Harper and Row.

Seguin, P. J. (1991). "Transactions Reporting, Liquidity, and Volatility: An Empirical Investigation of National Market System Listing." University of Michigan, Mitsui Life Financial Research Center working paper no. 91–21.

Smith, C. W., Jr. (1991). "Globalization of Financial Markets," *Carnegie-Rochester Conference Series on Public Policy,* 34, 77–96.

Stoll, H. R. (1989). "Inferring the Components of the Bid-Ask Spread: Theory and Empirical Tests," *Journal of Finance,* 44: 115–34.

Stoll, H. R. (1992). "Principles of Trading Market Structure." Vanderbilt University, Owen Graduate School of Management working paper no. 90–31 (revised).

CHAPTER 26

INTERNATIONAL ASPECTS OF SECURITIES MARKET REGULATION

Andrew Large

A close friend of mine advised me before I put my "head on the block" to take up the chairmanship of the Securities and Investments Board (SIB). "Andrew," he said, "what you've got to do is this: find the three things that need fixing and fix them. Forget the rest; they'll either take care of themselves or you can leave them for the next guy."

Well, I must confess after a year that I hope he was right. I've certainly identified the three things that I think need fixing. But I'm humble enough to suggest that fixing them may well outlive my term of office.

Two of the three are really quite domestic and relate to out-of-date regulations involving retail services. Trying to handle the arcane aspects of selling life insurance is not everyone's cup of tea. And, in the United States, the securities regulators must be relieved that they don't have to do it. Trying to create an enforcement culture and policeman mentality in "the land of self-regulation" is not so easy; neither is fitting our Financial Services Act, passed in 1987 by enthusiastic politicians, into a legal structure that goes back to the Magna Carta.

But the third is, quite simply, the most daunting. Helping to shape the regulatory framework to govern *international* financial transactions now and in the future. These are mainly wholesale market transactions and need to be treated differently from retail services. The regulatory requirements vary enormously from country to country, and pulling these together without increasing the regulatory burden of red tape and bureaucracies is certainly a difficult job. But it is a vital one if free capital flows are to be continued and markets further integrated.

It is indeed worth reflecting on why this conference would not have taken place 20 years ago. For sure, there was international activity. The Euro market was beginning to take off. FOREX had been around for many years. There was even your friendly local stockbroker prepared to buy you foreign shares.

But only in the last 20 years has the equity market exploded on an international basis—helped, of course, by the development of derivatives and modern portfolio theory, and electronic communications, and skilled intermediaries. Investor demand has broken out of its domestic straitjacket, probably for good.

The problem, however, is that regulation has developed on a national basis. It has developed in response to national concerns about what was "broke" and needed to be fixed. Naturally enough, this differed among countries. Equity markets especially have been subject to distinct national characteristics and allowed to muddle along in their own traditional ways until something scandalous or threatening happens. Such as the BCCI and Maxwell affairs. Then politicians get involved, looking to punish the guilty and unvirtuous and to protect those whom they regard as innocent victims. Big side issues are involved with equities: the market for corporate control, governance of corporations, insider trading, among others. Until recently, however, no effort was made to harmonize internationally what proper market conduct was and was not. Now it becomes increasingly important that we do so.

International activity has increased exponentially. And, in this increasing internationalization of the marketplace, we find that intermediaries may be in one country, issuers in a second, and institutional or private investors in a third or fourth. They all behave in different ways and conform to their own domestic regulatory requirements.

It is worth looking at a few cases of what *was* "broke" in different countries and why, therefore, they adopted different objectives and regimes. In all cases it is worth reflecting that regulation tends to develop in response to something that a country feels *is* broken, something that is felt to be wrong. There is no "absolute" as far as investor protection is concerned. What sort of protections are being provided? And from what sort of hazards? Perceptions about what really matters are different in different places according to differences in culture and law and practice.

Take the United States, for example. Here, the perception back in the 1930s was that there were too many crooked people selling worthless securities to the innocent public, and this activity brought on the crash, followed by the depression. This was, of course, a vast oversimplification of the situation, one which few historians would accept on its own. But the public perception drove the regulatory response, the Banking Act of 1933, which included the famous Glass-Stegall provisions, the Securities Acts of 1933 and 1934, which provided disclosure standards for new issues and regulated conduct of market participants.

What about the United Kingdom? Well, the establishment and clubby world of the U.K. never really accepted that much *was* broken until the 1960s or 1970s. Then it was something different. It wasn't so much that crooked directors put out false information or, rather, that this was the perception. The problem in the U.K. was that, for one example, flashy stockbrokers earned too much, so they *must* be creaming too much off the investors. Another example was that life insurance salesmen earned too much, so they *must* be paid commissions that were too high. And it was that crooked slickers said they would manage your money for you, only to pocket it and run off to the Cayman Islands. So, in the U.K., it wasn't really disclosure and transparency that people were after, it was codes of behavior, codes of conduct of business for firms and individuals. As for stringing them up, well, that was something you left to the criminal judiciary which had developed plenty of experience since the Magna Carta.

What about Germany? Different again. First of all, the investors kept all their money in nice, safe bonds. (In France, it was under their beds.) So, equities were for the "big boys" only. And the big boys really didn't need much help. Second, the big universal banks and institutions didn't really see why their legitimate wishes to make money should be interfered with by transparency and disclosure or by changes in the approach to corporate control. No, what was broken in Germany was that a new insider dealing law had to be implemented—imposed by the Brussels bureaucrats maybe—but definitely to be implemented. They needed to construct an efficient edifice to confirm and stamp out insider dealing, and that has been their new regulatory impetus.

And what about Japan? Even more bizarre: No real regulation at all, just forms of "administrative guidance." I am sure many of us have been recipients of the famous phone call, "M.O.F.* says...." Besides, too many people were making too much money. For the private investor, the market, after all, had always been going up. (It reminds me a little of the unfortunate members of Lloyd's, the insurance market. They were also told that, for the last 200 years, you *always* made money.) And so why should investors worry too much that they were being subjected to practices within the intermediaries and professionals that just wouldn't have been tolerated in most countries? What was the stimulus for change? Well, first, the music began to slow down. The market began to crumble. So, you *could* lose money after all. Second, the profits of the intermediaries were so high that they looked like fat cats. Third, foreign investors began to question the wisdom of dealing and investing where the practices were so bad. And, fourth, the government moved the goal posts so that behavior that had at one time been unofficially condoned was all of a sudden sufficient to have you locked up and ostracized.

I think this comparison of the origins of equity-market regulation in different countries tells us something. It explains perhaps why it is that the *objectives* of regulation differ so much from one country to another. But different regulatory systems have distorting influences. They can and do interfere with the free movement of international capital. As a free market man, I believe that we should have a system in today's electronic world where the full potential for capital movement is not impeded. Otherwise, economic and social development will be hindered to the detriment of the very investors whom the regulation is designed to protect. This is the real case for harmonization as a means to eliminate regulatory inefficiency. We all know that investor protection means different things to different people. But the question is, how can we use regulation to dismantle existing inefficiencies and create a fair marketplace without introducing a new set of inefficiencies that may be as bad as the ones we just got rid of?

How can we regulators respond to all of this? The first lesson, it seems to me, is to accept one basic truth: In regulation, nothing is black and nothing is white. Everything is a shade of gray. The question is, what should the shade be? What are the costs and what are the benefits? How can regulators approach the question of efficiency? Living as we do in a noncommercial environment (which as regulators we are con-

---

* Ministry of Finance (of Japan).

demned to do), there is no such thing as a commercial bottom line. I suppose that was the big culture shock I experienced personally when moving from being a banker to being a regulator. For regulators, the absence of a bottom line affects their whole credo. Their behavior will tend to be defensive—always defending some Holy Grail or objective, which may well have been correct at an earlier date but which has no incentive to move on with changing requirements in changing markets.

Let me give you a couple of topical examples where, in my view, there is no absolute right or wrong but where regulatory harmonization has proved difficult because of different objectives. We have in London right now the issue of post-trade transparency. Put quite simply for those who are not used to this piece of regulatory jargon, if you are a position-taking market maker, then if you are required immediately to publish large positions that you take on your books, such post-trade disclosure is helpful to market efficiency. But it may enable you to be picked off by your competition. Some market makers have complained that this hurts their profits and, therefore, is bad for the market in the long run. Full transparency would force firms to retreat from market making and take their capital and the liquidity they offered to provide investors with them. So, the market makers asked the London Stock Exchange for, and received, a "temporary" lifting of the post-trade reporting requirement. It is still lifted.

Now regulators in total transparency regimes would take a pretty dim view of this. It would not be consistent with their view that investors might be denied relevant information for periods of time; those same investors, consequently, might deal in ways that they wouldn't have if they had known all the facts. Other regulators might give other reasons. They might insist on order matching as a way of creating liquidity. They might query how the integrity of a derivative market could be guaranteed if the prices available to it from the cash market were not reflective of reality on a real-time basis. If your objective is total transparency, you will cry "foul." If your objective is improved liquidity, you will cry "fine."

Take another case, the amount of capital needed to support equity positions. Now, if your objective is that under no circumstances could a securities house be allowed to fail (because this could hurt investors), then you should have a very high level of capital cover, even if this added significantly to costs (also incidentally borne by the investors) and even if it meant that investors dealt offshore. But if your objective is to protect private investors through a compensation fund to ensure that costs are minimized and to encourage firms to use and focus on more sophisticated techniques and to encourage big investors to adopt a greater degree of caveat emptor in dealing with the investment industry, then you will come up with a different solution—certainly one demanding less ongoing capital support. Again, there is no black and there is no white—only "better" or "worse" solutions.

What all this means is this: Before harmonization of regulations can happen, the regulators have to accept that yesterday's objectives must always be capable of being looked at afresh. You have got to look at the opportunity cost of *not* altering your objectives, just like you have to do with respect to your portfolios if you are a fund manager. In all cases, I believe that the regulator should go back to first principles: not so much "We do it that way because that's how we do it," but more "What are hazards today or in the future of this activity to investors and to the integrity of the marketplace. How real are the hazards? What is the most cost-effective way of controlling them? And to what degree?"

Some of the mechanisms that will cause harmonization over time are, I think, quite passive. It may sound trite, but just as people travel and watch TV, so their attitudes change. Freer trade causes commercial barriers and legal obstacles gradually to be diminished. Generally, people's views on the standards of regulation that they are looking for will be conditioned by an increasingly sophisticated understanding of the markets and products on offer. Pressures of this sort will, in fact, *cause* change. I mentioned pressures from abroad that already have caused change in Japan. Pressures within the European Community have caused change in most countries in Europe. And pressure from the United States affects regulation in the United Kingdom.

Pressures and serendipity, however, may not be enough to reach a greater degree of understanding so that the costs of regulation can be set at levels that really reflect the benefits. A positive effort to harmonize must also be made—not blindly or stupidly, but where the hazards are the greatest. We have a number of parties who can, and increasingly do, try to wrestle with the issues and to reach better conclusions.

The European Commission attempts this as between its members. The Bank for International Settlements attempts it among the banks worldwide. The International Organisation of Securities Commissions attempts it between securities houses worldwide. Stock exchanges attempt it bilaterally and through the Fédération International des Bourses des Valeurs. Bilateral discussion takes place between most regulatory bodies. I believe that significant progress is actually being made, starting off by having better understanding as to what other peoples objectives are and by pointing out that maybe objectives and standards need adapting or adapting one's own. In addition to this, the legal systems evolve. Case law develops with experience of regulation in different countries (for example, insider trading). Of course, public opinion hardens as it becomes aware of market rigging, insider trading, and other practices.

What practical evidence do we now see of a push toward more effective internationalization of regulatory practices and standards? Let us take Europe. Here we now have enacted laws to prevent insider dealing. They won't be easy to implement, partly because of the reality that the more you try to define insider dealing, the more elusive it can become. So, enforcement won't be easy. A harmonized approach to insider dealing *is* in the cards for Europe. That, in turn, will help to improve the fluidity of capital flows within Europe as people's confidence in the integrity of the market is built.

Again in Europe, let us take the issue of the rights of minority shareholders. This is an important area within the market for corporate control. Foreigners have fought and won cases establishing such rights in France, Belgium, and Germany. Ultimately, this will work through to the benefit of investors both in those countries and elsewhere.

So what is the bottom line? Fair markets need openness, but regulation should be as light as possible. Wholesale markets, in particular, can look after themselves, and overregulation in the name of protection of nonexistent retail investors may be unnecessarily onerous. Of course, each marketplace needs enforcement of standards and integrity. It needs market surveillance and a willingness to show teeth. Firms must be adequately capitalized, particularly as nonbank intermediaries take bigger positions. But regulators must accommodate pace of innovation. They need to recognize that objectives and standards need to be dynamic, not defensive. Sensible attempts to improve harmonization need to be reinforced. In that way, capital markets will expand. The cost of capital will be lowered. And investors, in the broadest sense, will be benefited.

CHAPTER 27

THE LONDON EQUITIES MARKET

Stephen Wells

This conference is titled Technological, Competitive, and Regulatory Challenges, and I want to talk about regulatory challenges and how those challenges affect the London equity market.

For practical purposes at the moment the London equity market is the same thing as the London Stock Exchange. I say "for the moment" because there are competitive challenges on the horizon, and I shall finish my talk by opening up the discussion on the competitive impact of regulation.

Before that, I want to set the scene with some basic dimensions of the market. After that I want to describe some of the features of how the market works. As you might expect, it is different from how it looks on the surface. These features are important because of their impact on regulation. Then, finally, I want to examine some of the challenges to the market.

BASIC DIMENSIONS OF THE LONDON EQUITY MARKET

The London equity market is, in fact, two markets: domestic equities and foreign equities. The two markets have different participants, different rules, and different business structures.

The London Stock Exchange domestic equity market is dominant in the field; it has not serious domestic competitors at the moment, and its market share of domestic business is close to 100 percent. Of course, there is business in U.K. stocks outside the United Kingdom—several U.K. companies have an international following. The main focus of this is in the United States, where both the New York Stock Exchange and NASDAQ do significant volumes in certain U.K. stocks. For example, New York trading in Glaxo frequently exceeds London trading.

The last decade has seen a major reduction in transaction costs in the domestic market, mainly for large trades. As an illustration, Figure 27–1 shows the average institutional commission rate since 1981, depicting the drop and, more recently, the apparent stabilizing at about 0.23 percent for commission deals. In fact, the apparent stability masks a continued decline as a result of the growth of soft commissions (about 13 percent of all commission revenues).

Over the same period, trading volumes have expanded and velocity has increased (see Figure 27–2) in terms of total turnover, mainly because of the growth of dealer-to-dealer trades. But it has been more stable in terms of customer business—funds are not turning over their

FIGURE 27–1
Institutional Commissions (excluding net bargains)

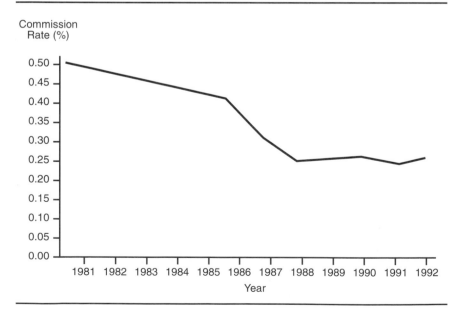

FIGURE 27–2
Velocity of U.K. Shares

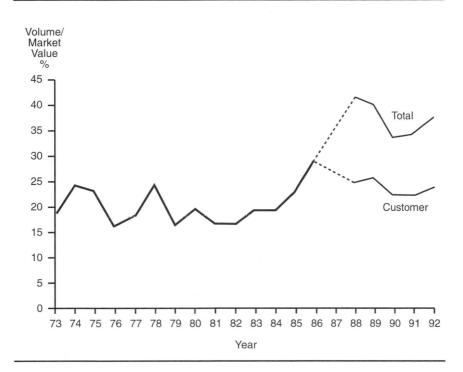

portfolios much more often than they have always done.

In foreign equities, the London Stock Exchange is the largest market for cross-exchange business, that is, trading in foreign equities. Trading on the exchange by our member firms in foreign equity in the first nine months of 1993 came to £412 billion, compared to a domestic equity figure of £406 billion. Volumes have grown rapidly in recent years. Figure 27–3 shows the monthly volume of business since 1990. The London market's importance and dependence on foreign equity trading are unique, and, as Figure 27–4 shows, the market represents all the major economies and some minor ones.

One sector never really succeeded, and that is the U.S. sector, which remains one of the smallest sectors. There are various possible explanations for this. The most likely is that the flow of business is U.S. money into foreign stocks. U.S. funds have no need to come to the

FIGURE 27–3
Monthly Volumes—January 1990 to September 1993

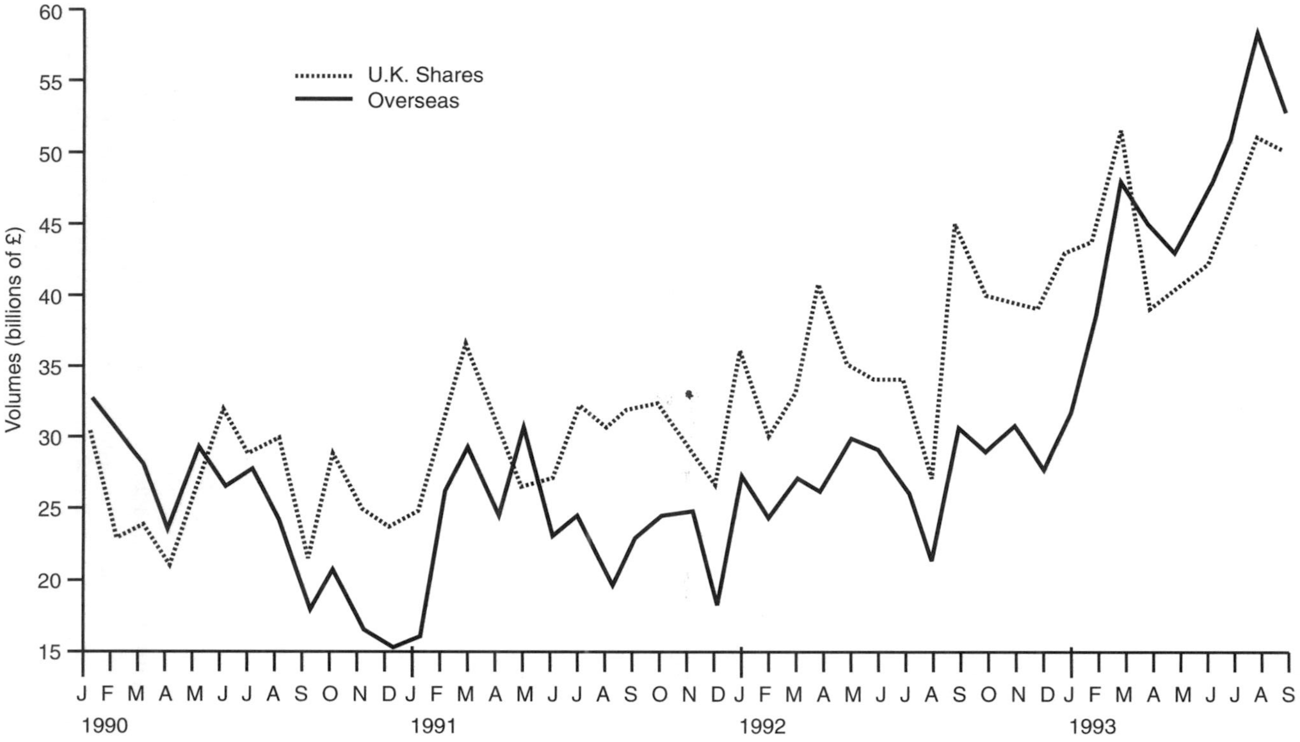

FIGURE 27–4
Breakdown of Overseas Equity Turnover in London, 1992–1993

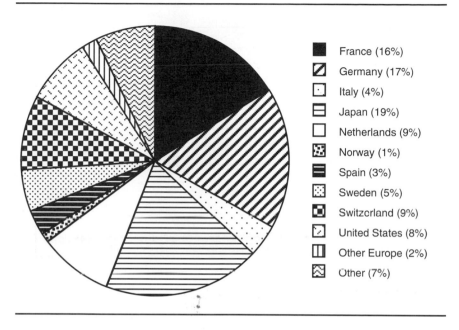

France (16%)
Germany (17%)
Italy (4%)
Japan (19%)
Netherlands (9%)
Norway (1%)
Spain (3%)
Sweden (5%)
Switzerland (9%)
United States (8%)
Other Europe (2%)
Other (7%)

London market for U.S. stocks! The London market is a gateway to Europe and Japan, not the United States.

MAIN FEATURES OF THE MARKETS

The London equity markets are dealer markets. You could say they are like NASDAQ, but, at the same time, not like NASDAQ. Figure 27–5 shows a SEAQ screen for North-West Water (a privatized utility). I will not labor through the details; anyone who has seen a NASDAQ screen will recognize the main features. But there is one point worth highlighting because it reflects other aspects of the market, and that is the size of the quotes. For North-West Water the quotes are mainly firm in 50,000 shares—over half a million dollars—quite a serious commitment of capital.

The SEAQ International screen (Figure 27–6) for overseas equities is very similar.

FIGURE 27–5
Representation of SEAQ Screen

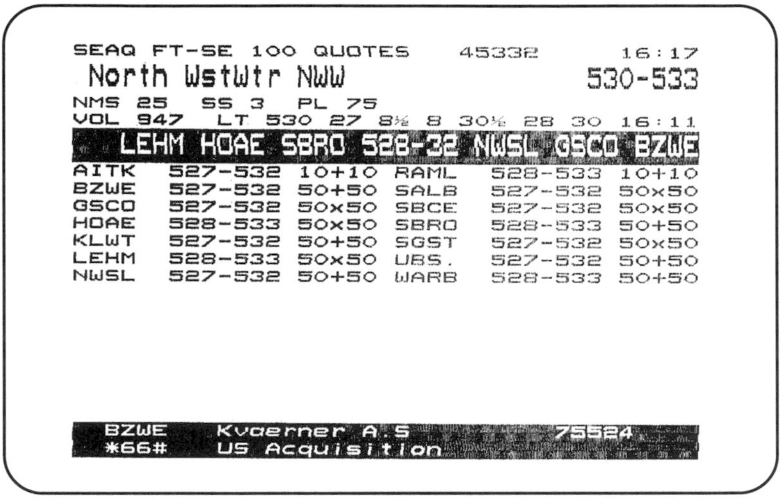

```
SEAQ FT-SE 100 QUOTES     45332        16:17
North WstWtr NWW                    530-533
NMS  25   SS  3   PL  75
VOL  947   LT  530  27  8½  8  30½  28  30  16:11
   LEHM HOAE SBRO 528-32 NWSL GSCO BZWE
AITK    527-532  10+10  RAML    528-533  10+10
BZWE    527-532  50+50  SALB    527-532  50x50
GSCO    527-532  50x50  SBCE    527-532  50x50
HOAE    528-533  50x50  SBRO    528-533  50+50
KLWT    527-532  50+50  SGST    527-532  50x50
LEHM    528-533  50x50  UBS.    527-532  50+50
NWSL    527-532  50+50  WARB    528-533  50+50




   BZWE    Kvaerner A.S           75524
   *66#    US Acquisition
```

FIGURE 27–6
Representation of SEAQ International Screen

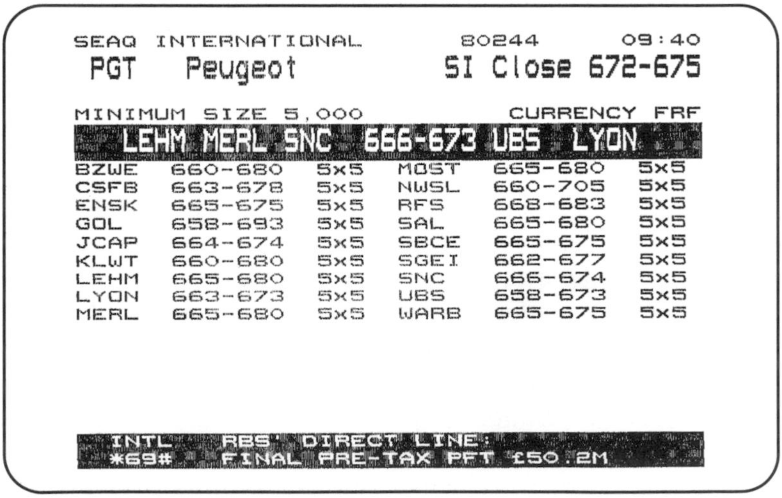

```
SEAQ  INTERNATIONAL      80244       09:40
PGT   Peugeot          SI Close 672-675
MINIMUM SIZE 5,000            CURRENCY FRF
   LEHM MERL SNC 666-673 UBS LYON
BZWE    660-680  5x5  MOST    665-680  5x5
CSFB    663-678  5x5  NWSL    660-705  5x5
ENSK    665-675  5x5  RFS     668-683  5x5
GOL     658-693  5x5  SAL     665-680  5x5
JCAP    664-674  5x5  SBCE    665-675  5x5
KLWT    660-680  5x5  SGEI    662-677  5x5
LEHM    665-680  5x5  SNC     666-674  5x5
LYON    663-673  5x5  UBS     658-673  5x5
MERL    665-680  5x5  WARB    665-675  5x5




   INTL    RBS' DIRECT LINE:
   *69#    FINAL PRE-TAX PFT £50.2M
```

Market makers are committing themselves to substantial positions and substantial risks. And they really do by taking those positions; these are not upstairs placing. Figure 27–7 shows the position movements for one of the market makers in Kingfisher Group (a retailer) for a period in January 1993. Those positions are large and have to be laid off, either with clients, with other market makers, or through the interdealer brokers.

Of course, the sizes of quotes are there to attract the main customers, institutions. The U.K. market is highly institutional: about 70 percent of domestic equity is owned by U.K. savings institutions and about 15 percent by foreign investors, again, largely institutions.

Domestic trading is similarly dominated by institutions (see Figure 27–8). U.K. and foreign institutions make up about 83 percent, and even more so in foreign equity (Figure 27–9), where U.K. and foreign institutions make up 92 percent.

And the final important feature: the London equity markets are negotiation markets. There are proprietary order routing systems for smaller trades, but practically all substantial, that is, institutional, deals are transacted over the phone. The SEAQ and SEAQ International quotes are firm but are really just the starting point. Negotiation established whether the market maker will improve on the screen price, and usually he will.

Firm quotes offer a one-way option to investors, *all* investors, and market makers adopt defensive tactics in making their screen quotes so as to cover themselves against the least attractive trades. Where the trade suits the book or where the market maker knows the customer, then price improvement is normal.

Figure 27–10 shows the proportion of trades at different values where the price is better than the bet bid or offer. As you can see, over 60 percent of larger trades improve on the screen price. So smaller investors are much more likely to be paying the screen price, that is, they will tend to pay more than institutions—not always (one market maker undertakes to better his screen quote for small orders) but usually.

So, in summary
- The markets are decentralized. In a real sense there are multiple centers pulled together through the SEAQ screens and the IDBs.
- The boundaries are difficult to define. For exchanges with electronic order matching systems or with trading floors, the scope of the exchange's business is obvious, but not so in a decentralized market.

FIGURE 27–7
Trade by Trade Market Maker Position (Kingfisher)—January 1993

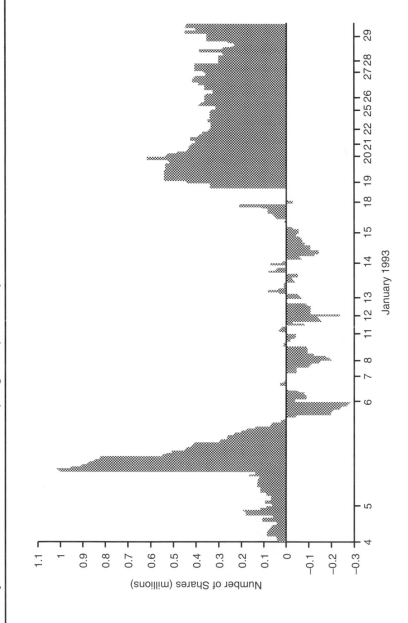

FIGURE 27–8
An Institutional Market in U.K. Shares

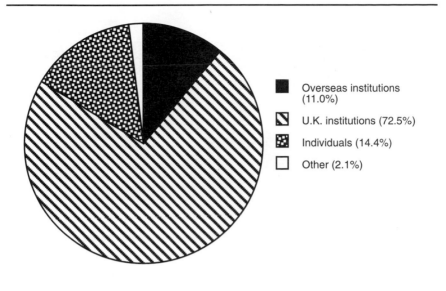

■ Overseas institutions
(11.0%)

▨ U.K. institutions (72.5%)

▨ Individuals (14.4%)

□ Other (2.1%)

FIGURE 27–9
An Institutional Market in Overseas Shares

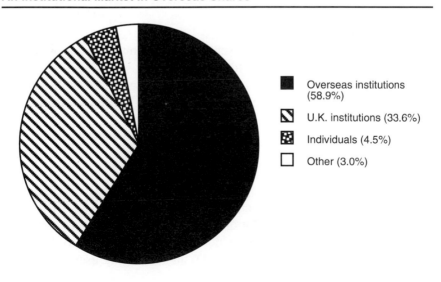

■ Overseas institutions
(58.9%)

▨ U.K. institutions (33.6%)

▨ Individuals (4.5%)

□ Other (3.0%)

FIGURE 27–10
Beating the Best Bid and Offer—April through June 1993

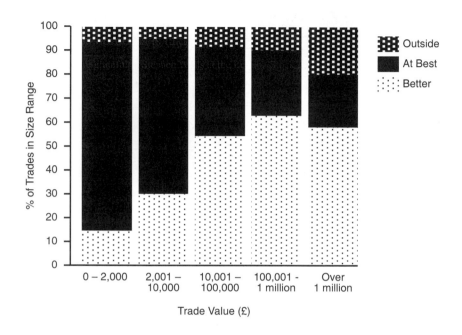

- The London markets are essentially institutional markets, which are used by individual investors, and this imposes its own regulatory challenges. Individual investors require and get a high level of investor protection, but the regulation can chafe for institutional investors.

CHALLENGES

What are the main regulatory challenges in the future? The SIB is producing a review of the regulation of investment exchanges, and this review will come into a market which is considering how to deal with the Investment Services Directive (ISD) and diverging user needs—the two main challenges.

The Investment Services Directive

The directive sets out the European law on securities business. It was a political compromise which sets out the *minimum* standards for regulated markets. Like all political compromises, there is a lot that is unclear in the wording, and this still has to be worked out before the directive comes into force at the end of 1996, just over two years away.

One thing is clear: it will radically alter the structure of the securities market in Europe. Whatever the detail, the main effect will be to allow each firm of intermediaries to be a member of every European stock exchange. At the moment, they have subsidiaries in each country, and each subsidiary is a member of the local exchange and only of that exchange. Under the ISD, the situation becomes closer to the situation here in the United States, where firms tend to be members of more than one exchange.

It will open up the European market. It is a lot like an open-skies policy for airlines. But it is more than that, because most current market regulation of operations assumes one-to-one relationship—one firm to one exchange. Following the ISD, the relationship moves, as Figure 27–11 illustrates, from a one-to-one relationship into a one-to-many relationship. At the same time, note that most major stocks will be listed on all the major exchanges. And also note the disappearance of trading floors. The question for exchanges is which transactions are regulated by which exchange? And what does the term "on-exchange" really mean in that environment?

Diverging User Needs

Institutions are our main customers, and their needs are beginning to change. Over the past seven years, transaction costs have fallen sharply, so execution costs have not really been much of an issue for them. Immediate execution has been available at a low cost, so there is little call for much else.

I don't think that will continue forever. Costs may rise, and the gradual awakening of pension scheme trustees is a certainty. The U.K. market is beginning to see people who are positioning themselves to offer low-cost trading services. Whether this will succeed or not, I don't know, but the demand is beginning to be there.

On a similar tack, there is a growing need for different regulatory

FIGURE 27–11
Impact of the Investment Services Directive—Now...

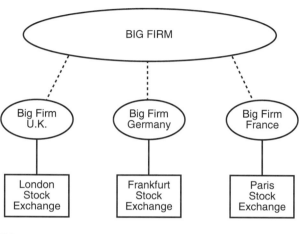

...And in 1996

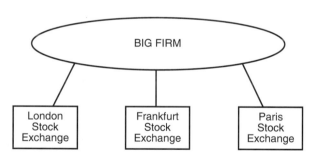

regimes for different types of users. It is very obvious that institutions and individual investors have different expectations and needs of regulation. Most markets have made some steps in that direction, either by opening certain types of trading for professionals only or by allowing for company issues aimed at sophisticated investors. This has gone by the name of segmentation, and it seems to me to be an essential feature of our markets in the future. If it is not, then the business will move to where it is.

Segmentation raises difficult issues in itself. At the simplest level, what must be done to ensure that prices for the same asset in different market segments move in step? Or, must anything be done? Can we leave it to the markets to solve? The Amsterdam Stock Exchange is implementing a two-tier system in which a form of specialist is responsible for arbitraging the retail and wholesale segments. Will that be enough?

ENDPIECE

I have tried to give you a brief flavor of the main regulatory challenges facing us in London. There are many more, which I have not mentioned. Some of the challenges you have seen already, and your regulators have responded with varying degrees of success.

The lesson we draw is that regulation and the trading system must be appropriate to the users' needs. They must be customer-driven. If they are not, the customers can go elsewhere, and fine regulation and trading systems are nothing without customers.

This may mean segmented markets, and the challenge for the London Stock Exchange—and for all stock exchanges—is to produce a mix of appropriate regulation which meets the needs of different types of investors within the overall need for fairness, investor protection, and pricing efficiency.

That implies that regulators must compromise and choose among second-best solutions—tiresome and difficult. But then, that is the way of the world.

CHAPTER 28

BLOCK TRADING ON THE LONDON STOCK EXCHANGE

Oliver Hansch
Anthony Neuberger

INTRODUCTION

The handling of block trades has been a controversial matter on the London Stock Exchange (LSE) ever since the market was reformed at the time of Big Bang in 1986. Much of the argument has centered around the issue of disclosure. The argument has widely been seen as one between transparency and openness on the one hand and provision of a deep and tight market able to meet the needs of institutions on the other.

The problem of handling block trades is not unique to London or to other quote-driven markets. Many order-driven markets, including, for example, the New York Stock Exchange and the Paris Bourse, provide special mechanisms for putting together large transactions off the floor. As Pagano and Röell (1990), among others, point out, most markets incorporate both quote- and order-driven features. Whatever the mechanism, it takes time to find counterparties to an unusually large order. There are difficult issues about what information should be made available while this process is taking place.

The authors are grateful to Stephen Wells at the London Stock Exchange for the provision of the data.

The purpose of this chapter is not to argue one way or the other on the transparency issue. That has been done in a number of other places.[1] The purpose of this chapter is to examine the cost of doing large trades relative to small ones. At first sight, the appropriate measure of cost might appear to be the difference between the trade price and the midprice at the time of the trade. But that is not adequate. The success of a trading strategy can only be evaluated once the inventory and information impact of the trade have been fully absorbed by the market.

Previous research on block trades has mainly focused on price impacts associated with them [see, for example, Kraus and Stoll (1972), and Holthausen, Leftwich, and Mayers (1987, 1990)]. A number of other papers have attempted to evaluate trading costs, some for block transactions, on U.S. exchanges. Typically they use either an investor- or a market-oriented approach. In the former category, Berkowitz, Logue, and Noser (1988), and Chan and Lakonishok (1993), among others, compare the price at which institutional trades are done with contemporary prices in the market, such as the volume-weighted average price over the day and open-to-trade and trade-to-close returns. The market-oriented category comprises the work by Hasbrouck and Schwartz (1988) and Hasbrouck (1993). They try to infer overall trading costs on an exchange by looking at the short-run times-series behavior of prices.

Both approaches have shortcomings. Collins and Fabozzi (1991) discuss several investor-oriented trading cost measures and the problems associated with them. The main problem with market-oriented studies is that they only measure trading costs (or market quality) for the market as a whole and not for particular types of trades, such as block trades which are at the center of our attention.

Our approach is somewhat different. As Stoll (1993) points out, trading costs and the gross revenues of intermediaries are the opposite sides of the same coin. An understanding of the way intermediaries make money, how they deal with the order flow, what trades they make money on, and what trades they lose money on, will cast light on the nature of trading costs.

Such a program of research presupposes that one can distinguish between public trader and intermediary. But in practice, the distinction is not clear cut. In markets (such as the CATS-type equity markets, as in Toronto, Tokyo, or Paris) where public orders transact against a public limit order book, it is tempting to identify market orders with the public and limit orders with intermediaries. However, this runs the danger of confusing execution tactics with economic motivation. A public trader may well believe that the best way of doing business is to post limit orders which are adjusted as the market moves, and he may only use market orders if the limit orders fail to execute within a certain period of time. Conversely, the most effective way for an intermediary to take advantage of a temporary deviation from what he perceives as the equilibrium price may be to execute a market order.

An alternative way of differentiating is to identify certain agents as intermediaries and examine their trades. This is the approach followed by Hasbrouck and Sofianos (1993) in their study of the New York specialist. It is also used in this chapter. It, too, is not perfect; registered market makers may on occasion back their long-term views about price trends, and their clients may trade tactically, buying when the price is low, expecting to resell at a profit a few minutes later.

This chapter uses transaction data from the London Stock Exchange. The data are described in the first section below. The second section looks at the overall profitability of market making and attempts to break down the market maker's activity between order matching and position taking. We find that order matching appears to be consistently profitable, while position taking (that is, holding large inventory positions) produces highly erratic profits which are indistinguishable from zero.

Market makers take trades which *ex ante* they know are likely to be unprofitable. Market makers generally appear to lose money when they buy and are already unusually long or when they sell and are unusually short. Why do they do this? It cannot be a readiness to sacrifice profits in order to get lower risk because these trades worsen inventory imbalance. It is not because of any obligation to make a continuous market, for they are under no such obligation.

The most plausible explanation appears to lie in the desire to maintain a reputation. It is costly and time consuming to shop an order between market makers. If news of the intended order reaches the market before the deal is consummated, prices are likely to move against the trader. So a trader (or his broker) will want to approach a market maker who is known to make consistently good prices. An opportunistic market maker who ties his prices too closely to the state of his own book is unlikely to get much order flow. If a market maker wants the order flow which is profitable, he must also be prepared to make competitive quotes on the orders which are likely to be unprofitable.

One of the key features of the London market is that market makers are prepared to quote prices in large size. For the more liquid stocks, one percent of public transactions by number account for almost one-third of the volume. Transactions of £1 million or more in value are commonplace, occurring on average once per day or more. The third section of the chapter, therefore, examines some of the largest transactions to see whether these transactions are profitable. Although the evidence is not conclusive, it suggests that the very large trades are not profitable in themselves, but that they allow the market makers who do the trades to make somewhat higher profits subsequently than their competitors.

THE DATA

The Trading System[2]

Any member of the exchange is free to register as a market maker in any share. Registered market makers are obliged to quote firm two-way prices at which they are prepared to deal; these quotes are carried on the Stock Exchange Automated Quotation (SEAQ) screens, which are available to all LSE members. The screen carries the name of the market maker and the size up to which his prices are firm. The minimum size for which the market maker can quote is the Normal Market Size (NMS). NMS varies from stock to stock but corresponds roughly to 2.5 percent of average daily volume.

A member of the exchange who wishes to deal with a market maker will contact him by phone and negotiate a price, which may be better than the price the market maker is quoting on the screen. Once the trade is concluded, it has to be notified to the exchange within three minutes. The quantity and price of the transaction are then published on the SEAQ screen; however, for large trades (over three times NMS) details are only published after a delay of 90 minutes.

Member of the stock exchange are free to deal directly with each other, bypassing the market makers, but are required to notify the LSE; and these trades are published in the same way as other trades. Traders are free to deal off-exchange. While there is little hard information on this for obvious reasons, it is generally believed that off-exchange trading is rare. Some of the shares (marked with a superscripted *a* in Table 28–1) were also traded in ADR form, and details of ADR trades have not been included in the data set.

Market makers can deal with each other directly or through the intermediation of an Inter-Dealer Broker (IDB). Only market makers can deal through the IDB. A market maker wishing to trade a block of shares through the IDB notifies the IDB of the quantity and price; the bid or offer is published on the IDB screen available only to market makers, who can then trade the block. Trading is anonymous. For the market as a whole, intermarket maker business accounts for about one-third of the total business by value.

Members of the public who wish to trade on the LSE must trade through a member of the exchange. The member may act either purely as a broker, doing the trade with a market maker or with another broker. or he can act in dual capacity, taking the trade onto his own book.

The Data

The sample consists of 25 liquid stocks quoted on the London Stock Exchange. All the stocks were members of the FT-SE 100 Index. The data set consists of all transactions on the LSE in those shares over the period from October 1991 to March 1992. For each transaction the record shows the time and date of the transaction, its price, the size of the trade, an indicator to show whether the buyer and the seller were registered market makers in the stock, and a code identifying the two parties to the trade (the broker or market maker, as the case may be). The identifying code does not allow one to identify the party by name, nor are the codes the same across stocks.

The data for price, quantity, trader identity, and type are likely to be accurate since they are used for surveillance and settlement purposes. There is some doubt about the accuracy of the date and time stamps. This is discussed more fully in Lee (1989, ch. 4).

In preparing the data, certain transactions were removed from the record. When a transaction is notified erroneously to the exchange, it is reversed by a second transaction on the transaction record which is specially identified as a so-called contratransaction. In general the original transaction can be identified confidently by matching the size, direction, and price, and both transactions were removed. Also, there were a small number of transactions (identified as such on the original data file) which are the result of the exercise of options (so-called traditional or over-the-counter options, not exchange traded). These are recorded as occurring at the exercise price of the option and were removed from the record. Finally, a number of anomalous entries for zero quantity or zero price were also removed.

Summary statistics on the stocks in our sample are provided in Table 28–1. As can be seen, activity varies widely, from £1 million of turnover per day up to nearly £20 million per day. In terms of number of public trades, the range is even wider being between 14 and 450 trades per day. For all the stocks in the sample, the majority of the turnover by value is between the public and market makers. Interdealer volume is between 40 percent and 70 percent of the size of public volume.

ORDER MATCHING AND POSITION TAKING

Theoretical Considerations

Conceptually one can distinguish between two functions of a dealer: a passive, order matching role, and an active, position taking role. For example, Madhavan and Smidt (1992) distinguish two roles of the New York Stock Exchange specialist:

- a market maker passively providing liquidity to accommodate transitory order imbalances;
- as an active investor maintaining a long-term position consistent with his portfolio objectives, while profiting in the short term from information about impending order imbalances.

In their paper Madhavan and Smidt model these two facets of the specialist function and show how they affect the price formation and inventory adjustment process. They then use transaction and quote data from a specialist to infer the significance of these two effects and conclude that both are important.

This chapter follows a different approach to explore similar issues. On the London Stock Exchange there are many competing market makers in each stock. They are not under any obligation to make a continuous market; their only obligation is to quote firm bid and ask prices in normal market size at all times when the market is open. Brokers are under an obligation to secure "best execution" for their clients. This is normally interpreted to mean the best price, though there may be other factors which an investor is interested in (such as the effect of the trade on the market if the client wishes to make further trades in the same stock.)[3]

It is therefore natural (though, as we will show, not entirely realistic) to think of the market as one where market makers compete freely

TABLE 28–1
Summary Statistics of Stocks in Sample

| Company Name | Number of Market Makers | Public Trades | | Inter-Market Maker/ Public Trading (by value) |
		Turnover (£m/day)	Frequency (trade/day)	
Abbey National	19	7.3	122	57%
Allied-Lyons	13	2.3	39	54
Anglian Water	17	5.4	59	47
Argyll Group	12	1.1	14	40
Associated British Foods	18	5.2	233	58
BAA	21	9.3	203	58
BTR[a]	18	11.4	181	54
B.A.T. Industries[a]	15	1.1	41	51
Bass[a]	17	6.8	107	46
Blue Circle Industries	17	2.1	37	63
BOC Group	16	4.3	62	57
British Aerospace	19	6.2	93	48
BET[a]	14	3.3	78	39
British Gas[a]	20	12.6	456	62
BP[a]	21	18.6	282	72
BT[a]	21	13.2	265	68
British Steel[a]	19	5.8	138	45
Cable & Wireless	21	9.4	179	52
Cadbury Schweppes[a]	19	4.2	100	58
Commercial Union	16	2.3	34	58
Courtaulds	14	2.5	45	39
Eurotunnel[a]	14	2.1	61	66
Enterprise Oil	17	3.4	20	59
Fisons[a]	20	9.9	147	49
General Accident	13	2.8	36	44
Average (equally weighted)	17	6.1	121	54

[a] Traded also in ADR or other form, so data is partial.

with each other for every public order and where the market maker who makes the best bid or offer gets the deal. If this view were right, it would be quite feasible to follow a strategy of bidding only for certain categories of trade, where categories are defined by information available to the market maker at the time the order is placed. For example, one could follow a strategy of only taking large orders or of maintaining inventory levels between certain bounds.

From this it is but a short step to taking transaction data and creating "synthetic strategies." A synthetic strategy is a subset of public orders defined by some *ex ante* rule. Of particular interest in the context of the debate on passive versus active market making is the profitability of strategies with strict position limits. We will show that such a strategy was consistently profitable. The complementary strategy of acting countercyclically (that is, buying when market makers are already long and selling when they are short) produced lower and much more erratic profits in general. Indeed, it is not even clear that these trades as a group were profitable at all.

It is tempting to conclude from this that market makers are foolish; if they stuck to order matching, they would make money. By position taking, they take on large risks for no clear returns. But it is implausible that such irrational behavior should persist. There are other, more plausible explanations which involve the impossibility of picking and choosing between trades. A market maker can only do those public trades which come to him. The synthetic strategy implicitly assumes that turning down public orders has no effect on future order flow.

This may not be realistic. Trades are negotiated bilaterally between the market maker and the broker. The market maker's quote constrains the possible outcome but does not determine it. Negotiating is costly, both in time and also because it may lead to information leakage. If a broker negotiates but fails to agree on a deal with a market maker, the failed deal may have a market impact which makes it more difficult or more expensive to trade with another market maker. For that reason, brokers may be unwilling to offer a deal to a market maker who has a reputation for making a poor price when the trade does not suit his book.

The only way a trader can tell whether a price is good or bad if he does not negotiate with other market makers is to compare the prices with the quotes on the screen. This may mean that market makers may negotiate prices which are at a discount to screen prices even when they do not want to take the trade. They will do so in order to maintain a reputation for making consistently competitive prices. This, in turn, implies that the costs faced by a public trader also vary across trades.

The Evidence

Our sample consists of 25 stocks. On average there are 17 registered market makers per stock, but many of them are fairly inactive. Estimates of the profitability of inactive market makers are very noisy because most of the profit or loss comes from positioning. We therefore restrict attention to the market makers who had a market share of 3 percent or more by volume. If one adds the number of market makers in each stock together, one gets a total of 208, many of whom will be the same firm in different stocks. This gives an average of just over 8 market makers per stock, each with at least 3 percent market share. Together they account for 92 percent, or £15.1 billion turnover out of a total public trading volume of £16.5 billion.

The first step is to calculate market maker profits. Trading profits can be defined[4] as:

>   increase in cash over period
> *plus*   closing inventory at midprice
> *less*   opening inventory at midprice.

Trading profits are then divided by public volume to get profit margin.

The problem in applying this formula is that we do not know the opening inventory level. We assume that they start with their desired inventory level.[5]

The average profit margin across the sample as a whole (total profit over total turnover) was 8.9 basis points[6] (that is, 0.089 percent; we measure profit margins in basis points which we abbreviate as *bp*). The mean profit margin averaged across market makers (equally weighted) was slightly higher at 11.9 bp.

This might suggest that smaller market makers tend to have higher margins. To test this, we regressed profit margin against market share. The slope coefficient is +0.0150, so a one percent increase in market share is associated with a 1.5 bp *increase* in profit margin. But the coefficient, while of some economic significance, is statistically insignificantly different from zero (the *t*-statistic is 1.05), and the regression has very low explanatory power (R^2 of 0.5 percent).

We tried a number of other models, using interdealer volume, difference between maximum and minimum inventory levels, and average trade size as explanatory variables; we found no models of profitability levels with significant explanatory power.

This negative result is disappointing but not surprising. In a market with free entry, there should be no economic rents, so there may be no systematic differences in profit margins to discover.[7] But even if these differences exist, our tests may not find them because they are not very powerful, for two reasons:

1. *Measurement error.* We assumed that the initial inventory level was zero for each market maker. If this is wrong by an amount equal to just one day's trading volume for a particular market maker, this will induce an error in the profit margin of some 20 bp for that market maker (assuming an annual volatility of the share price of 30 percent).

2. *Noise.* Actual profits are highly volatile. Market makers take large positions which they may hold over several days or weeks. The profit margin figures for the larger market makers is distributed with a mean of 11.9 bp but the standard deviation is 290 bp.

Synthetic Strategies

As a way of getting round these problems, we have studied the profit characteristics of certain synthetic trading strategies. The strategies are quite simple trading rules. We imagine three market makers, A, B, and C. They share out the entire public order flow between them. A has first call on any trades, then B and C get the residual. A has a strict position limit of, say, 100,000 shares. He starts with zero inventory and takes all public orders which do not leave him more than 100,000 shares either long or short. He cannot split orders. So any trade which would take him outside his limit is passed on to one of the other market makers.

Since we know his initial inventory, there is no error in estimating profits. And since his final inventory is strictly bounded and likely to be only a small fraction of turnover, his long-term positioning profits are small. A's profits or losses can be regarded as profits from order flow matching rather than from position taking.

There will be many public trades which A cannot take. They then go to B who has the same position limit as A. He will tend to do less trade than A and will normally buy when A is long and sell when A is short. His strategy is more speculative than A's. He tends to buy when the public has been selling consistently and to sell when there has been a run of buying. He will tend to hold positions for longer and make more of his profits or losses from position taking. Finally, there is market maker C, who does all the public trades which the other two market makers are unwilling to take.

Given the very different volumes of trading in each of the shares and the differences in share price levels, it makes little sense to set the control levels for the strategies at 100,000 shares for each stock. What we have done, therefore, is to set the limit for each stock equal to one-tenth of one day's average public volume. Depending on the stock, therefore, the limit on A's inventory position lies anywhere between £100,000 and £2 million.

The results of the exercise are set out for each of the 25 shares in the sample in Table 28–2. The first three columns of numbers show the proportion of public turnover accounted for by each of the three synthetic market makers. As can be seen, A on average takes 38 percent of the public order volume, B takes 8 percent, and C accounts for the balance of 54 percent. The proportion varies across stocks—the stocks with a higher trading frequency tend to get more balanced trade, so A has a relatively larger share. A's share gives some indication of how balanced the trade in that particular stock is. We make use of this observation later.

The next four columns show the market makers' margin (measured as profit divided by turnover, expressed in basis points). Looking at the equally weighted average figures at the bottom, market maker A appears to make 22 basis points on turnover. The margin is positive in every one of the stocks.

Market maker B makes a loss of –8 basis points on average. He loses money 16 times out of 25, which is just significant at the 5 percent level. He does worse than A on all but two of the stocks, which is statistically highly significant.

This suggests that trading as B does—that is, buying when market makers collectively are long and selling when they are short—is less profitable than a simple inventory control strategy, and these trades may actually on average lose money, even before taking into account any transaction costs.

This result may seem counterintuitive. First, since B's trades are identified on an *ex ante* criterion, it appears that market makers could identify these trades as unprofitable and, therefore, avoid them. Second, the trades B is doing are, by definition, risky trades. He is buying when the market is already long and selling when it is short. Since he is taking risky trades, one might have thought that he would be able to earn a higher return than A.

Market maker C's performance is highly erratic. That is not perhaps

TABLE 28–2
Profits from Synthetic Trading Strategies

Stock	Market Share by Strategy (in %)			Profit/Turnover (in basis points)			
	A	B	C	A	B	C	All
Abbey National	55	11	34	11	−5	−85	−23
Allied-Lyons	17	6	77	28	16	30	29
Anglian Water	46	11	42	17	1	−33	−6
Argyll Group	14	3	83	19	9	−16	−11
Associated British Foods	41	9	51	19	−12	−70	−29
BAA	56	10	35	14	2	−17	2
BTR	50	9	41	19	−6	−56	−14
B.A.T. Industries	25	4	71	55	13	28	34
Bass	53	10	37	12	−5	−217	−75
Blue Circle Industries	26	7	68	28	39	175	129
BOC Group	36	11	53	13	−12	−3	2
British Aerospace	44	10	47	30	−12	47	34
BET	37	9	54	22	−30	36	25
British Gas	56	10	35	14	−30	12	9
BP	51	8	42	25	−13	3	13
BT	47	9	44	12	0	62	33
British Steel	40	8	52	32	−5	−192	−88
Cable & Wireless	53	12	36	23	−2	8	15
Cadbury Schweppes	48	9	43	16	5	−100	−35
Commercial Union	19	4	77	18	−47	30	25
Courtaulds	7	1	92	33	43	−24	−19
Eurotunnel	21	3	76	55	−74	340	267
Enterprise Oil	24	6	70	14	−11	−116	−78
Fisons	63	10	27	10	−50	−5	0
General Accident	30	8	62	18	−7	28	22
Average (equally weighted)	38	8	54	22	−8	−5	10

surprising, given that he is taking large trades and necessarily has large inventory profits and losses. The average profit margin is −5 basis points. He loses money in 13 out of the 25 stocks. His profits are indistinguishable from zero. C does better than A in only 8 out of the 25 stocks; this is significant at the 5 percent level. C beats B 14 times out of 25, but this is not significant.

The evidence presented so far suggests that transactions can be divided into two classes. One class is very much more profitable than the other; indeed, it appears that the first class accounts for more than 100 percent of the profits, while the other class is actually loss making. The profitable class consists of small orders (certainly no bigger than 20 percent of average daily volume) and excludes sequences of trades which are all one way. The unprofitable trades consist both of those which are large (C) and those where the public is a large net seller or net buyer. From the investor's point of view, these results imply that small, retail-sized orders are more expensive to execute than large, institutional ones.

What does not come out clearly from this data is whether the unprofitability of strategy C is due specifically to the fact that the market maker is taking on large trades or whether it is simply the consequence of having an unbalanced inventory position, as in strategy B. It is to this we now turn.

LARGE TRADES

The definition of a large trade is bound to be arbitrary. It is also a relative rather than an absolute concept. For the purposes of this chapter we have defined a large trade as one of the top one percent in that particular stock in terms of number of shares. Thus, a 500,000-share or a £1 million trade in one stock may be regarded as large in stock A but not in stock B.

To give some idea of the size distribution, we have broken down the large trades into four different classes. Summary statistics are provided in Table 28–3. The top one percent of public trades account for nearly one-third of total volume. The very largest trades are widely varying in size, as reflected by the high coefficient of variation and difference between mean and median, but the other three classes are much more compact. In all cases, what we call a large trade is substantially larger than three times Normal Market Size, and the trade is only published with a delay of 90 minutes.

We then exclude from our sample,

- large trades which occur within the first 50 trades in our sample period or within the last 300 trades, so as to ensure a full window period of [t–50, t+300];
- large trades which occur less than 50 trades after a previous large trade, the purpose being to avoid double-counting linked transactions.

TABLE 28–3
The Distribution of Large Trades[a]

Category	Mean (£ millions)	Standard Deviation (£ millions)	Median (£ millions)	Share (%)
Top 0.25 percentile	3.50	3.81	2.55	15.3
0.25–0.5 percentile	1.51	0.49	1.38	6.9
0.5–0.75 percentile	1.16	0.35	1.07	5.6
0.75–1 percentile	0.93	0.29	0.92	4.4
Top 1 percentile	1.78	2.18	1.23	32.2

[a] For each stock, the top four quarter-percentiles of public orders by size were identified. The table gives the mean, standard deviation, and median for each category across all 25 stocks. It also shows the proportion of total public volume accounted for by each category.

Each large trade is treated as an event. An "event window" is then constructed extending from 50 trades before the large transaction to 300 trades thereafter. The window was chosen because it appeared to capture the period over which significant inventory effects could be observed. The actual time period of the event window varied widely from stock to stock—the 350-trade window corresponding to anything between one and 25 trading days average volume. We varied the window size, but the results were not significantly affected.

Inventory Changes

The first point we addressed was whether the market maker who does the large trade trades out of his position rapidly, and whether the trade is passed back to other public investors, or whether it is traded with other market makers. The set of charts (Figures 28–1 through 28–4) illustrate what happens.

Figure 28–1 takes as its central event a large public purchase, where "large" means among the top 1 percentile of public trades by size. For each such event, the change in each market maker's inventory from *trade* −50 to *trade* +300 is calculated. Arbitrarily setting the initial inventory level to zero, the inventory position of the market maker who does the trade—and of all the other market makers—can be calculated. The inventory is then normalized by dividing the inventory by the size of the large trade. Finally, the normalized inventory figures are simply averaged across the entire sample of large trades.

FIGURE 28–1
Impact of Large Trades on Market Maker Inventory (top 1% of trades)—Large Buys

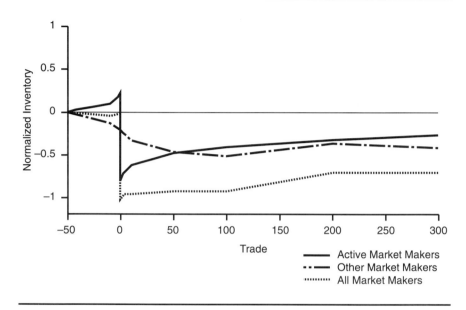

Figure 28–1 shows that the market maker who is to do the trade tends to build up inventory in advance of the large purchase, so the normalized inventory level rises to around 0.2. With the large purchase, the inventory drops by 1 (by definition) to –0.8. Over the course of the next 300 trades, they gradually reduce the inventory to end up with 40 percent of the original trade on their books.

The position of other market makers is almost the mirror image of this. They go short before the trade as the first market maker builds up inventory, and then they continue to build up inventory as the first market maker lays off his position. The net effect is that the market makers collectively stay virtually level until the trade. Their collective inventory then falls with the large purchase, and the market makers collectively then absorb the large trade.

Figure 28–2 shows that the position with large sales is almost identical, though in this case there appears to be some evidence that market makers' collective position actually gets larger with the elapse of time.

The pictures represent crude averages and, hence, convey no sense

FIGURE 28–2
Impact of Large Trades on Market Maker Inventory (top 1% of trades)—Large Sales

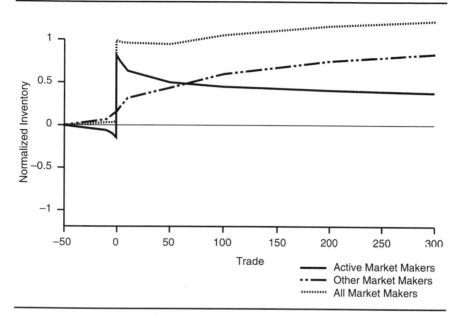

of significance. To get some idea of whether the pictures were representative, the pictures were plotted for each of the four sized subgroups. The pictures were very similar. The pictures for the largest category are reproduced as Figures 28–3 and 28–4.

The way that the market maker's inventory moves prior to the large trades has a number of possible explanations. The market maker's inventory position may cause him to price aggressively and get the deal. Also, any errors in recording the time of a trade will cause the laying off of the trade to look as if it occurred before the trade.

Profitability

We can look at profitability of the large trade. There are a number of interesting questions which our data allow us to investigate:

1. Is the large trade profitable, taken by itself? This is, is the price at which the market maker trades better or worse than the equilibrium

FIGURE 28–3
**Impact of Large Trades on Market Maker Inventory (top 0.25%
of trades)—Large Buys**

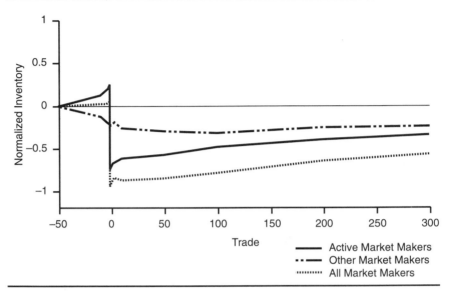

FIGURE 28–4
**Impact of Large Trades on Market Maker Inventory (top 0.25%
of trades)—Large Sales**

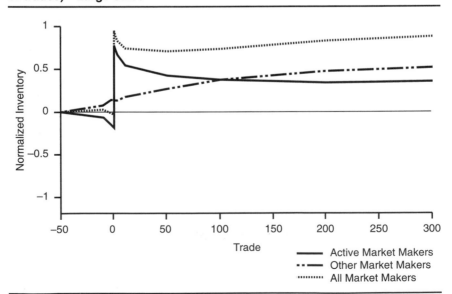

price level once the trade has been digested by the market? This is the question which is probably of most interest to the trader, since the price difference is the price he is paying for immediacy.

2. Does the market maker who does the large trade make money as a result of it, either directly or by subsequently positioning himself? The market maker may make money on the trade but still lose money overall because of the cost of trading out of his position. The opposite is also possible—he loses money on the trade itself but uses the information to make money subsequently by trading on his own account.

3. Are the other market makers who see less of the order flow disadvantaged as a result of not seeing the order flow? It is possible that a market maker will want to attract large orders, not because they are profitable, but because it is still more unprofitable to be a market maker where others have better information about the order flow?

Profitability of the Large Trade

We are concerned with the difference between the trade price and the equilibrium price given the trade. The equilibrium price is unobservable, but as a proxy we can take the midprice some time later. The time period should be long enough for equilibrium to be reestablished, but too long a period increases the noisiness of the proxy. Holthausen, Leftwich, and Mayers (1990) find that price reversals take place very quickly, implying that permanent price effects are realized very shortly after the block trade. Their data, however, relate to the New York Stock Exchange where trades are published virtually instantaneously. Since in our case large trades are only published after a delay, it is more appropriate to look at a longer time horizon.

We have taken the price after 300 trades as a reasonable proxy and run the regression:

$$\frac{\overline{P}_{300} - P_0}{P_0} = \beta_0 + \beta_1 I_0 + \beta_2 Q_0^B + \beta_3 Q_0^S$$

where

$\overline{P}$	= midprice
P	= trade price
I	= 1/–1 for a buy/sell
$Q^{B/S}$	= value of trade if buy/sell and 0 otherwise

The dependent variable, the price change, is actually the sum of two effects:

- the difference between the trade price and the midprice at time t;
- the change in the midprice between time t and $t+300$.

The first element would suggest a value of $\beta_1 < 0$. Insofar as spreads for large trades are an increasing function of size, this would be reflected in a negative value of β_2 and a positive value of β_3. The second effect, the change in the midprice following the trade, is likely to work in the opposite direction. It would reflect any information effects (a public buy suggesting that the share is undervalued) and price pressure as the market makers endeavor to balance their inventory (a public buy would force them to raise prices to encourage public sales).

The results of the regressions are set out in Table 28–4. In general, the size and direction of the large trade has very limited power in explaining subsequent price changes. In the first regression, where the price change is explained by the direction of the large trade only, the

TABLE 28–4
The Pricing of Large Orders [a]

| | Parameter Estimates (standard errors in brackets) | | | |
| | β_1 | β_2 | β_3 | |
Restriction	(bp)	(bp / £1m)	(bp / £1m)	R^2
$\beta_2 = \beta_3 = 0$	5.9 [10.5]			0.04%
$\beta_2 = -\beta_3$	18.5 [13.5]	−7.7 [5.2]	7.7 [5.2]	0.35%
Unrestricted	20.7 [13.6]	−1.9 [6.8]	15.9 [8.0]	0.60%

[a] This table reports the results of the regression:

$$\frac{\bar{P}_{300} - P_0}{P_0} = \beta_0 + \beta_1 I_0 + \beta_2 Q_0^B + \beta_3 Q_0^S$$

where

$\bar{P}$	= midprice
P	= trade price
I	= 1/−1 for a buy/sell
$Q^{B/S}$	= value of trade if buy/sell and 0 otherwise

under a number of parameter restrictions. The sample set consists of 728 large trades (the top one percent in each of 25 stocks by value).

coefficient is positive but is not significant (*t*-statistic of 0.6). The positive sign would imply that the long-term price will on average be 5.9 basis points higher than the price at which the public trader has bought a large block and 5.9 basis points lower after a large public sale.

Taking the result at face value, it suggests that the large trade, by itself, is marginally unprofitable to the market maker. Looking at the other two regressions in Table 28–4, there is mild evidence that the profitability of the trade to the market maker (as a percentage of the trade value) improves as a function of the trade size. This may be more pronounced in the case of public sales than buys, but the difference is not significant.

To summarize then:

- The bid-ask spread on large trades appears to be insufficient to compensate for their price impact. There is, therefore, some evidence that the permanent price effect exceeds the spread.
- There is weak evidence that the bid-ask spread widens with trade size faster than does the price impact, so ensuring that the very largest trades are, on average, profitable.

It appears then that the large public trader in this period was able to trade without paying any premium for immediacy; indeed, he may actually have got a discount. This result stands in contrast to the predictions made by many microstructure models, for example, Easley and O'Hara (1987), which predict large trades to be more costly to do than small ones.

Profitability of the Market Maker Doing the Large Trade

So far as the market maker who is doing the trade is concerned, the relevant question is the profitability of the large trade and the subsequent trades which the big trade entails. These trades may be driven by the desire to bring inventory under control. To investigate this, we have calculated the market maker's aggregate profits on his trades from t–50 to t+300. Again profits on each trade are calculated by valuing the shares bought or sold at the midprice at t+300. This is equivalent to calculating the profit assuming the market maker starts with zero inventory at t–50 and liquidates his inventory at t+300 at the midprice.

The market maker who does the large trade does on average make money over the period. The average profit per large trade is £3,740 with a *t*-statistic of 2.72. Other results are that:

- profits are independent of the direction of the large trade (regressing profits on direction give a t-statistic of 0.08);
- profits arise almost entirely on trades which take place after the large trade (profits on trades from t–50 to t+10 average –£30; the profit on trades in t+10 to t+300 average £3,770;
- profits in the window t–50 to t+10 are correlated with trade size. The larger the trade, the greater the profit. The regression is:

$$\pi = -£3,000 + 18.9 \times 10^{-4} \times Q_0P_0 \qquad R^2 = 1.53\%$$
$$(3.20)$$

where

$\quad \pi \quad$ = Profit in (t–50, t+300)
$\quad Q_0P_0$ = value of large trade

Trading profits in this time window are dominated by the large trade, and the dependency of profit on trade size largely reflects the way that the price of the large trade also improves (from the market maker's perspective) with size.

- the market maker appears to lose money on the large trade and on the immediately preceding trades when the large trade is not very large, but to make money on the very largest trades;
- the profits on trades after the large trade are significantly positive but are not related to the size of the large trade.

The market maker doing the large trade makes little or no money on it directly. He makes some profits on subsequent trades, and these profits amount to some 12 bp of the trades he carries out. This is similar to the profit margin of market makers in the whole six-month period. As noted above, if it is costly to unwind positions, one might expect the market maker to lose money in his trades following a large trade. If large trades carry information which is not immediately incorporated in prices, one might expect the market maker to make profits on his trades following the large trade. The fact that his profits are indistinguishable from normal trading profits suggests that either the effects are negligible, or else that they are of similar magnitude and therefore offset each other.

Profitability of the Other Market Makers
If the large trade is informative, then one might expect the other market makers who have not traded to be at an informational disadvantage.

They would lose money to the first market maker either by trading with him directly or, more plausibly, by getting the public order flow he deliberately avoids. To test this, we looked at the aggregate profits of all the other market makers. In the period t–50 to t+300, they made £6,500 as against £3,740 for the market maker who does the trade. When these profits are expressed as a proportion of the total volume of trading they have done, the figures are not enormously different. The market maker who does the trade makes a profit equal to 12.1 bp on his turnover as opposed to 8.8 bp for the other market makers. A test both of the relative magnitudes and of the frequency with which the one market maker beats the many reveals no significant difference between the two at conventional significance levels.

CONCLUSIONS

There are dangers in trying to draw wide and sweeping conclusions from a limited set of data, drawn from one particular market at one point in time. But some points do seem to emerge fairly strongly. Perhaps the most striking is the degree of cross-subsidy between different types of trade. It appears that all the gross trading profits of market makers can be attributed to under half the volume of trading. We do not fully understand why this cross-subsidy takes place. One possibility is that market makers need to offer competitive prices at all times if they are to attract order flow.

But whatever the reason, such cross-subsidy has important implications. It suggests that a competing mechanism such as a small order crossing network might be able to attract substantial business and seriously threaten the viability of market making as currently practiced.

Another implication is methodological. If there is an important degree of cross-subsidy, then the observable trade-to-trade price changes must be seen as the result of two forces. The first is the change in the equilibrium value of the stock. The second is the change in the profit element. Much research in the field of microstructure implicitly or explicitly assumes that the profit element is either constant or uncorrelated with other factors of interest. The present chapter casts doubt on the assumption, at least so far as the London Stock Exchange is concerned. It remains to be seen whether this degree of cross-subsidy also exists in other market structures.

Large trades do not seem to be profitable in themselves. In general, traders can deal in size at prices which are actually better than the equilibrium value of the stock. It is only for the very largest trades that this does not hold. Having done the large trade, there is no evidence either that the market maker ends up with benefits in the form of better information on which he can then make money, or that he has an inventory position which is costly to unload.

We have also found no evidence that the profits of other market makers are particularly depressed by the presence of the large trade.

NOTES

1. The Office of Fair Trading (1990) looks at transparency on the LSE. Franks and Schaefer (1991) looks at the empirical evidence. Wells (1993) is a more recent review of the key issues. For an international view, see IOSCO (1992).
2. A detailed description of the trading system can be found in Schwartz (1991).
3. For a discussion of the best execution concept and its meaningfulness on the London Stock Exchange, see Wells (1992).
4. This is similar to the definition of specialist profits in Hasbrouck and Sofianos (1993).
5. Market makers have stock borrowing privileges which make it quite easy to maintain an average zero inventory. But if market makers prefer to be long on average, then our measure of trading profit will exclude any gains or losses on the long-term position. This seems appropriate since the profits are not strictly attributable to the market making function.
6. This looks somewhat low compared with the global figures reported in the *Stock Exchange Quarterly* (spring 1992). There, dealing profits of member firms are given as £815 million for 1991, of which three-quarters are on equities and equity derivatives. Taking equity dealing profits as £600 million and equity turnover (customer business) as £234 billion gives a profit margin of 26 basis points. However, this also includes trading profits of nonmarket makers and profits on less-liquid stocks where margins are likely to be higher. Further, it appears that profits in the last quarter of 1991 were rather lower than through the rest of the year.
7. Of course, we are measuring gross profit, not economic rents. Even if there are zero rents, profit margins may vary because of differential risk exposures or different cost levels corresponding to different strategies. But, in fact, we find no evidence of that.

REFERENCES

Berkowitz, S., D. Logue, and E. Noser. (1988). "The Total Cost of Transactions on the NYSE," *Journal of Finance,* 43:1 (March), 97–112.

Chan, L., and J. Lakonishok. (1993). "Institutional Trades and Intra-day Stock Price

Behavior," *Journal of Financial Economics,* 33, pp. 173–99.

Collins, B., and F. Fabozzi. (1991). "A Methodology for Measuring Transaction Costs," *Financial Analysts Journal,* (March–April), pp. 27–36.

Easley, D., and M. O'Hara. (1987). "Price, Trade Size, and Information in Securities Markets," *Journal of Financial Economics,* 19, pp. 69–90.

Franks, J., and S. Schaefer. (1991). "Equity Market Transparency," *Stock Exchange Quarterly,* (summer).

Hasbrouck, J. (1993). "Assessing the Quality of a Securities Market: A New Approach to Transaction-Cost Measurement," *The Review of Financial Studies,* 6:1, 191–212.

Hasbrouck, J., and R. Schwartz. (1988). "Liquidity and Execution Costs in Equity Markets," *Journal of Portfolio Management,* (spring), pp. 10–16.

Hasbrouck, J., and G. Sofianos. (1993). "The Trades of Market Makers: An Analysis of NYSE Specialists," *Journal of Finance,* forthcoming.

Holthausen, Robert W., Richard W. Leftwich, and David Mayers. (1987). "The Effect of Large Block Transactions on Security Prices," *Journal of Financial Economics,* 19, pp. 237–68.

Holthausen, Robert W., Richard W. Leftwich, and David Mayers. (1990). "Large-Block Transactions, the Speed of Response, and Temporary and Permanent Stock-Price Effects," *Journal of Financial Economics,* 26, pp. 71–95.

IOSCO (International Organisation of Securities Commissions). (1992). "Transparency on Secondary Markets," (December).

Kraus, Alan, and Hans R. Stoll. (1972). "Price Impacts of Block Trading on the New York Stock Exchange," *Journal of Finance,* 27: (June), pp. 569–88.

Lee, R. (1987). "Market Making on the U.K. Stock Exchange." Oxford University Ph.D. thesis.

Madhavan, A., and S. Smidt. (1992). "An Analysis of Daily Changes in Specialist Inventories and Quotations." University of Pennsylvania, The Wharton School working paper.

Office of Fair Trading. (1990). "Trade Publication and Price Transparency on the International Stock Exchange," (April).

Pagano, M., and A. Röell. (1990). "Trading Systems in European Stock Exchanges: Current Performance and Policy Options," *Economic Policy,* vol. 10.

Schwartz, R. (1991). *Reshaping the Equity Markets: A Guide to the 1990s.* New York: HarperBusiness. (Reissued by Business One Irwin, 1993).

Stoll, H. (1993). "Equity Trading Costs in-the-Large," *Journal of Portfolio Management,* (summer), pp. 41–50.

Wells, S. (1992). "Price Improvement and Best Execution," *Stock Exchange Quarterly,* (spring).

Wells, S. (1993). "Transparency in the Equity Market: The Publication of Last Trades," *Stock Exchange Quarterly,* (spring).

CHAPTER 29

A PROGRAM TO INCREASE THE LIQUIDITY OF SHARES IN THE FRENCH EQUITY MARKET

Bertrand Jacquillat
Robert A. Schwartz
Jacques Hamon

INTRODUCTION

Major change occurred in the French equity markets in 1986 when the Paris Bourse reformed its trading system, abandoning its nonelectronic call market and introducing Cotation Assistée Continu (CAC), an order-driven, electronic continuous market which opens with a call.[1] The innovation was largely motivated by the threat of competition from London's new quote-driven, competitive dealer system, Stock Exchange Automatic Quotation (SEAQ). Nonetheless, many orders for French shares are flowing to London which seems to indicate that CAC's liquidity remains insufficient.

Supplying liquidity to a market, when public investors/traders do not appear capable of supplying it to themselves, is the classic economic function of a dealer. In London's quote-driven market, liquidity is provided by dealers who post quotes against which public participants can trade. In so doing, the dealers profit from the bid-ask spread and from short-run price volatility.

Just as dealers profit from short-run price swings that are attributable to a market not being perfectly liquid, so too may limit order traders profit.[2] In CAC's order-driven, continuous market, liquidity is provided by limit orders. That is, the limit orders placed by some public traders establish the prices at which other public participants can trade by market order. Like CAC, most major equity markets around the world are order-driven. For example, the U.S. and Toronto stock exchanges are order-driven markets where specialists (who are dealers) also supply liquidity to stocks that have been assigned to them. The Tokyo, other Far Eastern, and Australian exchanges are order-driven markets that do not include dealers or specialists.

How may liquidity be enhanced in an order-driven market, other than by incorporating a dealer into the trading system? The question is of critical importance for Paris's CAC market because London's SEAQ dealers are offering customers an attractive alternative. We address the issue in this chapter. Specifically, we focus on an innovation that is being implemented in France: the introduction of a facility designed to counter imbalances in order flow so that more appropriate prices may be established and trading costs lowered for the aggregate market.

The facility, PIBAL (Programme d'Intervention en Bourse pour l'Amélioration de la Liquidité), enables corporations themselves to be the source of additional liquidity for their own stocks. Using the corporation's own shares and cash, a fund is set up by the corporation and operated by a fiduciary to buy shares in a falling market and to sell shares in a rising market according to a prescribed formula, directly adding liquidity to the market.

PIBAL will also bring additional liquidity indirectly, because the mere existence of a liquidity fund should attract more investors. The effect will be self-reinforcing: when a transactions network includes a larger number of participants, counterparties can more easily find each other in time and in place, and transaction prices are expected to be in closer alignment with underlying equilibrium values.[3] This positive effect of a larger trading network explains why order flow attracts order flow, and it gives a large market center, such as the London Stock Exchange, a strong competitive advantage.[4]

Corporations should be involved in market making. Because liquidity is, *ceteris paribus,* associated with higher share prices, liquidity facilitates the capital-raising ability of the listed companies. Further, as will be shown below, the market making function of PIBAL might in fact be profitable for the companies that implement it. The concern about

involving corporations in market making is that they might use the position to manipulate the price of their shares. PIBAL eliminates this possibility because (1) the liquidity program is a fully articulated procedure
with publicly known parameters and (2) the fund is managed by a
fiduciary.

In the second section of this chapter, we describe how PIBAL enhances liquidity and present the essential features and parameters of the
program. The third section describes the profitability of the fund itself,
and the fourth section contains our concluding comments.

THE LIQUIDITY PROCEDURE

PIBAL brings liquidity to the CAC market in addition to that which is
naturally provided by traders who place limit orders. Let us use basic
economic concepts concerning supply and demand to see how this
works.

The price of a stock is determined in the marketplace by the intersection of the market's demand curve to hold shares and the supply
curve of shares outstanding. If the number of shares outstanding for a
stock is fixed, which it typically is, the supply curve is vertical. If the
supply curve has some elasticity, however, shifts in the market's demand
to hold shares have a smaller impact on price, and the reduction in the
impact is greater the less elastic is the demand curve. And transaction
costs and other impediments to trading cause the market's demand curve
to be relatively inelastic in the short run. From an economist's perspective, the key to the liquidity procedure is that, by changing the number
of its shares outstanding, a corporation can give its supply curve some
elasticity. From an investor's perspective, the company is adding liquidity to the market and dampening price volatility.

PIBAL's impact on share price is depicted in Figure 29–1. Assume
a sell imbalance develops for a stock and that the market for that stock is
thin (illiquid). Being thin, the market is not able to absorb the order
imbalance (as demand shifts from D_1 to D_2) without a large price decrease occurring (price falls from P_1 to P_3). However, the corporation,
through PIBAL, can absorb some of these sell orders by buying back its
shares (the buy back is $N_1 - N_2$ shares). The repurchasing provides
liquidity to the market and contains the downward price movement
(price falls only to P_2). Or, if a buy imbalance occurs, the company can
dampen an upward price movement by issuing shares. In effect, the firm

FIGURE 29–1
PIBAL's Impact on Share Price

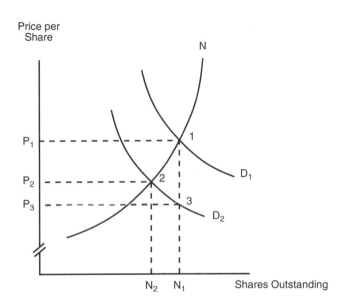

has given its supply curve of shares some elasticity. As is shown below, PIBAL simply calls for a company to specify its supply elasticity and to use it to calculate the size of the buy and sell orders that it will place. For that purpose, the company sets up a fund with cash and shares that will be used to supply liquidity and/or shares to the market when imbalances occur.

The Liquidity Formula

Schwartz (1991) has suggested that the corporation's supply curve of shares be given the constant elasticity form

$$\text{Number of shares outstanding} = g(\text{Price})^S \qquad (29.1)$$

where g is a location parameter and S is the elasticity that describes the supply responsiveness of the number of shares outstanding to the change in the market price per share. That is,

$$S = (\text{order size/shares outstanding}) \div (\text{price change/price}) \quad (29.2)$$

The following illustration shows how S can be set by the company. Assume that a company's stock price is FF135, that it has 100 million shares outstanding, and that average daily trading volume is 300 thousand shares. The company may decide that at the current price level, an order of 60,000 shares (which is .06 percent of shares outstanding and 20 percent of its average daily trading volume) would supply an appropriate amount of liquidity to the market. Let the price triggers for a company's liquidity trades be set at 5 percent intervals. S would then be .012 (the 0.06 percent change in shares outstanding, divided by the 5 percent change in price). If, alternatively, the firm decides to buy or to sell only 50,000 shares given its average daily trading volume, S would be set at .01. The lower the value of S, the less intensive the corporation's liquidity program is.

With the value of S established, solving equation (29.2) for order size gives the liquidity formula,

$$\text{Order size} = S \times (\text{price change/price}) \times \text{shares outstanding} \quad (29.3)$$

Because S is positive, a price decrease results in a negative order size, which is interpreted as a corporate buy order that reduces the number of shares outstanding. Or, a price increase triggers a corporate sell order, which would increase the number of shares outstanding.

Once S is set, it does not change as price and the number of shares outstanding vary from their initial values, but the number of shares bought or sold does change. In the above example, where S is equal to .012, the number of shares purchased at FF128.25 would be 60,000. Following the trade, the company will have 99,940,000 shares outstanding $(100,000,000 - 60,000)$. If the price then drops another 5 percent to the trigger at FF121.80, the next liquidity purchase would be 59,964 shares $(.012 \times .05 \times 99,960,000)$.[5]

PIBAL Trades Are Made in a Call Market Only

In call market trading, as orders arrive over a period of time, they are cumulated for simultaneous execution in a single multilateral trade, at the single price that best reflects the market's demand to hold shares. The call market's procedure of focusing (batching) the orders for execution at a specific point in time, naturally increases the liquidity of the market and, in so doing, contributes to the stability of price.[6]

CAC's opening for its Section 1 and 2 stocks, like that of Toronto's CATS, Tokyo's CORES, and Australia's SEATS, is an open book electronic call auction. Between 9:00 a.m. and 10:00 a.m., aggregated buy and sell quantities at each price are displayed, and all participants can watch the market as it forms. As new orders arrive, they are continuously aggregated and sorted, and the indicated clearing price—the price that would be struck if the call were held at that moment—is continuously updated. The indicated clearing prices are shown on the screen, as are the limit orders on the book.[7] Starting at 10:00 a.m., the clearing takes place and gives rise to the first quotes of the day.[8] CAC's thinnest issues (Section 3 stocks) have now been returned to call market trading only (two calls are held per day, at 11:30 a.m. and at 4:00 p.m., respectively). In the calls used for all three sections, PIBAL orders would simply be another determinant of the clearing price.[9]

Liquidity trades cannot be effectively made in a continuous market because the orders would retard the adjustment to a new equilibrium and, in so doing, benefit some traders unjustifiably. To see this, suppose a stock's equilibrium price falls from FF135.5 to FF125.5 with a corporate liquidity fund order having been entered at FF128. In the continuous market, the stabilization purchase would be made at FF128. However, there is no reason to enable a public trader to sell at FF128 when the new equilibrium price is FF125.5, and a transaction price at FF128 would be misleading for the market and costly for the corporation. In a call market, clearing prices simultaneously reflect all orders, including those entered for liquidity purposes, and the PIBAL order would execute at FF125.5. Thus, an electronic call is the only suitable type of market in which substantial capital can be committed to enhancing liquidity.

Rules and Procedures for Operating PIBAL

Certain rules have been established to control the operations of the liquidity fund:

1. *Liquidity orders are entered in the call market only* (as discussed above).
2. *Liquidity trades are made only as the market price at a call hits or crosses trigger prices that are set at discrete, fixed percentage intervals.*

Trigger prices are set by the corporation at discrete percentage intervals to create a spread that allows the procedure to be profitable for the fund. Thus, like a traditional market maker, the fund may profit from price reversals by buying at discretely lower values and selling at discretely higher values (see "Profitability of the Fund" below).

Setting the trigger prices *at prespecified percentage intervals* assures that the number of shares outstanding (and, hence, a firm's capital structure) would not change *at any given price level* as prices fluctuate and PIBAL purchases and sales at an array of other prices are made. If the corporate liquidity orders were alternatively specified in relation to the size of a price change over a period of time (such as a trading day), the PIBAL order would depend on how quickly a price was reached, not just on the price that was reached. With liquidity orders being "path dependent," corporate purchases in a falling market would generally not equal subsequent sales if price were to rise back to a previous level (and vice versa). Thus, the number of shares outstanding would drift and capital structure would change. Setting the price triggers at fixed percentage intervals and ignoring the speed at which a trigger is reached avoids this problem.

3. *The values that determine the number of shares to be purchased or sold in a liquidity transaction (S, the percentage spread between trigger prices and the number of shares outstanding) are publicly known. The liquidity repurchase commitment is for a fixed maximum number of shares. A company must give at least one month's notice before lessening its liquidity commitment. The liquidity trades are made by a fiduciary.*

This rule addresses the concern that corporate involvement in market making could allow the firms to use the procedure inappropriately to manipulate their share prices. The manipulation problem is dealt with by having liquidity orders entered according to a prescribed procedure by a fiduciary. So that the liquidity orders are known with certainty in advance, the company must give sufficient notice before lessening its liquidity commitment.

4. *The fund is large enough to make all required purchases if prices were to decrease by 50 percent or to increase by 100 percent from its current value. The size of the fund is adjusted whenever the firm issues new shares or repurchases shares for nonliquidity-providing purposes.*

Rules 3 and 4 exist because a commitment to provide liquidity can be destabilizing if traders believe the fund will back down in the face of a large order imbalance. These rules should prevent the procedure from suffering from this vulnerability.

Most of the rules and conditions set by the stock market authorities in their General Rulings are met in the context of the liquidity fund procedures. Other rules that have been imposed by the French Capital Market regulatory authority, the Commission des Opérations de Bourse (COB) are:

5. *The fund may purchase shares only on a downtick and sell shares only on an uptick.*

    This rule has been established for corporations which have discretionary, opaque, and nonpublicized (although authorized) intervention programs to prevent them from manipulating their stock price. COB's reason for this rule is not clear, given that the liquidity trades would be made in CAC's call market in a fully publicized and transparent manner.

6. *In principle, order size should not be greater than 25 percent of the average transactions volume measured on the last five trading days preceding its intervention.*

    This rule had already been established by COB to avoid manipulation of nontransparent corporations. The desirability of retaining it is not clear.

PROFITABILITY OF THE FUND

The expected return for a financial asset depends on two factors: risk and liquidity. As mentioned above, risk constant, liquid stocks are expected to be priced higher or, alternatively, to command lower expected rates of return than less liquid stocks. This is apparent in the French equity market. For the 150 largest French stocks, the liquidity premium, measured as the difference in risk-adjusted expected returns of the most and least liquid quintiles (with liquidity proxied by the log of free-float), was between .5 and 1 percent.[10] The stock of the most liquid company commanded an expected rate of return that was 400 basis points lower than the least liquid stock in the sample.[11] Thus, increasing liquidity will lower the cost of equity capital for corporations.

The maximum cost of such a program is the maximum possible cost of buying shares in accordance with the liquidity procedure, if share price were to decrease without reversal from its current level to zero. It can be shown that, for S sufficiently less than unity, the maximum percentage cost is approximately equal to, but less than, S.[12] For the example shown above, with 100 million shares outstanding, a stock price of FF135.5, and S set at .012, the maximum cost of purchasing at every trigger price, would be approximately FF8.1 million, which is less than one percent of market capitalization.

The reason the maximum cost is so low is that markets are thin compared to the number of shares outstanding. That is, there are not many orders on the book or on the trading floor relative to the number of shares outstanding. Therefore, a small corporate purchase or sale could provide the liquidity required to greatly reduce short-run price fluctuations.

Actual costs would be considerably lower than the maximum cost, however. In fact, the evidence suggests that the PIBAL operation will itself generate revenues. The reason is that the liquidity program is a form of limit order trading strategy that has been shown to generate positive returns for investors who, having reasonably well-balanced portfolios at current market prices, do not incur a substantial opportunity cost if their limit orders do not execute. For further discussion, see Hamon, Handa, Jacquillat, and Schwartz (1994a), ch. 5, p. 76, of this volume.

Limit order trading is profitable if share prices are sufficiently volatile in the short run. This is demonstrated by Handa and Schwartz (1994) in a study using NYSE 1988 trade data for the 30 Dow Jones Industrial Average stocks, and by Hamon, Handa, Jacquillat, and Schwartz (1994b) in a study that used all stocks listed on the Paris Bourse for the period March 1, 1990, to April 30, 1991. The findings show that limit order trading provides higher returns than trading with market orders when the limit orders execute.[13] The results are explained as follows.

Because order imbalances can temporarily drive prices away from equilibrium values, trading profits are generated when an order imbalance is corrected and price reverts back to its previous level (a process referred to as mean-reversion). In other words, if a public participant places a buy limit order below a stock's current price and a sell imbalance develops that drives the price down, the limit order will execute. When price returns toward its former level after the buy/sell imbalance is worked out, the limit order trader will have profited from the execution because of the reversal that followed.

Limit orders may thus be used as a "volatility capture" trading strategy. This involves placing a network of limit orders around the current quotes so that buy orders will execute as price decreases, and sell orders will execute as price rises. After each execution, a new limit order is entered to keep the network intact. To assess the profitability of placing limit orders as a pure trading strategy, inventory must at some future time be restored to its starting position at end-of-period market prices. Profit is then measured by the total value of the sales, less the total cost of the purchases (including the final inventory-rebalancing trade). Handa and Schwartz found the pure trading strategy to be profitable for their sample of NYSE stocks, and Hamon, Handa, Jacquillat, and Schwartz found the strategy to be profitable for their sample of CAC stocks.

Like the "volatility capture" trading strategy, PIBAL calls for placing a network of limit orders on both sides of the market. With mean-reversion, buy and sell triggers can be successively, and profitably, hit. As discussed above, mean-reversion is caused by order imbalances having an accentuated impact on price because of illiquidity, the problem CAC is facing. In this situation, the liquidity fund faces a no-lose situation. If the program is profitable, it confirms that there was a lack of liquidity, as predicted. By adding liquidity to the market for the issuing corporation's shares, the fund will suppress the mean-reverting process, making its activities less directly profitable. In the process, however, the liquidity of the market for its shares will have increased, short-run price volatility will have been dampened, and the firm's share price will be higher.[14] So, either way, whether the program is directly effective or not, the corporation and its shareholders will benefit from the liquidity fund's operations.

CONCLUSION

The short-run instability of stock market prices is causing concern in France as it is elsewhere around the globe. This chapter has presented a procedure, PIBAL, that is structured to make the Paris Bourse more efficient by enhancing the liquidity of shares traded on the exchange. This is accomplished by having corporations set up "liquidity funds" that allow shares to be purchased in falling markets and sold in rising markets. The procedure is similar to a limit order trading strategy that has been shown to be profitable in both the United States and in France.

The implementation of PIBAL would best be coordinated with an expanded use of electronic call market trading. PIBAL trades should be made in a call market environment only, and PIBAL orders should be a part of every call. This innovation would offer investors excellent liquidity. The benefits will enhance portfolio performance for buy-side participants and should enable the Bourse to compete with considerably more success in the global equity markets.

NOTES

1. This is the case for CAC's more heavily traded "Section 1 and 2" stocks. For thinner "Section 3" issues, CAC's market is called twice, and there is no continuous trading at all. Sections 2 and 3 stocks are traded in the cash (spot) market. Section 1 stocks are those traded in the Bourse's forward market only.
2. For further discussion, see Handa and Schwartz (1994).
3. Trading is costly in a less liquid market for several reasons: (1) bid-ask spreads are wider if a market lacks depth (there are few orders at prices in the close neighborhood above and below the price at which shares are currently trading), (2) market impact is large if a market lacks breadth (the best buy and sell orders exist in limited volume), and (3) excessive volatility occurs if a market lacks resiliency (short-run price changes due to temporary order imbalances do not quickly attract counterpart orders quickly to the market). That a network exhibits "positive network externalities" is further developed in Economides (1992) and Economides and Schwartz (1995).
4. See Jacquillat and Schwartz (1993) for an analysis of the causes and consequences of the divergence of order flow from the CAC market to London.
5. For a more detailed discussion, see Schwartz (1991).
6. Moreover, because all crossing orders execute at a common clearing price, participants can put limit prices on their orders without risking being "picked off" by other traders. Thus, the submission of priced orders is encouraged, which further increases the liquidity of the market. For a discussion of the efficiency of call market trading, see Economides and Schwartz (1995). We further suggest in Jacquillat and Schwartz (1994) that the Paris Bourse broaden its use of call market trading (calls should be held three times per day) to enhance this alternative to trading in its continuous market. This will lower the costs of trading for constituents, enhance CAC's liquidity, and thereby attract order flow back from London.
7. When the Paris market turned from a price scan auction (where participants are physically present at the call) to a call-continuous electronic call market in 1989, early order disclosure was often used by many traders for gaming purposes. To prevent this, among other purposes, a fixed fee on top of the normal commission is charged every time an order is placed in the order book in the preopening call. As a consequence, trading volume in the opening call is on average below 15 percent of total daily trading

volume. Insofar as the call system is a superior trading system compared to the continuous market for the reasons discussed in Economides and Schwartz (1995), early order disclosure should be encouraged in call market trading by using time priorities and by charging lower—and not higher—commissions for orders placed earlier in the entry period that precedes the call.

8. Market orders are executed after limit orders and are always executed on the limits of the order book: buy orders are matched with the best upper limit and sells with the best lower limit. If the number of stocks in the limit order book at that price is insufficient to execute all market orders, the excess market orders are entered as limit orders at the price at which the market orders were partially executed. If the order book is thick, the first transaction is made soon after 10 o'clock. For the first six months of 1990, Hamon and Jacquillat (1992) report average lags of 29 seconds and 2.5 hours for the largest and smallest deciles of stocks (about 35 each) negotiated on CAC, respectively.

9. As is true for all orders in call market trading, PIBAL orders do not execute at the price at which they are placed but at the common clearing price. Thus, if the PIBAL order has been entered at FF128 and the clearing price is FF125.5, the share repurchase will be made at FF125.5.

10. As discussed above, liquidity may be measured by a stock's bid-ask spread or by the magnitude of an asset's short-period price instability. Alternatively, liquidity can be proxied by transaction volume or by the number of shares issued and outstanding (i.e., market capitalization or free-float, market capitalization less controlling interest).

11. See Associés en Finance (1993).

12. See Schwartz (1991).

13. If the limit orders do not execute and a "forced" purchase is eventually made, then the market order strategy, on average, yields higher returns.

14. Under present market conditions, for each 10 basis points in the reduction of the expected return on a stock due to increased liquidity, its market capitalization would increase by roughly one percent. This is to be compared with the yearly opportunity cost of resources committed to the fund which is roughly 0.25 percent or 2.5 percent in present-value terms. This is a fixed cost, whereas the benefits of the program can lower the expected return by a larger multiple of 10 basis points. In the extreme example provided earlier in the chapter of the least liquid stock in the sample of the 150 French largest capitalizations which commanded an expected rate of return that was 400 basis points higher than the most liquid stock, hypothetically the value could increase by as much as 40 percent for the same 2.5 percent opportunity cost.

REFERENCES

Associés en Finance. (1993). "Entreprises, organisez vous-même la liquidité de vos titres," *Lettre Financiére,* 23.

Economides, Nicholas. (1992). "Network Externalities and Invitations to Enter," New York University, Stern School of Business discussion paper no. EC-92-2.

Economides, Nicholas, and Robert Schwartz. (1995). "Electronic Call Market Trading," *Journal of Portfolio Management,* forthcoming.

Hamon, Jacques, and Bertrand Jacquillat. (1992). "Le marché français des actions, Études empiriques, 1977–1991," PUF.

Hamon, Jacques, Puneet Handa, Bertrand Jacquillat, and Robert Schwartz. (1994a). "Market Structure and the Supply of Liquidity," ch. 5, this volume.

Hamon, Jacques, Puneet Handa, Bertrand Jacquillat, and Robert Schwartz. (1994b). "The Profitability of Limit Order Trading on the Paris Stock Exchange," New York University, Stern School of Business working paper.

Handa, Puneet, and Robert Schwartz. (1994). "Limit Order Trading," New York University, Stern School of Business working paper.

Jacquillat, Bertrand, and Robert Schwartz. (1994). "Divergence of Order Flow from the CAC Market to London," work in progress.

Schwartz, Robert. (1991). *Reshaping the Equity Markets: A Guide for the 1990s.* New York: HarperBusiness (reissued by Business One Irwin, 1993).

CHAPTER 30

THE GERMAN EQUITIES MARKET

Reto Francioni

TOWARDS A NEW STRUCTURE

The German financial market presently faces challenges that arise from the country's unification, European integration, and the political and economic development in East European countries.

The German unification of 1990 as well as the need for a steady modernization of the world's third largest industrial nation requires an efficient financial market for allocating investment capital. Germany's geographic location, the traditional links to our eastern neighbors and the experience in building up a free market economy gives the country's financial market a key role as the channel for international capital to flow into Eastern Europe's emerging economies. Europe's political and economic integration, with its program for a common internal market at the same time, puts the German financial market into stronger competition with other European markets.

In view of these economic and political developments and in order to strengthen its position, the German equities market is undergoing a reshaping process. The aim is to establish a marketplace for national and international investors and issuers that allows them to trade at low costs with a high degree of transparency through a set of modern trading systems.

The German Exchange (Deutsche Börse AG) was established with effect from January 1, 1993, to play a key role in modernizing the German marketplace—as the common roof for the Frankfurt Stock Exchange (FWB), the German Options and Futures Exchange, *Deutsche Terminbörse* (DTB), the German Securities Deposit (DKV), and the Computer Centre of the German Stock Exchanges (DWZ). (See Figure 30–1.) Its mission is to integrate financial market services and systems and to develop new ones in orientation to market participants' needs.

One of the new organization's success factors is the trading system infrastructure in the German spot and derivatives markets that it can provide today. Part of this infrastructure is an integrated exchange trading and information system (IBIS) which, in its latest version, has been running in parallel to the Frankfurt floor-based exchange and seven regional exchanges since April 1991. IBIS also serves as the day-long underlying market for the derivatives market, the German Options and Futures Exchange (DTB). The DTB is a fully electronic market that has been operational since January 1990, being today the world's largest screen-based system for trading derivatives including futures.

The organizational effort for strengthening the German financial markets embodied in the Deutsche Börse AG has its political equivalent in the reform of Germany's legislative setting for exchanges, securities trading, and financial services. The draft law, which is expected to be presented to the German cabinet this autumn and passed by parliament in early 1994, aims at assuring investor protection and market transparency on a level with the international standard today.

Central issues of that law will be (1) that insider-trading violations are made punishable by jail and fines, (2) that a supervisory office for securities will be created, and (3) that supervision of trading on the bourse floor will be reinforced.

GERMANY'S ECONOMY AND THE SIZE OF ITS FINANCIAL MARKETS

The size of an economy determines the capitalization of its financial markets. A high capitalization enlarges market liquidity and, thus, the attractiveness for investors. Germany as one of the world's leading industrial nations with the largest economy in Europe (see Figure 30–2) has, because of these facts and its economic stability as well as its

FIGURE 30–1
The Deutsche Börse AG—Structure of Ownership

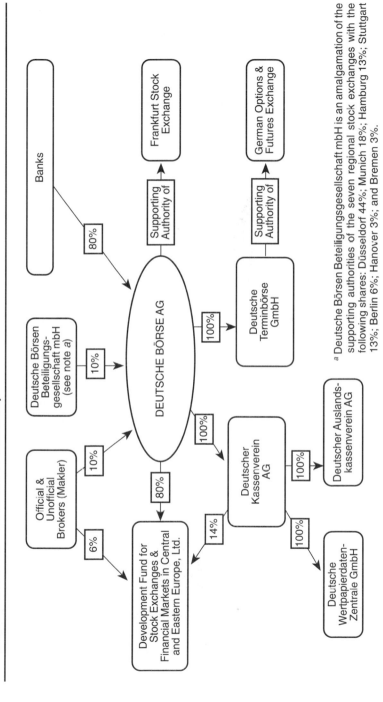

Banks

Official & Unofficial Brokers (Makler)

Deutsche Börsen Beteiligungsgesellschaft mbH (see note a)

80%

10%

10%

6%

DEUTSCHE BÖRSE AG

Supporting Authority of → Frankfurt Stock Exchange

100% → Deutsche Terminbörse GmbH

Supporting Authority of → German Options & Futures Exchange

80% → Development Fund for Stock Exchanges & Financial Markets in Central and Eastern Europe, Ltd.

100% → Deutscher Kassenverein AG

14%

100% → Deutscher Auslandskassenverein AG

100% → Deutsche Wertpapierdaten-Zentrale GmbH

[a] Deutsche Börsen Beteiligungsgesellschaft mbH is an amalgamation of the supporting authorities of the seven regional stock exchanges with the following shares: Düsseldorf 44%; Munich 18%; Hamburg 13%; Stuttgart 13%; Berlin 6%; Hanover 3%; and Bremen 3%.

Source: Deutsche Börse AG

FIGURE 30–2
Germany's Gross Domestic Product

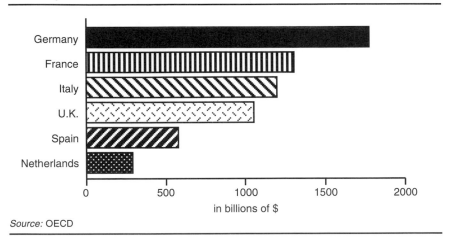

Source: OECD

international competitiveness, high potential to attract the interest of international investors. Stability of its currency and the position of Germany between the nations of the European Community (EC) and East Europe are factors that will further strengthen Germany's financial markets.

The correlation between an economy's potential and the size of its financial markets is obvious when looking at Germany's bond market (Figure 30–3), which is the largest in Europe. Major factors through which the market has gained its present size are a change in the policy of replacing certificates of indebtedness by exchange-traded bonds, a modification of the mode of placement and the admission of foreign banks as members of syndicates.

In contrast to the market for bonds, the share market does not represent the size of Germany's economy (Figure 30–4). The reason for this fact is that most German midrange enterprises, which are most important to the German economy, are not exchange-listed. One historical reason for this is the German system of universal banks, which allows a large number of companies to gain capital for investments through credits. Germany has more than 1,500 companies, each with more than 1,000 people employed. Only 665 of these companies were exchange-listed at the end of 1992, which hints at the market's potential for capitalization in the future.

FIGURE 30–3
Germany's Bond Market Size

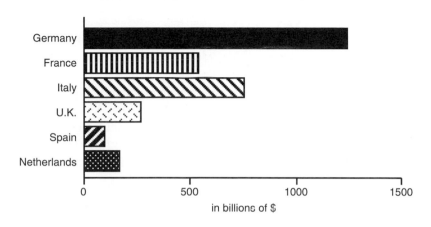

in billions of $

Source: BRI

FIGURE 30–4
Capitalization of the German Stock Market

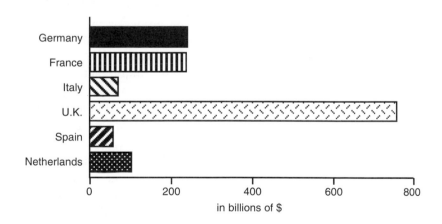

in billions of $

Source: Financial Times, Indices/Datastream

MARKET STRUCTURE AND TRADING VOLUME

Floor Trading

Germany's stock market presently is the fourth largest in the world. Germany's largest marketplace for stocks and bonds, the leading bourse in Germany, is the Frankfurt Stock Exchange with a market share of up to 70 percent of exchange-traded securities in Germany (Figure 30–5).

All German "blue chips" are traded in Frankfurt. Also, the German stock index, the Deutscher Aktienindex (DAX) is calculated each minute from prices of trades in the 30 DAX stocks in Frankfurt. Trading takes place on the floor, with trading hours from 10:30 a.m. to 1:30 p.m. in an auction-style order-driven market.

Orders are routed to the trading pits of the official brokers by BOSS, an electronic order routing and order book system, or they are revealed to the market by open outcry. The opening and closing procedure follows the principles of an auction call market. The matching of orders and determination of the trading price is performed by the brokers continuously or in batch-trading mode: all market orders are guaranteed to be executed. For limit orders, execution is guaranteed at the market price or better. Unlike the specialists at the New York Stock Exchange, brokers have the right, but not the obligation, to act as the counterpart for trades under certain conditions. Settlement takes place via the BÖGA system which enables (t+2)-day settlement in Germany.

IBIS

Running parallel to floor trading, IBIS, the integrated stock exchange trading and information system, forms a nationwide market for trading in the leading German shares, 30 of them being DAX shares, and bonds and warrants as well. IBIS accounts for one-third of all trading in DAX-listed shares in Germany.

IBIS is an order-driven system that allows entry of firm bids and offers in anonymous trading mode from 8:30 a.m. to 5:00 p.m., thus being a whole-day underlying market for the DTB. Members linked up with the system can transmit up to three bids and offers on the sell- as well as the buy-side of the market for each stock. With each bid and offer, the volume which the participant is willing to buy or sell has to be submitted. For each stock, bids and offers entered are displayed according to priority of time and price, every participant has the possibility to

FIGURE 30–5
Trading Volume of Equities in Germany and the Share of the Frankfurt Stock Exchange

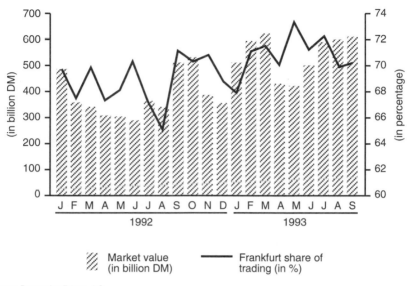

Source: Deutsche Börse AG

accept the indicated bids or offers because they are binding. Bids and offers have to be submitted at minimum volume of 100 or 500 (depending on the type of share) which makes IBIS a market system especially suited for block trades. The system has thus attracted a considerable share in trading of DAX-titles since it went operational (see Figure 30–6).

IBIS trades are directly routed to the BÖGA settlement system through which floor transactions are also settled. This means that an existing settlement organization that is reliable and which operates at low cost is used for the IBIS system. Transactions are settled on the second working day following the day the trade was made. Transaction confirmations and the delivery lists are entered directly via a system link into the system participant's electronic data-processing system.

The Deutsche Börse AG has the managerial as well as the financial responsibility for IBIS as a system that is not only accepted and utilized nationwide but also competes with stock exchange systems abroad as well as with off-exchange trading. Through IBIS, significant success has been achieved in shifting the dealing formerly done by telephone before

FIGURE 30–6
Trading Volume of DAX Shares in the IBIS System

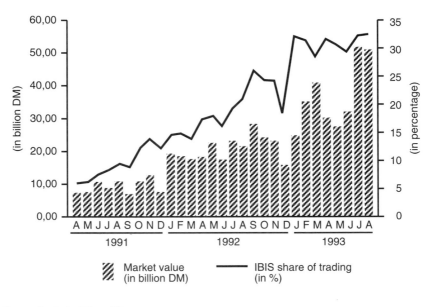

Market value
(in billion DM)

IBIS share of trading
(in %)

Source: Deutsche Börse AG

and after stock exchange business hours back into the exchange system.

DTB

DTB, the German Futures and Options exchange, was launched in January 1990. Before then, derivatives were relatively unknown in Germany—no financial derivative exchange existed—and even a change to the law governing financial instruments was required to enable the DTB to operate. The DTB also set new standards in being Germany's first fully computerized and automated exchange, making no use of the traditional open outcry trading approach..

DTB offers dealers and investors throughout the world a market for standardized deutsche mark denominated futures and options contracts in German stocks, the DAX index, and German fixed-income instruments (see Figure 30–7). Traders connect directly to the DTB via a nationwide electronic network, making it possible for market participants to carry out complete trading, clearing, and support transactions in options and futures from their offices in a matter of seconds. The simul-

FIGURE 30–7
DTB Products

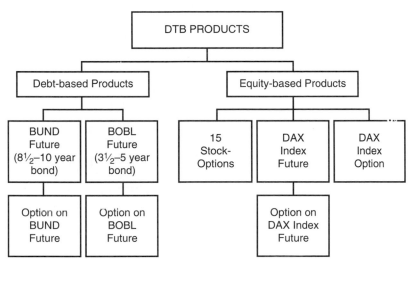

Source: DTB

taneous automatic clearing of transactions is completely integrated into the DTB system.

DTB now has 83 member firms, of which 40 percent are subsidiaries of foreign-based institutions. Over 900 individual traders are connected to the system and actively trading from throughout Germany, and DTB has already installed trading screens outside Germany.

The size and liquidity of the market has grown very rapidly. DTB currently trades about 200,000 contracts per day on average (see Figure 30–8 for monthly trading volume). In just three years DTB has become Europe's largest equity derivative exchange, Europe's largest options exchange, and the third largest derivative exchange overall in Europe. Indeed, DTB's DAX option is the world's largest index option contract.

Trading at DTB, like on IBIS, is anonymous. The market is opened with a call auction procedure and then proceeds as a continuous auction. The order matching principle is used with bids and offers being matched instantaneously and automatically by the DTB computer system whenever prices touch. Orders are given priority by price and time. Details of trade price and volume are instantaneously sent to all parties and relevant information is automatically sent to the clearing system.

FIGURE 30–8
DTB Contract Volume

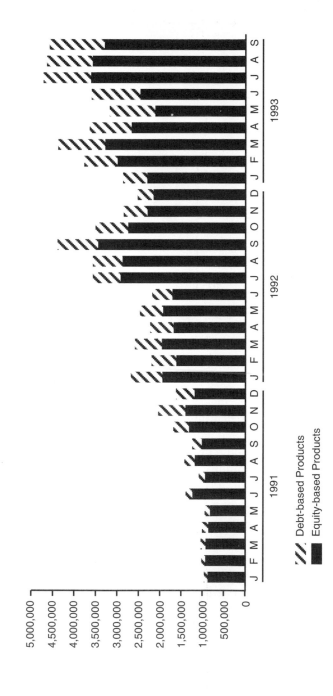

Source: DTB

The central system handling the order flow also provides full facilities to incorporate competing market maker quotations into the order matching system. DTB therefore combines the key features of an order matching system with the key features of the market maker quotation system. In addition, the close real-time informational links between the DTB and IBIS order flows improves market liquidity and transparency.

THE SECURITIES MARKET ACT AND THE
EUROPEAN FINANCIAL SERVICES DIRECTIVE

The Minister of Finance will present to parliament a draft for an extended Securities Market Act this autumn. By this act, market supervision in Germany will be regulated in a new way to reach the level of international standards. In addition, the Directives of the European Community on insider trading and transparency as well as the Investment Services Directive will be partly transformed into national law by this act.

Far-reaching authority for market supervision will be transferred to a Federal Supervisory Agency for Securities markets, being assigned to the Ministry of Finance. It will be granted the competence to prosecute cases of insider trading, which under the new law will be punishable by fines and jail. The Agency will also be competent for cooperation with market surveillance authorities abroad, for example, the U.S. Securities and Exchange Commission. This agency will be part of the three-level surveillance which also comprises institutions of Germany's regional administrations and bodies of the exchanges.

The German exchanges already perform a range of tasks and exert a range of authorities. According to the German exchange act of today, they enact rules and regulations, set a catalog of exchange fees, grant admission to the exchange and for participation in stock exchange trading. As self-regulating organizations, the exchanges are, by the new act, held to install offices for market surveillance as independent bodies. Their task is a continuous tracing of the trading process and the obligation to support the regional as well as the federal supervisory agencies.

In anticipation of the Investment Services Directive of the European Community, due to come into force December 31, 1995, Germany, as a member state, has already started to transfer part of that directive's requirements (via the Securities Market Act) into national law.

The Investment Services Directive gives financial services providers, credit institutions, and investment firms, with authorization in their home country a European passport that entitles them to offer their services all over Europe. The directive's enactment also means that the need to found an incorporation in the host country (for example, as a bank) to become a stock exchange member will be relieved. A U.S. investment house, for instance, will have the possibility to serve all European marketplaces with branches of one independent subsidiary in Europe.

For the European exchanges, the directive means that they can offer their services and systems, for example, their electronic trading systems like IBIS, to members all over the European continent. These new opportunities will strongly enhance the flexibility of market participants and, thus, the competition between the suppliers of securities services.

OUTLOOK

With the foundation of the Deutsche Börse AG, the prerequisites have been established for improved harmonization in the fields of information, trading, and clearing and settlement, in both the spot as well as the derivatives markets. The Deutsche Börse AG can gain a decisive competitive advantage against other international capital markets, if success can be achieved in harmonizing the spot market and the options and futures market to an optimum extent. The harmonization should also include the respective clearing and settlement system. One of the next challenges on this path of greater integration can be the establishment of a unified clearing and settlement system for the cash and derivatives markets. This would allow position keeping in one system and "net risk determination" for these positions. Competing systems abroad have up to now mostly provided only individual parts of the total range of transaction services on the securities market.

Clearing and settlement are only two phases in the trading process. Trading seen as a whole means to use a chain of different exchange services. The cost-efficient provision of these services, a major success factor for exchanges, requires a systematic utilization of computers in the service chain. IBIS and DTB as fully electronic markets are the first representatives of the new generation of exchange systems to come up in Germany.

CHAPTER 31

THE INTERMEDIATE MARKET IN MEXICO: AN APPLICATION OF THE CALL MECHANISM

Bernardo González-Aréchiga

The Intermediate Market is one of the Mexican stock market's responses to the challenges of equity and efficiency in an economy characterized (as in all developing countries) by high levels of poverty, insufficient domestic savings, inefficient channeling of resources towards production, and competition (that is not always loyal) with other financial sectors in the process of globalization. In the case of Mexico, the following structural challenges have been identified:

1. The diversification of products that are created, issued, and distributed by Mexican intermediaries, as well as the operational mechanics in Mexico. The improvement of the trading, clearing, and settlement infrastructure.
2. The creation of a "level playing field" for offering financial services, as well as for the intermediation of securities and derivative products. This sort of "field" must be attained among listed and over-the-counter markets and domestic and foreign markets.
3. An increase in the liquidity and depth of the financial domestic and foreign markets.

The author is grateful to Jaime Díaz Tinoco and Javier Villa Zárate for their assistance.

4. The adoption of prudential international standards for the capitalization and administration of risk, without ignoring the availability of resources and infrastructure in Mexico.
5. A reduction in the financing cost differential between the large exporting companies and small- and medium-sized companies. When the country's borders were opened to trade, large Mexican corporations began to have access to sources of international financing with an average cost in pesos of 12 percent (taking devaluation into consideration); medium-sized companies subject to bank financing have faced rates greater than 30 percent.

GENERAL BACKGROUND OF THE MEXICAN STOCK EXCHANGE

During recent years, the Mexican Stock Exchange has been one of the most successful emerging markets in the world, in terms of the rate of growth of its capitalization value and the increase in its liquidity and yields. This transformation has been very rapid and has been accompanied by changes of equal depth in the operational and financial infrastructure, in regulations and the composition of instruments and investors.

The analysis of certain indicators from the Emerging Markets Data Base of the International Finance Corporation (IFC)[1] and the Mexican Stock Exchange (BMV)[2] leads to the following conclusions:

1. Mexico was the largest emerging market in the world: at the end of 1992, with a capitalization value of $139 billion. Following Mexico in importance were Korea ($107 billion), Taiwan ($101 billion), and Malaysia ($94 billion). Mexico was considered to be ranked eleventh in the world at the end of 1992, ahead of Italy, Spain, Australia, Austria, Belgium, and Denmark. The value of the Mexican market at the end of 1993 was $200 billion.
2. The Mexican market's rate of growth during the period from 1983 to 1992 was 46.3, while the median rate for emerging markets was 9.3, and 3.1 for developed markets. International growth was only 3.3. In the IFC sample, only Portugal and Indonesia experienced higher growth rates.

3. The amount corresponding to the value traded in Mexico was $44.5 billion in 1992, placing Mexico in third place among emerging markets and in fourteenth place at the international level. The value traded in 1993 was $62.6 billion.

4. The volume traded in Mexico in the last decade grew by a factor of 40.1. This rate of expansion is 1.7 times greater than the emerging market average and 4.4 times greater than developed markets. The most rapid growth has occurred since 1990.

5. The turnover ratio for Mexico was 37 percent in 1992 and placed the country in eleventh place at the international level. It should be pointed out that the most liquid market, according to this indicator, is Germany (241 percent), followed by Thailand (209 percent). The United States market is in sixth place (60 percent), the United Kingdom in ninth place (40 percent), and Japan in eighteenth place (23 percent).

6. Compared with the sample of emerging markets, Mexico has experienced slow growth in the number of listed corporations; during the past decade, there was 19.6 percent growth in listings in Mexico, while the average for emerging markets was 96.4 percent.

7. The value traded in the Mexican market has tended to be concentrated in a reduced number of series of shares. For example, as of the end of 1993, 61 percent of the total value traded had been carried out with 20 series, from a total of 388 series.

8. Medium-sized corporations have reduced their participation in the stock market in Mexico. In 1990, for example, 28.3 percent of the total placements in the market were carried out by medium-sized corporations; by 1991, this amount had decreased to 1.34 percent of total placements and fell to zero for 1992 and 1993.

The above information indicates that the Mexican market has been one of the most active markets in international terms. However, it can also be observed that trading has been concentrated in a small number of highly traded series of shares. Medium-sized corporations have discontinued their financing through the stock market, while the number of shares of medium, low, and minimum marketability have increased. Resulting negative effects have been felt in terms of the market's liquidity, making it necessary to adopt new measures to increase liquidity.

STRUCTURAL MEASURES ADOPTED FOR INCREASING THE MARKET'S LIQUIDITY

In July 1989, the Mexican Stock Exchange began calculating a market-ability index[3] in order to establish benchmarks to classify shares in terms of their marketability: high, medium, low, minimum, and null. Important operational repercussions have resulted from use of the index, which has been the basis for:

1. Allowing short selling and securities lending (not subject to international arbitration) only for shares of high marketability.
2. Authorizing the issuance of warrants securities, only for shares of high marketability.
3. Establishing segmented "haircuts" on brokerage firms' capital for the distinct categories of marketability.
4. Establishing liquidity requirements for the formation of mutual funds' portfolios.
5. Requiring minimum liquidity levels for the collateral put up by short sellers with borrowed shares, or for the hedge and collateral on warrants issued.
6. Rating the transactions between brokers and their clients.
7. Regulating the issuance of warrants by corporate entities.

Independent from the marketability index, recent regulations call for liquidity to be used as a reference for the marking to market of securities. In addition, the degree of marketability is a determining factor when mutual funds calculate the number of investors to whom shares are distributed. Equivalencies are established by the BMV in its regulations. Due to the above reasons, liquidity has become one of the most important regulatory and operational concerns. The main reasons for promoting liquidity include:

1. Stabilization criteria (uptick rule) for operations against brokerage firms' own positions.
2. Deregulation of the commissions charged by brokerage firms.
3. Issuers' rebuying practices.
4. Trading and unlisting programs for shares with low liquidity.
5. Automation of market operations.
6. Improvement of the quality, timeliness, and coverage of information.

7. Increased information available for international arbitration.
8. Reduction in the commissions and fees charged by the stock exchange.

Given the high priority of liquidity, in May 1991, the National Securities Commission (CNV) requested that 67 corporations to increase the float in public hands, carrying out road shows and other activities in order to increase their liquidity. This program led to the canceled registration and unlisting of 16 companies in 1994. 14 in 1992, and 11 in 1993. The prerequisite for unlisting was a public offering to repurchase shares in the hands of minority investors, in accordance with the Commission's standards.

THE INTERMEDIATE MARKET[4]

In this context, the Intermediate Market seeks to (1) encourage the listing of new corporations that traditionally have been excluded from stock market financing, (2) reduce the gap between the financing costs that exist for large exporting corporations and medium- and small-sized corporations, and (3) find structural measures for increasing the market's overall liquidity. The last will be achieved by means of the BMV's division of the stock market into two sections: section A for trading the instruments of large corporations and section B (the Intermediate Market) for trading Mexico's medium-sized corporations.

Securities are designated to one of the two sections of the stock market by taking into consideration the corporation's net worth. The following definitions have been adopted: Medium-sized corporations are those with net worth between $7 million and $32 million. Large corporations have a net worth greater than $32 million. In the new section, it is possible for medium-sized corporations to place common stock, preferred stock, nonvoting stock, and convertible bonds.

It should be noted that the CNV has authorized the placement of preferred stock on the Intermediate Market as a means of strengthening investor confidence, since legislation prohibits the placement of this type of instrument in section A. Nonvoting stock is also eligible. The issuance of bonds that can be converted into stock is authorized, provided that the stock has been registered in the National Registry of Securities and Intermediaries that is operated by the CNV in accordance with the Securities Market Law. In addition, it is foreseen that series of shares that achieve levels of high marketability, upon previous BMV request and CNV authorization, can serve as underlying securities for warrants and be traded in operations involving the borrowing of securities and short selling.

It is important to note that foreign investment and favorable fiscal treatment are allowed, in that for both Mexican and foreign individuals, capital gains are tax-exempt, as long as the transactions are carried out at the Stock Exchange.

OPERATIONAL ASPECTS OF THE INTERMEDIATE MARKET

The operation of the Intermediate Market is regulated by the Securities Market Law. Article 14 of that law establishes that the characteristics of securities and the terms of placement must guarantee significant circulation and avoid detriment to the market, in addition to wide circulation in relation to the size of the market or issuer. The issuer must prove solvency and liquidity, follow policies of market participation that are congruent with investors' interests, and provide information to the CNV and the investing public. Article 14 also establishes that issuers must not interfere in the process of setting prices.

Circular 11–22 indicates the following criteria for listing securities on the Intermediate Market:
- A record of three years of operations as a corporation.
- Net worth of at least $7 million and no larger than $30 million.
- Profits shown by the sum of the financial results from the previous three fiscal years.
- At least 30 percent of the issuer's paid-in capital must be placed on the market.
- A minimum of 100 shareholders after the placement.

These requirements were designed to protect investors and increase market liquidity. The maintenance requirements imply that the issuer continually have on the market at least 20 percent of the documents representing its capital stock, held by at least 50 investors (see Table 31–1).

The Intermediate Market includes forms of trading that decrease securities' transaction costs and assure transparent mechanisms for setting prices which reflect prevailing market conditions. Trading is carried out in an automated manner, depending on the liquidity involved, and is flexible: one auction daily, one or two auctions weekly, or continuous trading.

At the time a security is listed, it is traded through a daily auction. After a certain period of time that allows for the evaluation of marketability, the Stock Exchange determines the most appropriate frequency for trading, based on the opinion of the issuer and the brokerage firms. The CNV authorizes issuers with high marketability to operate with a mixed timetable: opening and closing auctions combined with continuous trading.

Trading can be carried out with the use of limit orders (that is, orders that establish the maximum purchase price or minimum selling price) and firm orders (that cannot be withdrawn and only improved in their price).[5]

In order to support information revealed to the market, the Mexican Stock Exchange plans to establish discounts on commissions for orders presented in a timely fashion, as well as for large volumes.[6] On the other hand, definite orders facilitate controlling any attempt to manipulate prices at auctions.

The algorithm of the electronic book permits multilateral trading with the simultaneous participation of various buyers and sellers at a sole price, in accordance with the Mexican Stock Exchange regulations. The rules respect price and time priorities. The process for assigning orders[7] is:

- During a predetermined time period (60 minutes), intermediaries introduce, purchase and sell orders into the electronic book.
- The orders are collected and organized by the electronic book, based on the prices and times of presentation.
- Buy orders are sorted from highest to lowest, starting with the bid with the highest price, while sell orders are sorted from the lowest to the highest price.
- At the conclusion of the time for introducing orders, the algorithm finds the compensation price that maximizes the volume of transactions.
- The compensation price determines which orders will be executed. Only bids with selling prices that are equal to or less than the compensation price, or buying prices equal to or greater than the compensation price will be executed.

TABLE 31–1
Listing and Maintenance Requirements (BMV Circular 11–22 and Internal Regulations)

Concept	Section A[a]	Section B[b]
Listing Requirements	Article 14[c]	Article 14[c]
History of Operations[d]	3 years	3 years
Minimum Net Worth[e]	100 million new pesos	20 million new pesos[f]
Profits	Included in the total results of the previous 3 fiscal years	Included in the total results of the previous 3 fiscal years
Public Offering of Subscription or Sale of Stock	15% of the company's paid-in capital[g]	30% of the company's paid-in capital[g]
Minimum Number of Stockholders[g]	200	100
Registration Maintenance Requirements[h] Minimum Net Worth	50 million new pesos	10 million new pesos
Public Shareholdings	12% of the issuer's paid-in capital	20% of the issuer's paid-in capital
Minimum Number of Stockholders	100	50
Level of Marketability Required by Exchange	(1) Low to high, or (2a) 4 transactions per month in a series; (2b) 6 transactions per month in all issuer's series or have 0.5% monthly turnover or not comply with note *d* below.	

[a] Securities section, subsection A of the RNVI's Section A of the Capital Market.
[b] Securities section, subsection B of the RNVI's Section B of the Capital or Additional Market. The BMV Commission may authorize the registration in section B for one year of any issuer who so requests, provided that it meets the requirements of section A.
[c] The listing requirements stated in Article 14 of the Securities Market Law must be complied with.
[d] In the case of mergers or divisions, accreditation must take place with respect to the merged or divided company. Controlling companies whose subsidiaries meet the requirement are exempt.
[e] Based on official financial statements or on limited external auditing three or fewer months in advance.
[f] There may be exceptions for companies which, in the judgment of the CNV, have high growth potential.
[g] Once shares have been placed.
[h] Compliance with registration maintenance requirements will be checked annually in April and May.

- All transactions are carried out at a sole price.
- When the maximum volume is provided by diverse prices (tied bids at different prices), the bids of the two extremes are taken into consideration.
- Ties are broken as follows:
  If there is excess supply, the lower of the two prices is chosen.
  If there is excess demand, the higher price is chosen.
  If there are equal numbers of buyers and sellers, two alternatives exist: (1) The price closer to the most recent price will be the compensation price. (2) If both prices are equidistant from the most recent previous price, the higher price is chosen as the compensation price.
- Once the execution price is selected, the electronic book will generate the corresponding transactions.

The Intermediate Market began operations on July 12, 1993, with a single listed company. At the end of September 1994, there were seven listed companies (Controladora de Farmacias, Médica Sur, Ferrioni, Giconsa, PyP, Dixon, and Nutrisa), and five additional entities were in the last stages previous to listing (RGC, Hoteles Casa Grande, Grupo Mac′ma, La Central, and Grupo Propulsa). The turnover rate, measured as the ratio of value traded and total company capitalization value, of the Intermediate Market is larger than the average for the equity market.

CRITERIA IN THE EVENT OF NONCOMPLIANCE

Current regulations call for the Mexican Stock Exchange to carry out, during April and May of each year, an evaluation of each and every issuer's compliance with the maintenance requirements.[8] The results must be sent to the CNV. In the event of an issuer's noncompliance, the rules indicate the following:

1. The BMV must identify the form of noncompliance and agree with the issuer to request from the CNV and the BMV a reclassification of the issuer's registration from section A to section B. This change will be possible, provided that the issuer meets the maintenance requirements for section B.
2. The BMV must identify the form of noncompliance and agree

with the issuer to adopt a program to maintain its registration. The exchange will inform the Commission (CNV) of the form of noncompliance and recommend that the issuer adopt a program to diversify shareholdings, increase trading, or correct any other infraction, within a time period based on market conditions.

3. When, as a result of noncompliance, the issuer decides to unlist the stock and cancel its registration in the securities section (*sección de valores*) of the National Registry of Securities and Intermediaries (RNVI), the majority stockholders are required to make a public offering. The stock should be repurchased at the highest of the following two values: (a) the average closing price within the previous 30 business days or (b) book value per share according to the last financial statements.

4. The BMV must identify the form of noncompliance and, provided that the issuer does not resolve to adopt a maintenance program or fails to meet the time limits agreed upon for doing so, the exchange will inform the CNV of the form of noncompliance and recommend suspension from registration and listing. The BMV will proceed to delist and the CNV will cancel the issuer from the register and will request the majority stockholders' purchase offering in accordance with the company's articles of incorporation. This can also be requested in the event of the issuer providing any false or misleading information.

5. The CNV will temporarily exempt the issuer from compliance with the minimum requirements of shareholdings by public investors or with the minimum number of stockholders for the temporary acquisition of shares by the issuers themselves.

In April 1994, the BMV is due to check on compliance with the maintenance requirements for stock registered in sections A and B, which could lead to reclassifications to the Intermediate Market of the registrations of a substantial number of issuers currently in section A. Only the maintenance requirement is considered as established in the BMV's B4.15/02 communication which refers to the requirement that the listed securities register at least a monthly turnover ratio of 0.5 percent. It is estimated that as a result of their noncompliance at year-end 1993, nearly 10 percent of section A issuers could be transferred to the Intermediate Market.[9] The process will be finished by the end of 1994.

THE REGULATORY PACKAGE CREATED BY THE INTERMEDIATE MARKET

The Intermediate Market is ruled by CNV guidelines and by BMV internal regulations. Some of those rules are as follows:

1. Circular 11–22. General guidelines that establish listing and maintenance norms of the issuers placed in subsections A and B of the Securities Section of the RNVI.
2. Regulations for the Organization of the National Registry of Securities and Intermediaries (RNVI). Subsection B of the Securities Section of the RNVI is created and composed of the stock registered in the additional section (the Intermediate Market) of the Mexican Stock Exchange.
3. Circular 11–18. Modification to the general guidelines that simplify price setting practices and criteria and the elaboration of pricing reports for the issuers registered in subsection B, Securities Section of the RNVI.
4. Circular 11–23. Simplification of forms and frequency for the presentation of economic, accounting, legal, and administrative information for subsection B, Securities Section of the RNVI issuers.
5. Circular 10–128. General guidelines for the reception of buy/sell orders and the assignment of operations made with stock of subsection B issuers of the Securities Section of RNVI.

Within this regulatory package it is recognized that certain exclusive operations must be made in section A of the market or with high liquidity stock. These special operations are:

1. Extraordinary orders. This transaction is regulated under Circular 10–128.
2. Package orders. This refers to transactions made on the trading floor as a package in order to be assigned subsequently to a number of clients. It is regulated under Circular 10–128.
3. Global orders. Regulated under Circular 10–128.
4. International arbitration.
5. Operations with stock warrants. These transactions can only be made with high liquidity stock. In order to be able to trade

securities registered in section B, the CNV must grant authorization as per request from BMV.

6. Net sales operations. Authorization must be granted by the CNV for this type of operation, as per request from the BMV.

CONCLUSIONS

The creation of section B of the stock market to negotiate securities issued by medium-sized corporation should contribute to increase efficiency of the stock market to obtain and then channel financial resources to productive activities. Because of the characteristics of the Mexican economy, this market represents a great potential for financing medium-sized corporations that must compete with larger corporations having access to credit markets with lower interest rates than those they are offered.

For the intermediaries, the Intermediate Market constitutes an opportunity to consolidate a market niche and allows for a wider range of alternatives for the investment of capital from their own accounts. Should these objectives be achieved, the Intermediate Market should contribute to increase liquidity and diversification of the Mexican market. Under these conditions, higher competitiveness for the market as a whole can be expected.

NOTES

1. IFC, *Emerging Stock Markets Fact Book*, 1992, 1993.
2. BMV, *Anuario Bursátil*, var. issues.
3. The marketability index is a standardized geometrical index that is constructed from five indicators: number of operations, volume of shares traded, amount traded, capitalization value, and the lots of shares traded in volume. See the methodology in *Indicadores Bursátiles*, published monthly by the BMV.
4. The Intermediate Market project was initiated by the CNV. The Mexican Stock Exchange developed the conceptual aspects of its operation and designed the market structure, as well as the operation infrastructure and standards. Important input took the form of a seminar carried out in Mexico City under the auspices of the Interamerican Investment Corporation, with the participation of Robert Schwartz (NYU) and Steve Wunsch (AZX, Inc.).
5. See Articles 286 and 287 of the BMV's Internal Regulations.
6. Articles 292 and 293 of the BMV's Internal Regulations.

7. See Mexican Stock Exchange, *Operations Manual for Trading.*
8. See Articles 88, §§ 2, 3, and 4 of BMV's Internal Regulations.
9. It was estimated with reference in BMV, *Indicadores Bursátiles* (December 1993).

BIBLIOGRAPHY

Comisión Nacional de Valores. (1991). *Estudio de Factibilidad para Desarrollar un Mercado Accionario Intermedio.* Mexico City.

Comisión Nacional de Valores. (1993). "Ciculares varias," *Diario Oficial de la Federación,* 13 April. Mexico City.

Domowitz, Ian. (1991). "Automating the Continuous Double Auction in Practice: Automated Trade Execution System in Financial Markets," in D. Friedman and J. Rust (eds.), *The Double Auction Market.* Boston: Addison-Wesley Publishing Co.

Fedération Internationale de Bourses de Valeurs. (1992). *Requirements and Procedures for Listing Securities.* Paris.

Friedman, Dan. (1991). "The Double Auction Market Institution: A Survey," in D. Friedman and J. Rust (eds.), *The Double Auction Market.* Boston: Addison-Wesley Publishing Co.

Hayck, F. (1992). "The Use of Knowledge in Society," *American Economics Review,* 35: 4, 1945.

International Finance Corporation. (1991, 1992, 1993). *Emerging Stock Markets Fact Book.* Washington, DC.

Jackson, N. (1992). "Request for Proposal for a Call Auction Securities System." Washington, DC: Interamerican Investment Corporation.

Mexican Stock Exchange. (1991, 1992, 1993). *Anuario Bursátil.* Mexico City.

Mexican Stock Exchange. (1991, 1992, 1993). *Anuario Financiero.* Mexico City.

Mexican Stock Exchange. (1991, 1992, 1993). *Indicadores Bursátiles.* Mexico City. Published in December each year.

Pagano, M., and A. Röell. (1989). "Auction and Dealership Markets: What is the Difference?" London School of Economics, Financial Markets Group discussion paper no. 125.

Resnick, Bruce. (1989). "The Globalization of World Financial Markets," *Business Horizons,* November–December.

Rust, J., J. H. Miller, and R. Palmer. (1991). "Behavior of Trading Automata in a Computerized Double Auction Market," in D. Friedman and J. Rust (eds.), *The Double Auction Market.* Boston: Addison-Wesley Publishing Co.

Schwartz, Robert A. (1991). *Reshaping the Equity Markets: A Guide for the 1990s.* New York: HarperBusiness. Reprinted by Homewood, IL: Business One Irwin, 1993.

CHAPTER 32

SHANGHAI EQUITIES MARKET

Jianping Mei
Yimin Zhou

THE REBIRTH OF CHINA'S SECURITIES INDUSTRY

China's stock markets comprise two stock exchanges in Shanghai and Shenzhen, officially opened in December 1990 and July 1991, respectively. Shanghai is undoubtedly playing the role of a national market, while Shenzhen serves as a local market for the booming Pearl Delta region. Although still in their infancy, the two exchanges are playing an increasingly important role in the reform of the Chinese economy and in raising capital for the fastest growing economy in the world (see Figure 32–1).

The existence of the China securities market can be traced back as far as 1888, when a securities market started in Shanghai to trade foreign shares. The Shanghai government enacted its first regulations governing the trading of securities in 1914. In 1920 China's first securities exchange was officially opened in Shanghai; other securities exchanges opened later in Beijing and Tianjin. There were 24 companies listed on the Shanghai Stock Exchange. Because of many civil wars among warlords, trading was focused on government bonds, mostly issued to finance those wars.

The authors would like to thank Wang Beijun, executive vice president of Shanghai International Securities Co., Ltd., for providing some of the data used in this study.

FIGURE 32–1
China's Real Economic Growth (Gross National Product)

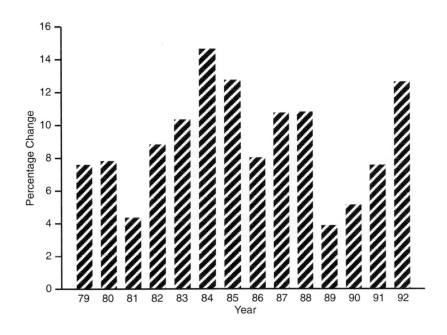

The securities exchanges were closed, and all securities were abolished soon after the Communist Party took over in 1949. China's securities market resumed its development in the early 1980s, when China's economic reform program called for a market-oriented economy. Since then, China's security industry has undergone a breathtaking growth. Following is a summary[1] of the major developments of the market:

1982 Annual issues of State Treasury bills started.
1984 First issue of shares in Shanghai.
1985 First issue of bonds by state-owned financial institutions.
1986 Creation of an over-the-counter (OTC) market for the trading of shares.
1987 First issue of short-term corporate bonds.
1988 Creation of OTC market for the trading of Treasury bills.

1990   Opening of Shanghai Securities Exchange. Trading of Treasury bills, bonds, and shares started on centralized securities exchange (December 19).
Opening of Securities Trading Automated Quotations system. Trading of Treasury bills started on nationwide computerized system.

1991   Official opening of Shenzhen Stock Exchange (July 3). Opening of the stock market to foreign investors. First issue of shares (B shares from Shanghai Vacuum Electron Device) to foreign investors.

1992   Trading of B shares started on Shanghai Securities Exchange and Shenzhen Stock Exchange (February).
Establishment of the State Council Securities Commission and China Securities Supervisory Commission as the central regulatory bodies of the China securities market (October 26).

THE TREMENDOUS GROWTH OF CHINA'S SECURITIES INDUSTRY

The Case of Shanghai International Securities Co., Ltd.

The Shanghai International Securities Co., Ltd. (SISCO) was established on July 18, 1988. Taking advantage of the growing demand of privatization and the need for external financing, the firm grew from an eight-person firm to a financial powerhouse with over a thousand employees in just five years (see Figures 30-2, 30–3, and 30–4). Profits surged, increasing from RMB 16,000 in 1992 to RMB 73,000,000 in 1992. By the end of 1992, the firm had helped convert 24 state-owned enterprises into shareholding corporations and had assisted more than 60 institutions to raise over RMB 7 billion ($795 million) through private placement or underwriting. The firm has also established a close working relationship with international investment powerhouses such as Merrill Lynch and Nomura. According to the income statement released by the firm, the return on equity was 110 percent for 1992.

THE SHANGHAI EQUITIES MARKET

At present, there are four major types of securities in China: Treasury bills issued by the government, bonds issued by financial institutions,

FIGURE 32–2
The Explosive Growth of Trading Volume at Shanghai
International Securities Co., Ltd. (SISCO)

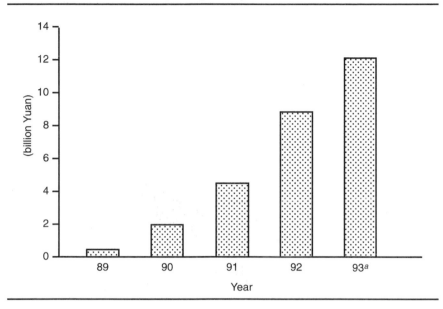

FIGURE 32–3
The Rapid Expansion of SISCO—Number of Employees

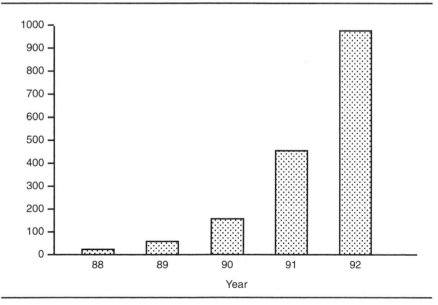

FIGURE 32–4
Profit Growth of Shanghai International Securities Co., Ltd.

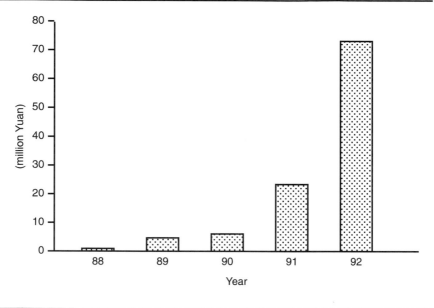

corporate bonds issued by business enterprises, and equity shares. There is also limited trading in futures and options in some unauthorized local markets.

Shares in China are divided into four categories according to type of ownership:

1. **State shares**—owned by the government, not listed.
2. **Enterprise shares**—owned by other corporations, transferable among Chinese corporations, not listed.
3. **Individual shares**—issued to the public (A shares) and traded on secondary markets.[2]
4. **B shares**—issued to foreign investors and traded on secondary markets.[3]

State shares still account for a majority of the total issued shares; however, there are some exceptions. The government generally plays a passive role in the firm's management while collecting dividends for the Treasury. Enterprise shares are generally cross-financing by Chinese corporations, and they can be transformed into individual shares with approval from the security exchange.

State shares, enterprise shares, and individual shares are classified as A shares. B shares are shares restricted to foreign investors, including investors from Hong Kong and Taiwan.

At the end of 1992, the total amount of securities outstanding stood at around RMB 330 billion. The new issues of securities, including shares, Treasury bills and bonds, financial bonds, and enterprise bonds is estimated to have exceeded RMB 100 billion in 1992.

The Shanghai Securities Exchange (SSE) was founded in November 1990 and opened for trading in December 1990. The SSE was the first centralized securities exchange in China. The exchange, which is a nonprofit-making legal entity regulated by the Shanghai branch of the People's Bank of China, organizes trading of listed securities and provides clearing, settlement, and custodial and registration services. Total market turnover of SSE amounted to around RMB 50 billion in 1992, up from RMB 1.6 billion in 1991. The annual trading volume is expected to exceed RMB 200 billion this year.

Members   Membership of the exchange is limited to securities companies and other financial institutions licensed by the Shanghai branch of the People's Bank of China. At present, the exchange has about 200 members, including 134 securities companies from 25 provinces, municipalities, and autonomous regions, which are all financial institutions approved by the government to deal in securities business. There are capital and operational requirements for member firms. Many foreign brokerage firms also have special seats on the exchange.

Trading   Trading is carried out through a computerized automatic matching system which executes each transaction based on the price priority and time priority. Trading information is displayed on an electronic screen in the trading hall and transmitted electronically to trading desks in the exchange hall and to members' offices all over China.

When entered into the computer terminal on the trading floor, trading orders are automatically matched by the central computer according to price and time priority. Share transfer is made at the same time that a deal is automatically done by the computer. Share trading is carried out in a paperless way. The transaction is recorded into a computer database, and no printed physical share is required. The computer system is capable of handling 100,000 transaction daily.

Settlement and Clearing   Settlement, share clearing, transfer, registration, and depository of A shares are performed centrally by the Securities Exchange. An independent clearing agent, the Shanghai Securities Clearing and Registration Corporation (CRC), was set up in March 1993 to provide independent services on B share registration, cash clearing, and custody.

After a transaction is struck, its settlement and delivery is carried out by a central depository system. Settlement and delivery are carried out on the basis of net settlement. Payment and securities receivable and payable are settled through book entry. Time of settlement and delivery for A shares is one business day.

When applying for securities to be listed, the issuer should submit to SSE such documents as a report for listing, company prospectus, balance sheets, and income statements. The documents will be examined by the SSE in light of its provisional regulation and will be verified by the relevant securities authorities for approval of listing, suspension, or termination. By the end of 1992, 75 securities were listed on the Shanghai Securities Exchange. They included 37 Treasury bills and bonds, 29 A shares, and 9 B shares. The number of A shares listed is expected to double in 1993. On average, trading of shares accounts for more than 90 percent of the total market turnover; trading of B shares accounts for less than 5 percent. Market capitalization of listed companies in Shanghai amounted to RMB 51 billion at the end of 1992.

Prior approval from the People's Bank of China is required if an investor plans to subscribe for or to increase his shareholding to more than 5 percent of the total issued share capital of any listed company. There have been reports that some firms tried secretly to acquire a large amount of shares of other firms in order to exercise influence. However, because of the existence of state shares, it is quite difficult to take over a Chinese company.

FOREIGN OWNERSHIP AND B SHARES

Foreign investment and loans to China totaled $17 billion last year, more than double the $4.2 billion figure for 1991. Since last year, the government has opened up many business sectors to foreign investment, even inviting foreign companies to participate in infrastructure and resource development. Direct foreign investment is permitted in most industries in China in three different forms of foreign-invested enterprises: equity joint-ventures, cooperative joint-ventures, and wholly foreign-owned enterprises. At the end of 1991, the People's Bank of China approved the first issue of shares available to foreign investors (B shares from Shanghai Vacuum Electron Device). B shares are denominated in RMB and settled in foreign currencies (U.S. dollars for Shanghai and Hong Kong dollars for Shenzhen).

The purchase of B shares, trading, dividends, and cash distributions are all paid in foreign currencies based on the latest market exchange rates in the Foreign Exchange Transaction Centers. Except for the restriction on the status of the shareholders, B shares have the same rights and obligations as A shares.

The Primary Market   All issues of B shares must be approved by the People's Bank of China. In general, an issuer of B shares must be a limited liability shareholding company and should have adequate foreign currency revenues to pay dividends and cash distributions. In addition, an appropriate prospectus, including the last three years' financial statements and earnings forecasts should be prepared. "B shares may be issued by way of a public offer or private placement. The lead underwriter/manager of a B share issue should be an authorized domestic securities company, which can invite authorized foreign securities companies to participate in the underwriting of the issue. Most of the B share issues so far have been carried out through private placements to institutional investors."[4]

The Secondary Market   Trading of B shares is only allowed on the two official stock exchanges. No short-selling or selling of a purchase before settlement is allowed. All trading expenses related to B shares are payable in foreign currencies. It is understood that there is no capital gains tax on B share investment and no tax on dividends received from the holding of B shares.

A simply study of the Shanghai B share index shows that the B share is more volatile compared to other country's indexes. However, as panel B of Table 32–1 shows, the correlations of B shares with other country indexes are extremely small—even negative—suggesting great diversification benefits can be achieved by including the B shares into one's investment portfolio.

Reforms of Accounting System   The importance of having listed companies' financial accounts prepared in accordance with international accounting standards (IAS) has been recognized by the government.[5] It has taken several steps to bridge the gap between domestic accounting practice with IAS:

1. Allowance of foreign accounting firms to open joint-venture offices

TABLE 32–1
Weekly Capital Gains for Seven Stock Indexes in
Local Currencies[a]

Panel A: Summary Statistics

	France	Germany	Hong Kong	Japan	Shanghai B Shares	U.K.	U.S.
Mean	0.0034	0.0060	0.0079	0.0034	–0.0096	0.0014	0.0006
Standard Deviation	0.0284	0.0220	0.0311	0.0272	0.0703	0.0157	0.0132

Panel B: Correlations among Weekly Returns

	France	Germany	Hong Kong	Japan	Shanghai B Shares	U.K.	U.S.
France	1.0000	0.6898	0.2770	0.2908	–0.0653	0.6702	0.5342
Germany		1.0000	0.2679	0.1379	0.1103	0.5696	0.3684
Hong Kong			1.0000	0.1769	0.2338	0.2217	0.0521
Japan				1.0000	–0.0071	0.1984	0.2799
Shanghai B					1.0000	–0.1096	–0.0418
United Kingdom						1.0000	0.5680
United States							1.0000

[a] The sample period for this table covers July 1992 – September 1993. Units on returns are percentage per week. Returns do not include dividends.

in China.[6]

2. The setting up of MBA programs in major universities in order to increase the number of qualified accountants to more than 100,000 by the end of the century.
3. Requiring all B share issuing companies to have their annual financial statements audited and certified by international public certified accountants in accordance with IAS.
4. Implementation in May 1992 of a new set of regulations for accounting and principles for shareholding enterprises.
5. Government implementation of a new set of rules governing Chinese enterprises' financial affairs and of a unified accounting standard and principles beginning July 1, 1993.

FIGURE 32–5
Shanghai A Share Index

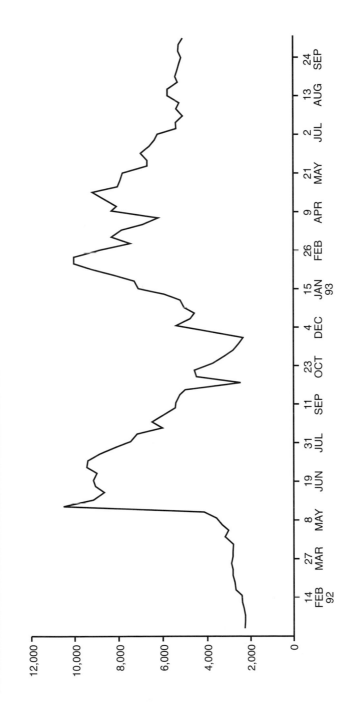

Source: Bloomberg

FIGURE 32–6
Shanghai B Share Index

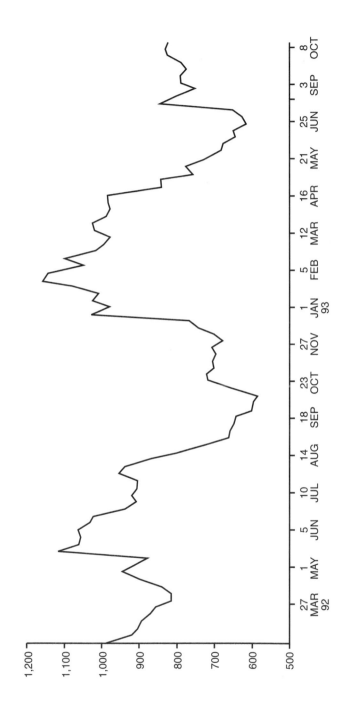

Source: Bloomberg

PROBLEMS AND FUTURE OPPORTUNITIES

In order to become a serious playground for world institutional investors, the Chinese security industry needs to build a financial infrastructure that will provide (1) effective hedging instruments for exchange-rate
risk, (2) efficient trading mechanisms, (3) rigorous and consistent regulations, and (4) sufficient disclosure of macroeconomic and corporate
information.

Investors also need to be aware of the following major political
risks that may affect the returns of their investment in the short run:
- First, the growing disparity between Chinese farmers and city
  residents may cause political unrest.
- Second, an overheating economy may cause high inflation which
  could worsen the income disparity and cause serious currency
  devaluation.
- Third, though corruption provides a way around the rigid bureaucratic system, it also undermines the legitimacy of government.
- Fourth, the loss of most-favored nation (MFN) trading status could
  be a serious blow to China's most dynamic coastal economy and
  lead to a stock market crash.

Despite the above potential problems, China offers some very
unique investment opportunities for investors.

First, because of its size, the Chinese economy has so far grown
quite independently of other world economies. China's stock markets
are affected mostly by its own political environment and other local
factors. This is easily seen in Table 32–1, in which we calculated weekly
capital gains for seven stock indexes in local currencies. As expected,
the Shanghai B share index is the most volatile; however, it is the only
index which has *negative* correlations with other indexes.

Secondly, despite the high volatility, the potential reward for participating in the world's biggest economic boom since the Industrial
Revolution seems to justify the risks taken. With a literate, hard-working
labor force (with a $1.4 per day minimum wage), China has huge poten-
tial for further development and could maintain its high growth rate well
into the next century.

> The Industrial Revolution, which started in England in the eighteenth century,
> changed the way of life for one quarter of the world's population living in
> Western Europe and North America. It created huge amounts of wealth for
> those who took the risk and participated in the process. But that is history now.

The Chinese modernization, which started in 1978, is also rapidly changing the way of life for another quarter of the world's population living in Asia. This is certainly an historical opportunity not to be missed.[7]

NOTES

1. See *China Stock Market Review*, Swiss Bank Corporation, January 1993.
2. See Figure 32–5 for the history of Shanghai A Share Index.
3. See Figure 32–6 for the history of Shanghai B Share Index.
4. See *China Stock Market Review,* Swiss Bank Corporation, January 1993, for a list of B share offerings and their leading underwriters.
5. The key deviations from IAS include (1) no provision for bad or doubtful debts or for inventory obsolescence, (2) capitalization of certain expenditures which would have been written off immediately under IAS, (3) dividend accounting for subsidiaries and associates, (4) no restatement of monetary assets and liabilities denominated in foreign currencies to reflect fluctuations of exchange rates, and (5) net income to include bonuses and incentive wages paid to the workers. See *China Stock Market Review,* Swiss Bank Corporation, January 1993, for details.
6. So far, Arthur Andersen, KPMG Peat Marwick, Coopers & Lybrand, Price Waterhouse, Deloitte Ross Tohmatsu, and Ernst & Young have established joint-venture accounting firms in China.
7. See *The China Report*, Prudential Real Estate Investors.

CHAPTER 33

DEREGULATION OF JAPANESE PENSION FUND MANAGEMENT

Kazuhisa Okamoto

INTRODUCTION AND BACKGROUND

The Japanese stock market rose 3720 percent between 1965 and 1989 and declined 63 percent in two years and eight months between 1990 and 1992. This decline is one of the symbols of many changes Japan is now experiencing. The changes are driven by market forces—the same forces which demolished the wall in Berlin and dissolved the USSR. The changes extend from the economy to political scenes, social structures, the way business have been conducted, and the way of life of common people. The uniqueness of Japan, which had long been preserved in an environment closed to the outside world, is now beginning to be eliminated in the wake of global market forces.

THE CLOSED FINANCIAL WORLD OF JAPAN

The financial market of Japan, especially the pension fund market, is not an exception. Until recently, cross-holdings of shares among corporations and financial institutions have always created a tight supply and demand condition in the stock market. (See Figure 33–1.) The economy was always growing. Corporations were young and expanding, and earn-

FIGURE 33–1
The Closed Financial World: The Good Old Days?

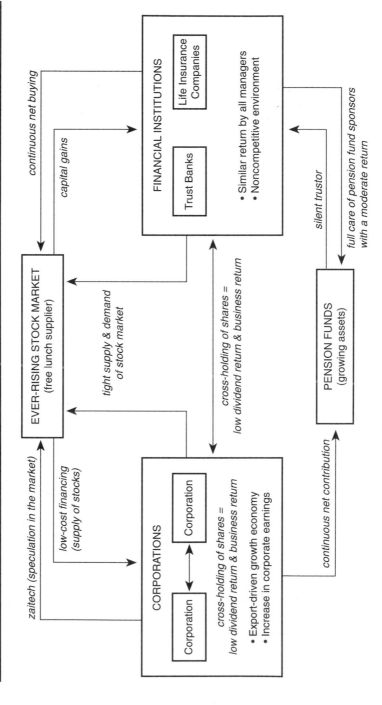

Source: Wells Fargo Nikko Investment Advisors Japan Limited.

ings were always rising. They have been consistent net contributors to their pension funds. Pension fund assets have been rising, and management of the assets was exclusively in the hands of life insurance companies and trust banks. These institutions paid only modest returns while providing comprehensive pension fund management services. Financial institutions, managing the assets, kept buying equities, and capital gains were accumulated in their own portfolio as unrealized gains. Corporations exploited the rising stock market and financed a huge amount of money at an extremely low cost of capital. Part of the money was put back into the stock market in the form of *zaitech* (financial engineering) operations.

Now the stock market's "free lunch" is gone. Corporations are suffering from poor business conditions, and financial institutions have lost most of their hidden unrealized profits. For the first time in its history, pension funds are facing a hard time. Returns have deteriorated from trust banks and life insurance companies on which pension funds had been totally relying upon.

The value of Japanese pension assets as of March 1992 stood at ¥165 trillion or $1.57 trillion. This is expected to rise to ¥305 trillion ($2.9 trillion) by March 2001 (see Figure 33–2). In spite of this growth rate, which is one of the highest in the world, the industry is extremely closed and has been monopolized by life insurance companies and trust banks. Current ratio of the assets managed by investment advisory companies (IACs) is a mere zero to 3 percent, depending on the type of pension funds. In fact, only four years ago it was about zero. It would not be surprising if this ratio goes up to 30 percent by the year 2000. A combination of growth in the assets and an increase in the share constitute a double play for IACs. The role here for IACs is to advocate rational investing. Whoever introduces rational investing, instead of the old-fashioned "trust me" investment method, will win the game in the long run.

EMERGENCE OF INVESTMENT
ADVISORY COMPANIES

The most important event in the history of Japanese corporate pension funds has probably been the decision to allow IACs to enter into this market. Up until March 1990, the industry had long been monopolized

FIGURE 33–2
Pension Funds: High Growth in a Closed Environment—Growth in Pension Fund Assets

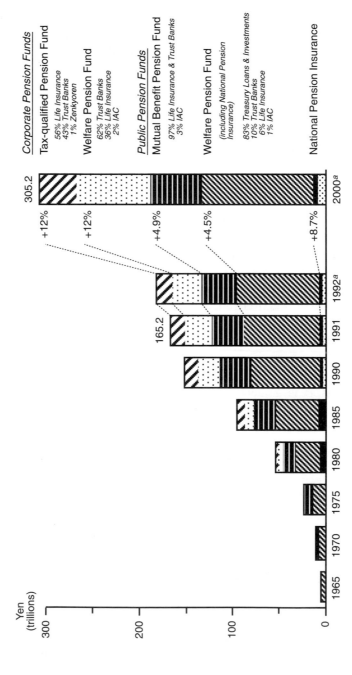

a Estimated.

Source: Wells Fargo Nikko Investment Advisors Japan Limited.

by commingled funds run by life insurance companies and trust banks. Everything—that is, complete management of pension plans, from actuarial calculations and estimating of future liabilities to investment operations—was basically done behind the curtain of these two type of financial institutions. In addition, law required individual managers as well as the overall plan to observe the 5:3:3:2 Rule in their asset mix.[1] Still, all problems caused by these irrationalities were hidden because the market continued its ascent. It was "the good old days" for plan sponsors and managers.

IACs were legally acknowledged as a formal member of Japan's financial society by the IAC Law in 1986. Increasing volatility of the stock market and an expectation for a rapidly aging society created the necessity to reexamine the way assets had been managed. Obviously, there was a very strong resistance from life insurance companies and trust banks. The government had to make a category of assets called "new money" and introduced some deregulation within that category. As a result, IACs were allowed to enter into this business and, for new money, the 5:3:3:2 Rule was lifted with the exception of the principal-guaranteed asset requirement.

In order for pension funds to take advantage of such deregulation, it was necessary to pension funds to first accumulate new money after receiving a qualification approval (*nintei*) and formal approval (*ninka*) from the Ministry of Health and Welfare. Furthermore, the plan must have at least eight years of history and its new money cannot exceed one third of the plan's total assets. Also, the minimum allocation amount to a manager of new money was set at ¥1 billion.

Though it was only partial deregulation, these changes represented a small crack in the wall. In December 1991, further deregulative measures were achieved for non-Japanese IACs as a result of very strong pressure from the financial community overseas.

THE PENSION FUND ASSOCIATION RECOMMENDATION

In April of this year, the Pension Fund Association made a very important recommendation for deregulation of pension fund investment activities. Shown below are deregulation after 1990 and needed future deregulation:

Deregulation after April 1990

December 1991
For IACs with majority ownership by foreign capital
- minimum allocation lowered to ¥500 million
- minimum principal-guaranteed asset at 30 percent

April 1993
Recommendations for deregulation by Pension Fund Association
- 5:3:3:2 Rule imposed on each pension fund
- 5:3:3:2 Rule imposed on each money manager
- Elimination of distinction between old money and new money

July 1993
Elimination of distinction between old money and new money (to be enacted)
Abolition of minimum allocation requirement

Needed Future Deregulation

- Abolish asset mix mandate for managers
- Abolish asset mix mandate for overall plan
- Change book (acquisition) cost to market-based accounting
- Allow IACs to manage public pension funds and tax-qualified pension funds

CHANGES IN THE LAW

In July, following the recommendation from the Pension Fund Association, the government announced that the distinction between old money and new money will be eliminated. This means that the deregulation made for new money is now applicable to all assets. I think this decision is as important as the deregulation in April 1990 that permitted IACs to enter the pension fund market. The background is that there were very poor investment performances of trust banks and life insurance companies in the last three years and a mounting of foreign pressure to reduce entrance barriers.

It is unlikely that some limiting conditions, such as the eight-year history requirement or the one-third restriction, will be set as a transition for complete deregulation. In spite of that, according to my calculation, assets which can be managed relatively freely will increase from ¥3 trillion for 400 plans to ¥10 trillion for 1,100 plans when the law is enacted next year. Besides, these restrictions are temporary in nature and are likely to be eliminated in several years.

Table 33–1 shows the major pension funds in Japan. Please remember that all these large funds are managed by traditional, old-fashioned,

TABLE 33–1
Major Pension Funds in Japan, March 1993

	Assets (in billion $) [a]
Public Pension Funds	
Pension Welfare Service Public Corp.	140.3
PFA for Local Government Officers	61.6
Public School Teachers MAA	50.0
Prefectural Government Employees MAA	13.8
Police Personnel MMA	11.3
Tokyo Metropolitan Employees MAA	7.8
PFA for National Municipal Employees	7.6
Welfare Pension Funds	
Pension Fund Association	17.9
National Credit Union	5.2
Hitachi	3.9
Matsushita	3.8
Toshiba	3.3
Mitsubishi Electric	3.3
Japan Securities Industry	2.7
Toyota Motor	2.6
Honda Motor	2.6
Fujitsu	2.3
NEC	2.2
National Credit Association	2.0
Nissan Motor	2.0
Tokyo Pharmaceutical Industry	1.7
Saison Group	1.7
Sharp	1.5
Mazda	1.4
Sanwa Bank	1.3
Osaka Pharmaceutical Industry	1.3
Tokyo-to Electric	1.3

[a] Based on $1 = ¥115.

Source: Wells Fargo Nikko Investment Advisors Japan Limited.

balanced managers—no passive core, no specialty-active managers, and very little usage of consultants or performance measurements. When these assets are managed more rationally, there will be a tremendous impact on the characteristics of the stock market.

ANALOGY OF U.S. AND JAPANESE PORTFOLIO MANAGEMENT OF PENSION FUNDS

Figure 33–3 shows the history of the U.S. stock market (as indicated by the Dow Jones Industrial Average) with annotations of U.S. pension fund reforms. From 1949 to 1950, many corporate pension funds were established. Despite many irrational practices, things went well, since the market was bullish and assets were always growing. Around the mid-1960s, however, the market went into a "box," where the market seemed stalled. By the late 1960s, or 20 years after the drive to establish corporate pension funds, a lot of efforts to reexamine pension fund asset

FIGURE 33–3
U.S. Stock Market (Dow Jones Industrial Average) and Pension Fund Reforms

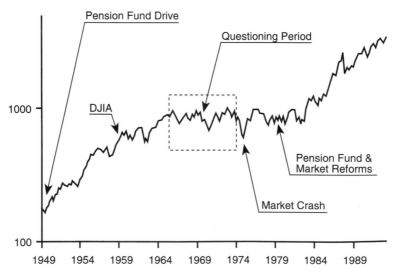

Source: Wells Fargo Nikko Investment Advisors Japan Limited.

management were made. These included recommendations by BAI in 1968, the Ford Foundation in 1969, and the Securities and Exchange Commission's report on institutional investors in 1971.

Due to the first oil crisis, the U.S. market declined more than 40 percent. This triggered changes in U.S. portfolio management. In 1973, we at Wells Fargo introduced the first S&P 500 index fund. In 1974, ERISA was implemented. In 1975 Charles Ellis published *Loser's Game*, and that year marked May Day with passive core strategy, use of consultants, performance measurement, and all that followed.

In Japan, a corporate welfare pension fund system was enacted in 1966 (see Figure 33–4). The market followed a basic uptrend, and assets grew. The questioning period started 20 years later. In 1985 the Pension Fund Law was revised. In 1986, the Investment Advisory Law was put into force. The market crashed in 1990, and today we see many changes beginning to evolve.

As it happened in the United States, now in Japan, 20 to 30 years after the corporate pension fund boom, there are trends for reform. This

FIGURE 33–4
Japan Stock Market (Nikkei Average) and Pension Fund Reforms

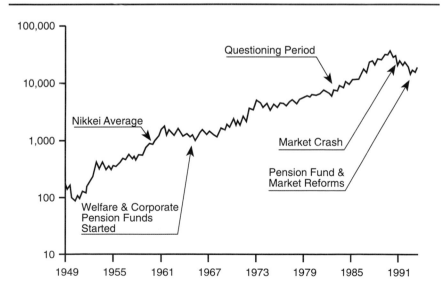

Source: Wells Fargo Nikko Investment Advisors Japan Limited.

is not just a coincidence. I think it is related to the maturity cycle of pension funds. When two or three decades pass, coupled with a market decline, irrationalities become intolerable and serious need for reform arises.

THE FUTURE OF THE JAPANESE PENSION FUND MARKET

In Japan now, it is obvious that market leaders are beginning to change. The leaders used to be corporations that (1) through cross-holdings, owned stocks of their friendly corporations and (2) indulged in *zaitech* operations using *tokkin* structures. The former category was looking for combined total return of investment and business. Low yield from investing was all right as long as they secured business from cross-holdings. The latter category was aiming at annual realized gains to boost business profits. In such an environment, no one cared much about rational investing.

Now, there is no question that the new leaders will be pension funds who have long investment horizons, who consider risks and returns, and who care very much about reducing costs.

This big shift of market leaders, which will occur over the next three to five years along with deregulative measures, will undoubtedly change the market characteristics, just as happened in the United States after the mid-1970s. In a sense, the Japanese market will become very similar to the markets in the western world. It will be closely linked to other markets of the world in terms of information and systems, in terms of trading activities, and in terms of rules and regulations. A lot of unique characteristics of the market currently existing in Japan will be lost. The market will be increasingly efficient. These are market-driven changes which are impossible to stop.

NOTES

1. The 5:3:3:2 Rule required pension funds to mix their assets in the following ratio:
    Principal-guaranteed assets (bonds, cash, and corporate bonds): $\geq 50\%$
    Stocks: $\leq 30\%$
    Foreign currency denominated assets: $\leq 30\%$
    Real estate, all at a book (acquisition) cost basis: $\leq 20\%$